Immature Playboys
and Predatory Tricksters

Immature Playboys and Predatory Tricksters:

Studies in the Sources, Scope and Reach of Don Juan

Edited by

CARMEN GARCÍA DE LA RASILLA

and

JORGE ABRIL SÁNCHEZ

Juan de la Cuesta
Newark, Delaware

On the cover: *Don Juan and the Statue of the Commander* (1835), Alexandre-Évariste Fragonard.

This project has been partially funded by the Ministerio de Educación, Cultura y Deporte in Spain through the Programa Hispanex para la Cooperación y Promoción Internacional de la Cultura.

Juan de la Cuesta Hispanic Monographs
An imprint of LinguaText, LLC.
Newark, Delaware 19711 USA
(302) 453-8695

www.JuandelaCuesta.com

MADE IN THE UNITED STATES OF AMERICA
ISBN: 978-1-58871-345-2

Table of contents

Acknowledgments

THE EDITORS OF THIS collection would like to express their gratitude to the many individuals that have contributed to its completion. We were honored by the active presence of a select group of scholars that accepted to attend and participate in our academic gathering at the University of New Hampshire-Durham in March of 2017. Their willingness to travel from several locations in the United States and overseas was crucial to the success of the symposium organized around the 400th anniversary of the first known performance of *El burlador de Sevilla* [*The Trickster of Seville*]. They offered their valuable work, time and expertise to this enterprise contributing with their essays and accepting editorial intervention with remarkably good disposition. We are also thankful to Frederick A. de Armas who agreed to serve as keynote speaker for the event. We also feel obliged to recognize the outstanding critical assessment of Edward H. Friedman in his prologue as well as Gregory Baum's fine translation of the essays of Alfredo Rodríguez López Vázquez, Ricardo de la Fuente Ballesteros and Carmen García de la Rasilla.

We are grateful to the Program Hispanex for the International Cooperation and Promotion of Spanish Culture from the Spain's Ministry of Education, Culture and Sports, and to the University of New Hampshire Center for the Humanities and the Office of the Provost and Vice President for Academic Affairs that funded our meeting through their generous grants, including the Class of '54 Academic Enrichment Fund. In addition, we wish to acknowledge the work of many people in various university offices for assisting us in hosting a successful symposium. At Juan de la Cuesta Hispanic Monographs we offer an appreciative nod to editors Michael McGrath and Michael Bolan and their staff for their prompt acceptance of this volume for publication and for their fast and helpful responses to our queries during the publishing process.

Prologue: Imagining Don Juan

EDWARD H. FRIEDMAN
Vanderbilt University

THE FIGURE OF DON Juan Tenorio has captured the imagination of spectators, readers, and writers over centuries. Don Juan is neither heroic nor, like Don Quixote, a complement in fame and familiarity, mock-heroic, but precisely the antithesis: a cruel seducer with few scruples and fewer commendable traits. There is something in Tirso de Molina's— or, for some, Andrés de Claramonte's—*El burlador de Sevilla* that invites analysis, interpretation, and adaptation of the title character and of the thematic reach of the play. *El burlador de Sevilla* offers a brilliant combination of seemingly disparate components, from sexual attraction and seduction to confession and salvation. The playwright's dependence on a structure based on a scheme of overdetermination is, arguably, a stroke of genius, a baroque thrust that keeps the consumer of the art object engrossed, busy, and, likely, inclined toward shifts in focus and reexamination of tentative conclusions. Is Don Juan, for example, an emblem of masculinity or an underachiever with low self-esteem and illusions of grandeur? Is the honor code a reflection of theological principles or an earthly intrusion into divine morality? Do women have agency, or are they solely functions of patriarchal values? Do language and rhetoric lead to truth or take the opposite route? And so forth. *El burlador de Sevilla* quite laudably might be labeled a play that keeps on giving.

The trickster moves from place to place, from woman to woman, and from one form of outrage to another. The play unquestionably satisfies the criterion of theater as spectacle through its construction and its varied locales and social environments. Don Juan Tenorio and his servant/conscience Catalinón are unifying presences. Catalinón could be called a baroque *gracioso*, not only a commentator on the action and a source of comic relief but also a representative of Catholic dogma that reminds his master of the need to repent in a timely fashion. A significant portion of the stage business of *El burlador de Sevilla* involves documenting the sins of Don Juan for the record. The female victims and the men affected by Don Juan's boldness constitute the essence of the plot, given that religious doctrine would be difficult to portray on stage. Each of the women is key to the sense of entitlement of the protagonist (or antagonist) and to the play's rendering of social strata, but perhaps Doña Ana de Ulloa is the most illustrative, for her father Don Gonzalo becomes her protector and, after his death at the hands of Don Juan, the "stone guest" that consigns the reprobate to hell. Don Gonzalo is a link between life and the afterlife and, simultaneously, an ingenious creative device geared to elicit excitement and awe. Don Juan has chosen to live on the edge, and he tests the boundaries of behavior, endurance, and protocol. He claims to understand the operating premises of salvation and heavenly grace, but he does not act accordingly or, paradoxically, he puts too much faith in the liberal nature of contrition.

It can be said that sinners are potentially more engaging than saints and that they therefore are stronger candidates for assignment as dramatis personae. Generally, plays about saints demonstrate a progression from sinner to saint, and more of the play will be devoted to the *before* than the *after*. The dialectics of crime and punishment, or of redemption and ruin, determine the unity of action of *El burlador de Sevilla*. The material in-between accentuates the dissoluteness of Don Juan, who preys upon women and scorns propriety and civility. He is unapologetic in his arrogance and audacity. This makes him, at once, repulsive and fascinating, as one observes his attempts to expand his list of conquests and to offend as many people as possible. Readers and viewers can expect a poetically just dénouement while enjoying the practice of transgression and impiety in settings that range from an Italian royal palace to a fishing village near Tarragona, to the court of Seville, and to a peasant marriage ceremony in Dos Hermanas. The deceived women are noble and humble, yet all are recipients of a misguided and iniquitous brand of sexual energy that bespeaks little of love or devotion.

Don Juan Tenorio is an emphatically complex character. He is attractive to women, but he frequently achieves victory through misrepresentation and always through duplicity. His inspiration never seems to be love or the appeal of a particular woman; rather, he disparages his victims and seeks victory for its own sake. The first time that he appears, having been in the bedroom of the duchess Isabela, and later with Doña Ana, he has gained entry by posing as another man and deluding a woman in the darkness. Don Juan acts cowardly, and he uses his nobility and his work as a gentleman to entrap his low-born victims. He is a liar and a cheat, with no concern for those whose rights and dignity he is ignoring. He betrays the trust of his companions and abuses the privileges of his rank, with only his charm and his social status to excuse his conduct. Catalinón informs him of the requisites of honor and, more decisively, of faith, but Don Juan establishes his own frames and guidelines. His self-absorption and insensitivity dominate the play. At the end, Tirso devises an earthly, if supernatural, means to wreak vengeance on the trickster: the invention of a statue that will accompany Don Juan on his infernal journey. The playwright formulates a spectacular climax that jointly applies the chain of events and the messages of the text. Tirso seems to have two audiences in mind: the theatergoers that hope to be entertained and enlightened (in that order) and the censors that will prioritize the didactic and doctrinal intentions over the visual and emotional features and the dramatic action per se. The expansive perspective allows for—and helps to account for—the special richness and intricacy of *El burlador de Sevilla*. The social structure, class distinctions, questions of gender, the multiple projections of honor, and the intersections of individualism and conformity are on display. As in baroque art in general, the spectator becomes a participant in the process of defining meaning, since reception is inscribed in the work itself.

Sin and treachery orient the linear development of *El burlador de Sevilla*, while the promise of salvation lies at its heart. Circumstances, primarily of his own doing, jeopardize Don Juan's chances for success on the eternal plane. Nonetheless, he remains confident of God's forgiveness. He mistakes free will (or free rein) for freedom from restrictions, and that precipitates his downfall. If one examines the parameters of the play, a number of topics—secular and spiritual—emerge: *machismo* and its underside, the objectification of women, favoritism due to the social hierarchy, the theory and practice of honorability, absolute and relative justice, and conceptions of the hereafter. Don Juan is the conduit from which the major subjects surface. Tirso the dramatist dialogues with Tirso the theologian, and it is conceivable that psychology, expressed through poetry, provides a nexus between the realms of the theater and religion. The world view of early modern Spain inflects *El burlador de Sevilla*, notably by way of the emphasis on honor, the strict social order, the baroque confluence of elements, and the obvious force of Catholicism. Tirso produces a conspicuously flawed protagonist that demands attention and that may seduce the spectator as he seduces his victims. Don Juan turns his shortcomings into compelling points of interest. Not surprisingly, an audience member may assume that the build-up of offenses will bear intriguing and dazzling consequences, yet there is more to the puzzle that is Don Juan Tenorio. Every interaction has double or triple interpretive options that relate respectively to Don Juan, to his interlocutor, to the context of the specific incident or speeches, and to Tirso's intervention as implied author (in an age of censorship). Society sets forth a diverse playing field, and theology deals with the mysteries of life and death. Models of behavior are broken, and pathways to heaven are prescribed but unheeded. If drama depends on conflict, Don Juan is, ironically and oxymoronically, the ideal negative exemplar and standard-bearer of chaos. He fails to learn, but he can teach others as he goes astray, as he violates the laws of man and of God. What saves him, in a manner of speaking, is the eloquence of a discourse generated by the playwright.

Tirso did not create *El burlador de Sevilla* in a vacuum. Prior works treat variations on the themes of honor, male and female stereotypes, and the road to eternity. In terms of the full scope of intertextuality, however, the play leaves an indelible mark on later writers and artists. Don Juan Tenorio becomes a universally recognized character, ripe for reappropriation. Tirso's text has—despite its sense of closure—a certain openness regarding the social, political, and doctrinal aims of the author. The elusive and bewildering Don Juan, in turn, lends himself to recasting. In Spanish literary history, the most famous of the rewritings is the Romantic play *Don Juan Tenorio*, by José Zorrilla. Zorrilla's Don Juan is, if anything, a bigger scoundrel than his predecessor. This Don Juan Tenorio takes pride in the exceedingly lengthy list of women that he has dishonored. He cannot refrain from betting on his prowess, especially if the wager permits him to deploy his resourcefulness and powers of deception, and, of course, to amplify the list. Zorrilla seems to strive to surpass Tirso in extravagant twists and in extreme measures. In *Don Juan Tenorio*, the protagonist actually falls in love with a noblewoman named Doña Inés, who will disrupt the template of Tirso's play. The Romantic (and romantic) version has Don Juan kidnap Doña Inés from the convent in which she had been housed, to then be confronted by her enraged father Don Gonzalo de Ulloa and reluctantly to kill him after pleading in vain for her hand. Returning to Seville some five years after his escape, Don Juan discovers that his family estate is now a pantheon, with statues of those for whose deaths he is responsible, including Don Gonzalo and Doña Inés, who succumbed to grief and to the pain of abandonment. Doña Inés has remained in purgatory, under the stipulation that she must save Don Juan or suffer damnation herself. As Don Juan is about to enter hell, he prays to God for mercy, and Doña Inés materializes with just enough time to redeem two souls.

The First Part of *Don Juan Tenorio* underscores the protagonist's role as transgressor and concludes with the death of Don Gonzalo, more accidental than premeditated. The Second Part opens with Don Juan's reappearance in Seville. In the pantheon, he responds to the signs of his earlier life and to the spirit of Doña Inés. Whereas Tirso crafts four female characters with distinct personalities and motives, Zorrilla highlights the undifferentiated qualities of Don Juan's victims; they are names on a list or fiancées of friends that must be humiliated. Contact is purely physical. With Doña Inés, the picture changes radically. Don Juan reacts to her from the beginning—before she enters the convent—as if she were a holy object. He abducts her, but does not stain her honor. He tries to convince her father that his intentions are honorable, and he begs for her hand. The master of desecration is uniquely touched by Doña Inés, that is, touched by love, a factor absent from his former relations with women. Doña Inés remains chaste throughout the play. Their love is unsullied, unconsummated. Don Juan is altered—reformed—by love, and, in this Romantic vision, love conducts him upward, with a pious partner that selflessly has tied her destiny to his. Zorrilla modifies the character of Don Juan Tenorio and the tenor of the play by electing to insert love into the design: love that softens the callousness and cruelty of Don Juan and that is personified in Doña Inés, the veritable protagonist of the Second Part. The playwright re-creates the pitiless *burlador* of Seville while adding a dimension to Tirso's characterization. Zorrilla's Don Juan has a capacity for love, for genuine feelings of respect and fidelity. If one cannot help but notice a lack of consistency or a suitable transition in the about-face, it might be conceded that Zorrilla picks symbolism over psychology. He introduces love into the equation and revamps the conceptual base of *El burlador de Sevilla*. Tirso seems most preoccupied with giving the wayward Don Juan his just deserts. Zorrilla bypasses theological polemics to propose that love—rather than well-timed repentance—can be a means of attaining divine rewards.

Tirso de Molina's Don Juan Tenorio is a libertine that seems to take pleasure in degrading and disgracing women. He takes a bit too literally the tenet that sinners can be saved if they confess before death, and ultimately time is not on his side. The unity of action of *El burlador de Sevilla* centers on the delineation of misdeeds and the eventual and inevitable punishment of the offender. The four exempla of dishonor and the exchanges with the statue of Don Gonzalo take up the dramatic space between the transgressions and the fiery demise of Don Juan. In this space of deferral between the exposi-

tion and the dénouement, Tirso has the opportunity to reveal the outlook
and attitudes of the protagonist in an array of venues and with an Italian
countess and, in Spain, with a fisherwoman, a noble lady, and a village bride.
Don Juan is steadfast and versatile, without compassion or empathy. Love is
at a far remove from his game plan. Don Juan amuses himself by demeaning
women, and this hardly stresses a laudable virility. His disdain and indiffer-
ence toward women mirror his problematic stance on religion. Tirso resorts
to the supernatural sphere in order to draw together the aggression and the
sacrilegious posturing of Don Juan: Don Gonzalo—aristocrat and statue—
is the avenging father and the escort into hell. José Zorrilla maintains the
ostentatious *machismo* of the protagonist by exaggerating his obsession with
statistics for his register. Rivalry substitutes for love until Don Juan meets
Doña Inés, who completely transforms his sentimental disposition. His feelings now have swung from contempt for women to idealization of a single
love object. In the Second Part of *Don Juan Tenorio*, Don Juan reexamines
his life and reclaims his lost love. In Zorrilla's vision, the roots of love remain
an enigma, but here love can transcend all barriers and transport the lovers to heaven. Doña Inés, who has no counterpart in *El burlador de Sevilla*,
becomes a symbol of love as an agent of redemption. Romantic drama more
often than not ends in tragedy; fate is the enemy. Zorrilla reverses the pattern
of his contemporaries and of his model, as he breaks away from the defense-
less women of Tirso's play to spotlight a truly admirable female character,
who can love God and reform the basest of delinquents through love.

The deep structure of *El burlador de Sevilla* has many elements in common with that of *Don Juan Tenorio*, yet the endings advance opposing reso-
lutions. Tirso has the malefactor pay for his irreverence, while Zorrilla posits
love as a catalyst for salvation and as a means of escape from pending doom.
In *El burlador de Sevilla*, Don Juan is a captivating but static character. The
situations differ, yet the persona is virtually unchanging. Much revolves
around his rejection of change. In *Don Juan Tenorio*, in contrast, the protagonist is a divided self, a perpetrator of evil before meeting Doña Inés and a
contender for redemption thereafter. Love influences his *modus operandi* and
his choices. Zorrilla teases the meanings of *faith* as he orchestrates the final
act of Don Juan, a decision—and a state of mind—that will bring him and
his beloved Inés to the gates of heaven. The setup for each play is similar, yet
the conclusions could not lie further apart. The moral and spiritual lessons of
El burlador de Sevilla are unambiguous, to an extent thanks to the repeated
intercession of Catalinón. Tirso's Don Juan himself—a braggart and a cal-
lous troublemaker—decidedly positions himself for retaliation from above.

Zorrilla's Don Juan starts from the same level of brazenness and abuse. He boasts of his exploitation of women and seems to be bereft of a conscience. He is struck down not by the wrath of God but by the previously unexperienced pull of love. He cannot avoid the killing of Don Gonzalo or the encounter with the statue of his nemesis, but, through Doña Inés's devotion to him and to God, Don Juan can delight in eternal life, a good fortune that he does not categorically deserve. Zorrilla may be more inclined to foreground the impact of love than to debate the nuances of repentance. In doing so, he bestows agency on the principal female character Doña Inés, whose heroism overshadows the anti-heroism of Don Juan.

The two classic Spanish versions of the Don Juan Tenorio story serve as templates for other works, scores of them, by artists such as Molière, Byron, Mozart, Unamuno, Valle-Inclán, Azorín, and Dalí, and by students of the human mind such as Freud, Jung, and Lacan. Tirso brings gender identity, misogyny, and salvation to the fore. Zorrilla intensifies the indiscretions and insolence of Don Juan before concentrating on the effect of Doña Inés (and, hence, of love) on the sinner. Adaptations in an assortment of media, along with critical and scientific commentaries, delve into the character, the themes, and the traditions associated with Don Juan Tenorio. Criticism on Don Juan addresses myriad issues and exhibits a broad spectrum of approaches. Every "reading" of Don Juan looks to the intertext and begins anew. Every commentary (or meta-commentary) should presuppose a thorough consideration of the text proper. The essays in this collection attest to the continued allure of Don Juan in his countless manifestations over time, space, and artistic mode. Some focus predominantly on textual analysis, while others scrutinize the text against other objects, some aesthetic, some not. A common thread is critical and theoretical dialogue that incorporates the text, social and cultural practices, literary conventions, and ideologies of many varieties. Literary history is part of history and part of the educational process. Literature encapsulates the ways in which people think, act, write, and move forward. In this case, *El burlador de Sevilla* becomes the *primum mobile* of essays that explore the construction and reconstruction—and, perchance, the deconstruction—of Don Juan Tenorio. Naturally, each essay bears the imprint or signature of its author, who examines a text or group of texts *a su manera*. The result is a compendium of meditations on Don Juan. The trickster stands at the center, while the complementary materials and the supporting cast enrich and enliven the image. There are still lacunae to be filled, and what is new can add dimensions and insights into what is old. Archetypes, one could submit, are made to be reevaluated and supplemented.

The essays, with impressive precision, cover important facets of the texts and take advantage of numerous methodologies. An early mystery regarding *El burlador de Sevilla* is its authorship. Tirso de Molina is the leading candidate, but Andrés de Claramonte has vigorous supporters. The structure of *El burlador de Sevilla*, which does and does not take place in the fourteenth century, complicates matters of space: real, fictional, and anachronistic. Women in the play are objects, but objects with voices that can be articulate, assured, and persuasive. Judgments on women's voices in the early modern period may promote a better understanding of feminine and feminist discourse in the present. From another slant, today's readers may feel removed from the theological disputes that inform the play and from the supernatural occurrences that mark the ending, and they may not relate easily to the signs of melancholy and lovesickness that could need contextualization, as well. The prevalence of these sensations in early modern literature and treatises of various sorts can aid in clarifying the depiction of the ailments attendant to love in *El burlador de Sevilla*. Since religion is a *sine qua non* of Tirso's play, it is not coincidental that productions of *Don Juan Tenorio* are a staple of All Souls' Day. Don Juan Tenorio is a character with a literary past and a notable refashioning, and he is a reminder of the cycle of life and death. Zorrilla's play can be seen as a theatrical venture and an allegory of the relation between the flesh and the spirit, with resurrection always in the background.

A beauty of criticism is the infinite depth of comparative studies, of juxtapositions without end. The essays assembled in this volume verify that stance. Following the outline of the cosmogenic theory of the pre-Socratic philosopher Empedocles, one can interpret the four women of *El burlador de Sevilla* as embodiments of the four basic elements and of the strife provoked by their interactions. Don Juan empowers the women and then steals their powers, and this, reductively stated, lands him in hell. Again, with recourse to classical antiquity, Don Juan and Doña Inés in *Don Juan Tenorio*—marked by an accent on the sense of touch—evoke the myth of Pygmalion and Galatea. Moving centuries ahead, one can note that Zorrilla's play influences Mozart and Da Ponte's *Don Giovanni*, which leads to the composition of comic melodramas on the Don Juan narrative for London's commercial theaters. The British takes on Don Juan rewrite the character, as befits the spirit of comedy. On a more serious side, the myth of Don Juan in the baroque and Romantic eras can be mediated by relations of authority and control as postulated by Michel Foucault and other theorists. In the domain of intertextuality, Don Juan and the aura of the character can be suggested as implicit ingredients of Gothic fiction. At the end of the nineteenth century and the beginning of the twentieth, writers in the Iberian Peninsula rethink Don Juan Tenorio, sometimes as a senior citizen that ruminates on the past. One such writer is Valle-Inclán, whose *Sonatas* put forth a new, elaborate, and striking thesis on the power of seduction. Another is Fernando Pessoa, of Portugal, whose *Book of Disquiet* contains a modernist reassessment of the phenomenon of Don Juanism and the bases, ethical and aesthetic, of seduction. Don Juan makes his way into pictorial art and popular culture in Spain and abroad. Illustrations, paintings, and costume designs interpret the protagonist and other characters through the style of the artist. Correspondingly, social types—in films, television, and "real life," in Spain, Latin America, and internationally—draw upon the legend of Don Juan.

There is a metonymical quality to the essays that comprise the collection. Each contributor uses a version, or versions, of Don Juan from which to analyze a relevant aspect of the text or to "bounce" the text off other texts and areas of inquiry. Tirso's *El burlador de Sevilla* is a play about faith, about society and its values and hierarchies, and about gender. The play's linear structure follows Don Juan's passage to hell. Tirso imbues Don Juan with a degree of magnetism that could threaten to conceal—at any given moment—the harshness and the heartlessness of his attitude toward women and toward religion. Albeit a transgressor of the highest magnitude, he is a mesmerizing presence on stage. His exchanges with a large cast of characters show his verbal and mental dexterity, yet charisma cannot offset the damnation that is his final sentence. Zorrilla's *Don Juan Tenorio* includes a last-minute reprieve attributable to love, a good woman, and the grace of God. Whether consciously or unconsciously, Zorrilla sanctions the refurbisher's freedom to alter—as drastically as deemed necessary—the primary intertext. These stimulating essays investigate the plays, their sources, their form and content, their internal logic, their theatricality (and meta-theatricality), their ideology, and their connections with other works of art and systems of thought. Don Juan and the plays about his "performances" are evocative because of the intricacies of the character, the plots, and the human and spiritual conflicts. Critical approaches, angles of vision, and comparative possibilities seem limitless. Don Juan Tenorio scarcely could be classified as an endearing protagonist, yet he can beguile a reader or audience—surely, if incongruously—through his very resistance to heroism and integrity, through his flight from virtue. The destructive personality notwithstanding, it is hard to get Don Juan, in any of his manifestations, out of one's mind. The trickster's elasticity may be his most salient feature and an analogue of his elusive motivations and those of his creators. Although we would like to think otherwise, removed as we are in time, space, and sensitivity, Don Juan's world is not entirely unlike our own, and while his defects may be hyperbolically rendered, we may recognize them in our neighbors and in ourselves. Societies change. Human nature, desire, strains of lawlessness, and the mysteries of the beyond do not. The literary past is more than accumulated works and critiques. It is a reading of (mutable) reality. The world is permanently and irrevocably a stage, and *virtuosos* of the stage never forget that *dictum*. As we contemplate the nexus of life and art, neither should we.

Introduction

Carmen García de la Rasilla and
Jorge Abril Sánchez
University of New Hampshire-Durham

I n 2017, Hispanists around the world celebrated the four-hundredth anniversary of the first known performance of *El burlador de Sevilla* [1630; *The Trickster of Seville*]. Despite the still heated debate about the identity of the author of this text—attributed both to Spanish playwrights Tirso de Molina and Andrés de Claramonte—the original play has enjoyed a long history of adaptations, appropriations, misappropriations, sequels, and translations of all kinds. Indeed, certain scenes, such as the encounter of Don Juan and his beloved in the balcony, have been revisited on multiple occasions by several dramatists. Furthermore, its main character, Don Juan Tenorio, an inveterate womanizer who does not find complete satisfaction in his enjoyment of women, has transcended the literary text and crossed interdisciplinary boundaries to become part of popular culture. Today, the term Don Juan refers to a man who enjoys a predatory sexual freedom at the expense of his victims and lacks emotional commitment or staying power. The archetype has re-emerged in the last decades in American academia, and many courses have been designed to explore the defining features of the villain in the text, in later adaptations, in movie versions, in the public sphere and in social media. This monograph will be in this sense required reading for many of these courses. At a time when academic institutions have engaged in intense conversations and debates about the nature and prevalence of sexual assault on university campuses, this volume will provide new analyses, interpretations and readings of some of these literary variants in connection with a wide array of theoretical approaches and sociopolitical contexts.

The editors of this book organized a conference at the University of New Hampshire in March of 2017 to commemorate this anniversary by re-examining the historical and literary evolution and transformation of the protagonist through different perspectives: contemporaries, later innovators, and modern audiences. Thanks to the financial support granted by the Center for the Humanities, the Department of Languages, Literatures and Cultures, the Department of Classics, Humanities and Italian Studies, the Department of Political Science and the Program for Women's Studies at UNH, the organizers put together an interdisciplinary academic meeting to discuss the nature of this archetypical character, his defining attributes, and the consequence of his *modus vivendi*, including the communication, transfer, transformation and (mis)use of the characteristics of the antihero in a number of artistic, literary, movie and theatrical creations. The symposium consisted of several panels organized around major aspects of *El burlador de Sevilla* and the character of the legendary seducer, the theme of apparitions and illusions, the issue of sexual immaturity and the translation, adaptation and re-interpretation of the character in Spain and abroad.

Professor Alfredo Rodríguez López-Vázquez opened the symposium with a special lecture on three works he provocatively argues were misattributed to Tirso de Molina: *El burlador de Sevilla*, *El condenado por desconfiado* and *El infanzón de Illescas*. The lack of documentary basis in support of these attributions casts doubt on the play's long accepted authorship, while further investigations point, according to López-Vázquez, to Andrés de Claramonte as the only possible creator of the myth of Don Juan. This intriguing, provocative and controversial opening underscored the mystery and debate that surrounds the legend as well as its persistent and "invasive" influence in the literature of other countries and epochs. Some essays gathered in this book contribute to reveal the scope and "predatory" reach of Don Juan in early modern and modern arts and letters, while other disclose essential keys to understand the myth and its cultural and literary influence from a historical, cosmological, psychological and sexual perspective.

The second segment of the book deals with the spaces and movements of the famous and infamous wandering Trickster. Frederick A. de Armas's "Constructing Don Juan's World: Women and the Cosmos in *El burlador de Sevilla*" argues that the new individualism and the new desire to revise the cosmos during the early modern period were instrumental in the creation of the character of Don Juan. Since *El burlador de Sevilla* brings forth a new and important myth that seems to counter the traditional or medieval cosmic perspective, de Armas investigates how the play questions the three levels of this cosmos and particularly the four basic elements and the uses of planetary and zodiacal images. He asks whether an orderly and harmonious universe, impeccably designed and governed, can survive the ravages of a Don Juan. The essay illustrates how Don Juan's tricks unleash a quasi-cosmic battle, one that leaves the heavens diminished as planetary women like those filed away in the Don's catalogue are made sickly and debased by the *burlador* and his ilk. Even the signs of the Zodiac suffer as Taurus and Capricorn are foregrounded as images of deceit. The cosmos is left reeling but seeking to right itself: seeking to balance the masculine and the feminine, as Empedocles prescribes.

Antonio Guijarro Donadiós studies the physical space where the libertine wanders with special reference to the fictionalization of the urban environment (physical, moral and vital) in *El burlador de Sevilla*. His purpose is to examine the confluence between two realities: those of Seville and Lisbon, two major centres with their own genuine vital spaces, their peculiar urban geography and their populations and mentalities. Guijarro Donadiós argues that their fictional conformations in interplay with the pieces of the dramatic mechanism and of Tirso's imaginary construction create the formalization of a fictional space and the articulation of the urban as a key functional element of the play.

The third section is dedicated to principles of perversion, hedonism and ludic theatricality that invariably govern Don Juan's world in most, if not all, of its literary versions. For instance, although Tirso de Molina's *El burlador de Sevilla* and José Zorrilla's *Don Juan Tenorio* reflect distinct contexts and sensorial boundaries, Charles Victor Ganelin examines how the most notable moments in both texts involve a special touch: the statue asking/demanding that Don Juan give him his hand. Throughout each play, Don Juan does "give his hand," the texts imply, to various women, only to deceive them, in order to satisfy a perverted sense of ecstasy. Elizabeth Harvey summarizes the importance of touching in general when she writes of this sense that it "establishes our sentient border with the world." Every time Don Juan reaches out, he conveys a distinct nuance to these events or moments, each one leading to his demise. Where *El burlador* couches the final, quasi-mystical grasp of the statue in theological terms, condemning Don Juan to hell, *Tenorio* converts damnation into apotheosis, redeeming him and redefining ecstasy. Zorrilla's presentation appears thus to be informed by a Platonic reading of touch in its dual capacity for pleasure or pain, reversing the "pharmakonic" effects we see in Tirso's *comedia*. By staging touch as redemption (another sort of ecstasy), Zorrilla also embarks on redefining Pygmalion as Don Juan shuffles off his mortal coil in his transformation into ethereal being, entwined in Inés's arms to create an image that anticipates Jean-Léon Gérôme's canvas *Pygmalion and Galatea.* Both incarnations of Don Juan are in thrall to touch and both become thrilled with its ecstatic possibilities. Ganelin's insightful analysis is corroborated by Ricardo de la Fuente's essay titled "José Zorrilla's Don Juan and His Games." This essay emphasizes the character's Dionysian concept of life as a game, which is the essence of tragedy. Like Ganelin, de la Fuente reveals the insubstantial identity of Don Juan, based on primarily theatrical games. As a hero of appearances and of disguise, he is a frivolous actor, whose body disappears into the collective body of the carnival. However, as Ricardo de la Fuente points out, his inconstancy is dissolved by the quietness of the marble of the statue, but only until the next festivity or performance. In "Valle-Inclán's Don Juan Beyond the Pleasure Principle," James Mandrell explores that author's *Marqués de Bradomín* as a problematic version of the *burlador*, taking as its point of departure the seemingly contrary identifications of the Marqués as a Don Juan and as a Catholic, which is to say, as a Catholic Don Juan. His attempt to understand the Marqués by following Valle-Inclán's instructions on how he is to be read, draws on his earlier work on Don Juan even as it traces the logic of Valle-Inclán's four seasons, the *Sonata de primavera* (1904), *Sonata de estío* (1903), *Sonata de otoño* (1902), and *Sonata de invierno* (1905). By addressing the ways in which the *Sonatas* work out the difficult relationship between love and death in the framework of texts that read as memoirs, as reflections on a past ranging from remote to recent, as well as a recasting of prior literary models, Mandrell demonstrates that the Marqués is a Don Juan in word and deed and that, moreover, he is part and parcel of the patriarchal and literary tradition pertaining to Don Juan.

Mandrell's essay works well as an introduction to the articles in Section Four, written from a feminist perspective. Robert E. Bayliss argues that Tirso de Molina's *comedia* serves as a useful point of departure for a broader understanding of the factors that contribute to the widespread sexual assault of female students on college campuses. His essay "Taking Back the Night: *El burlador de Sevilla* and Twenty-First Century Feminisms" examines the ways in which Tirso's play may enhance student awareness of the institutional and ideological roots of the issue and how our approaches to it have evolved from those of previous generations. Based on his experiences teaching *El burlador* in English translation in a First-Year Seminar, including a class visit by the Spanish feminist activist Lidia Falcón, Bayliss explains how teaching the play alongside subsequent adaptations (*Don Juan DeMarco, Don Juan Tenorio, Johnny Tenorio*) can deepen students' understanding of their own cultural problems while revealing profound differences between present-day strategies and earlier iterations of feminist criticism. In the same vein, Margaret E. Boyle underlines how the provocative model raised by *El burlador* four hundred years later has become a fascinating object of study, considering our present debates on "locker room talk," and the power of language over action, and most recently the #metoo movement. Building on past scholarship concerning women's roles within the dramatic world of the play, her essay ("When Women Say No: Don Juan and the Language of Protest") explores the complex ways in which language and sexual consent are tied together within character dialogue: overt and expressive declarations and accusations; scenes of misunderstanding, silencing or obscuring; and finally how words relate to modes of being and knowing.

Section Five includes several illuminating articles on the powerful legacy of the Spanish myth in various distant literary and cultural contexts and genres. Daniel Lorca studies José de Espronceda's adaptation of Don Juan in *El estudiante de Salamanca* from a Foucauldian perspective. With a focus on the evolving moral values of justice from the Baroque to the Romantic period, he points to the major changes in power relations during this era and how they affected Don Juan's literary and cultural transformation and reception in the nineteenth century. In any case, and as Vicente Pérez de León explains, the great freedom and creativity displayed in the sequels of Don Juan in that century were the result of the historical accumulation of receptions and traditions of the myth of Don Juan. Using a comparative approach, Pérez de León's essay contextualizes the *Giovanni burlettas* within the literary tradition of the "comic don Juan," associating these popular culture plays with related Spanish Golden Age donjuanesque characters and short picaresque plays about criminals or *jácaras*. As he points out, a few months after the successful performance of Mozart's opera *Don Giovanni* in London in 1817, several musical comic sequels on the Don Juan topic became theatrical successes. Two illustrative examples are the leading actress Lucy Vestris cross-dressed as don Giovanni, and the presence of the evocative and romantic character of Constatia Quixotte in *Don Giovanni in London*. This essay contextualizes these plays in the literary tradition of the "comic don Juan," with special emphasis on exploring the early mixed reception of the original Spanish myth in England, initiated in Shadwell's *The Libertine* (1676) and strongly influenced by Mozart's opera *Don Giovanni* (1787).

Clearly, by the early nineteenth century the character of Don Juan had become quite malleable. Fernando González de León focuses on the Gothic as the key transitional genre in the metamorphosis of the Spanish seducer. Basing his study on documentary as well as textual research, and tracing the origins of the Gothic notions of Don Juan to the original Spanish play and its various European adaptations in the seventeenth and eighteenth centuries, González de León uncovers the key role that the story of the Spanish seducer played in Walpole's *The Castle of Otranto* and the genesis of the Gothic genre, as well as in its later iterations both on the written page and on the stage in England and France. The gothification of Don Juan, he argues, reached an apotheosis in the figure of the Romantic vampire, a wandering, predatory and protean aristocratic trickster who operates as an implacable and uncanny reincarnation of the Sevillian libertine, clearly identified as such by the authors and audiences of the day, and eventually mutating into the greatest creation of a quintessential man of the theatre, Bram Stoker's *Dracula*. González de León then goes on to sketch the final and ultimate Gothic metamorphosis of Don Juan in a later Stoker novel dealing with the Spanish-American War, *The Mystery of the Sea*. In this romance of imperial Gothic, the parallel becomes explicit as the vampire Don Juan turns into Don Escoban, a brooding Spanish nobleman bent on resurrecting the might of Spain. Like Dracula, Don Juan and other foreign invaders and debauchers, Escoban refuses to adapt to modernity, stands against historical progress and represents an ancient and insidious ethno-cultural threat to Anglo-American global domination. As such, he, too, must spectacularly perish.

Lastly, Fernando Beleza studies Fernando Pessoa's version of Don Juan, whom he excludes from modernism, in tandem with the Romantic male subject, presenting him as a radically outdated form of masculine subjectivity with no place in his modernist literary imagination. Bernardo Soares, the narrator and fictional author of Fernando Pessoa's *The Book of Disquiet*, is in a myriad of ways the exact opposite of Don Juan. He is a lonely bookkeeper without any seduction skills, who works, lives, and writes his autobiography (*The Book* itself) on a single street of Lisbon's downtown district, which he rarely ever leaves. He is a man without qualities, and when it comes to seduction, he is an absolute failure. Yet, he does not envy, but, instead, mocks the Don Juans of early twentieth century Lisbon. By focusing on various passages of failed seduction, Beleza argues that Soares radically attempts to pulverize the figure of Don Juan—particularly in its Romantic incarnation—when writing in his fictional autobiography a quintessential modernist self.

Daniel Chávez's article also focuses on Don Juan as a model/anti-model of masculinity. If the history of Mexican masculinities, Chávez argues, reflects most of the different inflections present in western cultures, the combination of colonial heritage, cultural *mestizaje*, revolutionary violence and the pressures of capitalist modernity have given raise to contested if not conflicting forms of masculinity in the twentieth century. Born to a Libanese family from Tampico, Mauricio Feres Yázbek (1926-1989), who is also known as Mauricio Garcés, had a distinguished and eventful career in a country where actors from Middle Eastern cultures were often perceived as not "sufficiently" national. However, by a combination of certain cultural tropes embodied as a strategy of cosmopolitanism and sexual ambiguity, Mauricio Garcés established an artistic persona that moved from Don Juanismo to homosexuality, from chauvinistic bourgeois "Mexicaness" to affected cosmopolitan dandyism that ensured him an iconic presence in Mexican film and television for more than three decades.

A chapter devoted to great painters' interpretations of Don Juan closes the volume and brings us again to the mystery of his legend and to his perverted, hedonist and playful personality. As de la Rasilla contends in her essay, the lack of clear delineation of Don Juan's image in the original text has contributed to a situation in which each author and artist has constructed his own version of the character, generating a multiplicity of Don Juans. This fact also explains the painters' difficulty in capturing his physical appearance and the fact that our great conquistador, in spite of his universal popularity, has not, unlike Don Quixote, become an icon recognizable at first sight. It is not, therefore, strange that artists, instead of trying to recreate an impossible image, have been interested in exploring the moral and tragic dimensions of his personality or in representing concrete episodes from the drama (duels, amorous encounters, confrontations with the dead, etc.) in which an actor in the theater might breathe life into Don Juan. The great Spanish painter Ignacio de Zuloaga expressed the difficulties of composing a portrait of Don Juan "lo suficientemente representativo y a la vez lo suficientemente concreto para ser pintado" [sufficiently representative and at the same time sufficiently concrete to be painted], which brought his friend, and leading expert on the topic, Gregorio Marañón to point out that in terms of the visual arts one cannot speak of a single Don Juan but instead of many Don Juans (Marañón 83). But perhaps, this is not only true of the arts but also of literature, as the reader will see in the illuminating chapters of this book.

Had the editors of this book been more playful or adventurous, in other words, more like their subject, we could have named it *A Mirror for Don Juan* or, borrowing from Ricardo de la Fuente, *The Games of Don Juan*, since in so many ways that is just what the book is and what it offers. The alert reader will easily notice certain common themes running through most and perhaps all of the essays in this collection. The most important theme is, perhaps, conflict and transformation without loss of essential identity. The origins of Don Juan are difficult to elucidate with enough certainty and involve the confrontation of potential or possible authors and the challenge of minute investigation of words, nuances of language, and historical evidence for scholars concerned with clarification or detection. This notion of language as a weaponized indicator of identity runs across the various approaches and periods in this book and informs the work of Alfredo Rodríguez as much as it does that of Margaret Boyle; in other words, Don Juan becomes a motive and a source of linguistic disruption right from the start, and as Ganelin and de Armas persuasively suggest, the struggle may have cosmic connotations. There is also dormant or active thematic and generic conflict in the essays of Pérez de León, Mandrell, Beleza and González de León, and in their focus on the inherent tensions and continuities within the various nineteenth century or early twentieth century versions of the Don. Their contributions, and those of others, suggest that Don Juan was and remains a magnet and embodiment of all sorts of intense cultural confrontations and duels from which the fabled *burlador*, despite *burlas* at his expense, or even after much anathema and opprobrium, seems always to emerge artistically revitalized and newly relevant. These recurring concerns lend unity and coherence to a group of essays that presents a snapshot of early twenty-first century scholarship and brings together the two Spanish Don Juans as well as the many guises and disguises of their descendants.

This collection, though quite heterogeneous, relies on certain special assets that we hope will elevate its usefulness and value to the contemporary reader and scholar. It exhibits and employs a wide array of approaches to the study of Don Juan, from the historicist to the feminist to the Foucauldian, to name only a few of the perspectives. It is also remarkably interdisciplinary as it considers and analyzes the presence of Don Juan in a substantial variety of media, from plays to novels to paintings to film and television. It ranges widely in temporal terms and examines literary, artistic and historical moments and circumstances from the Renaissance to the twenty first century. Furthermore, there is an impressive demonstration of spatial reach in this collection, not only in the essays of Chávez and Guijarro Donadiós, but also in others that range from Spain to Latin America to remote or lateral locations of the English-speaking world. Again, in this important regard the collection closely resembles its subject in its versatility, its mobility, and its capacity to adopt new guises and disguises.

The Authorship of
El burlador de Sevilla

El burlador de Sevilla, El condenado por desconfiado and El infanzón de Illescas: Three Works Misattributed to Tirso de Molina

ALFREDO RODRÍGUEZ LÓPEZ-VÁZQUEZ
Universidade da Coruña

VERIFYING SOURCES AND A contrast of hypothesis are habitual heuristic processes in any field of knowledge to lay the foundations or to discard ideas handed down by tradition and anchored in a system of beliefs without documentary basis or theoretical consistency. The absence of a solid documentary basis in the attribution of these three works to Tirso de Molina is of a distinct rank: *El infanzón de Illescas* and *El burlador de Sevilla* do not appear in any of the five parts of Tirso's comedies, while *El condenado por desconfiado* appears in the *Segunda parte* published with colophon in Tarragon in 1634 without Tirso's authorization. The prologue indicates that only four of the twelve comedies included in the volume were his. As for the *Burlador*, printed in Seville but with false colophon from Barcelona in 1630, the attribution to Tirso in a very deteriorated text that was transmitted with grave errors by Roque de Figueroa's company, which in 1624 did not have this work in their repertoire, faces an important documentary problem: the version known as *Tan largo me lo fiáis* is printed in 1634-35 in Seville, this time in Calderón's name, and it has the guarantee of the fact that already in 1617 the same title was staged in Córdoba by Jerónimo Sánchez's company, in which very probably it is a *comedia nueva* [new comedy], that is, premiering in that season and in a year when Tirso de Molina is on the island of Santo Domingo, from where he will not return until 1618. For these reasons, the document on which the attribution of *El burlador de Sevilla* to

31

Tirso is based is, on the one hand, a collection and a fraudulent edition and, on the other hand, it has two contrary documentary proofs: the edition in Calderón's name of the same work but under another author's name, and the documentary verification that *Tan largo me lo fiáis* corresponds to the title and original text and that it opens in a year that is compatible with Tirso's hypothetical authorship only with great difficulty, and which should be considered a conjecture based on a printing that is a collection. A much greater documentary problem is posed by *El infanzón de Illescas*, which was never re-edited in Tirso's name until Hartzenbusch included it in his volume of the BAE, crossing texts edited in the seventeenth century in Lope de Vega's name and Calderón's name in a different text. The work is edited in a *suelta* [loose collection] under Lope's name around 1630-1640 and in the *Parte Cuarta* of Calderón's works edited by Antonio de la Cavallería in Barcelona in 1673, an attribution that Calderón himself rejected. The most complete and trustworthy document, which is also the oldest, is a manuscript copy made by Juan Francisco de Henao and dated to December 30, 1626 in Zaragoza, which indicates that the comedy is one of Andrés de Claramonte's. This attribution is corroborated by a second manuscript, with seventeenth century letters and a shorter text, with the name *El rey don Pedro en Madrid*, in which Claramonte is also identified as the comedy's author. To this point, then, the documentation, as one may see, does not support the attribution to Tirso of any of these three works and, instead, offers an alternative author, Andrés de Claramonte. This is corroborated by two manuscripts with different titles, a phenomenon that is also recorded in the case of *Tan largo me lo fiáis/El burlador de Sevilla*.

Passing from documentation to theory, we must distinguish between theories of a more general character and particular theories. The more general theories include the results of research into objective aspects of theater, like the evolution of metrical uses and thematic trends; partial aspects of concrete playwrights that imply (especially in the case of Lope and Calderón) a fixing of the corpus; the transmission of texts through theatrical companies or by means of unbound or broken-down editions; and other objective indices such as the appearance of poetic names like Belardo for Lope, Lauro for Luis Vélez, Clarindo for Claramonte, and other similar ones that should be considered in cases of doubtful attributions. In what pertains to the evolution of polymetry, the pioneering studies of Morley and Bruerton, continued by various analysts like Vern G. Williamsen, Diego Marín, and others, have allowed scholars to establish general constant principles in addition to the variations of particular uses. The methodology of distinguishing between works of certain attribution with dates of staging, doubtful works from imprecise periods of time, and works with alternative authors has revealed its effectiveness after the discovery of the Gálvez manuscript, which verified the hypotheses of Morley and Bruerton at over 95%. This means that we have general theories with reliable results in the case of Lope de Vega and works attributed to him, and in cases in which they have followed the same methodology, with important results concerning Tirso de Molina. This is the case with the doctoral research of Torre Temprano at the University of Navarra, which attempts to elucidate the attribution of *El condenado por desconfiado*. The analysis is based on a collation of all the metrical aspects of all twelve works included in Tirso's *Segunda parte* compared with the works of certain attribution from the remaining parts, which gives us a corpus of some fifty works of certain authorship to establish the relative fit of the dozen works of which Tirso only recognized four as his own. The methodological rigor with which this work is carried out brings with it the requirement that works of doubtful attribution in Tirso's corpus, such as *El burlador de Sevilla*, *La ninfa del cielo*, and *El infanzón de Illescas*—which many Tirso scholars include in order to also attribute *El condenado por desconfiado*, and which results in a distortion of the data—not be used. The fifty works of certain attribution allow scholars to obtain a very reliable metrical profile and objective results. According to this profile the twelve comedies of the *Segunda parte* are ordered according to their greater or lesser fit with the metrical profile of Tirso, and each of the texts is assigned a number in this order. The two comedies that correspond wholly to Tirso's profile are precisely the two whose final lines declare Tirso's authorship: *Por el sótano y el torno* and *Amor y celos hacen discretos*. The third work that matches Tirso's metrical profile, according to the criteria analyzed by Torre Temprano, is *Esto sí que es negociar*, which corresponds to a different transmission of *El melancólico*, which Tirso himself had included in his *Primera parte*. The fact that the three works, out of this collection of twelve, are also the ones that offer the greatest similarity with the corpus of Tirso's fifty comedies is clear support of the methodology by which Torre Temprano has worked. Therefore, the critical problem is reduced to identifying which could be the fourth text out of the remaining nine. Ángel Raimundo Fernández sets out this question in summary in his edition of *El condenado* in 1990:

> Tirso no indica cuáles son las cuatro suyas. Pero sobre tres de ellas toda la crítica está de acuerdo en que son de Tirso, desde Hartzenbusch, Cayetano Alberto de la Barrera, Emilio Cotarelo y también Menéndez Pelayo.

Dos (*Por el sótano y el torno* y *Amor y celos hacen discretos*) llevan el nombre de Tirso en los dos versos finales. La tercera (*Esto sí que es negociar*) es una refundición de otra (*El melancólico*), que es indudablemente de Tirso. Y en cuanto a la cuarta no hay acuerdo. Fue Agustín Durán el primero en señalar que se trataba de *El condenado por desconfiado*. Le siguieron en la atribución Hartzenbusch, de la Barrera y Menéndez Pelayo. Sostienen, en cambio, que no es obra de Tirso, Cotarelo y Mori, Manuel de la Revilla, Fernández Guerra, C. E. Aníbal, Gómez Baquero y Ángel Valbuena Prat. Doña Blanca de los Ríos volvió a reivindicar la paternidad en favor de Tirso, basándose en que se imprimió a nombre de él durante todo el siglo XVII y XVIII y que la duda de la autoría no se formula hasta 1878, por M. de la Revilla.[1]

[Tirso does not indicate which are his four. But for three of them, all the criticism is in agreement that they are Tirso's, from Hartzenbusch, Cayetano Alberto de la Barrera, Emilio Cotarelo, and also Menéndez Pelayo. Two (*Por el sótano y el torno* and *Amor y celos hacen discretos*) bear Tirso's name in the final lines. The third (*Esto sí que es negociar*) is a reworking of another (*El melancólico*), which indubitably is Tirso's. With regard to the fourth there is no agreement. Agustín Durán was the first to point out that it was *El condenado por desconfiado*. Hartzenbusch, de la Barrera, and Menéndez Pelayo followed him in this attribution. Cotarelo y Mori, Manuel de la Revilla, Fernández Guerra, C. E. Aníbal, Gómez Baquero, and Ángel Valbuena Prat hold, in contrast, that this is not Tirso's work. Doña Blanca de los Ríos also defended its origins in favor of Tirso, basing this on the fact that it was printed under his name in through the 17th and 18th centuries and that doubts of authorship did not arise until 1878, posed by M. de la Revilla.]

It is surprising that Ángel R. Fernández omits from this line-up Ruth Lee Kennedy, the Tirso scholar who has denied the work's authorship with the greatest abundance of arguments, and that he also omits the doctoral work of María Torre Temprano, who has corroborated this with a different methodology from R. L. Kennedy. Both authors are excluded, in effect, from the bibliography manipulated by the editor, who, in contrast, includes three

---

1   Tirso de Molina, *El condenado por desconfiado*, Madrid, Espasa-Calpe, 1990, pp. 15-16.

articles from Friar Rafael Hornedo,[2] published in the journal *Razón y Fe* in 1940 and 1948. It is also surprising that Fernández includes two short articles by Serge Maurel, but that he does not include the publication of his doctoral thesis in 1973, where, after analyzing the problem of the attributions of *El burlador de Sevilla* and *El condenado por desconfiado* in two extensive chapters, he concludes that there is no objective datum that supports these attributions. He also argues that buttressing a work of doubtful attribution with another work that is also of doubtful attribution is not very convincing; in the end, he suggests, without another candidate, they should still be considered Tirso's.

In reality, the problem of determining which are Tirso's four works included in the *Segunda parte* is less arduous than it seems. The three that fit with Tirso's metrical profile, according to Morley and Bruerton's methodology applied by Torre Temprano, are the three about which there is full agreement. But, in addition, there are another four that we know are not Tirso's: *La reina de los reyes*, which is Hipólito de Vergara's; and the two parts of *Próspera y adversa fortuna de don Álvaro de Luna* and *Cautela contra cautela*, all three Mira de Amescua's. With regard to *La reina de los reyes*, the classification of Torre Temprano placed it as the least similar to Tirso's profile, number twelve in his ordering. The two belonging to Mira de Amescua about don Álvaro de Luna were both among the four most distant from the profile. Therefore, out of the five most distant metrically from Tirso's model, four are today proven to be of other authors: Hipólito de Vergara and Mira de Amescua. The fifth of this group of works that do not belong to Tirso's profile is precisely *El condenado por desconfiado*, which is number eleven of this classification based on objective elements. The fact that the other four are documented as belonging to other authors seems sufficient guarantee to go further with the hypothesis that, in addition to not corresponding to Tirso's metrical model, the attribution of this work is only based on a doctrinal element: the fact that there is a theological message and that the only possible author who could write a work with such theological depth has to be a theologian. The work that Torre Temprano proposes as highly compatible with Tirso's metrical model is *La mujer por fuerza*. Already in his edition, Cotarelo had excluded *El condenado* and had set forth a gallery of arguments to support Tirso's authorship of *La mujer por fuerza*. Recently we have

---

2   The titles of Friar Rafael Hornedo's two articles make clear his methodological approach: "*El condenado* no es una obra molinista" and "La tesis escolástico-teológica de *El condenado*." It deals with research of a doctrinal nature, separate from the problem of authorship.

broadened and made more precise the objective elements that support this. In this sense, Torre Temprano's theoretical proposal is the first that supports this attribution with arguments that do not depend on previous beliefs, as occurs with the risky, erroneous, and apodictic attributions by Blanca de los Ríos, which some modern scholars still defend.

It is worth stopping for a moment to consider the argumentative and critical procedures that Blanca de los Ríos has used for her work on Tirso and, more concretely, for the cases of comedies included in the *Segunda parte*. The best example is the comedy *Siempre ayuda la verdad*. The illustrious Tirso scholar begins her exposition in an apodictic way: "Esta obra pertenece al ciclo galaico-portugués de Tirso" [This work belongs to Tirso's Galician-Portuguese cycle].[3] Having established that the work belongs to the Galician-Portuguese cycle, she moves on to comment on the alternate proposal:

> Don Luis Fernández-Guerra, amenísimo biógrafo del mejicano Juan Ruiz de Alarcón... incurrió en grave error crítico y en imperdonable injusticia al despojar a Tirso de este drama a todas luces tan suyo, y ahijárselo a Ruiz de Alarcón, ayudado por Luis de Belmonte, sin que Téllez tuviera arte ni parte en la creación de esta obra. Juicio tan infundado y tan erróneo que no se sabe definir si en él es mayor el absurdo que la injusticia. Porque sobre que Alarcón no la incluyó entre sus obras y Tirso la insertó en la *Segunda parte* de las suyas, el drama no ofrece un solo indicio por donde se relacione con el mejicano, y no contiene rasgo alguno por donde no se relacione con Tirso.

> [Don Luis Fernández-Guerra, the most pleasant biographer of the Mexican Juan Ruiz de Alarcón... ran into a grave critical error and an unforgivable injustice by stripping Tirso of this drama that in any light is his, and to give it to Ruiz de Alarcón, helped by Luis de Belmonte, and with Tellez having neither art nor part in the creation of this work. This is a baseless judgment and so erroneous that it is impossible to decide if there is more absurdity in it than injustice. Because in addition to the fact that Alarcón did not include it among his works and Tirso placed it in the *Segunda parte* of his, the drama does not offer a single indication with which to relate it to the Mexican, and it does not contain any trace by which it is not related to Tirso.]

---

3   Tirso de Molina, *Obras dramáticas completas*, vol. III, Madrid, 1962, p. 457.

One of the arguments that Doña Blanca puts forward in favor of Tirso is that the mention of Lisbon coincides with the description of Lisbon in *El burlador*. Another is that "El Rey Don Pedro el Bravo de esta comedia es un boceto del Rey Don Pedro el Justiciero de Tirso" [King Pedro the Brave in this comedy is a sketch of King Pedro the Just of Tirso" (p. 458). In reality, there is no comedy called *El Rey Don Pedro el Justiciero* in all of Tirso's work. Blanca de los Ríos refers to *El infanzón de Illescas*, published under Lope de Vega's name with the title *El Rey don Pedro en Madrid* and under Tirso's name in the nineteenth century by Hartzenbusch, based on its relationship with *El burlador de Sevilla*. Blanca de los Ríos accepts as given the idea that *El burlador* as much as *El infanzón de Illescas* are Tirso's, and as a result, *Siempre ayuda la verdad* also has to be Tirso's and that the alternative authorships are attempts to strip the Mercedarian of his works. She also takes for granted that *Cautela contra cautela* is Tirso's, and, based on this triple attribution, discredits Fernández-Guerra's proposal:

> Finalmente denunció el maestro, refiriéndose a Alarcón—a quien Fernández-Guerra pretendió regalar *El condenado*—"la manía que en estos últimos tiempos ha habido de aumentar su caudal dramático, atribuyéndole toda comedia expósita" (1). Y el escritor más gravemente atacado de esta manía de enriquecer a Alarcón fue don Luis Fernández-Guerra, que sobre donarle gratuitamente *siempre ayuda la verdad* y *Cautela contra cautela*, pretendió endosarle *El condenado*.

> [Finally the master denounced, referring to Alarcón—to whom Fernández-Guerra tried to give *El condenado*—"the mania that there has been recently for increasing his dramatic fortunes, attributing to him every foundling comedy" (1). And the writer who has been most gravely attacked by this mania to enrich Alarcón was don Luis Fernández-Guerra, who in addition to giving him gratuitously *Siempre ayuda la verdad* and *Cautela contra cautela*, attempted to dump *El condenado* on him.]

The qualification of "master" refers to Menéndez Pelayo, who is the quote (1) that de los Ríos uses. An argument from authority is used to support a prior belief, without providing documentation or a theoretical proposal that upholds that belief. And terms such as "denounce," "give," "mania," and "gravely attacked" are used for critical alternatives that are presented with argumentation. Blanca de los Ríos's real purpose is not to establish theoretical or documentary bases with regard to the problem of Tirso's *Segunda parte*, but instead it is what the illustrious Tirso scholar sets forth at the end of the paragraph: "La restitución de esta comedia a Tirso es un paso más para restituirle entera la *Segunda parte* de las suyas" [The restitution of this comedy to Tirso is one more step towards restoring the *Segunda parte* of his works to him whole]. In the face of this prior conviction we have documentation that proves that at least four of the comedies of this *Segunda parte* are not Tirso's, but instead are Mira de Amescua's and Hipólito de Vergara's, which supports the hypothesis that only four of the works may be attributed to Tirso, as he himself affirmed in the prologue. The consequence of this is the fact that *La mujer por fuerza, El condenado por desconfiado, Cautela contra cautela,* and *Los amantes de Teruel* cannot be Tirso's at the same time. Only one of them is Tirso's and, in the lack of documentation one must hold to objective theoretical evidence that all point towards the fourth comedy being *La mujer por fuerza.* It is necessary to lay out all of this because once again in 2013 *El condenado por desconfiado* was re-edited under the name of Tirso de Molina, taking as its central argument the fact that it is a theological comedy and using passages from *Cautela contra cautela* and from other works attributed to him as arguments of textual coincidence. This is a methodological problem based on a critical abuse contrary to the rules of research.

Before moving on to examine the case of *Tan largo me lo fiáis / El burlador de Sevilla,* it is necessary to clarify the empirical and heuristic problem of presenting beliefs or subjective convictions as argumentative proofs. The problem is epistemological in nature and is rooted in not distinguishing between five different levels of argumentative uses of very different value in relationship to critical problems:

a)   Documents and data
b)   Theories
c)   Hypotheses
d)   Conjectures and suppositions
e)   Beliefs and convictions

The support of documents and data in any field of knowledge is essential to establish the limits within which theories must be constructed. And the theoretical frame allows one to evaluate hypotheses that agree with theories. Hypotheses must be able to be corroborated and verified, and they must not be contradictory and should be set forth in keeping with objective principles. Conjectures, in fields in which objective elements are not available to elaborate hypotheses, can only be accepted in a provisional format and as mere

conjecture without argumentative value. The working out of "*ad hoc* conjectures" should be excluded because an *ad hoc* conjecture does not aim at
testing a hypothesis but instead at introducing previous beliefs or ideological
convictions within the frame of the hypotheses and at eliminating objective
analyses in order to introduce ideological and doctrinal debates. The perfect
example of an *ad hoc* conjecture is the idea that *El condenado por desconfiado*
is a theological work.

It is important to distinguish between simple conjectures and *ad hoc*
conjectures because in debates about doubtful attribution both types of procedures are used frequently. With regard to the comedy *Siempre ayuda la
verdad*, Fernández-Guerra's proposal should be considered a simple conjecture: both Ruiz de Alarcón and Luis de Belmonte are possible authors for a
work staged in 1623, a year in which both are active and have collaborated
on a comedy like *Algunas hazañas del marqués de Cañete*. One indication
that allows one to propose that we are dealing with a collaborative work is
Cotarelo's observation that the final lines of the work say, "Con este título
quiero/ que dé fin *nuestra* comedia" [With this title I desire / that *our* comedy end], which may be interpreted as an indication of double or triple authorship. Towards this period (1623) the fashion of collaborative comedies
had already begun, and Luis de Belmonte was its principal driver. Both Ruiz
de Alarcón and Mira de Amescua participated, together with Vélez de Guevara and Guillén de Castro, in this type of work, for which reason there is
a basis or indication to raise this conjecture. The methodology of analysis
would demand the availability of objective criteria and a sufficient corpus to
evaluate this conjecture as a hypothesis, a procedure that has not been carried out, with the result that this conjecture has not elucidated this work's
author. Opposing this conjecture on the basis of the conviction and belief
that it is Tirso's work and then using as an argument the fact that Tirso was
familiar with Lisbon is an *ad hoc* conjecture meant to allow one to maintain
a prior belief—a belief that has been refuted in theory and with documentary evidence. It would also be an *ad hoc* conjecture to propose that the work
is Mira de Amescua's because three of the other pieces in that volume are
his. What might be considered objective criteria to determine this doubtful
authorship? In the metrical plane, these might be specific, infrequent characteristics: a) beginning the work in *quintillas*, using, in only six *quintillas*, two
different kinds: ababa, aabba, without ordering them as three *coplas reales*. b)
Beginning the second act with a large passage of *octavas reales* and the use of
octavas reales in all three acts. c) The extensive passage in *tercetos encadenados*
in the third act, which coincides with the abundance of passages in *décimas*

and *endechas hexasilábicas.* We are dealing with a collection of very infrequent metrical characteristics all found in one work and, as Torre Temprano's analysis has revealed, these characteristics are foreign to Tirso's metrical practice. Fernández-Guerra's conjecture is proposed to resolve a documentary and critical lacuna and deserves further evaluation; Blanca de los Ríos's polemic is an *ad hoc* conjecture that is upheld by her previous conviction that the work is Tirso's. It is outside any objective criteria of analysis and is not in keeping with any of the data that we know about the *Segunda parte.*

Having clarified those five argumentative levels and their different critical validity, we will occupy ourselves with the problem of the attribution of *Tan largo me lo fiáis / El burlador de Sevilla.* Documents and data on this problem are clear: in 1617 Jerónimo Sánchez's company staged in Córdoba *Tan largo me lo fiáis,* a title that coincides with a printing in Calderón's name, dated by D. W. Cruickshank, according to typographical analysis, to 1634-35 in Simón Faxardo's press in Seville. In 1630 there had been published, in Tirso de Molina's name, the same comedy with variations in transmission from Roque de Figueroa's company, in a collection titled *Doze comedias de Lope de Vega y otros autores,* in which the play is edited in Tirso's name and with colophon in Barcelona, by Gerónimo Margarit. Cruickshank's same research has established that the edition is a collection of *desglosables* [selections from books that have been broken down or that are separable] and that the press from which they come is that of Franciso de Lyra in Seville. With regard to Roque de Figueroa we know that he performed in Seville in 1629, in June and in December, and we also know that in March of 1624 he did not have this work in his repertoire. There is also documentation for the fact that in 1625 Francisco Hernández Galindo's company staged in Naples a work called *Il convitato di pietra,* the same title that in 1626 Pedro Ossorio's company also stages in Naples. Thus, in light of this data and documentation, there are two different titles and two different authors for the same work, transmitted in two different ways. There are also two different *loas:* one at Seville in *Tan largo me lo fiáis,* and another at Lisbon in *El burlador de Sevilla.* The first one is spoken by Don Juan Tenorio, and the second by Comendador Ulloa. There is also a documentary fact that is evident: Tirso did not publish this work in any of his five volumes of comedies.

The problem of authorship can be summed up thus: either one of the two playwrights to whom the work is attributed in the two editions of 1630 and 1634-35 (Tirso and Calderón) is the author, or it is neither of them. What is sufficiently improbable is that the work be of both. These two hypotheses deserve equal consideration and should be upheld by objective arguments and not by previous beliefs and theological convictions. The traditional argument, before the discovery of *Tan largo me lo fiáis*, assumed that the author was Tirso. In the face of evidence that the work did not appear in any of the five *Partes* of the Mercedarian's comedies and that no document associated with Tirso alludes to this possible authorship, scholars elaborate an *ad hoc* conjecture and present it as an argument thus: the documentary evidence does not show that Tirso denies having written it, therefore "quien calla, otorga" [silence implies consent]. This is a matter of an *ad hoc* conjecture that arises from a previous belief and that cannot be proven, for which reason it lacks any value in a critical debate.

The first proposal to analyze the first hypothesis (that either Tirso or Calderón is the author) comes from Griswold Morley, in a pioneering article of his methodology: "The use of Verse-Forms (Strophes) by Tirso de Molina."[4] Morley analyzes the metrical typology of thirty-two of Tirso's comedies, and he compares the results with the comedies of doubtful attribution: *La firmeza en la hermosura, El infanzón de Illescas, El condenado por desconfiado*, and *El burlador de Sevilla*. In the case of *La firmeza en la hermosura*, his analysis concludes that "Although it differs somewhat in style from most of Tirso's work, and hence a little doubt has been cast upon it, there is no real reason to believe it another's."[5] As for *El infanzón de Illescas*, after laying out the problem of attributing the work to Tirso and the debates among Cotarelo, Menéndez Pelayo, and Hartzenbusch, he concludes the following: "the verse analysis may add its weight, which is entirely against Tirso's authorship. Such an insignificant use of *redondillas* is not to be found elsewhere on Tirso, and it is to my mind conclusive" (403). The same occurs with *El condenado por desconfiado*: "The verse-analysis, it will be seen, is all against Tirso." An expression such as "all against Tirso" is, in effect, conclusive: in fact, Morley, once he has put forward objective, metrical arguments against Tirso's authorship, adds arguments for stylistics and internal criticism: "Tirso certainly nowhere else can show a play with so few superfluities, with a plot so well hammered into shape, or one in which the main interest lies in the development of characters" (407). With regard to the results of collating the meter of those thirty-two works by Tirso with *El burlador de*

---

4   S. Griswold Morley, «The Use of Verse-Forms (Strophes) by Tirso de Molina», *Bulletin Hispanique*, 1911, pp. 387-408.

5   In any case, Morley expresses the following reservation: "The analysis certainly does not show sufficient cause to change the assignation, tho the play is exceptionally short (only *Amor y celos* falls below it) and it contains less *redondillas* than any other play analysed" (p. 403).

Sevilla, Griswold Morley notes that the text of *El burlador* "is corrupt and full of little gaps (...) this analysis throws no new light on the authorship of the play" (404) and finally that "the author of the play must remain dubious unless some piece of definitive evidence comes to light" (406).

The text attributed to Tirso with the title of *El burlador de Sevilla* is, indeed, very corrupt, and given that the documentation discovered in 2005 proves that the older text is *Tan largo me lo fiáis*, and that in this text there are only omissions at the end of the third act, it is necessary to return to the text. The collation of BS and TL allows one to assume the alternative hypothesis that neither of the two playwrights under whose name the two versions were published is that "author of the play" who, in Morley's words, "remains dubious." The alternate author has been associated with the play for over a century; Gerald E. Wade refers to him with an interesting suggestion: "Arturo Farinelli recuerda que Menéndez y Pelayo creía que Claramonte había intervenido en TL en la composición del trozo que describe a Sevilla" [Arturo Farinelli remembers that Menéndez Pelayo believed that Claramonte had intervened in TL in composing the section that describes Seville]. For a sufficiently long time, Claramonte's connection with *B* has been known. Four lines of the comedy, with minor changes, appear in Claramonte's comedy *Deste agua no beberé*. (There is no reason to doubt Claramonte's authorship of this comedy.) The lines are found at the beginning of *B*'s third act.

PATRICIO.   Celos, reloj de cuidados,
             que a todas las horas dais
             tormentos con que matais,
             aunque dais desconcertados.

[PATRICIO.   Jealousy, the timepiece of care,
             that every hour gives
             torments with which you kill me
             although you give them bewildered.]

One of these three conclusions seems necessary: 1) that the lines were taken from *B* for *Deste agua*, 2) that they were taken from *Deste agua* for *B*, 3) that the lines were copies from a common source.[6]

In reality, in this quote from Wade there are various errors: in the text of *El burlador*, the monologue is not spoken by Patricio but by Batricio; the text

---

6   Gerald E. Wade, "Hacia una comprensión del tema de Don Juan y *El burlador*," *Revista de Archivos, Bibliotecas y Museos*, 1964, p. 700.

that is reproduced is from *Deste agua no beberé*, lightly modified, in which the monologue is spoken by Juana Tenorio and the *redondilla* is perfect. The text of Batricio in *B* contains a rhyme error and another error of transmission: "Celos, relox y cuydado, / que a todas las horas days / tormentos con que matays, / aunque days desconcertados" [Celos, timepiece and care, / that every hour gives / torments with which you kill me / although you give them bewildered]. "Cuidado," in the singular, does not rhyme with "desconcertados," and it repeats the verb "days" where the text of *Deste agua* has "andays." In other words, the *redondilla* of *B* is defective, in contrast to the correct *redondilla* of *Deste agua*. The problem becomes clear if we approach the text of *Tan largo me lo fiáis*, in which this *redondilla* does not exist, but the situation is homologous or isomorphic to that of *Deste agua no beberé*: a monologue introducing a jealous character (Batricio / Juana Tenorio), with the character dialoging with jealousy, personified in the interlocutor:

	Tan largo me lo fiáis		*Deste agua no beberé*
Bat.	Zelos, átomos de amor	Juana.	Celos, reloj de cuidados
	y entre los ojos gigantes,		que a todas las horas dais
	a la muerte semejantes		tormentos con que matáis
	y al infierno en el dolor.		aunque estéis desconcertados.
	Dexadme, no me canséys		Gutierre Alfonso Solís
	con iras y desconsuelos		muchos años me sirvió
	que en lo azul parecéys cielos		y la palabra me dio:
	y como infiernos ardéys.		¿cómo no se la pedís?

	[*Tan largo me lo fiáis*		*Deste agua no beberé*
Bat.	Jealousy, atoms of love	Juana.	Jealousy, timepiece of care,
	and in the eyes enormous,		that every hour gives
	similar to death		torment with which you kill me
	and hell in their pain.		although you are bewildered.
	leave me, do not weary me		Gutierre Alfonso Solís
	with anger and grief		served me many years
	which in their blue look like heaven	and gave me his word:
	and burn like hell.		how do you not ask for it?]

In both cases the dramatic technique is the same: jealousy is mentioned, it is named, it is personified, and its figure is made into a metaphor (metaphor and prosopopoeia combined) and there is a dialogue or jealousy is cursed: "dexadme, no me canséis / ¿Cómo no se la pedís?" [leave me, do not weary me / how do you not ask for it?]. In TL, jealousy is called "átomos of amor" [atoms of love] and then it introduces the paradox that, although atoms, they are also gigantic. In DANB, jealousy is "reloj de cuidados" [time-piece of care] that instead of telling the hours gives torments. The dramatic problem is the same: how do you stage a jealous character in a way that is both dramatic and poetic? Both TL and DANB have the same year, 1617, as the documented date of staging. In the same year, and by the same company that staged *Tan largo me lo fiáis*—Jerónimo Sánchez's—another work of Claramonte is staged, *El secreto en la mujer*, in which that same dramatic situation is developed in a more complicated way based on the same elements of prosopopoeia and metaphor. The passage is homologous or isomorphic: Clavela expresses his jealousy in a monologue:

> Celos, si sois ilusión
>> y si os engendráis de nada,
>> si sois quimera fundada
>> sólo en la imaginación
>> ¿cómo vuestros actos son
>> tan claros y descubiertos,
>> y cómo en mil desconciertos
>> sois fieros y vengativos,
>> y atormentáis con motivos
>> si sois espíritus muertos?
>> Si sois hijos del no ser,
>> decid: ¿cómo sabéis tanto?
>> Y si sois fuego, en el llanto
>> ¿cómo os volvéis a encender?
>> No hay quien os pueda entender,
>> celos, en vuestro rigor,
>> que en amor sois lo mejor
>> y os levantan testimonios,
>> pero yo os llamo demonios
>> de las glorias del amor.   (vv. 1607-1626)

> [Jealousy, if you are an illusion
>> and if you are born from nothing,
>> if you are a chimera founded
>> only in the imagination
>> how are your acts

so clear and apparent,
and how in a thousand confused people
are you fierce and vengeful,
and you torment them with motives
if you are a dead spirit?
If you are child of non-being,
speak: how do you know so much?
And if you are flame, in grief
how do you reignite?
There is no one who can understand you,
jealousy, in your cruelty,
who in love you are the best
and people bear testimony of you,
but I call you a demon
of the glories of love.   (vv. 1607-1626)]

The dramatic situation is developed here in a more intense and complex way. Instead of *redondillas*, *décimas* are used, "buenas para quejas" [good for complaints], according to Lope. The fact that this comedy is staged the same year and by the same company as *Tan largo me lo fiáis* makes it impossible to hold that Claramonte is copying the dramaturgy of the other work, which is in its premiere, if we hold to Ángel García Gómez's observation.

These isomorphisms and homologies, unlike the similar passages in B and DANB, imply a dramatic style of composition, a dramaturgy identity that forces one to consider Claramonte's authorship for *Tan largo me lo fiáis* staged the same year as *El secreto en la mujer* and *Deste agua no beberé*. The similarities between *Deste agua no beberé* and *Tan largo me lo fiáis* had already been noticed, from Menéndez Pelayo and Cotarelo to Gerald E. Wade, but they had been explained as the influence of Tirso's lost text that Claramonte had refashioned to transform that lost text into *El burlador de Sevilla*. The similarities go beyond that *redondilla* of Batricio, which is not in *Tan largo me lo fiáis*. The plays coincide in the names of their protagonists, Juan/Juana Tenorio, Diego Tenorio, and the servant Tisbea, who also appears in masculine form as Tisbeo in *El secreto en la mujer*. The general vocabulary used in *Deste agua no beberé* coincides, as Wade has observed, with that of *Burlador/ Tan largo*. If we broaden the collation to other works of Claramonte, several structural traits call our attention: in the two versions of the first Don Juan, there is a long section praising a city, Seville or Lisbon. This is a trait that appears in datable works by Claramonte, as later, in 1612, is the case of *La católica princesa Leopolda*, in which a character, Friar Andrés, appears at the beginning of the first act in Bohemia to praise Valencia for a hundred and ninety-two lines—a length somewhere between the *loa* of Seville in TL and that of Lisbon in BS. In *El Nuevo rey Gallinato*, which was staged on two occasions in Salamanca, there is a *loa* to Zamora, a city close to Salamanca and that very probably was on the itinerary of Baltasar de Pinedo's company, where Claramonte was on those dates. For this reason, the practice of "inserción de una larga loa a una ciudad" [inserting a long *loa* to a city], which is foreign to Tirso's style of composition, is verified in Claramonte's corpus before the dates documented for the staging of *Tan largo me lo fiáis*.

Objective analysis of Claramonte's work, excluding works of disputed authorship, like *El infanzón de Illescas, Dineros son calidad*, or *La estrella de Sevilla* (three works in which the character Clarindo appears, Claramonte's own *nom de plume*), reinforces the attribution to Claramonte on a dramaturgical level closer to the principles of general composition of the Don Juan theme. I will summarize them in six elements of dramaturgy central to the myth: a) a friend who resorts to stealing another's identity in order to enjoy sexually another man's wife; b) the seducer who flees in order not to keep his promises of marriage; c) the murderer who receives his punishment from a dead man; d) the captious oath that brings divine providence into the question; e) offense given to the dead man's statue; f) the wild lover uncapable of controlling his erotic impulses. These six components of the myth are in all of Claramonte's works, the majority before 1617. These are the elements of content, the themes on which the stagecraft works, themes foreign to Tirso's authentic drama, who was the author of *Don Gil de las calzas verdes, El vergonzoso en palacio, El castigo del penséque, La prudencia en la mujer, La villana de la Sagra*, and *La celosa de sí misma*. In the case of Claramonte, these themes already appear in *El nuevo rey Gallinato*, that is, thirteen years before the premiere of *Tan largo me lo fiáis*, and they continue in later works like *La infelice Dorotea* and *El valiente negro en Flandes*. I will offer an example of each of these six themes that structure the Don Juan myth:

a) In *El secreto en la mujer*, Clavela, a woman courted by three different gentlemen, arranges for Ursino, the only one she loves, to come by night to enjoy her favors. Lelio, who by chance passes near the window, realizes that Clavela has confused him with Ursino and pretends to be him, grateful to the night for the deception:

CLAVELA ¿Eres Ursino?

LELIO   Sí soy.
CLAVELA A ti tu esposa se entrega,
         tuya soy tuya es mi alma.
LELIO   Mi bien, las ternezas deja,
         porque en mejor ocasión
         tendrán lugar las ternezas.
CLAVELA ¿Las postas?
LELIO   Aquí las tengo.
CLAVELA ¿Corren bien?
LELIO   Su ligereza
         les dio el viento, y yo imagino
         que como hipogrifos vuelan.
CLAVELA Pues vamos.
LELIO, *aparte:*   (¿Hay tal engaño?)
         ¡Oh noche oscura, tercera
         de sucesos prodigiosos,
         cierra tus ojos de estrellas! (vv. 686-699)

[CLAVELA ¿Is that you, Ursino?
LELIO   Yes, it's me.
CLAVELA Your wife delivers herself to you,
         I am yours, my soul is yours.
LELIO   My treasure, leave off with your tender words,
         because on a better occasion
         there will be time for tenderness.
CLAVELA ¿The horses?
LELIO   I have them here.
CLAVELA ¿Do they run well?
LELIO   Their lightness
         the wind gave them, and I imagine
         that they fly like hippogriffs.
CLAVELA Then let's go.
LELIO, *aparte:*   (¿Could there be such a deception?)
         ¡Oh dark night, go-between for
         prodigious events,
         close your starry eyes! (vv. 686-699)]

As with what happens between the Duchess Isabela in Naples, here
Clavela is also part of the plan for the nocturnal seduction; just as what Don

Juan Tenorio does in taking the place of the Duke and knowing the crime that he commits, here Lelio executes the deception under the cover of night. By always prioritizing the text of *Burlador*, which was transmitted with omissions, over the text of *Tan largo*, Tirso scholars have failed to quote the passage in which Don Juan thanks the night and the stars for the deception that he will carry out:

> gozarla sin miedo espero,
> la noche camina y quiero
> su viejo padre engañar.
> O estrellas que me miráys,
> dadme en este engaño suerte
> si el castigo hasta la muerte
> tan largo me lo fiáys. (vv. 2006-2012)

> [I hope to enjoy her without fear,
> the night is passing and I want
> to deceive her old father.
> Oh stars that look down on me,
> give me luck in this deception
> if the punishment until death
> you will hold off. (vv. 2006-2012)]

Clavela's confidence, when she discovers that the one who enjoyed her body was Lelio and not Ursino, is comparable to that of Isabela, who accepts the lie concocted by Don Pedro Tenorio and lies by saying that it was the Duke Octavio who dishonored her. Here Clavela does not hesitate in accepting marriage with Lelio because, as the servant Pánfilo says sarcastically, "él poseyó, y el que posee es beato" [he possessed her, and he that possesses is blessed] (vv. 890-91).

b) The seducer who flees in order not to keep his promise of marriage. Among the various examples of a seducer who flees, the most spectacular is doubtless that of *El valiente negro en Flandes*. It presents many structural homologies with *Tan largo me lo fiáis*. Captain Don Agustín de Estrada seduces Leonor in Mérida with the promise of marriage; like Tisbea or Arminta, Leonor wants guarantees, and once they are given, she fulfills her part of the bargain: "Amor, ya vencida estoy; / verme esta noche podéis/ si en el papel concedéis/ lo que decís" [Love, I am conquered; / you may see me tonight / if on this paper you concede / what you say] (f. 5a). The next day, after having enjoyed her, he leaves towards Flanders in order not to keep his promise. Captain Agustín de Estrada seduces by means of his word, as Don Juan does with Tisbea: "Con vuestra ausencia/ en esta ocasión quedara/ como sin sol queda el mundo/ metido entre sombras pardas" [With your absence / on this occasion I would be / like the world without the sun / thrust among dreary shadows] (f. 3b). Once the trick has been discovered, Leonor complains in a lyrical-dramatic speech in which her passionate outburst is homologous to that of Tisbea in *Tan largo*:

> Cielos, rayos me fiad,
>   sierpes, prestadme ponzoñas,
>   fieras, infundid en mí
>   la crueldad que hay en vosotras.
>   Burlóme un hombre, mas yo
>   más culpada que quejosa
>   es bien que esté, pues di el alma
>   con advertencia tan poca (VNF, f. 6b-7a)

> [Heavens, trust me with your bolts,
>   serpents, lend me your poisons,
>   wild beasts, infuse in me
>   the cruelty that is in you.
>   A man has mocked me, but I
>   more blamed than complaining
>   it is better to be, for I gave my soul
>   with little caution (VNF, f. 6b-7a)]

Like Tisbea, Leonor admits her own guilt for having let herself be deceived and after she curses the heavens so that they will give her their lightning bolts, like Tisbea. As with Tisbea, the complaints are in *romance* with a close in paired distichs—in this case, a few lines that Calderón will use for his *Alcalde de Zalamea*: "el añor del Soldado no es más que un hora / en tocando la caja, adiós, señora" [the longing of the soldier is no more than an hour / when the drum sounds, goodbye, lady] (VNF, f. 7a). When his interlocutor asks: "¿Vos queréis bien a Leonor?" [Do you love Leonor?], Don Agustín, as Don Juan Tenorio would have done if faced with the same question, affirms: "Quiérola como a gozada,/ que en la posesión se enfada / aunque se dilata, amor" [I love her as one I have enjoyed, / for in the possession love grows weary / even though it grows longer] (f. 18 a). In the same way as Don Juan Tenorio, Agustín de Estrada believes that the time will never come when he must fulfill his promise, but at the end the time does come, and the old black slave, who has risen to become a general and the master of the field, forces him to pay his debt.

c) The murderer who receives his punishment by means of a dead man. In *El Tao de San Antón*, a work that must be earlier than 1611 because it mentions Queen Margarita, who died that year, and which has a metrical schema typical of the period 1605-1610 (44.2% of *quintillas* against 23.8% of *romance*), Adaberto, Anatilde's lover, is betrayed by his servant Tiburcio, who seduces and abandons Anatilde and murders, on stage, Adaberto's other servant. After some wandering, Adaberto ends up killing, also on stage, Tiburcio and running away to the desert with Anatilde. Adaberto carries the guilt of having killed Tiburcio, and finally a resurrected San Antón imposes on him the penance of living as a hermit. In other cases, as in *El ataúd para el vivo y tálamo para el muerto*, the dead man who returns is an effect of perspective: Don Nuño, in order to enjoy Doña Brianda, who is married to Jorge de Ataíde, arranges for the King Don Juan to send him on a mission to Goa, and he orders that they kill him in secret. Jorge's trick is that he makes them believe he is dead, and he reappears six years later to take his revenge on the man who ordered his death—he, too, kills him on stage. The effect of the "muerte en escena" [on-stage death], like that of the Comendador in *Tan largo*, is typical of Claramonte and, as in the story of Don Juan and the Comendador, it serves to achieve the theatrical effects popular with public taste, contrary to Tirso's work, which is based on the complexity of the psychological analysis of its characters, the carefulness in the elaboration of the plot, and respect for the Aristotelian principle of not using on-stage deaths.

d) The captious oath that brings divine providence into the question. Let us remember the crucial moment in the story of Don Juan's tricks: the captious oath that he makes to Arminta, promising that, if he does not keep his word, a man should kill him (a dead man, since God will not permit a living one to do so). In *El gran rey de los desiertos*, Eudipo shares certain traits with Don Juan: both are murderers, and both have killed the man who stood in the way of their amorous passion, the Comendador Ulloa and King Delfo. Both, after the beginning of the third act, carry out a captious oath. This is Eudipo's:

mas el hombre que, engañado,
le dio crédito imprudente
y que, callando, consiente
matar a su mismo rey,
que da obligado, por ley,
a callar eternamente.
Y pues tan vil desconcierto
pude, callando, causar,
voto hago a Dios de no hablar
palabra en este desierto:
callar pienso hasta que un muerto
que venga de la otra vida
en nombre de Dios lo pida,
que, pues es cosa imposible,
será, en acción tan terrible,
el silencio mi homicida. (GRD, vv. 1902-1917)

[but the man who, deceived,
gave him imprudent credit
and who, keeping silent, consents
to kill his own king,
is obliged, by law,
to keep silent forever.
And since such evil confusion
I could cause, by keeping silent,
I swear to God not to speak
a word in this desert:
I intend to keep silent until a dead man
who comes from the next life
in the name of God asks me,
which, since it is an impossible,
will be, in such a terrible action,
silence my murder. (GRD, vv. 1902-1917)]

The end of the work shows Eudipo that for God nothing is impossible, and
that he can make a dead man return from the next life: in this case, San Onofre,
who resurrects in a wondrous dramatic effect,[7] and like a new *deus ex machina*

---

7   Stage direction: *Rásgase una peña y aparece* SAN ONOFRE *de rodillas, y a
un lado el cetro y la corona en una peña y los ángeles a sus lados.* [A rock breaks open

he arranges the play's ending. To Eudipo, in particular, he says that "Dios, que hables y perdones / a Silene, Eudipo, manda, / porque han sido los rigores / de su poder escarmiento" [God orders, Eudipo, / that you speak to and forgive Silene / because the rigors of his power / have been a lesson] (vv. 2490-3). It seems clear that what scholars have wanted to see as a theological element in *El burlador de Sevilla* is simply a recurring dramatic effect in Claramonte's theater.

e) The offense given to the dead man's statue. As is well known, in the theatrical mechanics of the Don Juan myth this element is essential: the offense to the statue of the dead man on sacred ground. It is what Fernando, the tragic protagonist of *La infelice Dorotea,* drags along as the hubris before the deeds that the spectator sees and that will culminate in the involuntary murder of Dorotea at the hands of her own husband, Fernando, who offends the statue of the dead man as he himself tells it in the play's first act:

> Llego a su sepulcro un día,
>   cuyos alabastros quiebro,
>   que no le temo por piedra
>   ni por bulto le respeto.
>   Llego donde reposaba
>   ya su embalsamado cuerpo,
>   porque siempre fue el agravio
>   autor de los sacrilegios.
>   La iglesia no le valió
>   al traidor después de muerto,
>   ni la hermosa arquitectura
>   de los alabastros tersos.
>   Salgo con él a la plaza
>   donde, a un encendido fuego,
>   pirámides de humo y llama
>   hizo sus pálidos huesos.

> [I come to his tomb one day,
>   whose alabaster I shattered
>   because I do not fear him because of stone

and San Onofre appears kneeling, at one side a scepter, a crown on the rock, and angels at his side] (GRD, p. 445).

nor do I respect him for their bulk.
I come to where rested
his embalmed body,
because grievance was always
the author of sacrileges.
The church did not avail
the traitor after death,
nor the beautiful architecture
of shining alabasters.
I go out with him to the plaza
where, on a burning fire,
pyramids of smoke and flame
his pallid bones make.]

The gesture of offending someone venerable by ripping out his beard, which is Don Juan's action in *Tan largo me lo fiáis*, is in other historical dramas by Claramonte, such as *El honrado con su sangre*, but the difference is in the fact that it deals with the effigy of a dead man and that the offense occurs in the church, as in *La infelice Dorotea*.

f) The wild lover incapable of controlling his erotic impulses. The figure of the "seductor erótico compulsivo" [compulsive erotic seducer] put in place by the Don Juan myth is based on two principles: the repetition of the tricks, and the story of instantaneous passion. The idea of the seducer who seduces and abandons is already in classic Greco-Latin literature, in figures such as Ulises (Circe, Calypso, Nausicaa), Jason, who abandons Medea, Aeneas, who abandons Dido, and Theseus, who abandons Ariadne. But an essential element to structure the myth of the seducer is in the technique of seduction, which cannot be fixed in the model of the nocturnal impersonator but rather in that of the *beau parleur* of the daytime. This is a matter of the articulation of convincing amorous discourse, the story of passion that exercises its effect on the seduced woman. There are many examples in Claramonte's work, but I will limit myself to that of the King Don Pedro, the king who appears in *Tan largo me lo fiáis*, Alfonso Onceno with his lover Leonor de Guzmán, the *Favorita* of Donizetti's opera. Don Pedro himself and his tumultuous love affairs serve as examples of Don Juan-style conduct. In *Deste agua no beberé*, where Don Pedro, Juana, and Diego Tenorio all appear, we have a splendid example of a wild lover incapable of controlling his erotic impulses. The scene with Don Pedro before Mencía de Acuña, whom he has just seen while bringing her candied preserves and a vase of water, expresses clearly that irresistible erotic impulse; Don Pedro's discourse is in the same tenor as that of Don Juan before Tisbea:

REY: Yo estoy ciego;
        si lo es, ¿cómo no sosiego?
        Mas, ¿quién habrá que sosiegue
        si entre dos manos de nieve
        me dais un vidrio de fuego?
        Fuego con agua templado
        me traéis, que, aunque encendido,
        en vuestras manos asido
        viene así disimulado;
        pero si parece helado
        el fuego que en ella hallé,
        si bebo, más sed tendré,
        que el licor que el vidrio fragua
        es fuego vestido de agua
        y así fuego beberé.
        Los dulces, sin ocasión
        vienen mi señora, acá,
        que donde esa boca está[8]
        los dulces ¿para qué son?
        Amor vierte colación
        en ellos mas liberal,
        y no es, a Portugal
        hacerle, señora, agravios,
        que en dulzura vuestros labios
        afrentan a Portugal.
        Mas, por haberlos traído,
        de los dulces probaré
        y del agua beberé,
        si es agua el fuego encendido.
        Hércules, señora, he sido,

---

8   In the edition of Claramonte's *Comedias* by Hernández Valcárcel, this line is omitted. It is also omitted in one of the two editions of this work in the seventeenth century, the one used by Mesonero for the BAE and again by Ebersole and Hernández Valcárcel.

y, si lo soy en la ira,
del agua helada que mira
el alma su incendio vea,
que es razón que Hércules sea
donde vos sois Deyanira. (DANB, vv. 292- 326)

[KING: I am blind;
if it is so, why do I not calm down?
But, who could calm down
if between two hands of snow
you give me a glass of fire?
  Fire tempered with water
you bring me, that, although burning,
held in your hands
comes to me in disguise;
but if it seems like ice
the fire that I find in it,
if I drink, I will be more thirsty,
because the liquor that the glass forges
is fire dressed as water
and thus I will drink fire.
  Sweets, for no occasion
come, my lady, here,
for where that mouth is
sweets ¿what are they for?
Love pours out collation
on them more liberal,
and it is not to cause grievances
my lady, to Portugal,
for in the sweetness of your lips
they offend Portugal.
  But, for having brought them,
I will try the sweets
and I will drink the water,
if hidden fire is water.
Hercules, my lady, I have been,
and if I am he in my wrath,
out of the frozen water that the soul
sees as its fire,

this is reason for me to be Hercules
where you are Deyanira. (DANB, vv. 292- 326)]

An objective analysis of Claramonte's dramatic work shows that themes, subthemes, motifs, and dramatic elements appear that characterize the Don Juan myth. If we center our analysis on the text of *Tan largo me lo fiáis*, the similarities reach the level of the repetition of specific lines and metaphors and syntax. Until now, the critical insistence on defending the attribution of *El burlador* and *El condenado* has been based on the absence of comparisons with other authors, more specifically with Claramonte, Vélez de Guevara, and Mira de Amescua. The case of *El condenado por desconfiado* is special because in this case the objective metrical analyses discard Tirso as an option. However, they are also not favorable for Mira de Amescua, since this type of analysis has been performed with a sufficient corpus of Mira's works, and the results have been compared with the metrical typology of five works of debated authorship. The normal procedure for research would require that we apply the same critical parameters to Claramonte, Belmonte, and Vélez de Guevara, which has not yet been done. Instead, scholars have continued to insist on the theological character of the work and to accept as a reference bibliography doctrinal articles about the dispute *De auxiliis*. No reliable heuristic procedures have been suggested, nor have there been verifiable or refutable hypotheses, but rather ideological conviction that introduce *ad hoc* conjectures to the debate. That is to say, a critical problem becomes a doctrinal discussion, and the church's doctrine is approached to settle a merely theatrical question.

In reality, this is no different from the suggestion that Menéndez Pelayo proposed in his day in order to attribute to Lope de Vega the works edited in his name spurious volumes or in loose collections, without any guarantee, and which did not appear in either of the two lists in *El peregrino en su patria*. Instead, in these works (*La estrella de Sevilla, El infanzón de Illescas, Dineros son calidad*) the first reliable indication of authorship is given by the appearance of a character named Clarindo, and even a character named Natilde, in *La estrella de Sevilla*, which is the poetic name of Beatriz de Castro, Claramonte's wife. In light of this evidence, which should have required objective analysis and critical comparisons, Menéndez Pelayo ('el maestro' [the master] in Blanca de los Ríos's terminology) established the idea that Claramonte used the name Clarindo to indicate that he was modifying Lope's previous work. This is a magnificent example of an *ad hoc* conjecture, one that cannot be proven and is alien to critical reason. That same principle, supported by Doña Blanca de los Ríos, is what has been applied to the problem of works of debated authorship. If this is correct, there should be more than a half dozen lost works by Lope de Vega and Tirso de Molina, of which no documentation has been found. This corresponds to Menéndez Pelayo and Blanca de los Ríos's desire, but not to any documented reality nor to the theories and facts that we know pertain to theater in the Siglo de Oro. From documentary evidence we know that Claramonte lived, performed, wrote comedies and poetic books in Seville from at least 1610 to 1617; we also know that he did all this under the protection of Don Juan de Ulloa and Don Fernando de Ulloa and also Gaspar de Saavedra, of the Sala de los Alcaldes de Sevilla, to whom he dedicates in 1617 the *Fracmento a la Inmaculada Concepción*. Throughout all those years, Tirso is in various Mercedarian monasteries, between Toledo and Estercuel, in Aragon, and he only appears in Seville just long enough to sail for Santo Domingo, where he will be until 1618. According to the legend of Tirso, in Seville there may have been a legend related to Don Juan Tenorio and the Comendador Ulloa, which Tirso may have heard and used to write *El burlador*, which stylistically and thematically is outside his dramatic style and which does not match his metrical practice. He would have written this during those weeks in Seville while he was waiting to sail for the Indies, and the immediate fame of this lost work would have led Claramonte to write *Deste agua no beberé* based on it. This would explain the similarities of the characters of Tenorio and Tisbea, the occurrence of some identical lines and stanzas, and the repetition of scenes in two works by Claramonte. It seems simpler, following William of Ockham, to assume that *Tan largo me lo fiáis* is a work more closely fitting within Claramonte's normal production, with his same metrical modes and the same dramaturgy that he uses in other works. It is also simpler to assume that the attribution to Tirso of the version transmitted by Roque de Figueroa is the work of the quick-witted editor who edited collections of *desglosables*, just as another editor in Seville would do with the attribution of the version of *Tan largo me lo fiáis* to Calderón, with the same desire to link the work to an author who would guarantee sales. Objective analyses, based on documentation, corroborated theories about the theater of the time, and the principles of debate about the hypotheses in contest show that the work is Claramonte's and that the text that is closest to the original is *Tan largo me lo fiáis*. The convictions and beliefs of Menéndez Pelayo and Blanca de los Ríos are based on *ad hoc* conjectures that cannot be proven and on the absence of methodological rigor to focus critical problems, with the result that attribution to Tirso de Molina should be considered a mere traditional belief based on doctrinal principles and refuted by documentary and critical means.

Works Cited

Atribuida a Tirso de Molina. *El burlador de Sevilla*. Ed. Alfredo Rodríguez López-Vázquez, Madrid, Cátedra, 2016 (edición 23ª ampliada).

Claramonte, Andrés de. *Comedias*. Ed. M.ª del Carmen Hernández Valcárcel. Murcia: Academia Alfonso X el Sabio, 1983.

———.*La infelice Dorotea*. Ed. Charles V. Ganelin, London: Tamesis Books, 1986.

———.*El secreto en la mujer*. Ed. A. R. López-Vázquez. London: Tamesis, 1991.

———.*La estrella de Sevilla. El gran rey de los desiertos*. Madrid: Cátedra, 2010.

———.*El valiente negro en Flandes*. Salamanca: Imp. de la Santa Cruz, 1745.

———.*El Tao de San Antón*. MS 16.937 BNM.

Fernández, Xavier A. *Las dos versiones dramáticas primitivas del Don Juan*. reproducción en facsímil de las ediciones príncipe. Madrid: Revista Estudios, 1988.

Menéndez Pelayo, Marcelino. *Estudios sobre el teatro de Lope de Vega*. Santander: Aldus, 1947.

Molina, Tirso de. *Obras dramáticas completas*. III. Ed. Blanca de los Ríos, complementos editoriales Luis Escolar Bareño. Madrid: Aguilar, 1962.

———. *El condenado por desconfiado*. Ed. Ángel R. Fernández. Madrid: Espasa-Calpe, 1990.

———.*El condenado por desconfiado*. Ed. Ysla Campbell. Madrid: Castalia, 2013.

Morley, S. G. "The Use of Verse-Forms (Strophes) by Tirso de Molina." *Bulletin Hispanique*, 1911.

Rodríguez López-Vázquez, Alfredo. *Andrés de Claramonte y El burlador de Sevilla*, Kassel: Reichenberger, 1987.

———.*Lope, Tirso y Claramonte. La autoría de las obras maestras del Siglo de Oro*. Kassel: Reichenberger, 1999.

Rogers, D. *Tirso de Molina. El burlador de Sevilla*. London: Grant & Cutler, 1977.

Wade, G. E. "Hacia una comprensión del tema de Don Juan y *El burlador*." *Revista de Archivos, Bibliotecas y Museos* n° 77, 1964.

———."The Fernández Edition of *Tan largo me lo fiáis.*" *Bulletin of the Comediantes* 20 (1968).

The Cosmological, Geographical and Spiritual Spaces of *The Trickster Of Seville*

Constructing Don Juan's World: Women and the Cosmos in *El burlador de Sevilla*

FREDERICK A. DE ARMAS
University of Chicago

SPAIN'S SEVENTEENTH CENTURY THEATERS invited spectators to revel in a space that represented the cosmos in its threefold structure. The main stage was the earth where humans carried out their daily business, made love and fought wars. Beneath the raised wooden platform was the infernal level. A trap door led to these depths from whence, at appropriately dramatic moments, demons would rise or humans would sink into hell. And above, a two-tiered balcony permitted a view of the celestial realm with angels, saints, pagan gods, planets, stars and constellations (Varey 23-36). The middle level was often suffused from what was above and threatened from the dangers below. But its cohesion stems from the four elements that order the world, albeit through its many mutations. The elements also help to structure the actions of a play—we need go no further than *La vida es sueño* and the confusion that arises from the absence of elemental qualities: "rayo sin llama, / pájaro sin matiz, pez sin escama / y bruto sin instinto" (Calderón vv. 3-5). Empedocles formulated the theory where the four roots constitute the unit that structures the world.[1] His fragments were collected in the Renaissance. Translated into Latin first by the German Xylander, they also appeared as *Empedoclis fragmenta* in Paris in 1573 (Fesbach 20). Empedocles impacted the thought of Marsilio Ficino, Pico della Mirandola, Giordano Bruno, Sir Walter Raleigh, Philip Sidney and many others (Bercovitch 72-73). The fragments describe how the elemental roots exhibit the potency of cosmos. First contained in a perfect sphere, held together by Love and

---

1 The fragments were translated by Simplicius, Stephanus, Xylander and others. Some could even be found in Natale Conte's *Mythologies*. (Berkovitch 76).

guarded by Strife, the globe was eventually shattered when Strife or hate intervened. The whole was fragmented and discrete forms were eventually perfected: As in grotesque paintings, heads would merge with vines; two torsos would come together until humans were formed.[2] Love and Strife continued to oppose each other in successive creations. Empedocles also points to the belief that through the study of the elements, human beings can gain health and longevity, perhaps immortality. He even claims to be able to bring men back from the dead (Fesbach 20, 26).[3]

Empedocles's elements echo the four humors that help to establish character, each ruled by a heavenly body. And the heavens in constant movement would often incline the will, as astrologers set out to understand its portentous moves: "estos globos cristalinos / que las estrellas adornan / y que campean los signos / son el estudio mayor" (Calderón, *Vida Es Sueño* vv. 620-632). The seven Ptolemaic planets together with the twelve signs of the zodiac would often reveal something about the action of the play that was being performed: *Las almenas de Toro* was structured under Taurus and Venus; *La estrella de Sevilla* was set under Saturn and Gemini; *El vellocino de oro* was ruled by Aries and Mars (De Armas, "Zodiacal plays"). And even at times we encounter the comingling of angelic and planetary orders as in *El pintor de su deshonra* (De Armas, "Jerarquías Pictóricas").[4] These were by no means recondite structures, influences or allusions during the early modern period. Even Don Quijote warns against the rage of casting horoscopes: "estas figuras que llaman judiciarias, que tanto ahora se usan en España, que no hay mujercilla, ni paje, ni zapatero de viejo que no presuma de alzar una figura, como si fuera una sota de naipes del suelo, echando a perder con sus mentiras e ignorancias la verdad maravillosa de la ciencia" (Cervantes 748). Thus, even the most ignorant of the *mosqueteros* who attended a theatrical performance

---

2   "In each half of the cycle, as the separation or unification proceeds, there is a cosmogony (generation of a cosmos or ordered world) and a zoogony (generation of animals). In the first half-cycle, under the increasing influence of Strife, a cosmos and then animals come to be. In the second half, under the increasing influence of Love, again a cosmos and animals come to be" (Parry).

3   Even in the modern world, where belief in these elements as a part of cosmos and even as magical elements has faded, the four still appear as structuring principles in literary texts. In T. S. Eliot's *Four quartets*, for example, each part celebrates one of the elements (Fesbach 15).

4   In this play Juan Roca as a tormented melancholy figure under Saturn is struck by Serafina, a new Venus, but also a Seraphim: "Quiere purgarse del veneno del amor así como los serafines purgan a los que están bajo su influjo" (De Armas, "Jerarquías Pictóricas" 221).

would seek to understand astrological references, much as they would often follow astrological forecasts as found in almanacs. Every conjunction, comet or eclipse would be accompanied by countless pamphlets propounding a different interpretation.[5]

This obsession with astrology would be found equally among kings and commoners. We know that every Habsburg ruler would have his horoscope cast at birth; that buildings could only be begun at an auspicious time: a special horoscope was cast for the building of the Escorial. Even courtly spectacle plays would often feature the heavens. In the *loa* to Calderón's *Fieras afemina amor*, for example, all twelve of the signs of the zodiac are used to praise Queen Mariana. Here, Capricorn wins out since it is the sign under which the Queen was born (Greer 1991: 157-78). Spain's cosmic theater would often point to the above and how it mirrors the below, weaving celestial lights and earthly times into an intricate pattern that is in itself a mirror of life. It is also the case that some *comedias* would eschew the heavens, or would even satirize astrological belief. While Lope de Vega, Ruiz de Alarcón and Calderón de la Barca would show a keen interest in astrology, Tirso de Molina would often move away from such prognostication. Since *La estrella de Sevilla* has been definitively attributed to Andrés de Claramonte, we can now point to the playwright's interest in astrology and the development of what has been called an "astrólogo estilo" (Brooks; Sturm).

According to S. K. Heninger the Renaissance believed in cosmos: "During the Renaissance as at most times in our intellectual history, the longing for order was so strong that the belief in cosmos persisted despite all evidence to the contrary.... And with increasing insistence and ingenuity, the dogma of cosmos was proclaimed" (147-148). At the same time, this cosmos was constantly under pressure from an individualism that set human beings at the center, and set them to observe new stars where none should be born, a maculate moon instead of a perfect orb. As Mario Domandi states, what had changed was the impetus to "understand the intelligible in and through the sensible—the universal in and through the particular" (ix). Indeed, as Enrique García Santo-Tomás has shown, the instruments of Galileo's New Science were even able to penetrate Spain during the Counter-Reformation. But while there was great curiosity, there was also great caution. Still, it was while Galileo sought to come to Spain around 1616 to show the uses of the

---

5   For a list of the many astrological tracts published in the Spanish Golden Age see Hurtado Torres; and for a typical almanac see Andrés de Li's *Repertorio de los tiempos*.

telescope, that Claramonte would be composing *Tan largo me lo fiáis*, the predecessor of *El burlador de Sevilla* (García Santo-Tomás 44).

It may be that this new individualism, this new desire to revise cosmos, was instrumental in the creation of the Don Juan myth. Ian Watt has suggested that four myths of modern individualism emerged during the early modern period, Faust, Robinson Crusoe, and two Spanish figures, Don Quijote and Don Juan. Figures of dissension and disorder seek to rise out of repressive societies, becoming over time almost mythical characters that grapple with communal values so as to free themselves. It would make sense that two of them arise during the Spanish Counter-Reformation. Don Juan emerges as a quasi-demonic personage that at the same time elicits grudging admiration as he manipulates a society and all its values and aspirations: honor, truth, piety, the desire for salvation, and the paternalistic authority embodied in a father and a King (Watt 90-118).[6] Since *El burlador de Sevilla* brings forth a new and important myth that seems to counter the traditional view of cosmos, I would ask if the play questions, transforms or reasserts cosmos through the new forces that challenge it. In other words, does an orderly and harmonious universe, impeccably designed, survive the ravages of Don Juan? Thus, I will examine the three levels of cosmos, and particularly the four elements and the uses of planetary and zodiacal images. To these will be added the uses of mythology.

Alfredo Rodríguez López-Vázquez points to an "hipótesis helenista" in the work,[7] one that brings together many of the threads of classical myths, that in the main deal with seduction, those of Aeneas, Jason and Ulysses.[8] We must also include the seducer par excellence, Zeus/Jupiter. One of the first critics to link Don Juan to mythology was Georges Gendarme de Bévotte, who saw him precisely as a new Jupiter. Does the chief of the gods preside

---

6   Watt underlines that his conception of myth is not that of a sacred tale as in classical mythology. Rather it is "a traditional story that is widely known throughout the culture, that is credited with a historical or quasi-historical belief, and that embodies or symbolizes some of the most basic values of a society" (xvi).

7   "hay dos tipos de estructuras míticas sólidas, conservadas en la tradición occidental, en la que el mito de Don Juan parece entenderse bien: la historia de un trickster o brulador... y que al final es burlado por alguien más astuto o cruel... [y] la historia del convidado de Piedra... la doble invitación tiene que ver con las leyes de la hospitalidad" (Rodríguez López-Vázquez 100).

8   A number of critics have pointed to one or more of these figures. For example, Américo Castro and Arturo Echevarren, have studied the figure of don Juan in terms of Aeneas. Other myths have also been studied. Marc Vitse, for example, refers to don Juan as a "Héctor de Sevilla" (186).

over cosmos or does he expose Don Juan's wanton paganism? How does a mythical and cosmic language figure in a play whose main character, as James Mandrell has argued, is guilty of "of linguistic perversion" (76).[9] Will this rebelliousness and perversion transform the language, style and structure of the play and lead to a critique of the cosmic vision in spite of the fearsome symmetry of images and events?

Without question, the play exposes the notion of Dante's counterpassion, as Don Juan is deceived and punished using the same means he utilized to deceive the women in his path; and there is no doubt that a reader or audience can contemplate Blake's fearsome symmetry as the ending recapitulates in a somber tone the images of transgression utilized by Don Juan.[10] More to the point in this inquiry is how the earthly elements, the celestial images (comprised of planets and signs of the zodiac) and the demonic exhalations are utilized in this *comedia* to reinforce or critique the tradition of cosmos.

I. Jupiter and the Elements

While in Calderón's *La vida es sueño*, the confusion of qualities and elements is foregrounded in order to present the fallen nature of the world and its inhabitants, as they seem to be headed towards a new Golden Age, *El burlador de Sevilla* seeks instead to represent each of the four women that Don Juan seduces in the play as embodying one of the elements.[11] Francisco J. Martín summarizes the structure: "Isabela is the character in the play who seems to be in possession of fire, or at least in a situation able to produce it 'quiero sacar una luz" (v. 9)... Tisbea represents water by definition... Doña Ana... would represent air, since her letter arrives to Don Juan 'por la estafeta del viento' (v. 1301)... Aminta... inhabitant of the countryside... represents earth" (Martín 33). Jupiter, although equated with air, is also master of the thunderbolt, signifying fire. As the chief of the gods and ruler of the two upper elements, he rules over elemental creation. Curiously, the four elements are embodied by the women in the play. Empedocles had specified that there were two male and two female elements: Fire and earth as masculine, ruled by Jupiter and Hades (Aidoneus); air and water as feminine, ruled by Hera

---

9   "Don Juan's failures to keep his promises therefore threatens the very discursive texture of the social fabric in a society in which speech is the one essential means of making a contract" (Madrell 76).

10   See, for example, the early essays by Marni and Rogers.

11   For citations, I am using the 1991 version of Rodríguez López-Vázquez which does not contain interpolations form *Tan largo me lo fiáis*. I have also consulted his 2016 edition.

and Persephone.[12] It is as if Don Juan's world is already askew, a place where only women can provide his elemental needs.

The nameless trickster ("hombre sin nombre" v. 15) who seems to attain vitality and daring, through his acquisition of women, is also a god-like figure, Jupiter, known for his many metamorphoses through which he seduces women.[13] Isabela may be fire, the highest of the four elements, but she is also Alcmena, who, when left alone by her husband Amphitryon as he goes to war, is seduced by Jupiter who takes on the form of her husband. Isabela, like Alcmena, thinks she is enjoying her beloved, but is in reality being deceived by Don Juan who in the darkness resembles the Duque Octavio. Shortened from its original form in *Tan largo me lo fiáis*, the scene acquires a crisp and mysterious brevity that is missing in the original.[14] Catalinón is missing—he would have been the play's analog of Mercury who would warn of any danger. Don Juan's forceful confrontation with his uncle, the lies that are crafted, and his dramatic escape, contrasts with the most popular version of the Alcmena story as found in Plautus's *Amphytrion*. Well-known in the Renaissance, it was often translated and imitated in the Spanish Golden Age (Quintero).

There are important deviations here that serve to paint Don Juan as a Jupiter *in malo*. After all, Don Juan forces others to lie for him thus augmenting the confusion in the court of Naples, while Jupiter comes clean in the end, honoring Amphytrion. In Plautus, Alcmena is able to miraculously give birth to twins, one of which is Amphytrion's son while the other is Jupiter's offspring Hercules. This latter would have been an ideal means of kingly praise in the play, since Hercules, according to legend, would help sire a line of Spanish kings. But no such allusion is found. Don Juan here and elsewhere will only confound rulers. In many ways, Don Juan from the start causes havoc, engenders lies, and even when it comes to the element of fire, we witness how he steals the light from Isabela "matarete la luz yo" (v. 9). His desire to consume the elements makes him into a force that in neither the

---

12   Aidoneus (Hades) was Persephone's husband. In Empedocles, Persephone is the only elemental deity not named directly since she was taken to the underworld. She is called instead Nestis.

13   For a somewhat different version of the thesis of Don Juan as Jupiter see De Armas ("Cortesano endiosado" 173-184).

14   Alfredo Rodríguez López-Vázquez argues that Isabela's role is shortened because, once Claramonte recovers his play around 1622 and proceeds to sell it to the company of Roque de Figueroa, the actress that plays the part of Isabela is less important than the one who plays Tisbea, whose role is augumented (Tirso 68).

Love nor Strife of Empedocles. He is more like a force that seeks to absorb the potential of cosmos.

Reborn from the sea water, where he has been shipwrecked, Don Juan now finds himself in Tisbea's arms, a woman that scorns the amorous advances of men, an *esquiva*, reveling in self-sufficiency.[15] As a new Aeneas, he will seduce and abandon this modern Dido: "lo mismo hizo Eneas / con la reina de Cartago" (vv. 900-901). And because she stands for water, he will burn her heart; burn her hut as he abandons her, as the image of Troy stands for the fire that consumes her heart, her hut and her honor (Arellano 122-123). Two opposing elements face each other, but in this case an inversion *contra natura* takes place as fire quenches water. It is as if Don Juan can now use the fire he acquired from Isabela at will. With his triumph over Tisbea, the trickster now controls two of the cosmic elements. Although it would seem that Jupiter has faded to give his place to Aeneas, such is not the case, as will be discovered later in the play. For now, we can only witness this seemingly unstoppable force of nature as it descends upon Seville.

Of course, Don Juan is not just ready to trick women, but also his supposed friends. When the Marqués de la Mota reveals that he is in love, Don Juan will immediately plot to seduce his friend's beloved, Doña Ana. This seduction will replicate the first, underlining the importance of Plautus in the plot. Once again, we find Don Juan disguised, as Ana becomes a second Alcmena. To reach her, Don Juan must kill her father. A word of caution: Empedocles had asserted that shedding blood with the knife or sword was the worst offense:

> There is an old condition, a decree of Gods
> eternal and sealed with extensive oaths,
> that if a spirit blessed with long-lasting life
> should by sin or error defile itself

---

15 Melveena McKendrick was the first critic to label her an *esquiva*: "The arrogant pride which leads her to reject love and disdain her suitors adds a new dimension to the Don Juan theme of pride and self assertion... She is above love... Tirso's disapproval of Tisbea is obvious. She is shown to be the victim not of Don Juan but of her own character» (158). Constance Rose goes even further: "In Tisbea, it would appear, the author has created a character for whom he has nothing but contempt.... And it is his intention to undercut everything she says by turning her very words against her" (48). I would look at Tisbea very differently, as a woman who strives for self-sufficiency albeit under the guise of petrarchism. In the end, she will journey to the court seeking justice.

with slaughter or forswear and oath
in the spirit of Strife, he shall wonder
thirty thousand years
apart from the blest,
born through time in various mortal forms
switching through the painful tracks of life.
The air haunts them into the sea
the sea splits them onto the land
the earth spurns them onto the sun
and the sunlight beats them into whirling air,
passed on by all
hated by each,
and I am one of them,
a fugitive from God, a wanderer
captivated by maniacal strife. (Lombardo 57-58)

Are we witnessing Don Juan's error? He has both slaughtered and fore-sworn an oath. Is he about to be condemned? Or, is he a fugitive, a wanderer, captured by maniacal Strife and not allowed to settle, drifting through life, performing his trickery again and again? Tricking every woman, every element, he is hated by each. As opposed to the condemned in Empedocles, he is not sent away by elemental forces, but is able to manipulate them. Is he something else not foreseen by this craftsman of cosmos? Is he someone who would challenge the ordered world; is he seeking to become a new kind of being who uses the old laws to attain unfathomable power and perhaps immortality of sorts?

Still, he steals wind or air from Ana—all that remains is earth. Indeed, he arrives unexpectedly at a rustic wedding where Batricio is to marry Arminta. The groom sees this as a bad omen, "mal agüero" (v. 1746).[16] Indeed, a song augurs not marital harmony, but the arrival of the trickster:

Lindo sale el Sol de abril,
con trébol y toronjil;
y aunque le sirve de estrella,
Aminta sale más bella (vv. 1684-1687)

---

16   On Batricio's motivation see Conlon (86-94).

The April sun has as its zodiacal sign Taurus, the bull, which figures Batricio as a deceived husband with the horns of a *cornudo*, a trait that is alluded to by Catalinón "si tiene de ser toro" (v. 1788). Don Juan himself points to Taurus as he readies to trick Arminda. In a lyrical passage that seems to clash with his intent, he exclaims:

> La noche en negro silencio
> se extiende, y ya las Cabrillas
> entre racimos de estrellas
> el Polo más alto pisan.
> Yo quiero poner mi engaño
> por obra, el amor me guía
> a mi inclinación, de quien
> no hay hombre que se resista.
> Quiero llegar a la cama.
> ¡Arminta! (vv. 2224-33).

Don Juan, then, seeks to trick at the time when the *Cabrillas* or Pleiades are highest in the night sky, thus guiding him. The Pleiades are seven bright stars (formerly sisters pursued by Orion) that rest within the constellation of Taurus. Thus they are a double sign for seduction. Don Juan becomes the pursuer of women like Orion. And, since these constellations rest within Taurus they recall the myth: Jupiter, disguised as a white bull, robbing Europa. And this myth is also that of Tisbea and even Isabela—only Ana escapes it. In the third and final act, Isabela comes from Naples in a ship in order to marry Don Juan. The ship makes a stop in Tarragona, where she meets Tisbea, who asks the duchess: "¿Sois vos la Europa hermosa / que estos toros os llevan?" (vv. 2213-14). Tisbea and Isabela soon realize that they are both Europa, having been deceived by the bull, by Jupiter, by Don Juan. It is as if the two women see themselves in an ancient myth, but one where Jupiter has been debased. In this new cosmos, Don Juan seeks to rule, to be the supreme god as he takes away from four women the powers of the four elements. He does recall Francisco J. Martín's hyperbolic statement: "Just as in the case of Count Dracula, our *burlador* must have a woman, a new woman each time, who for him will mean his very life" (43). Although not knowing Martín's words, María do Carmo Mendes has recently returned to this topic in an essay in *Dracula and the Gothic in Literature*. Here, she develops the equation pointing to numerous parallels: Don Juan, like the vampire, has aristocratic origins, has an immense allure but is a formidable threat to the social fabric. I would simply say that up to this point Don Juan is appropriating for himself the authority and structures of cosmos. He who controls the elements, it would seem, can control his environment. Don Juan signals the birth of a new order, one that emerges from a god's ability to seduce women, and from women's power to embody the elements. In a work that actually exalts the power of women, will they fully succumb to a new order that ironically demeans them?

II. CATALOGUES OF CELESTIAL WOMEN

In Seville, as Don Juan meets Mota, his partner in crime, he asks him about the availability of women. As the marquis gives names and qualities, Don Juan asks for more details. This type of *enumeratio* is quite common in the theater of the period and derives, ironically, from the catalogues of famous heroes that appear right before a battle in epic poems and in chivalric romances including the *Amadís*. This epic device was so common that Cervantes satirizes it in *Don Quijote*. Let us recall what occurs when the knight stands on a hillock to observe the battle between the armies of Alifanfarón and Pentapolín (actually, two flocks of sheep that seem to be headed for one another). At that point, he starts to name all the main warriors, giving them high-sounding and even ridiculous names: Laurcalo, Micocolembo, Brandabarbarán, etc (Cervantes 158). Perhaps because the conquest of a woman was often associated with the conquest of a city such as Troy, later writers crafted this new type of *enumeratio*. They may have also had in mind the pseudo-Hesiod epic fragments entitled *Catalogue of Women* where women bore children that would become great heroes. Numerous *comedias* exhibit a catalogue of women. In many cases, it is the servant of a lord who complies with his master's wishes and provides the names, qualities and availability of the women. In Lope de Vega's *Fuenteovejuna*, for example, the *Comendador* asks his servant or go-between, Flores, what women would be available to him at that moment. Pascuala is too busy getting married (v. 1059). But, Inés is ready to serve: "Para cualquier ocasión / te ha ofrecido sus donaires" (v. 1077-1078). As for Olalla she is well guarded by her jealous man: "Que su desposado / anda tras ella estos días, / celoso" (vv. 1066-1068). Flores, however, offers hope that the husband will become less vigilant and that the Commander will be able to enjoy Olalla's favors. In *El castigo sin venganza*, we find a similar catalogue as the Duke wishes to enjoy many women before marrying.[17] In Ruiz de Alarcón's *La verdad sospechosa*, Tristán tells his master, don García, about the women at

---

17   This takes place under the stars and moon as the world "luna" (vv. 16. 23) is repeated more than once. In addition, one of them is also a "serafín" (v. 36), conflating planetary and angelic orders.

court. While the chaste ones abide under the zodiacal sign Virgo, others are equally exalted. Married women appear as planets, while discreet daughters are fixed stars.[18] But many are courtesans who do not even reach the heavens, becoming comets and exhalations (vv. 309-352). Most important for our purposes is the catalogue found at the beginning of Claramonte's *La estrella de Sevilla*. As king Sancho IV enters the city, he fails to gaze at the Seville's architectural beauties, asking his minister to describe the beautiful women who stand in balconies around him. Arias thus creates a catalogue and offers to obtain any of them for Sancho, even though they are noblewomen. James F. Burke has explained that they actually embody the seven Ptolemaic planets, not in their celestial order, but as they are structured in the days of the week, beginning with Leonor de Ribera as Sol/Sunday, and ending with Estrella as Saturn/Saturday (Burke 137-156).

With these structures in mind, let us return to *El burlador de Sevilla*. As in *La estrella de Sevilla* we find here a total of seven women. But they all seem to be prostitutes.[19] Mota explains that the court has changed and many of them are not worth having. Some, such as Inés and Constanza are too old; Teodora has suffered from "el mal francés" (v. 1217); while Julia "con sus afeites lucha" (v. 1223). The two sisters at the conclusion of the catalogue recall those in *La estrella de Sevilla*, while the term "blancas" in both *comedias* serve as a play on coins.[20] In both catalogues, the last woman is the one that attracts most attention. In this case it is doña Ana de Ulloa, the woman that Mota loves and that Don Juan will seek to seduce and who stands apart from the prostitutes as a noblewoman. While it is quite possible that the seven women in this catalogue may also refer to the seven Ptolemaic planets, with the ex-

---

18   The "bellas casadas" are planets "porque resplandecen mas" (vv. 309, 312); discreet daughters are "estrellas fijas" (v. 327); while their mothers ironically are "errantes" (v.328).

19   For Pendzik the exact number is not clear. She points to a long list: "Inés, Constanza, Teodora, Julia, the two sisters and their mother, and several others still harder to identify who are referred to as a group (*el barrio de Cantarranas*) (167). In my count, I foreground six Inés, Constanza, Teodora, Julia and the two prostitutes. The mother belongs to a parenthesis made by Mota, while a neighborhood does not necessarily count. To the six prostutes, I add Ana who is associated to the prostitutes only in that both Mota and Don Juan have recourse to them.

20   In the *El burlador*, one of the two sisters is described as: "Blanca, y sin blanca ninguna" (v. 1235). Her name may be Blanca but she lacks coins (money). In *La estrella* we read: "muy prolijo el alemán / pues de dos en dos están / juntas las blancas ansí" (vv. 84-86). In this pun, German bankers seem quite generous, offering double the coins.

ception of Ana, they all seem wasted, old, consumed by their trade. They represent a fallen world, a world that exhibits the results of the trickster's excessive desires. Susana Pendzik refers to these and other women as figures "bonded by their absence" (167). She adds that "the text's evocation of 'invisible women' is to be understood as an *invocation* to the silent voices of those who do not have a place in the overall scheme of the World's Order" (Pendzik 168). Perhaps this new kind of debased catalogue also reflects the new discoveries where the heavens are no longer perfect. The maculate moon may be a sign of fallen women, a fallen world, and the disintegration of cosmos.

This invisibility also has to do with Don Juan's understanding that these women cannot help him to absorb the vitality of the cosmos. From this list of planetary prostitutes, only Ana can do so as she becomes the element of air. Indeed, Don Juan receives a message intended for Mota "por la estafeta del viento" (v. 1301). She may also, like Estrella, be a new Saturn, a darkened Sun: "Un manto tapado, un brío / donde el puro sol se esconde" (vv. 1138-1139). Furthermore, this third *burla* is to take place at exactly eleven o'clock at night. Don Juan has given Mota the wrong time, he is to go to Ana at midnight. The twelfth sign of the zodiac belongs to Pisces, ruled by Venus. Don Juan offers Mota the amorous delights of Venus, but tricks him in so doing. He will go to her, instead, at the eleventh hour or sign, Aquarius, the night house of Saturn.[21] Twice Saturn appears to Don Juan: first as a darkened Sun and now as the ruler of Aquarius. As the planet of tragedy, death and the occult sciences, it promises ill fortune. And sure enough, Don Juan kills Ana's father, don Gonzalo, during this escapade.

III. THE GHOSTLY STATUE
Seeking refuge in a church in Sevilla, Don Juan encounters the tomb of don Gonzalo. This is followed by Don Juan's insult as "buen viejo, barbas de piedra" (v. 2403), as he invites the dead man to dinner. Beyond the traditional folk tale, we may well ask how is it that a statue is transformed into a ghost from the beyond. Echoing *Dineros son calidad*, where the statue of King Federico comes to life and rises from Purgatory when enjoined by Octavio,[22]

---

21   There are scattered references to the signs of the zodiac in the play. Catalinón refers to Octavio as "Sagitario de Isabela, / aunque mejor diré / Capricornio" (vv. 1145-46).

22   Count Federico had lent most of his money to King Enrique of Naples, who is then killed by Ludovico, who usurps the throne. The impoverished Federico lives away from the court. Towards the end of the play, his son, Octavio, challenges Enrique's statue to a duel. Eventually, it acknowledges that it has come to life in order

here the statue of don Gonzalo is revivified so that it can come to Don Juan's Inn for dinner and then invite the trickster for dinner at the church. Although the tradition of revivified stone goes back at least to Ovid and the classical world, here it may have to do with the four elements. Let us remember that Don Juan had yet to appropriate earth as he kills don Gonzalo. Thus the Commander adopts earth's stone to return and through it, he can access all the other elements, in particular the fires below. Would an audience, viewing the spectacle, recall that this was a moment that reveled in automata? In 1615 Salomon de Caus published a book on the subject where he imagines a machine that can act/move on its own, "if it is maintained by the four elements of which it is composed" (Grillner 94). Does the revivified statue, in its use of the elements, echo Don Juan?

Slowly, the trickster loses his powers, and he cannot wound the statue, which now is mere air. In a feat of counterpassion, don Gonzalo fights fire with fire, taking the fiery Don Juan to the fires of the underworld. The time for the dinner is ten o'clock at night. Following the previous times that we have related to the signs of the zodiac, ten corresponds to the sign of Capricorn, and it was this very sign that Catalinón assigns to Duke Octavio, since he is a cuckold: "aunque mejor dire / Capricornio" (v. 1147). Don Juan is taken at this very hour and in a sign that also belongs to Saturn, planet of the occult and of death as a type of counterpassion, as a kind of retribution for cuckolding so many men. Furthermore, according to neo-platonic and hermetic treatises, Cancer and Capricorn are the two gates or passages for souls that come to earth and depart this world. Porphyry explains that souls are born through Cancer and at death go back to the other world through the gateway of Capricorn (Ulansey 61; Richer 64).

As Don Juan takes Gonzalo's hand, he loses many of his earthly powers, much as he had gained them by giving his hand in marriage to Tisbea and Arminta. He loses his rule over earth, no longer a Jupiter whose thunderbolt stands for the element of fire. Instead, he will burn in the fires of the underworld. Curiously, it is the women in the play that had empowered him through their elemental essences.[23] Don Juan understood their hidden

---

to return the money owed to Federico. Only this way can it leave the torments of purgatory (De Armas, "(Un)Earthly Treasures" 127).

23   Ruth Lundelius and others have asserted that the four women deceived by Don Juan are victims of their own weaknesses: "Tirso… is able to exhibit and castigate a number of traditional exemplars of errant women" (12). Lundelius further explains: "the inordinately prod and disdainful [Tisbea], the irresponsible rebel against paternal authority [Ana], the incontinent flouter of the precepts of

power, their discontent in a world that did not give them their due. Let us remember that Empedocles had defined two male and two female elements: Fire and earth as masculine, ruled by Jupiter and Hades (Aidoneus); air and water as feminine, ruled by Hera and Persephone. Now Gonzalo as earth or Hades is able to take Don Juan to the Underworld.

In conclusion, Don Juan's tricks have unleashed a quasi-cosmic battle, one that has left the heavens diminished as planetary women are made sickly and debased by the *burlador* and his ilk. Even the signs of the zodiac suffer as Taurus and Capricorn are foregrounded as images of deceit. Paradoxically, Don Juan has also empowered women as embodiment of the four elements, only to steal their powers. But as he reaches for Ana, who is both air and Saturn, he unleashes his own destruction, given that the seventh Ptolemaic planet is the giver of the highest wisdom, but also the malefic destroyer of ignorance, thus empowering the guest of stone. Ana's father as stone and earth, the as yet undefiled element, takes Don Juan away from this earth. After all, earth, in Empedocles' system, can also stand for Hades where the trickster must go.

Cosmos is left reeling, but seeking to right itself: There must be a balance between the masculine and the feminine, as Empedocles prescribes. The end may not be the dawn of a perfect age where violence against women, the shedding of blood and the breaking of one's oath will never occur. But it is a world with lesser threats, or so it seems. If Don Juan sought to become an individual through an elemental rebellion, Galileo beats him at his own game, through the metamorphoses of the heavens. The maculate moons and luminaries point to a moment of inflection where gender and other hierarchical positions can be questioned, something that would have been impossible in Don Juan's Ptolemaic universe. Don Juan fails because he never questions cosmos; he never seeks to go beyond stratified visions of a structured world and a hierarchical society. He only wants the power to control all that surrounds him. Even though he seems to relish a prostituted heavenly structure, he is unaware that such a vision brings visibility and voice to the invisible and debased women in the catalogue of conquests; and even though he steals the

church and state [Isabela], and the foolish social climber [Arminta]" (12). Susana Pendzik, on the other hand, asserts that the work reflects "the female's profound discontent with the impositions of patriarchal order" (179). Ignacio Arellano adopts a posture midway between condemnation and praise: "En conjunto las mujeres del burlador participan de los defectos morales y sociales que caracterizan a la mayoría de los personajes del trama" (137). They may all share in deffects, but the women of *El burlador de Sevilla* embody the elements that allow for a new society to be reborn.

elements from four strong women, he cannot see that the roots of creation may be threatened by strife, but are held together by a love that he can never envision.

Works Cited

Arellano, Ignacio. *Arquitecturas del ingenio: Estudios sobre el teatro de Tirso de Molina*. Pamplona: Instituto de Estudios Tirsianos/ Universidad de Navarra, 2001.

Bercovitch, Sarcan. "Empedocles in the English Renaissance." *Studies in Philology*, vol. 65, no. 1, 1968, pp. 67-80.

Brooks, J. L. "*La estrella de Sevilla*, admirable y famosa tragedia." *Bulletin of Hispanic Studies*, no. 32, 1955, pp. 8-20.

Burke, James F. "The *Estrella de Sevilla* and the Tradition of Saturnine Melancholy." *Bulletin of Hispanic Studies*, no 51, 1974, pp.137-56.

Calderón de la Barca, Pedro. *Fieras afemina amor*. Edited by Edward M. Wilson. Kassel: Reichenberger, 1984.

———. *La vida es sueño*. Edited by Ciriaco Morón. Madrid: Cátedra, 1998.

Cassirer, Ernst. *The Individual and the Cosmos in Renaissance Philosophy*. Mineola, NY: Dover Publications, 2000.

Castro, Américo. "El don Juan de Tirso y el Eneas de Virgilio." *Semblanzas y estudios españoles*. Princeton, NJ: Princeton University Press, 1956.

Cervantes, Miguel de. *El ingenioso hidalgo don Quijote de la Mancha*. Edited by Francisco Rico. Madrid: Punto de Lectura, 2007.

Claramonte, Andrés de. *La estrella de Sevilla*. Edited by Alfredo Rodríguez Lopez-Vázquez. Madrid: Cátedra, 1991.

Conlon, Raymond. "Batricio in *El burlador de Sevilla*: The Pathology of Sexual Honor." *Tirso's don Juan: The Metamorphosis of a Theme*. Edited by J. M. Sola-Solé and G. E. Gingras. Washington, DC: The Catholic University of America Press, 1988, pp. 86-94.

De Armas, Frederick A. "El cortesano endiosado: espectáculos paganos en *El burlador de Sevilla*." *Hipogrifo: revista de literatura y cultura del Siglo de Oro*, no. 1, 2013, pp.173-184.

———. "Zodiacal Plays: Astrology and the Comedia." *A Confluence of Words: Studies in Honor of Robert Lima*. Edited by Wayen H. Finke and Barry J. Luby. Newark, DE: Juan de la Cuesta, 2011, pp. 59-76.

———. "De jerarquías pictóricas, planetarias y angélicas en *El pintor de su deshonra*." *Calderón: del manuscrito a la escena*. Edited by Frederick A.

de Armas and Luciano García Lorenzo. Madrid: Iberoamericana, 2011, pp. 209-26.

————. "(Un)Earthly Treasures: Spirits as Wealth in *Dineros son calidad.*" *Indiana Journal of Hispanic Literatures*, vol 1, no. 1, 1992, pp.115-133.

Domandi, Mario. "Translator's Introduction." *The Individual and the Cosmos in Renaissance Philosophy.* By Ernst Cassirer. Mineola, NY: Dover Publications, 2000.

Echevarren, Arturo. "La figura de Eneas en el teatro español del Siglo de Oro." *Silva: Estudios de humanismo y tradición clásica*, no. 6, 2007, pp.91-117.

Feshbach, Sidney. "Empedocles: The Phenomenology of the Four Elements in Literature." *Analecta Husserliana*, no 23, 1988, pp. 9-64.

García Santo-Tomás, Enrique. *The Refracted Muse: Literature and Optics in Early Modern Spain.* Translated by Vincent Barletta. Chicago: University of Chicago Press, 2017.

Gendarme de Bevotte, Georges. *La legende de don Juan.* Paris: Hachette, 1908.

Greer, Margaret Rich. *The Play of Power: Mythological Court Dramas of Calderón de la Barca.* Princeton, NJ: Princeton University Press, 1991.

Grillner, Katja. "To See the World as a Limited Whole: Human and Divine Perspectives in the Works of Salomon de Caus." *Chora 3: Intervals in the Philosophy of Architecture.* Edited by Alberto Pérez-Gómez and Stephen Parcell. Montreal: McGill/Queens University Press, 1999, pp. 79-102.

Heninger, S. K. *Touches of Sweet Harmony: Pythagorean Cosmology and Renaissance Poetics.* The Huntington Library, 1974.

Hurtado Torres, Antonio. *La astrología en la literatura del Siglo de Oro.* Alicante: Instituto de Estudios Alicantinos, 1984.

Li, Andrés de. *Repertorio de los tiempos.* Edited by Laura Delbrugge. London: Tamesis, 1999.

Lombardo, Stanley. *Parmenides and Empedocles: The Fragments in Verse Translation.* Eugene, OR: Wipf & Stock, 2010.

Lope de Vega, Félix. *El castigo sin venganza.* Edited by Antonio Carreño. Madrid: Cátedra, 1990.

————. *Fuente Ovejuna.* Edited by Juan María Marín. Madrid: Cátedra, 2004.

Mandrell, James. *Don Juan and the Point of Honor. Seduction, Patriarchal Society and Literary Tradition.* University Park: Pennsylvania State University Press, 1992.

Marni, A. "Did Tirso Employ Counterpassion in *El burlador de Sevilla*?" *Hispanic Review*, no. 20, 1952, pp. 123-133.

Martín, Francisco J. "The Presence of the Four Elements in *El burlador de Sevilla*." *A Star-Crossed Golden Age: Myth and the Spanish Comedia.* Edited by Frederick A. de Armas. Lewisburg, PA: Bucknell University Press, 1998, pp. 30-45.

McKendrick, Melveena. *Women and Society in Golden Age Spanish Drama.* London: Cambridge University Press, 1974.

Mendes, Maria do Carmo. "Who's Afraid of Don Juan: Vampirism and Seduction." *Dracula and the Gothic in Literature: Vampirism and the Arts.* Edited by Isabel Ermida. Leiden: Brill/Rodopi, 2015, pp. 273-294.

Molina, Tirso de (atribuido). *El burlador de Sevilla.* Edited by A. Rodríguez López-Vázquez. Madrid: Cátedra, 2016.

———. *El burlador de Sevilla.* Edited by A. Rodríguez López-Vázquez. Madrid: Cátedra, 1991.

Parry, Richard. "Empedocles." *The Stanford Encyclopedia of Philosophy* (Fall 2016 Edition). plato.stanford.edu/archives/fall2016/entries/empedocles/ . Accessed 23 March 2017.

Pendzik, Susana. "Female Presence in Tirso's *El burlador de Sevilla*." *Bulletin of the Comediantes,* no. 47, 1995, pp. 165-180.

Quintero, María Cristina. "The Interaction of Text and Culture in Spanish Renaissance Translations of Plautus' *Amphytruo*." *Bulletin of Hispanic Studies,* vol. 67, no. 3, 1990, pp. 235-252.

Richer, Jean. *Sacred Geography of the Ancient Greeks: Astrological Symbolism in Art, Architecture and Landscape.* Albany: State University of New York Press, 1994.

Rodríguez López-Vázquez, Alfredo. "Ulises, Jasón, Eneas y Don Juan: la urdidumbre textual del mito de Don Juan." *Academia,* www.academia.edu/28431870/Ulises_Jas%C3%B3n_Eneas_y_Don_Juan_la_urdimbre_textual_del_mito_de_Don_Juan . Accessed 23 March 2017.

Rogers, Daniel. "Fearful Symmetry: The Ending of *El burlador de Sevilla*." *Bulletin of Hispanic Studies,* no. 41, 1964, pp. 141-159.

Rose, Constance. "Reconstructing Tisbea." *The Golden Age Comedia, Text, Theory and Performance.* Edited by Charles Ganelin and Howard Mancing. West Lafayette, IN: Purdue University Press, 1994, pp. 48-57.

Ruiz de Alarcón, Juan. *La verdad sospechosa.* Edited by Alva V. Ebersole. Madrid: Cátedra, 1982.

Sturm, Sarah, and Harlam Sturm. "The Astronomical Metaphor in *La estrella de Sevilla*." *Hispania,* no. 52, 1969, pp. 193-197.

Ulansey, David. *The Origin of the Mithraic Mysteries: Cosmology and Salvation in the Ancient World.* New York: Oxford University Press, 1989.

Varey, John. *Cosmovisión y escenografía: El teatro español en el Siglo de Oro.* Madrid: Castalia, 1987.

Vitse, Marc. "Las burlas de don Juan: viejos mitos y mito nuevo." *El mito en el teatro clásico español.* Edited by Francisco Ruiz Ramón and César Oliva. Madrid: Taurus, 1988, pp. 182-195.

Watt, Ian. *Myths of Modern Individualism: Faust, Don Quixote, Don Juan, Robinson Crusoe.* New York: Cambridge University Press, 1997.

Woods, Michael J. *The Poet and the Natural World in the Age of Góngora.* New York: Oxford University Press, 1978.

The Fictionalization of the Space in *El burlador de Sevilla y convidado de piedra*[1]

Antonio Guijarro Donadiós
Worcester State University

This essay traverses the multiform appearances of spaces in *El burlador de Sevilla y convidado de piedra*, attributed to Tirso de Molina and published in 1630. During the journey from Naples to Seville of Don Juan and those who follow and chase him, there is a confluence between realities:

one, those of the places themselves, with their own genuine vital spaces, their peculiar urban and rural geography and the human material that inhabits them will become evident;

and two, fictional transformations: the pieces of the dramatic mechanism and of the dramaturg's imaginary construction that create the formation of the fictional space and the articulation of it as functional and key to the play.

Confronting the rigid norms that the space imposed as an integral part of the dramatic unit, the Spanish playwrights of the Golden Age adopted a posture of creative freedom, they prioritized the action over space and time. Each action required its own time and space.[2] This doesn't mean that the pieces in the seventeenth century lacked verisimilitude, but that each one of the scenes possessed its own time-space unit. On top of that, the action also superseded historic reality such as in *El burlador*. The characters, even though they belonged to an earlier age, expressed seventeenth century values which resulted in a historic space full of anachronisms. For example, the one

---

1 I would like to thank Erica C. Sines for the help with the translation of this essay.

2 For a study of *mise-en-scene* of *El burlador,* see Navas Ocaña.

pointed out by Marc Vitse, where Juan I of Portugal and Alfonso XI of Castile share the same time frame (23) or as Alfredo López-Vázquez mentioned, referring to the Spanish Conquest of America in a play that takes place in the 14th century (Tirso 1996, 31).

Tirso—according to Enrique García Santo-Tomás—was a travelling friar that knew of diverse locations and he used many of these impressions in the construction of legendary spaces and atmospheres (Tirso 2007, 13). While the motive of travel does not structure the play (the trajectory itself is not mentioned), Don Juan and Catalinón leave Naples and appear in Tarragona and from there to Seville. It is not less true that the thematic tool of movement, not only by Don Juan, but by many of the male and female characters that accompany him, brings the distinction of specific places and spaces to the play. As Francisco Ruiz Ramón has pointed out, "la pieza teatral responde, estructuralmente, a una concepción dinámica de la acción, aquí consonante con el vivir del protagonista" (*Historia* 207). "Protagonista éste—adds Ruiz Ramón—cuya esencia estriba en existir en el más puro y radical de los presentes. Don Juan Tenorio solo cree en el aquí y ahora porque su vida es ser aquí y ahora" (*Historia* 208). The dynamism of the character whose ignorance of the distance of death is repeated throughout the play, "¡Qué largo me lo fiáis!" (v. 905) and carries with it more the notion of time suspended in space, not only physical, but also symbolical.[3]

Based on the discipline of postmodernist political geography in favor of a humanistic approach rather than a positive science where space becomes anchored in the experience of human life, not as something to look at or describe, but rather to live and experience, Edward Soja, the late urban theorist, following in the tradition of the work by French Marxist urban sociologist Henri Lefebvre, updated Lefebvre's concept of the spatial triad with his own concept of spatial trialectics which includes thirdspace, or spaces in which "everything comes together... subjectivity and objectivity, the abstract and the concrete, the real and the imagined [...] everyday life and unending history" (57). Soja conceives the space as a material product, an expression that configures a society and insists on the symbolical importance of what mental maps and imaginary landscapes contain, where we find a continual relationship of domination between city and country, urban and periphery, and as such, giving importance to human geography, the establishment between social relationships according to social practice. In this context, I propose that the study of the representation of certain emblematic spaces

---

    3   Quotes are from the eighth edition by Alfredo Rodríguez López-Vázquez published by Cátedra in 1996.

that appear in the play (imagined, seductive, supernatural, profane, sacred, domestic, marginal, urban, rural, pastoral, nuptial, maritime, diurnal, nocturnal, even of absences) determine the rest of the components of the piece, as is the construction of the characters and of the dramatic action.[4]

El burlador is constructed in a symmetrical way around the central location where the action develops, three in the first act (Naples, Tarragona, and Seville), one in the second (Seville), and three in the third (a town called Dos Hermanas, Tarragona, and Seville).[5] The piece begins in media res in the Royal Palace of Naples, in a room where there is consensual carnal love and sex between an unmarried couple, the Duchess Isabela and Don Juan—although she thinks she is with her lover, the Duke Octavio. As occurs in a similar event later in the play, we suppose that Don Juan has intercepted a note, and has gone to Isabela's rooms in place of the Duke Octavio. Even though a palace, religiously speaking, is not that different from the outskirts of Seville, that will appear later on, where the prostitutes are and as such, sex: the carnal encounter that occurred, under the promise of marriage, and with that the potential to climb the social ladder, is not that different that an economic transaction. The fact that the Duchess has invited a lover into her rooms is morally scandalous, and even worse, as John E. Varey affirms, that the invitation is to the Royal Palace "es algo que va contra el honor personal del Rey" and, I would add, transforming the palatial space into a wanton one (141). The trick occurs inside a space that is domestic and nocturnal, it is surprisingly easy for Don Juan to enter the chamber, an intimately feminine space with difficult access inside another space, and the palace which we imagine to be well-guarded. Isabela shows herself as a woman who lets her suitor dishonor her, thinking she is securing her prospect of marriage, but does not even find light by which to enjoy looking at his face.

As in all urban enclaves, there is a rich and a poor Naples; interestingly, in El burlador, only the rich side appears. Naples, both as Court and embassy, is a maritime city at the shores of the Mediterranean with a direct connection with Spain. The action in Naples develops in various spaces: the palace itself, which includes Isabela's room where the action begins, and the tower, where

---

4   For diverse and innovative studies of space in Spanish Golden Age plays, see the enlightening works by García Santo-Tomás.

5   Francisco Ruiz Ramón states that "El Burlador, lejos de ser un texto descuidado o improvisado, refleja una precisa y clara estructura cuyo recurso fundamental de configuración es el principio de la bipolaridad"; at the same time, the critic argues his reasoning "en torno a tres niveles: de forma, ideológico y mítico" (El Burlador 905).

she is taken prisoner after her carnal exchange with Don Juan; and later Octavio's foyer where they want to take him to prison, the same situation as Isabel and the tower. It is important to note that there is a constant in the play where those against the imperative moral code must be locked away—let's not forget that the same thing will happen later on with the Marquis of la Mota. The fiction transmits a space occupied by the higher class, where the lower class of Naples does not appear, although primitive instincts do, those of betrayal, deceit, and lust.

After the discovery of Don Juan in Isabela's chamber, Don Pedro, his uncle, ambassador of Castile to the Court, instead of arresting his nephew, tells him to go to Sicily or Milan, another anachronism, since they were not Spanish territories in the 14th century, when *El burlador* takes place, but were in the seventeenth century when the play was first performed. In the same light, how many of the audience members at that time had ever even been to Naples? Unlike Seville, an urban space that all the characters, even the outsiders, seem to know in the play.

Since the very first moment, we perceive that Don Juan is in a constant state of flight; from the very first verse of the play "por aquí/ podrás salir" (vv. 1-2) he was already fleeing the scene: Don Pedro tells Don Juan "Tu padre desde Castilla a Nápoles te envió" (vv.85-87). Interestingly, Naples is shown as a city that has embraced Don Juan and he responds by offending it by the way he acts. The King of Naples finishes the scene using the metaphorical use of the space to elevate his complaint: "no importan [...] murallas/ fortalecidas almenas/para Amor" (vv. 173-175); a spatial symbolism that the Duke Octavio reiterates only a few verses later when, with maximum expression of courtly love, states that he has been "guardando, ausente y presente/el castillo del honor" (vv. 206-207).

With Isabela locked in the tower, her space of seclusion, Don Juan and Catalinón flee to Spain directly by sea—which was largely an unknown form of transportation—and Octavio is also on his way to Spain. The characters leave frenetically and must leave their comfort zone, from a hedonistic courtly space to get to a decadent one. Through the maritime space, that of the Mediterranean, a sea, it appears, that gets rid of the bad: Don Juan and "pirates" (v. 425) as the work itself indicates, is how they arrive in Tarragona, in a violent way, after a shipwreck which will contrast soon afterwards with the sea as a seductive space. On his way to Seville, Don Juan will have to stop in this country space, a small fishing village living a peaceful life, full of "cabañas de amor" (v. 415) and "chozas de paja," (v. 565), away from walls of the great Palace of Naples. This is somewhat paradoxical when during the sixteenth and seventeenth centuries they built walls or solidified fortresses to defend the city and its surroundings from continuous wars and pirate attacks. Piracy on the Mediterranean coast provoked the exodus of the people from the shores to the more secure interior. In order to control pirate attacks, defense towers were built along the coastline, such as the Torre de la Mora.[6] Don Juan, the same as in the palatial space, will penetrate Tisbea's bedroom, an intimate feminine space, also insurmountable. In this case, the anachronism is a social one: perhaps Tisbea (and Arminta later) did not realize—and by that extension, the audience either—that a wedding between her and a gentleman of the court would have never occurred. Tisbea, again using the metaphoric use the space, exclaims "mi pobre edificio queda/hecha otra Troya en llamas" (v. 990) and Don Juan continues on his way to crowded Seville, the most populous city in Spain at the end of the 16th century along with Naples (Domínguez 79).

The scene between Tisbea and our libertine hangs in suspense to introduce a scene much discussed by critics between the King Don Alfonso de Castilla y don Gonzalo de Ulloa, where don Gonzalo makes a very large elegy about Lisbon, whose function, according to Ignacio Arellano, consists in "establecer un contraste moral entre dos mundos, el de don Juan, y el ideal de Lisboa" (344).[7] This pause in the action establishes the mythical and ideal model of Portugal, which will be compared to the Babylonian Seville, and, by extension the Spanish Empire. Lisbon, as with Naples, appears described as a city and embassy full of wonders, connected to the Atlantic Ocean, a sea, it appears, that leads to the good, with a connection to the Americas and the Indies, where they speak of Goa, a Portuguese colony, and of Ceuta and Tangier in Africa, exalting the great conquests made by the neighboring country. Alexia Dotras has established an analysis based on the hierarchy of elements present such as the extension as a symbol of strength, with more fervor and religious spaces than Rome, natural beauty, nobility, rising economy, and discoveries. Lisbon, and by extension, Portugal, appears surrounded "by a halo of perfection and idealism, it appears as a rich, thoughtful, and even magical city" (131).

---

6   See Recasens.

7   For a more detailed account of the vision of Lisboa, see Vitse, Fraticelli and Zamora. Also, Mercedes de los Reyes Peña justifies the praise of Seville in Golden Age narratives "dentro del contexto contrarreformista de la España Barroca" (480).

The second act begins in the palatial space of Seville where the King of Castile (Alfonso XI) and the King's Ambassador to Naples appear.[8] The Duke Octavio arrives, as the stage directions indicate, with "ropa de camino" (v. 1086), not as a castaway, but as a "peregrino/ mísero y desterrado" (vv. 1086-1087). Contrary to Naples, the streets and underworld of Seville do appear here. It's important to understand something that may have escaped the critics, the only mention of Mount Vesuvius in the play is made in Don Juan's exclamation when he sees Duke Octavio away from his Neapolitan shore:

DON JUAN   ¿Quién pensara,
duque, que en Sevilla os viera?
¿Vos Puzol, vos la Ribera
desde Parténope clara/ dejáis (vv. 1158-1160).

Rodriguez López-Vázquez lets us know that Puzol is a celebrated location amongst the country folk of Naples, famous for its solfatare (191). If Puzol is the Neapolitan space where Don Juan y Octavio are coming from, this provides a metaphorical linking of the Devil and Don Juan, as Sandra L. Brown has argued in a brief, but exceptional article. She identifies how our hero "stands out as a social counterpart to the Biblical figure Lucifer" (63) studying the imaginary associated with Don Juan: he is likened to a snake, he is possessed of fire, he is being sent by the Devil (when the Burlador intrudes on the wedding of Batricio and Arminta), the meal that Gonzalo serves Don Juan only minutes before the latter's death includes scorpions and serpents, "things symbolic of evil and Satan" (64). Therefore, not only the imaginary symbols that Brown demonstrates, but the space where Don Juan comes from completely determines the construction of the diabolic appearance of the libertine.[9]

The space where both of them see themselves and move easily is the *mentidero*, a merchant-lined open space where couples stroll together: "en Gradas os aguardamos" (v. 1535) says the Marquis of la Mota, but it's also

---

8   Regarding the social critique in relation to the spaces through which our libertine goes through, Varey has noted that "la obra ataca con cierta dureza la condición moral de España, ejemplificada por una de sus ciudades más importantes, Sevilla, contrastando al mismo tiempo la vida de la ciudad con la de la aldea" (136).

9   Brianda Domecq refers to Don Juan as "la expresión de la Reforma dentro de una sociedad fundamentalmente teocéntrica y medieval, cuya bandera principal en la Contrareforma" (11). She sees Don Juan as a character without ideals, inability to love, and closely tied to the Devil.

a commercial space that gained great fame for the thievery and outbreaks of violence that were a daily occurrence (Piñero 202).[10] A shared space appears next, the tavern of los Pajarillos, a place where a dialogue about prostitutes mentions the streets Candilejo where they identify the prostitutes by the space they occupy in the neighborhood of Cantarranas, where low-class prostitutes lived, and those of the "rameras caras" on the Calle de la Sierpe, who were of high-class (213).[11]

They speak of places of prostitution in Seville (which are real) against the idealized image of Portugal that brings with it the reference to Doña Ana, cousin to the Marquis of la Mota: "Es hermosa" (v. 1259) Don Juan asks, "Es extremada" (v. 1260) Mota responds. Just like Lisbon appears against a backdrop of the ugly prostitutes, so emerges Doña Ana. Both characters traverse through a Seville of gallantries, a space completely lacking in seduction since it is entirely present in prostitution.

Another supposed private area that stops being one is the prostitute Beatriz's house, where Don Juan goes to sleep with her without paying. To enter the closed space, he has to approach the lattice window and, as the Marquis tells him, "decid Beatrís" (v. 1532) to enter. The violation of the prostitute and her space that Mota does tricked by Don Juan barely receives attention in the play, maybe as a testimony to the extension the practice had at the time, and because one could say such a thing to the audience of the time without causing much scandal.[12] However, it is of great importance since the play will pass from the theme of the *burlador* to that of the *convidado de piedra*. The strategy used by Don Juan to hang the blame on the Marquis of la Mota is to make him believe that both of them are going to sleep with the prostitute. The Marquis yields the meeting and even his own cape to deceive her, but in reality, he:

10   See also *Diccionario histórico*.

11   For a detailed study of the public prostitution laws in Seville at that time, see Moreno.

12   There is no need to talk about the moral condemnation or the social rejection that has always accompanied prostitution. It was actually not prohibited in the seventeenth century, but regulated. For example, when calling on "casas de arrepentidas," method of control and surveyance had been established. Therefore, the law did not pursue women for prostitution, but for practicing it outside the regulations. What is also interesting is that prostitution was relegated to the peripheral spaces of Madrid, while it took place in the urban center of Seville. For an analysis of prostitution in Castile, see Menjot. For Madrid specifically, see Villalba.

a) facilitates his own disgrace and,
b) starts a chain of events that lead to Don Gonzalo's death.

Mota states "La mujer ha de pensar/ que soy yo" (vv. 1543-1544), a prediction that comes true, but not with the woman he believes, since don Juan, with the Marquis' cape, will not go to Beatriz's house, but to play a trick on Doña Ana, the cousin and lover of the Marquis of la Mota and the daughter of Don Gonzalo. As we know, don Juan will terminate the Comendador's life and will continue to make it appear as if the Marquis is guilty, who after roaming the streets of Seville, on his way home, is chased by an angry crowd carrying torches that makes it all the way from the Plaza of the Alcazar to direct him towards the incarceration space—which contributes even more to the degradation of the character—and afterwards put his head on a spike.

The metaphoric language of the space appears again at the beginning of the duel between Don Juan and Don Gonzalo. The father claims:

> DON GONZALO. La barbacana caída
> de la torre de mi honor
> echaste en tierra, traidor
> donde era alcaide la vida (vv. 1572-1575)

Don Juan has destroyed his daughter's honor and now he must defend her with his life, which is usually more common in cloak-and-dagger plays.

At the end of the second act, we find a Don Juan, exiled and defamed, on his way to Lebrija. He stops in Dos Hermanas, a famous location where they made bread to cover the demand in Seville, and as such, it was well-known by the audience (Piñero 64). Here, the hospitality and the sacrament of matrimony is what Don Juan breaks in this space of *locus amoenus*. This idyllic location: "sitio hermoso," space of happiness, of innocence, appears as very different from Seville where in a matter of seconds we went from death to a wedding of "más colores el prado" (v. 1701) and the spacial metaphors continue: "montes en casa hay de pan, Guadalquivides de vino, Babilonias de tocino" (vv. 1752-1754), and as a contrast, the deception of Arminta, in whose abode, in the wee hours of the night, as we recall, Don Juan enters surreptitiously. In this case, in addition to marriage, he also promises jewelry—material cultural artifacts: "virillas, clavos de oro, gargantillas, perlas y sortijas" (vv. 2097-2105), which is one of the few moments we find expressions of material culture to support the conquest of the main character. In an interesting way, contrary to what is happening in Madrid in the seventeenth century, Don Juan is not attracted by the immediate pleasure that material goods offer (only the letter and the cloak appears as artifacts), but by Seville as a scenic motivation where the dramatized actions and the presence of the nocturnal space continues.

Castaways as well, Isabela and Fabio arrive in Tarragona and after their encounter with Tisbea, in their search for Don Juan, change course towards Valencia: "ciudad bella" (v. 2161) to have fun, as a place to stop on their way to Seville. A more interesting place that they choose over Madrid, we can suppose that the diversion comes from watching theater since it was a constant amongst the Valencian oligarchy.[13]

Don Juan and Catalinón are staying at an inn hidden in the street. Unlike others characters in the play, they room in a space that is not their own, where the door is locked behind them. It is worth noting that the female characters are locked or hidden away (in towers, in their bedchambers), but Don Juan locks his own self away out of fear of revenge for his actions. On their way, they pass the chapel where don Gonzalo's tomb is. This inn appears as a space of fantasy, of supernatural dramatic action, where both fiction and reality take place: "sombra, fantasma o vision" (v. 2484).

Meanwhile, at the Palace, an attempt at a duel happens between Don Diego and Octavio. That is interesting because the palace is not a marginal space, it is not a place for duels, clearly Don Juan is distracting the people and keeps distorting the spaces to make them his own: he obliges people to duel in a royal space (of kings and queens) rather than in the street at night and he enters easily into what are supposed to be private spaces such as the females' bedchambers.

Female spaces frequently appear as spaces of refuge—"fuese al sagrado Doña Ana/de mi señora la reina" (vv. 1679-1680) or "con mi nombre profanó/ el sagrado de una Dama" (vv. 2605-2606)—they are denominated the *sagrado* or private bedchamber of a lady. According to the *Diccionario de Autoridades, sagrado*: "usado como substantivo, se toma por el lugar que sirve de recurso à los delinqüentes, y se ha permitido para su refugio, en donde están seguros de la Justicia, en los delitos que no exceptúa el Derecho." Along the same lines as *Autoridades, sagrado* is also defined as "la cosa que por su destino, o uso es digna de veneración y respeto" or "lo que segun rito está dedicado a Dios y al culto Divino." Therefore, *sagrado* is a polyvalent space (sacred, profane, female) that Don Juan violates with a large amount of thematic and ambient paganism with the subversive use of the sacred space of the Church,

---

13   See Mouyen (113-114).

not converted anymore into a place of refuge for the libertine, but, on the contrary, his place of destruction, even with the warning by Catalinón "la iglesia es tierra sagrada" (v. 2285). One can appreciate a space that feeds off literature as much as the city inspires and generates literature itself, between landscapes located in a fiction that is more domestic and a reality made action.

At the same time, it is paradoxical how the King names Don Juan "Gentilhombre de mi Cámara/ es Don Juan, y hechura mía" (vv. 2632-2633), and opens up his own private space to such a fortunate libertine, protected and respected by the King. A *gentilhombre* was one of the most distinguished charges amongst the King's servants whose function was to assist in dressing and undressing him, accompany him when he went out in his carriage, another private space that the main character occupies.

One final consideration remains for this essay: the multitude of invitations contained in the play. Many scholars have argued that the *El burlador* comes down to the double dinner invitations in the third act.[14] However, in exploring the potential significance of the invasion or not of personal space through invitations, it also worth analyzing the diverse invitations since they are a constant throughout. First, Isabela extends an invitation to the Duke Octavio, which he does not receive, but Don Juan, invading the Duchess's personal space since he was not the one invited. After taking advantage of her, Don Juan asks for confirmation of the carnal encounter "dame, Duquesa, la mano" (v. 18) which she refuses and then calls out for rescue; unlike Tisbea who lets Don Juan come in the cabin, first as an act of charity, after Don Juan and Catalinón's shipwreck—"que a mi choza les llevemos" (v. 674)—and later on, insinuating:

> TISBEA: Ven, y será la cabaña
> del amor que me acompaña
> tálamo de nuestro fuego. (vv. 951-953)

something she herself reiterates further:

> TISBEA: Del agua derrotado
> a esta tierra llegó un Don Juan Tenorio
> difunto y anegado;
> ampárele, hospédele en tan notorio

---

14   See MacKay.

peligro, y el vil huésped
víbora fue a mi planta en mi tierno césped. (vv. 2226-2231)

The Marquis of la Mota invites Don Juan to take his place in a nocturnal
rendezvous to deceive Beatriz: "Vamos, y poneos mi capa/para que mayor
lo deis [el perro]" (vv. 1524-1525); Ana invites the Marquis of la Mota to her
room via a note—that Don Juan also intercepts—: "Para vos, Marqués, me
han dado/un recaudo harto cortés" (vv. 1376-1377); Gaseno invites Don Juan
to take part in the wedding, and therefore shares in the blame for the disgrace that follows—but neither Batricio nor Arminta, the newlyweds, had
extended the invitation—:

GASENO: Venga tan gran caballero [Don Juan]
             a ser hoy en Dos Hermanas
             honra de estas nobles canas. (vv. 1758-1760)

Don Juan accepts the invitation: "Con vuestra licencia quiero/sentarme
aquí" (v. 1777-1778), and situates himself next to the bride, invading her personal space as much as that of the groom who should be sitting there; Batricio lets his discomfort be known:

BATRICIO: Si os sentaís
             delante de mí, señor,
             seréis de aquella manera
             el novio. (vv. 1779-1782)

Don Juan continues the adulation of Arminta: "Hermosas manos tenéis/
para esposa de un villano" (vv. 1800-1801) and invades her personal space by
taking her hand, as he does with all women during the play: (*Tómale* Don
Juan *la mano a la novia*) (234) and says when confronted with the rejection
by the bride:

DON JUAN: ¿Por qué la escondéis?
ARMINTA: No es mía (vv. 1807-1808)

Later on, he presents himself, uninvited, to her bedroom for pleasure:

ARMINTA: ¿Quién llama a Arminta?
             ¿Es mi Batricio?

DON JUAN: No soy
             tu Batricio.
ARMINTA: Pues, ¿quién?
DON JUAN: Mira
             de espacio, Arminta, quién soy.
ARMINTA: ¡Ay de mí! ¡Yo soy perdida!
             ¿En mi aposento a estas horas? (vv. 2032-2038)

On the other hand, Don Juan invites Catalinón to sit with him at dinner with poor manners:

DON JUAN: Catalinón,
             siéntate.
CATALINÓN: Yo soy amigo
             de cenar de espacio.
DON JUAN: Digo
             que te sientes. (vv. 2338-2343)

He makes him sit, later on, near a statue of Don Gonzalo reiterating: "Siéntate" (v. 2393) and "Siéntate, Catalinón (v. 2398), wanting him to share his personal space. Don Juan insists that the statue eat dinner with him, and the statue repeats the invitation back to him, but asks him to swear it on his honor and asks to shake his hand "dame la mano no temas" (v. 2499) and later on "que me abraso, no me aprietes" (v. 2847) he burns himself literally how Tisbea was burned metaphorically. The symbolic value and the dramatic unit that the Comendador asks for Don Juan's hand is clear, in the same way he did to his female victims asking their hand in marriage. As we have seen, Don Gonzalo will ask for Don Juan´s hand and with that gesture start him on his path to perdition. However, Don Juan continually invades the public and private spaces of others—of course never the other way around. He lacks his own space and is rarely personally invited.

Ultimately, in this construction of reality, Don Juan's behavior crystallizes, in which a series of speeches from various aesthetic traditions come together, where a tension between immediate pleasure takes place and almost nothing is tangible, everything revolves around trickery and deceit. The play offers, in reality, a vision of the space—real and imagined—that reveals a surprising familiarity with the rural and urban fabric for this trickster, this modern myth that lacks, invades, and takes charge of the fictionalized space, and also tries to survive—without succeeding—in a time without time.

Works Cited

Arellano, Ignacio. *Historia del teatro español del siglo XVII.* Madrid: Cátedra, 2008.

Brown, Sandra L. "Lucifer y El burlador de Sevilla." *Bulletin of the Comediantes* 26.2 (1974): 63-64.

Diccionario de Autoridades. Madrid: Gredos, 1963.

Diccionario histórico de las calles de Sevilla, dirigido por Antonio Collantes de Terán Sánchez, Josefina Cruz Villalón, Rogelio Reyes Cano y Salvador Rodríguez Becerra. Sevilla: Consejería de Obras Públicas y Transportes de la Junta de Andalucía/Excmo. Ayuntamiento de Sevilla, 1993.

Domecq, Brianda. "Don Juan y el Burlador de Sevilla: una interpretación." *La Palabra y el Hombre* enero-marzo 25 (1978): 7-17.

Domínguez Ortiz, Antonio. *Historia de Sevilla. La Sevilla del siglo XVII.* Sevilla: Universidad de Sevilla, 1984.

Dotras, Alexia. "Lisboa soñada por Tirso de Molina." *Hipogrifo* 3.2 (2015): 125-134.

Fraticelli, Barbara. "La creación de un espacio imaginario: los españoles y Lisboa." *Revista de Filología Románica* III (2002): 317-326.

García Santo-Tomás, Enrique. "Early Modern Geographies: Teaching Space in Tirso de Molina's Urban Plays." In *Approaches to Teaching Early Modern Spanish Drama.* Ed. Laura R. Bass and Margaret R. Greer. New York: MLA, 2006.

———. "El espacio simbólico de la pugna literaria." *El teatro del Siglo de Oro ante los espacios de la crítica. Encuentros y revisiones.* Ed. Enrique García Santo-Tomás. Iberoamericana/Vervuert, 2002. 31-58.

———. *Espacio urbano y creación literaria en el Madrid de Felipe IV.* Madrid: Iberoamericana, 2004.

———. "Tráfico barroco: urbanidad y urbanismo en *Las Bizarrías de Belisa de Lope de Vega.*" *Bulletin of the Comediantes* 5 (2000): 31-53.

MacKay, Dorothy E. *The Double Invitation in the Legend of Don Juan.* Stanford: Stanford University Press, 1943.

Menjot, Denis. "Prostitutas y rufianes en las ciudades castellanas a fines de la Edad Media." *Temas Medievales* 4 (1994): 189-204.

Moreno Mengíbar, Andrés and Francisco Vásquez García. "Poderes y prostitución en España (siglos XVI y XVII): El caso de Sevilla." *Criticón* 69 (1997): 33-49.

Mouyen, Jean. "Las casas de comedias de Valencia." *Teatros del Siglo de Oro: Corrales y Coliseos en la Península Ibérica.* Ed. José María Díaz Borque. *Cuadernos de Teatro Clásico* 6 (1991): 91-122.

Navas Ocaña, Maribel. "Hacia una reconstrucción espectacular de *El burlador de Sevilla y convidado de piedra* de Tirso de Molina." *En torno al teatro del Siglo de Oro: actas de las jornadas* I-VI. Ed. Heraclia Castellón Alcalá, Agustín de la Granja, Antonio Serrano Agulló. Almería: Instituto de Estudios Almerienses, 1991. 89-103.

Piñero Ramírez, Pedro and Rogelio Reyes Cano. *Itinerario de la Sevilla de Cervantes. La ciudad en sus textos.* Sevilla: Junta de Andalucía/Caja San Fernando, 2005.

Recasens Comes, Josep Mª. *La Ciutat de Tarragona.* Barcelona: Barcino, 1966.

Reyes Peña, Mercedes de los. "El espacio urbano de Sevilla." *Homenaje a Frédéric Serralta. El Espacio y sus representaciones en el teatro español del Siglo de Oro.* Eds. Françoise Cazal, Christopher González y Marc Vitse. Universidad de Navarra: Iberoamericana/Vervuert, 2002. 451-495.

Ruiz Ramón, Francisco. *Historia del teatro español I.* Madrid: Alianza, 1967.

————. "El Burlador de Sevilla y la dialéctica de la dualidad." *Estado actual de los estudios sobre el Siglo de Oro: actas del II Congreso Internacional de Hispanistas del Siglo de Oro.* Vol. 2. Ed. Manuel García Martín. Universidad de Salamanca: Ediciones Universidad de Salamanca, 1993. 905-912.

Soja, Edward. *Thirdspace. Journeys to Los Angeles and Other Real-and-Imagined Places.* Cambridge: Polity Press, 1996.

Tirso de Molina (atribuida a). *El burlador de Sevilla.* Ed. Alfredo Rodríguez López-Vázquez. Madrid: Cátedra. 1996.

Tirso de Molina. *Don Gil de las calzas verdes.* Edición de Enrique García Santo-Tomás. Madrid: Cátedra, Letras Hispánicas, 2007.

Varey, John E. "Crítica social en *El Burlador de Sevilla.*" *Cosmovisión y escenografía. El teatro español en el Siglo de Oro.* Madrid: Castalia, 1987. 135-155.

Villalba Pérez, Enrique. "Notas sobre la prostitución en Madrid a comienzos del siglo XVII." *Anales del Instituto de Estudios Madrileños* 34 (1997): 505-519.

Vitse, Marc. "La descripción de Lisboa en *El Burlador de Sevilla.*" *Criticón* 2 (1978): 21- 41.

Zamora Vicente, Alonso. "Portugal en el teatro de Tirso de Molina." *Biblos* XXIV-I (1948): 1-41.

Don Juan's Principles: Perversion, Hedonism and Ludic Theatricality

Don Juan Tenorio, Touch, Pygmalion:
Perverse Ecstasy and Ecstatic Perversion

CHARLES VICTOR GANELIN
Miami University

THE TWO CHARGED TERMS in my title, "perverse" and "ecstasy," are not intended to be understood in a psychoanalytic context in a study dedicated to a figure who has elicited a legion of such readings; rather my brief essay explores these concepts in ways closer to their original meanings: "pervertere": Latin for "overturn, ruin, corrupt"; and "ekstasis," from the Greek, "put out of place" (*Oxford Dictionary of English Etymology*). I use them to link to two related ideas in the respective denouements concerning Don Juan from *El burlador de Sevilla* (*Burlador*) to Zorrilla's *Don Juan Tenorio* (*Tenorio*), though with the primary emphasis on the nineteenth-century play: the myth of Pygmalion and Galatea (the name given to the statue in the eighteenth century), particularly the animation of Doña Inés's statue, and the concomitant sensorial aspect of touch. The most notable moments of both these plays involve a special touch: in *Burlador* Don Juan promises marriage to his victims not with a vow to God but often to a body part (hands, eyes), culminating in Don Gonzalo's statue demanding Don Juan's hand; in *Tenorio*, Don Juan's obsession with Doña Inés trades on a repeated play of hands, incorporating the touch of Don Gonzalo's statue but concluding with an outstretched hand toward Doña Inés in the final step of his salvation. Each Don Juan satisfies his perverted sense of ecstasy in his respective conquests, and an ecstatic sense of perversion as he flouts social conventions. Don Juan constantly seeks to define relationships on his own *physical* terms constituted by an imposition of physical contact. The extensive sense of touch serves as Don Juan's conduit to control, for touch, as Elizabeth Harvey has written, "establishes our sentient border with the world"

95

("Portal" 386). Each time Don Juan approaches the liminal space between his convoluted world of moral inversions and the universe of prevailing social norms his touch conveys a distinct nuance to the events he sets in motion and rends the taut fabric of social construction. The issue of touch and how and what it communicates is decidedly one-sided in _Burlador_ whereas the issue assumes greater complexity in _Tenorio_ through Doña Inés's status as near-novitiate, her removal from the convent, and her physical death joined to her "spiritual" continuance. As she approaches the frontier between the here and the beyond, she, too, imparts a touch that metamorphoses. The two plays naturally reflect distinct contexts and sensorial boundaries. Where _Burlador_ couches the final, quasi-mystical grasp of the statue in theological terms, condemning Don Juan to hell, _Tenorio_ converts the final touch—from the spirit of Doña Inés and not from the statue of Don Gonzalo—to apotheosis and transcendence, redeeming Don Juan, subverting perversion, and redefining ecstasy. The moment of Don Juan's conversion is also a turn in Spanish Romanticism, itself an expression of a wide-ranging spiritual, philosophical, and artistic crisis (Cardwell 146).

The particular element of _Don Juan Tenorio_ that focuses on questions of perversion, ecstasy and touch is Zorrilla's appropriation of the Pygmalion myth. In the play, the Sculptor admires and reveals his infatuation with the statues in the pantheon that now occupies the space of the Tenorio palace; however, the statues, particularly the one of Doña Inés, have an effect primarily on Don Juan. Briefly, the myth tells of the sculptor Pygmalion who becomes enamored of his sculpture of his ideal female and prays to Venus to grant it life, which the goddess does (_Metamorphoses_, X.242-298). Zorrilla took advantage of Pygmalion's growing popularity in later-eighteenth- and nineteenth-century Spain owing, in part, to Jean Jacques Rousseau's treatment in his 1770 play _Pygmalion_, a text that was to inspire the British Romantics before having its influence felt in Germany and western Europe in general (Joshua 38). Catherine Jagoe finds that the Pygmalion motif appears frequently in nineteenth-century Spain especially in works by men about women (44). Though Jagoe's remarks concern Galdós's 1878 _La familia de León Roch_, Pygmalion served the Romantics earlier in the century quite well. The Romantic artist frequently isolated himself from others, searching for his muse generally in the form of a woman or ideal female who is not part of the physical world (Rueda 100). Ana Rueda provides a way of presenting artistic creative urges through exploration of metamorphosis, where the Pygmalion story fits ideally:

la reanimación de la estatua se convierte en motivo de terror para una mente ya atormentada y abocada al ámbito de las sombras. Si la visión del artista penetra en las capas más profundas de las cosas, es para descubrir un sentido de maldad, de poderes oscuros que controlan su destino y que lo atormentan en el proceso (100-01).

Rueda sees a distinction between many of the male statues that appear in Romantic texts and specifically that of Doña Inés in Zorrilla's play; she notes that Inés, a "fetiche de pureza" for Don Juan (112), undergoes continual transformations into shadow, soul, and spiritual flame, the opposite trajectory found in the Pygmalion story where stone becomes flesh. The inversion of the myth allows Don Juan to trust Inés and accept her entreaties to save his soul. She creates a new Don Juan—not to mention a new Romantic hero—and entices him to be transformed into heavenly spirit and not be consigned to hell. To understand the impact of the scene, I begin with the first act of the second part of *Tenorio*.

Don Juan has returned to Seville and finds the palace converted into a pantheon. The sculptor, bidding adieu to his creations, takes pride in his work in the pantheon attributing to himself demiurgic qualities invested in the renown his creations will bring him:

> ¡Ah! Mármoles que mis manos
> pulieron con tanto afán,
> mañana os contemplará
> los absortos sevillanos
> /.../
> ¡Oh!, frutos de mis desvelos,
> peñas a quien yo animé
> y por quienes arrostré
> la intemperie de los cielos;
> el que forma y ser os dio
> va ya a perderos de vista;
> ¡velad mi gloria de artista,
> pues viviréis más que yo!" (vv. 2656-59; 2668-75).

The sculptor speaks to bringing life to stone ("yo animé") despite nature's challenges; the "intemperie de los cielos" could also be read metaphorically as the violence Don Juan had wrought on his victims, leaving the sculptor to create a permanent monument of beauty to the transitory suffering inflicted on the individuals. The artist becomes the Pygmalion figure only insofar as he has created a "living" statue out of the raw material, admires his handiwork, and leaves it to his creations to ensure his fame. The sculptor exits, leaving Don Juan to wander among the marble images of those whose death he has caused. The creator's art begins to come to life as Don Juan first implores the statue of Doña Inés to intercede on his behalf, then leans against it as of to lend the strength of his body to his plea:

> si es que de ti desprendida
> llega esa voz a la altura
> y hay un Dios tras esa anchura
> por donde los astros van,
> dile que mire a don Juan
> *llorando en tu sepultura.*
> (Se apoya en el sepulcro . . .; un vapor que se levanta del sepulcro oculta la estatua de doña Inés. Cuando el vapor se desvanece, la estatua ha desaparecido.) (vv. 2968-73; ensuing stage directions)

The physical proximity of body against the tomb as well as Don Juan's intimations of a benevolent God put in motion the process that will save Don Juan's soul as it appears that he has somehow imbued the statue with sentience.

Zorrilla's Don Juan, as well as the seventeenth-century model, is in thrall to touch and becomes either fearful of or thrilled with its ecstatic possibilities. Tactility between humans is a cornerstone of civilization and conducive to pleasure, but tactility between human and stone brings with it numerous complexities. Theodore Ziolkowski details that the two most prolific themes of talking statues in the European tradition are the legend of Venus, and the Ring as told by William of Malmesbury in c. 1125, and Don Juan (951). *Burlador* presents a statue drawn upon legend and representing divine justice, but by comparison with the statuary in *Don Juan Tenorio Burlador*'s stone guest appears almost two-dimensional, given that Romantic philosophies of the "world soul" led to a belief in the sentience of statues (960). As a result, the sensorial aspect of *Burlador* focuses more on perversion of the social order despite the ecstatic moment of Don Juan's conveyance to hell. Don Juan defies the long-established, nearly universal connection of the sense of touch with fundamental trust (Tuan 78). *Tenorio* endows the protagonist with a legitimate tenderness missing from *Burlador* and recontextualizes Don Juan's path by attempting to balance overweening perverse acts and growing ecstatic moments with Doña Inés. The turmoil that this Don Juan has brought forth—a rejection of the abject suffering characteristic of the Romantic hero such as Don Álvaro—occurs in the context of Carnival and the masks Don Juan has donned (outlaw, exotic, different, violator). Unlike the temporary transformations of the world-turned-upside-down, his actions cannot be undone. Yet the path to absolution for the perpetrator culminates in the apotheosis of the final scene of a literally inspired statue of Doña Inés. Despite the intent of Don Gonzalo's statue to lead Don Juan to hell, Doña Inés's spirit (most likely in human form) intervenes in order to convert him into an ethereal being:

> (Don Juan se hinca de rodillas, tendiendo al cielo la mano que le deja libre la estatua [de Don Gonzalo]. . . . Doña Inés toma la mano que don Juan tiende al cielo.
> . . . Heme ya aquí,
> don Juan; mi mano asegura
> esta mano que a la altura
> tendió tu contrito afán
> y Dios perdona a don Juan
> *al pie de mi sepultura.*
> (Stage directions; vv. 3770-75)

The moment of outstretched hands of both Doña Inés and Don Juan draws attention to touch not only as a signifier of trust but as transmitter of knowledge, here through the threat of a horrifying *confutatis maledictis*, condemnation to the flames of woe. (The scene is almost iconic, bringing to life not just a statue but Michelangelo's ceiling in the Sistine Chapel.) Don Juan in *Burlador* vitiates the social structure and the individuals who represent it (honor, women and authority) and his disappearance into those flames responds to his failure to seek the grace that two centuries later Inés extends to his literary successor. *Burlador* presents Don Juan as the Socratic pharmakon who appears to have eaten and drunk from the concoctions laid out in the purgatorial dinner: *alacranes* and *hiel*. In *Don Juan Tenorio* the protagonist becomes purged from society without the implication of the state-church apparatus found in *Burlador*; the transformation from violator to saved being brings about the end of perversion—a post-Carnival, Lenten state—as well as an implementation of ecstasy in spiritual terms. The statue-turned-spirit of Doña Inés fulfills her role as "creator" in its own right, granting redemption—new life, eternal life—through touch to Don Juan. (I elaborate below.) By staging touch as redemption it becomes a quasi-mystical ecstasy as the redeemed, exclaiming ¡Clemente Dios, gloria a Ti! (v. 3806) stands outside both his former self (ecstasy) and his mortal remains. Touch in its multiple possibilities offers a fluid pathway between the one touched and the one touching; the sense always has the potential to convey ecstasy. Early Modern ascetic and mystical texts (San Juan de la Cruz's "Noche oscura del alma" or Santa Teresa's "Muero porque no muero") exhibit this conceit most commonly, though in *comedias* like Tirso's *La celosa de sí misma* one character cannot contain his joy at the memory of having just glimpsed a certain woman's hand (Ganelin, "Confusing Senses"). More often in other texts, specifically those of Cervantes, the sense of touch—or lack thereof—objectifies (*La española inglesa*), impedes full social integration (*El licenciado vidriera*), or questions mystical ecstasy itself (*Don Quijote*, I.XVI, with Maritornes) (Ganelin, "Cervantes's Exemplary," and "Saliendo"). The crowning Counter-Reformation achievement of touch's transformative effect is Bernini's *Ecstasy of Saint Theresa* (completed in 1652), depicting the mystic's enthrallment as the arrow held by the angel is about to pierce her heart with divine illumination and the erotics of the unitive moment. This and other striking images are shared across the arts, and the various statues, paintings and other icons in their insistent portrayal of divinely-inspired joyful suffering represent variations of ecstasy.

Touch in the nineteenth century takes on distinct shadings from the Early Modern examples, given a change of focus not only from Descartes writings but also in the wake of John Locke's 1690 *Essay Concerning Human Understanding*, which exhibits a "shift toward a more corporeal conception of the 'common sensorium' or seat of the soul" (Vila 3). The Enlightenment's proclivity for expressing senses become "materialized," it could be argued, in language itself. Andrew Bennett, in a study of language and the body, argues that in Romanticism "embodied perception of nature is itself a 'language': it is, indeed, a 'language of the sense' that underlies the transcendence of the material or embodied, of language or the written" (77). A poem fragment by Keats defines new considerations of touch's effect and links Bennett's assessment of the senses and language to a specific episode in *Tenorio*:

> This living hand, now warm and capable
> Of earnest grasping, would, if it were cold
> And in the icy silence of the tomb,
> So haunt thy days and chill they dreaming nights
> That thou would wish thine own heart dry of blood,
> So in my veins red life might stream again,

And thou be conscience-calm'd—see here it is—
I hold it towards you.
(Keats, Poetry Foundation)

It is not difficult to see Keats's imagery in the final scene of apotheosis as well as in the cruel touch of Don Juan as he dispatches rivals and foes. At the same time, touch in *Tenorio* also carries a political significance. Elizabeth Amman's arguments on the nineteenth-century policy of disentailments (*desamortización*)—the Spanish government's usurpation of non-income-producing lands and buildings—vis-à-vis the conversion of Tenorio land to a pantheon, recall that properties in aristocratic entail in addition to Church properties were called *mano muerta* (the legal term is "mortmain") (518). The government's practice, which took place in liberal Spain between 1835-1856, is reflected in Don Juan's own expropriations. Amann brings to bear Don Juan's purchase of a house on his Part II return to Seville from a man who had lost everything, we are told, owing to misfortune over a woman (519), but his acts go further: he enters a building off-limits to most males (the convent), expropriates Inés by removing her from the Church's protection (Part I Act III title, "Profanación," suggestive of perversion in itself) in order to place her in daily currency as part of (his) civilian life. The change in Doña Inés's status is instigated through his letter read to her by attendant Brígida and which she had held in hand after it dropped from her book: by touching the same paper as Don Juan had touched it communicates his "essence"; Doña Inés's immediate reaction is to exclaim "¡Ay! Se me abrasa la mano / con que el papel he cogido" (vv. 1602-03). Leaving aside the angel/devil dichotomy of traditional readings, the effect of Doña Inés's holding the letter is to familiarize, demystify and sensitize both the object and the hand that now holds it (Ganelin, "Museum" 79). The letter had anticipated his arrival, had prepared her for his presence in flesh and blood, effecting a transformation sealed by his mellifluous words and fearful proximity, if not suggestive caresses. Pérez Firmat has noted: "The letter is Don Juan's equivocal *don*, a poisonous gift that passes from hand to hand disseminating its venom. It is also an instrument of usurpation, a gift that possesses the receiver rather than being possessed by her" (272). The challenge becomes, for those who hear this letter along with Inés—Brígida, or we as spectators—to define this object as a fetish (the object contains the power) or anti-fetish (the social structure contains the power) (Debary and Gabel 126). The choice is an aporia, a duality wherein the cause of the object's effect is either in the object or in the human who projects the effect onto the object. (Hennion and Latour 9). Inés's reaction does little to resolve the doubt:

¡Ay! ¿Qué filtro envenado
me dan en este papel,
que el corazón desgarrado
me estoy sintiendo con él?
¿Qué sentimientos dormidos
son los que revela en mí?
¿Qué impulsos jamás sentidos?
¿Qué luz, que hasta hoy nunca vi?
(1.3.3.1732-39)

Don Juan induces an awareness of Doña Inés of her own sensuality as if she were made of marble and he has sculpted away all that hid her emotions. The letter induces Inés's confusion realized in her growing ecstatic reaction to it, emanating perhaps fetishistically from Don Juan's seemingly perverse seduction. Inés finds herself in a precarious emotional state brought on by the "accidental" discovery of Don Juan's letter, for she is in the process of changing form from cloistered to "free," though Don Juan's act exchanges one manner of imprisonment for another. Pérez Firmat also observes that the letter has passed through the walls of the convent, just as statues step down from their pedestals or penetrate the walls of Don Juan's dining room (*Literature* 23). The letter is both instrument and altered object, a sign of physical barriers, reflective of the very malleability of solid surfaces; this, in turn, is the underpinning of the Pygmalion myth in its ability to transform the inanimate to the animate.

Images of letters and persons passing through normally impassable constructs have the effect of perverting (turning around, reversing order) social structures; where Pérez Firmat speaks to penetration of convent and palace walls, implicit are sensual and sexual overtones that inform fundamental actions of *Tenorio*. Naturally, Don Juan's letter to Doña Inés, Brígida's recitation of it, and Don Juan's and Doña Inés's encounter are central to this idea (and central structurally to the play). Kaja Silverman has written that beyond sexual penetration, "all other sexual activities belong either to the category of 'fore-play', in which case they are strictly subordinated to 'end-pleasure', or perversion (185-86)." And perversion, she argues, "strips sexuality of all functionality, whether biological or social . . . Perversion also subverts many of the binary oppositions upon which the social order rests," including life and death (187). Silverman's definition may seem extreme in the context of this particular play, but Don Juan's earlier evisceration of social norms has not been completely cast off. His seduction of Inés, both in his arranging her removal from the convent and his presence at her side in his home, had originated in a bet and so has no real "biological or social" value as it exists beyond acceptable social practice. One result is that his perversions affect everyone in contact with him. Don Juan of *Burlador* is a man for all senses who succumbs to an unmitigated perversion of their pleasures in search of an ill-defined and essentially non-existent ecstasy; Don Juan of *Tenorio* moves from his outlandish self-representation in the "duel" with Don Luis to searing introspection at the close of the play, what Judith Arias calls a "process of interiorization" (30); the step is also from a self-isolated voice (he moves alone, incognito, cold and distant) to one that becomes re-incorporated, quite literally, into a heavenly body. Both of these changes penetrate the walls Don Juan Tenorio has built around himself, enabling a restoration—or perhaps a reconstruction—of the social order, a move away from perversion.

Three episodes in Zorrilla's text underscore Don Juan's transformation. The first occurs during the rendezvous at the tavern in Act I with Don Luis:

> Salí de Roma, por fin,
> como os podéis figurar:
> con un disfraz harto ruin
> y a lomos de un mal rocín,
> pues me querían ahorcar.
> Fui al ejército de España;
> mas todos paisanos míos,
> soldados y en tierra extraña,
> dejé pronto su compaña
> tras cinco o seis desafíos.
> (vv. 471-480)

Followed soon thereafter with lengthy boast:

> Por dondequiera que fui,
> la razón atropellé,
> la virtud escarnecí,
> a la justicia burlé
> y a las mujeres vendí.
> Yo a las cabañas bajé,

yo a los palacios subí,
yo los claustros escalé,
y en todas partes dejé
memoria amarga de mí.
(vv. 501-510)

Throughout this *relación* don Juan gathers speed and energy; at the outset
he narrates his deed in a relatively straightforward manner, but, as the depth
of his perversions becomes clear in his "egocentrismo hedonista"(Gies 547),
the first-person line-ending verbs create a series of oxytone (*agudo*) verses (vv.
501-510) as if to emphasize the depravity of his actions. The second stanza (vv.
506-510) reinforces the effect as four of the five verses begin with "yo." The
section closes, as many have noted, with Don Juan referring to himself in the
third person, rendering himself subject and object, subject to no authority
and object only of himself.

A third set of incidents trades on forms of the word "sentido." As Don
Juan and Brígida discuss his preparations to carry the two women from the
convent, Don Juan reacts to Brígida's description of Inés after having read the
letter:

Tan incentiva pintura
los sentidos me enajena,
y el alma ardiente me llena
de su insensata pasión.
(vv. 1306-09).

"Insensata" can mean, beyond "sin sentido," "que carece absolutamente de
prudencia y cordura" (Zerolo, s.v. "insensato"). Don Juan is outside of himself,
ecstatic at the thought of Inés, though the violence he practices will recur soon
with Don Luis and Don Gonzalo. As he finally is alone with Doña Inés Don
Juan's sensuous speech moves beyond glib patter and smooth seduction:

Y estas palabras que están
filtrando insensiblemente
tu corazón, ya pendiente
de los labios de don Juan,
y cuyas ideas van
inflamando en su interior
un fuego germinador

no encendido todavía,
¿no es verdad, estrella mía,
que están respirando amor?
(vv. 2194-2203)

"Insensiblemente," defined by the *Real Academia Española* as "de manera
impercetible, de manera inconsciente o sin darse cuenta," characterizes his
awakened love for Inés with his sinuous rhythms that pierce her and move
inward, what Pérez Firmat calls an "acoustic insemination" (273). Don Juan
believes he is breathing life into (inspiring) a young woman previously held
prisoner in her "triste cárcel sombría" (v. 2169), imbuing her with human
emotions that chisel away at the image of Inés as "garza" or "paloma," fashioned into a silent object. Don Juan-as-sculptor (Pygmalion) of the human
infuses passion in what he sees as his "creation," in turn enabling his salvation
during the play's closing scene where the "creation" turned into spirit inverts
the Pygmalion/Galatea relationship:

Heme ya aquí,
don Juan; mi mano asegura
esta mano que a la altura
tendió tu contrito afán,
y Dios perdona a Don Juan
al pie de mi sepultura.
(vv. 3770-75)

The intertwining of Don Juan Tenorio's hand and the *mortmain*—"the tes-
tamentary clutch of the past on the present," in Katherine Rowe's words
(15-16)—reflects on Don Juan's yielding his inheritance both literally and
metaphorically. His hand becomes a literal *mano muerta* while it paradoxically has brought "life" to Doña Inés, while her literally dead hand infuses
eternal life in the act of forgiveness and mercy. Don Juan had caressed Doña
Inés with his words, with his tone, but Inés extends the hand, the touch that
will permeate Don Juan with divine grace and forgiveness, "tactility's capture
within the net of language" (Harvey, *Sensible* 14). This act is the true incon-
trovertible touch, this act undoes the many perversions he had committed,
this act "removes" Don Juan literally from himself, places him literally outside of his self in the play's culminating, ecstatic moment.

A commonplace of *Don Juan Tenorio* criticism brings to bear that Zorrilla himself was not happy with his play. Yet the author has followed a long line

of artistic purveyors to ensure that Don Juan and his many female and male victims of his do not become mere "nomenclatures of invisibility" (Mathem Shiferraw, in quite a different context). The evolution from *Burlador* to *Don Juan Tenorio, pace* the intermediate/intermediary stages, moves from descent to ascent, from condemnation to apotheosis. In Zorrilla's hands Don Juan Tenorio awakens from what Stephen Daedalus will later call the "nightmare of history," for his ecstatic perversions and perverse ecstasies define changing mores and evolving figurations of the story and myth. The effect on spectators or readers in bringing the text to life occupies the same metaphorical field where Pygmalion touches the statue (whose prime example is Jean Léon Gerôme's 1890 painting.) The touch of the sculptor's skin on the ivory he has fashioned into an adored object "is the locus of a subjective project of relation to the world, and illustrates how physiological and psychological domains cannot be separated," as Penelope Deutscher offers on touch's effect (105). This brings us back to the sculptor of the pantheon's numerous statues. Ràfols holds that "the sculptors chisel has turned [Don Juan Tenorio's victims] into pure representations" (262). These cold manifestations of those Don Juan has harmed are not just "empty signifiers" (262), as Ràfols writes, but facets of a creator's work, which he has so admired, coming to "life," however temporarily. They may be *emptied* of earthly life, but their power to signify knows no diminishment, brought back into the sentient world by the sculptor's and Don Juan's touch.

The exquisite poetry we find in both plays instills in readers, spectators and listeners the haunting perversion of Don Juan and his distinct fates. The panoply of the senses, but especially touch, throughout these two dramatic pieces makes it logical to bring my arguments to a close through other sensorial images. Both iterations of Don Juan—and perhaps all of them in between—have been "cut by the whips of the five senses," in Robinson Jeffery's spectacularly dramatic wording, in their pain-inducing perversions and ecstasies. The apotheosis in Zorrilla's play harks back to John Donne's "The Extasie": "Our soules, (which to advance their state,/Were gone out,) hung 'twixt her, and mee, /And whil'st our soules negotiate there,/Wee like sepulchrall statues lay" (vv. 15-18). We move beyond the reach of ecstasy and perversion, and literally out of sense in a profoundly physical way. Don Juan Tenorio moves beyond the earthly bonds, and in hearing Inés's pleas from her disembodied self, the voice, in Susan Stewart's words, becomes a "metonymy to the body as a whole (108)." He cannot "touch" the voice, yet it touches him. The sounds emanating from her Spirit escape the limitations of closure (see Stewart 111), and what is shuffling off the mortal coil if not moving away from the bonds, toward closure of his life on earth.

Works Cited

Amann, Elizabeth. "Writing and Revenue in Zorrilla's *Don Juan Tenorio*, *Hispanic Review*, 85, 2008, pp. 513-31.

Arias, Judith H. "The Devil at Heaven's Door: Metaphysical Desire in *Don Juan Tenorio*. *Hispanic Review*, 61, no. 1, 1993, pp. 15-34.

Bennett, Andrew. "Language and the Body." In *The Cambridge Companion to the Body in Literature*. Edited by David Hillman and Ulrika Maude. New York: Cambridge University Press, 2015, pp. 73-86.

Cardwell, Richard A. "'El Lord sublime': Byron's Legacy in Spain." In *The Reception of Byron in Europe*. Edited by Richard A. Cardwell. London: Thoemmes Continuum, 2004, vol. 1, pp. 144-63.

Classen, Constance. *The Deepest Sense. A Cultural History of Touch*. Urbana: University of Illinois Press, 2012.

———, ed. *The Book of Touch*. New York: Berg, 2005.

Corbin, Alain. *Time, Desire and Horror: Towards a History of the Senses*. Translated by Jean Burrell. Cambridge, UK: Polity, 1995.

Debary, Octave/Gabel, Philippe (2010): "Seconde main et deuxiéme vie. Objets, souvenirs et photographies." In *L'Objet de main en main/El objeto de mano en mano*. *Melanges de la Casa de Velázquez*, 40 no. 1, pp. 123-42.

Deutscher, Penelope. "Desiring Touch in Sartre and Beauvoir." In Classen, *The Book of Touch*, 102-105.

Diccionario de la Real Academia Española. 2016. http://www.rae.es.

Diccionario enciclopédico de la lengua castellana. Composed by Elías Zerolo, et. al., two vols., Garnier Hermanos, 1898.

Donne, John. "The Extasie." *Complete English Poems*. Edited by C. A. Patrides, updated by Robert Hamilton. London: Dent, 1994, pp. 48-50.

Ganelin, Charles Victor. "Cervantes's Exemplary Sensorium, or the Skinny on *La española inglesa*." In *Beyond Sight: The Other Senses in Iberian Literature*. Edited by Steven Wagschal and Ryan Giles. Toronto: University of Toronto Press, 2018, pp. 167-185.

———. "Confusing Senses and Tirso de Molina's *La celosa de sí misma*." *Bulletin of Spanish Studies*, vol. 90, nos. 4-5, 2013, 619-38.

————. "¿Saliendo sin ser notada? Lo anti-místico y lo anti-erótico en *Don Quijote*." *AnMal Electrónica*, vol. 32, 2012, 352-80.

————. "Don Quixote as Museum." *Cervantes in Perspective*. Edited by Julia Domínguez. Madrid: Iberomericana, 2013, pp. 71-84.

Gies, David T. "Don Juan contra Don Juan: Apoteosis del romanticismo español." *Actas del Séptimo Congreso de la Asociación Internacional de Hispanistas*. Edited by Giuseppe Bellini. 2 vols. Rome: Bulzoni, 1982. vol. 1, pp. 545-51.

Harvey, Elizabeth, ed. *Sensible Flesh: On Touch in Early Modern Culture*. Philadelphia: University of Pennsylvania Press, 2003.

————. "The Portal of Touch," *American Historial Review*, vol. 116, no. 2, 2011, pp. 385-400.

Hennion, Antoine, and Bruno Latour. "Objet de lard, objet de science. Note sure les limites de l'anti-fétichisme," *Sociologie de l'art*, vol. 6, 1993, pp. 7-24.

Jagoe, Catherine. "Krausism and the Pygmalion Motif in Galdós's *La familia de León Roch*." *Romance Quarterly*, 39, no. 1, 1992, pags. 41-52.

Jeffers, Robinson. "Promise of Peace." poemhunter.com/poem/promise of-peace/.

Joshua, Essaka. *Pygmalion and Galatea. The History of a Narrative in English Literature*. London: Ashgate, 2001.

Keats, John. "This living hand." poetryfoundation.org.

Mandrell, James. *Don Juan and the Point of Honor. Seduction, Patriarchal Society, and Literary Tradition*. University Park, PA: Penn State University Press, 1992.

Oxford Dictionary of English Etymology. Edited by C. T. Onions. New York: Oxford University Press, 1966.

Ovid. *Metamorphoses*. Trans. Rolfe Humphries. Bloomington, IA: Indiana University Press, 1955.

Pérez Firmat, Gustavo. "Carnival in *Don Juan Tenorio*." *Hispanic Review*, 51, 1983, pp. 269-81.

————. *Literature and Liminality: Festive Readings in the Hispanic Tradition*. Durham: Duke University Press, 1986.

Ràfols, Wilfredo de. "Writing to Seduce and Seducing to Write about It: Graphocentrism in *Don Juan Tenorio*." *Revista Hispánica Moderna*, 50, no. 2, 1997, pp. 253-65.

Rodríguez López-Vázquéz, Alfredo. *Andrés de Claramonte y El burlador de Sevilla*. Kassel: Reichenberger, 1987.

————, ed. *El burlador de Sevilla*. Madrid: Cátedra, 1990.

————, ed. *El burlador de Sevilla*. 2nd ed. Madrid: Cátedra, 2016.

Rowe, Katherine. *Dead Hands. Fictions of Agency, Renaissance to Modern.* Stanford, CA: Stanford University Press, 1999.

Rueda, Ana. *Pigmalión y Galatea: Refracciones modernas de un mito.* Madrid: Fundamentos, 1998.

Shiferraw, Mahtem. "Nomenclatures of Invisibility." academyofamericanpoets.com.

Silverman, Kaja. *Male Subjectivity at the Margins.* London: Routledge, 1992.

Spell, J. R. "Pygmalion in Spain," *The Romanic Review*, vol. 25, 1934, pags. 395-401.

Stevens, Wallace. "Of Modern Poetry." *The Collected Poems of Wallace Stevens.* Corrected edition, 2nd ed. Edited by John S. Serio and Chris Beyers. New York: Vintage, 2005.

Stoichita, Victor. *The Pygmalion Effect: From Ovid to Hitchcock.* Translated by Alison Anderson. Chicago: University of Chicago Press, 2008.

Tuan, Yi-Fu. "The Pleasures of Touch." In Classen, *The Book of Touch*, pp. 74-79.

Vila, Anne C. "Introduction: Powers, Pleasures, and Perils of the Senses in the Enlightenment Era." In *A Cultural History of the Senses. In the Age of Enlightenment.* Ed. Anne C. Vila. Vol. 4 of *A Cultural History of the Senses.* General Editor Constanc Classen. New York: Bloomsbury, 2014, pp. 1-20.

Watteau, Fabienne and Pierre Rouillard, "L'objet et la main," *Mélanges de la Casa de Velázquez*, 40, no. 1, pp.11-16.

Ziolkowski, Theodore. "Talking Statues?" *Modern Language Review*, vol. 110, no. 4, 2015, pp. 946-68.

Zorrilla, José. *Don Juan Tenorio.* Edited by Luis Fernández Cifuentes with a preliminary study by Ricardo Navas Ruiz. Barcelona: Crítica, 1993.

The Late Don Juan Tenorio: Valle-Inclán Beyond the Pleasure Principle

James Mandrell
Brandeis University

> Estas páginas son un fragmento de las "Memorias amables," que ya muy viejo empezó a escribir en la emigración el Marqués de Bradomín. Un Don Juan admirable. ¡El más admirable tal vez! Era feo, católico y sentimental.
>
> (*Sonata de primavera; Sonata de estío* 22)

WITH THESE WORDS, VALLE-INCLÁN leads us into the world of his Marqués de Bradomín, claiming at one and the same time two apparently distinct ways of interpreting the narrator of the *Sonatas*, that, on the one hand, the Marqués is a Don Juan and, on the other, that he is an ugly, sentimental Catholic. Although these claims are individually comprehensible and indeed not necessarily mutually exclusive (Unamuno's Hermano Juan comes to mind), the conjunction of the carnality of Don Juan with the spirituality—if not the carnality—of orthodox religion as found in the *Sonatas* provokes problems in the reconciliation of that which is seemingly blasphemous, Don Juan, with that which is sacred, religion. These problems are not unlike those associated with Azorín's Juan de Prados y Ramos, or Hermano Juan, of the later novel *Don Juan* (1922). Both Valle-Inclán's *Sonatas* and Azorín's *Don Juan*—even though far different one from another in tone and effect—elucidate a primary characteristic of what can perhaps coyly be referred to as the late Don Juan. The late Don Juan is neither an agent of social anarchy nor opposed to the Church, but, rather, operative within the world of the divine, such that the *burlador* seems to become spiritual in and of himself, possibly even a "good" Don Juan.

The tradition of the "good" Don Juan probably begins in Spain in earnest with José Zorrilla's *Don Juan Tenorio* (1844) and includes Jacinto Octavio Picón's *Dulce y sabrosa* (1891). But it represents, I would argue, a form of cultural seduction in the service of male fantasies. In the story of the "good" Don Juan, as in Zorrilla's *Don Juan Tenorio*, woman fulfills man's desires, she saves him morally and spiritually, such that, in Luce Irigaray's words, the woman becomes a "sexual imaginary" in which she serves as "a more or less obliging prop for the enactment of man's fantasies" (25). Still, the question of the *burlador*'s social function as well as that of his spiritual nature remains for discussion; and it takes on a peculiar cast in Valle-Inclán's version of Don Juan, especially in light of those who would adduce a mystical spirituality in the *Sonatas*. When read in a mystical or spiritual light, it appears possible that Valle-Inclán's Marqués escapes those theories of Don Juan and seduction that emphasize the negative—social conformity at any price—at the expense of the positive—true love and freedom from social restrictions. The Marqués becomes the exception, whether or not he proves this or that rule.

I wish to explore here Valle-Inclán's version of the *burlador* in terms of the seemingly contrary identifications of the Marqués as a Don Juan and a Catholic, as a Catholic Don Juan. My attempt to understand the Marqués as Valle-Inclán indicates he is to be read will draw on my earlier work on Don Juan even as it traces the logic of Valle-Inclán's four seasons, the *Sonata de primavera* (1904), *Sonata de estío* (1903), *Sonata de otoño* (1902), and *Sonata de invierno* (1905). By addressing the ways that the *Sonatas* work out the difficult relationship between love and death in the framework of texts that read as memoirs, as reflections on a past ranging from remote to recent, as well as recastings of prior literary models, I hope to demonstrate that the Marqués is a Don Juan in word and deed and that, moreover, he is part and parcel of what I understand to be the patriarchal and literary tradition pertaining to Don Juan.

Few texts play so openly on the paradox at the heart of the amorous reflections of a narrator close to death as Valle-Inclán's *Memorias del Marqués de Bradomín*, by which I mean that the four texts comprising the *Sonatas* take up time and again, in ways major and minor, the effects of time on the experience of love, the disparity between the past and past loves, and the imminence of the death of a solitary narrator, in this instance the Marqués. The contrast between youth and senectitude as well as between the plenitude of love and the emptiness of death—what Valle-Inclán refers to elsewhere as "una armonía de contrarios" (131)—is particularly significant in the *Sonatas* because the Marqués returns to its descriptive force at key moments in his account of his life and amorous encounters. It appears not only as a means of explaining the occasion of his story, as at the beginning of the *Sonata de invierno*, where the Marqués laments, "Como soy muy viejo, he visto morir a todas las mujeres por quienes en otro tiempo suspiré de amor . . . . Hoy, después de haber despertado amores muy grandes, vivo en la más triste y más adusta soledad del alma y mis ojos se llenan de lágrimas cuando peino la nieve de mis cabellos" (*Sonata de otoño; Sonata de invierno* 121). It also recurs in the language of the narration and the substance of the experience of love, as in the *Sonata de otoño*, where the Marqués remarks:

> Todavía hoy el recuerdo de la muerta es para mí de una tristeza deprava-
> da y sutil: Me araña el corazón como un gato tísico de ojos lucientes. El
> corazón sangra y se retuerce, y dentro de mí ríe el Diablo, que sabe con-
> vertir todos los dolores en placer. Mis recuerdos, glorias del alma perdi-
> das, son como una música lívida y ardiente, triste y cruel, a cuyo extraño
> son danza el fantasma lloroso de mis amores. (*Sonata de otoño; Sonata
> de invierno* 115-16)

In this brief reflection on the death of one of his paramours, Concha, the Marqués points to the subtle sadness of death as well as to its erotic shadings, now courtesy of the devil, both in the conversion of pain to pleasure and in the invocation of the image of his memories of sobbing as they dance to a tune at once livid and fervent, sad and cruel.

If the connections between love and death form the paradoxical nature of many narratives of memory in general and if the radical difference be-tween the decay of the present and the glories of love in the past center the *Sonatas* in particular, the Marqués leads us to suspect that the conjoining of love and death is not so much a paradox but a normal part of human experi-ence. Where there is love there is death, but a death in which loss and decay are seen as potently erotic. And, in fact, the commingling of love and death found in the *Sonatas* suggests the Spanish tradition of mystic discourse. Yet the mixture of love and death found in mystic verse—the love in death and death in love in the experience of the Divine and all that is eternal—is far different from what the Marqués describes as an all too carnal desire limited by time and provoked or at least witnessed by all that is not holy. When, at the end of the first of the *Sonatas*, the *Sonata de Primavera*, the Marqués con-cludes with the possibility of yet another vision of yet another beloved, we see how he himself is linked to the devil, and this gives the lie to the nature of the paradox being invoked in these *Memorias* and of a principal literary subtext:

> ¡Pobre sombra envejecida, arrugada, miedosa, que vaga todavía por aquellas estancias, y todavía cree verme acechándola en la oscuridad! Me contaron que ahora, al cabo de tantos años, ya repite sin pasión, sin duelo, con la monotonía de una vieja que reza: ¡Fue Satanás! (*Sonata de primeravera; Sonata de estío* 100)

With these parting words, we as readers recognize the need to take Valle-Inclán at his word as found in the epigraph to the *Sonatas*: in effect, the *Memorias* represent nothing more but certainly nothing less than the *vita amatoria* of a Catholic Don Juan who is, as tradition would have it, linked to the devil; and the literary tradition surrounding the *burlador* informs the paradox between love and death even as that seeming paradox resolves into the paradoxical tropes characteristic of mystic poetry.

But what exactly is a Don Juan? Common sense tells us that he is someone who is renowned as a womanizer, a seducer, and we can easily see in the Marqués a version of the *burlador* in the multiple seductions of which he speaks. We could also say that stories of Don Juan—the literary texts to which Don Juan has given rise as well as the critical and interpretive approximations—revolve around one basic action, seduction. Yet, in the context of Valle-Inclán's *Sonatas*, to isolate seduction is to leave to one side a significant aspect of Don Juan's story as embodied in the Marqués de Bradomín, to say nothing of later avatars of the character. As Don Juan himself puts it in Zorrilla's *Don Juan Tenorio*:

> Por donde quiera que fui,
> la razón atropellé,
> la virtud escarnecí,
> a la justicia burlé,
> y a las mujeres vendí. . . .
> A quien quise provoqué,
> con quien quiso me batí,
> y nunca consideré
> que pudo matarme a mí
> aquel a quien yo maté. (ll. 501-05, 516-20)

In Zorrilla's account, Don Juan is famed both for tricking women *and* for killing men. And as the tallying of Don Juan's and Don Luis de Mejía's lists proves, it is not the number of women which the two men seduced that is important in and of itself. Rather, it is seduction in conjunction with death that rests at the heart of Don Juan's story (ll. 646-55). Whereas the gift of seduction is usually viewed as the primary attribute of Don Juan, Zorrilla's two rakes evidence as much if not more interest in death, a fact that is rarely mentioned in the critical tradition surrounding Don Juan.

To be sure, the traditional story of the *burlador* comprises two aspects, serial seductions and what is referred to as the double invitation, or love and death. This suggests that, as a character and like the mystics, Don Juan takes part in a narrative in which love and death are not in opposition but work in tandem. Such might be the case if we consider that the experience of love leads to Don Juan's death. But there are significant discrepancies between presentations of mystic encounters on the one hand and the exploits of Don Juan on the other, discrepancies that reveal profound differences. Mystic poetry expresses union with the divine in terms of sexual experience in which the carnal is also divine and in which death brings eternal life. Don Juan's seductions are anything but spiritual; and, depending on the version of the tale, his death, although a result of seduction and perhaps leading to salvation, as in Zorrilla's *Don Juan Tenorio*, is not an instance of an experience of the divine leading to eternal life. Nevertheless, it *is* possible to argue that, at least in some versions of his story, the desire articulated by Don Juan replicates that of the mystics, that his love, if not simultaneously carnal and spiritual, leads to spirituality through the carnal. In this way, Don Juan becomes part of the tradition he initially flaunts; the sinner is brought into the fold.

It would, however, be a mistake to overlook the importance of death per se in stories relating to Don Juan. In Sigmund Freud's own schema, Eros, or the life instinct, is but half of a story in which the corresponding part is found in Thanatos, or the death instinct. But if Eros is the most obvious part of the story—since Freud himself never writes of Thanatos and is only reported to have used the term in conversations with Ernest Jones (Laplanche and Pontalis 425)—this means that, as in Don Juan's story, Thanatos is the absent or repressed half of Freud's *Beyond the Pleasure Principle*.

For Freud, Eros, as the life instinct or pleasure principle, functions as a force that, "by bringing about a more and more far-reaching combination of the particles into which living substance is dispersed, aims at complicating life and at the same time, of course, preserving it" (*The Ego and the Id, Standard Edition* 19: 40). It is also "a tendency operating in the service of a function whose business it is to free the mental apparatus entirely from excitation or to keep the amount of excitation in it constant or to keep it as low as possible" (*Beyond the Pleasure Principle, Standard Edition* 18: 62). An instinctual force, the pleasure principle stands in apparent opposition to the death instinct, which drives the individual towards the ultimate lowering of tension, towards death (Laplanche and Pontalis 336). Freud notes in *Beyond the Pleasure Principle*, "the aim of all life is death" and "the organism wishes to die only in its own fashion" (*Beyond the Pleasure Principle, Standard Edition* 18: 38, 39). But this means, as Freud also points out, that the "pleasure principle seems actually to serve the death instincts" (*Beyond the Pleasure Principle, Standard Edition* 18: 63), that Eros does not so much stand in opposition to Thanatos as complement it. Jean Laplanche affirms, "Eros is the gatherer and tends to form perpetually richer and more complex unities. . . . Eros is what seeks to maintain, preserve, and even augment the cohesion and the synthetic tendency of living beings and of psychical life. . . . what appears with Eros is the *bound and binding form* of sexuality." In contrast, "the death drive is the very soul, the constitutive principle, of libidinal circulation" (*Life and Death* 108, 123-24).

The distinction between Eros as a mature drive implicated in the sustenance of the individual through bound relationships and Thanatos, the libido that circulates unchecked, moving towards the death of the individual, allows us to identify the Don Juan of *El burlador de Sevilla* as similar to Eros, as bringing others together in socially productive ways even as his libido drives him through *la petite morte* to his real death. This is also the point of Miguel de Unamuno's late Don Juan, *El hermano Juan* (1939). As Unamuno's Juan explains to his "victims," "Metí entre vosotros la discordia, pero para traer la reconciliación." Thus, Juan concludes, "Mi destino no fué robar amores, no, no lo fué, sino que fué encenderlos y atizarlos para que otros se calentaran a su brasa. . . . Los antiguos, que fueron unos niños, me llamaron Cupido, el arquero" (*Obras completas* 5: 808, 815).

With respect to Zorrilla's Don Juan, the case is somewhat different. Don Juan's erotic function serves not to bring those around him into conformity with specific social ends but to bring about his own introduction into the body politic and social; at the same time, however, we also find that Doña Inés is seduced into saving Don Juan, as befits one version of the Romantic heroine. If the contrast between *El burlador de Sevilla* and *Don Juan Tenorio* could not be more starkly evident—a drive towards death upon the fulfillment of Don Juan's erotic function as opposed to a drive towards the death of Don Juan in his absorption into society—neither could the emphasis on death in Zorrilla's drama: death becomes the occasion of society's reaffirmation of the importance of ritual marital bonds.

With the late Don Juan Tenorio, however, with Don Juan after Zorrilla, the situation is somewhat different. Death either is entirely absent, as in Jacinto Octavio Picón's *Dulce y sabrosa*, or strangely, even comically, displaced, albeit with tragic consequences, as in Clarín's *La Regenta* (1884-1885). Still, these transformations are not particularly remarkable, given the protean quality of Don Juan and his story. With respect to Don Juan and death, the overdetermination and subsequent displacement of death betoken yet another twist in the narrative of patriarchal society and culture, which is where Valle-Inclán's *Sonatas* come in.

Although the pertinence of the *Sonatas* to the literary tradition surrounding Don Juan is ostensibly debatable, it is nevertheless undeniable that the Marqués de Bradomín takes great pains to portray himself in terms of Don Juan, as is the fact that Valle-Inclán chooses to present the Marqués as a seducer in his twilight years. Ignacio-Javier López suggests that in this regard the Marqués is but a pale imitation of Zorrilla's Don Juan, an inversion of the character (135-150). And yet, in the *Sonata de Primavera*, the Marqués ardently desires the convent-bound María del Rosario, recalling Zorrilla's Doña Inés and her seduction by Don Juan; in the *Sonata de Estío* he pursues the Niña Chole; in the *Sonata de otoño* he seduces the dying Concha once again and then sleeps with her sister Isabel, recalling the many betrayals of various Don Juans; and in the *Sonata de invierno* he assaults the virtue of María Antonietta. Perhaps, though, when all is said and done, the death of the *burlador* is no longer the point, either as a form of punishment or as a token of social integration. Rather, the emphasis on and the eroticization of death in these texts becomes more pressing and is therefore the key to reading them in the tradition of the *burlador*.

Take the first of the *Sonatas*, the *Sonata de primavera*, which opens with the belatedness that characterizes many of the Don Juans previous to the Marqués de Bradomín. In Tirso's *El burlador de Sevilla*, the Comendador informs Don Juan that he has no time to repent: "No hay lugar; ya acuerdas tarde" (l. 2762). Zorrilla's Don Juan faces a similar fate; when he asks God to take pity on him, once again the Statue answers, "Ya es tarde" (l. 3770). This concern with tardiness allows Gustavo Pérez Firmat to suggest in a brilliantly quirky reading of Zorrilla's *Don Juan Tenorio* that "all of the *Tenorio* is permeated by an 'originality neurosis,' an obsessive worry of tardiness or epigonism" (20). The same obsession with originality turns up in the *Sonata de primavera*, but only briefly, as the specter of prior tradition is done away with in the first few paragraphs. The Marqués—who travels to Liguria to bestow upon on Monsignor Estefano Gaetani, Bishop of Betulia, a cardinal's cap—arrives in time to witness the Monsignor's death. And the story that begins with a death ends with one, too, this time with the death of María Nieves, a child whose name voices her purity. In fact, the death of the child demonstrates the displacement typical of the late Don Juan, the Don Juan who bears but does not endure death.

As the *Sonata de primavera* draws to a close, the Marqués senses that he is about to obtain an admission of desire from María Nieves' oldest sister, María Rosario. In a passage linking together cause and effect, seduction with a painful sobbing frenzy, the Marqués presents us with a sign of deathlike pleasure in which the woman whose death *in* or *from* the pleasures of love serves to bring pleasure to a Don Juan:

> Y mi voz fué tierna, apasionada y sumisa. Yo mismo, al oírla, sentí su extraño poder de seducción. Era llegado el momento supremo; y presin-tiéndolo, mi corazón se estremecía con el ansia de la espera cuando está próxima una gran ventura. María Rosario cerraba los ojos con espanto, como al borde de un abismo. Su boca descolorida parecía sentir una vo-luptuosidad angustiosa. Yo cogí sus manos, que estaban yertas. Ella me las abandonó sollozando, con un frenesí doloroso . . . .
>
> Yo tenía lágrimas en los ojos, y sabía que cuando se llora, las manos pueden arriesgarse a ser audaces. ¡Pobre María Rosario, quedóse pálida como una muerta, y pensé que iba a desmayarse en mis brazos! (*Sonata de primeravera; Sonata de estío* 91)

María Rosario's momentary lapse into the remote possibility of carnality is checked by the intrusion of her youngest sister, upon whom María Rosario bestows the caresses that she cannot give to the Marqués, and this despite the fact that he detects in her eyes "una mirada tímida y amante" (*Sonata de primeravera; Sonata de estío* 93). The sexual death with which María Rosario flirts while speaking to the Marqués eventually becomes real yet displaced in the death of María Nieves. The fall into sin that the oldest sister contemplates in the demonic form of Valle-Inclán's version of Don Juan finds fulfillment in the youngest sister's fall into the garden, the very garden in which so many of the darker scenes of the story are set.

The conflation of seduction, *la petite morte*, and deaths that are all too real recur in the second of the *Sonatas*, the *Sonata de estío*, in the person of the curiously savage Niña Chole and the emotions that she provokes in the

Marqués. When the black man is pulled back into the water by the sharks with "un alarido horrible," the Marqués detects on the Niña Chole's lips an "inquietante sonrisa" such that

> mis labios, aún trémulos, pagaron aquella sonrisa de reina antigua con la sonrisa del esclavo que aprueba cuanto hace su señor. La crueldad de la criolla me horrorizaba y me atraía. . . . La trágica muerte de aquel coloso negro, el mudo espanto que se pintaba aún en todos los rostros, un violín que lloraba en la cámara, todo aquella noche, bajo aquella luna, era para mí objeto de voluptuosidad depravada y sutil. . . . (*Sonata de primavera; Sonata de estío* 124)

The Marqués's obedient response to the Niña Chole's cruelty, phrased as the relationship between a slave and his "señor," to say nothing of the peculiarly erotic valence given death, points to the Spanish tradition of mystic discourse mentioned earlier. San Juan de la Cruz is typical in his appropriation of the paradoxes structuring mystic thought in that he mixes pain and pleasure, erotic or sexual fullfillment and spiritual union with the deity. If the opening lines of the *copla* "Que muero porque no muero" play most patently on the twists and turns of Christian faith and paradoxes of death in life and life in death—"Vivo sin vivir en mí, / y de tal manera espero / que muero porque no muero"—it is San Juan's "Llama de amor viva" that puts all of the different elements together in a macabre lament that would not be out of place in the decadent spirituality of Valle-Inclán's Marqués de Bradomín: "¡Oh llama de amor viva, / que tiernamente hieres / de mi alma en el más / profundo centro! / . . . . / ¡Oh cauterio suave! / ¡Oh regalada llaga! / ¡Oh mano blanda! ¡Oh toque delicado!" (40-41).

The macabre spirituality characteristic of mystic verse is most apparent in the *Sonata de otoño*, but it is not entirely absent from the *Sonata de invierno*, in which the peculiar nature of the eroticization of death is also seen:

> No se llega a viejo sin haber aprendido que las lágrimas, los remordimientos y la sangre, alargan el placer de los amores cuando vierten sobre ellos su esencia afrodita: Numen sagrado que exalta la lujuria, madre de la divina tristeza y madre del mundo. ¡Cuántas veces durante aquella noche, tuve yo en mis labios las lágrimas de María Antonieta! Aún recuerdo el dulce lamento con que habló en mi oído, temblorosos los párpados y estremecida la boca que me daba el aliento con sus palabras:
>
> —No debía quererte . . . Debía ahogarte en mis brazos, así, así . . .

Yo suspiré:
—¡Tus brazos son un divino dogal! (*Sonata de otoño; Sonata de invierno*
203)

This passage recalls quite clearly the *Sonata de otoño*, in particular another
scene of love, this time between the Marqués and the dying Concha. Indeed,
from the proleptic yet strangely distant reference to the renewal of an old
love in the first paragraph of the *Sonata de otoño*, "El viejo rosal de nuestros
amores volvía a florecer para despojarse piadoso sobre una sepultura" (*Sonata de otoño; Sonata de invierno* 31), the narrative returns time and again
to the issue of death, both as a sexual and an existential possibility, until the
moments immediately prior to Concha's death when the Marqués implores
his dying lover, "¡Azótame, Concha! ¡Azótame como a un divino Nazareno!
¡Azótame hasta morir! . . ." (*Sonata de otoño; Sonata de invierno* 109). The
deliciously ambiguous final phrase—in which the questions of whose death
and what kind of death it will be remain momentarily open to speculation—
demonstrates the confusion of pain and pleasure, carnal knowledge and, in
Freud's terms, the sudden reduction of all tension.

In the end, however, it is Concha who dies, yet again in an ambiguous
presentation of what are either the final moments of sexual pleasure or the
final moments of earthly existence:

Cerró los ojos estremecida, y mis brazos la abrigaron amantes. Me pare-
ció que en sus labios vagaba un rezo . . . .
Quedamos en silencio. Después, su boca gimió bajo mi boca.
—¡Yo muero!
Su cuerpo, aprisionado en mis brazos, tembló como sacudido por mortal aleteo. Su cabeza lívida rodó sobre la almohada con desmayo. Sus pár-
pados se entreabrieron tardos, y bajo mis ojos vi aparecer sus ojos angus-
tiados y sin luz. (*Sonata de otoño; Sonata de invierno* 109)

However, sexual pleasure is confused with mystic union, it is clearly a woman
whose death is in service to the pleasure of the Marqués, despite his tender
lamentations. What we find in the *Sonatas*, then, is a version of Don Juan's
story in which death is displaced from the *burlador* to the *burlada*; and in
these texts the woman does not sacrifice herself to the redemption of Don
Juan, but simply to his pleasure. If it would be pushing it to claim that the
Sonatas, because of their ambiguous presentation of death in a sexual guise,
verge into pornography, there is nevertheless every reason to recognize in

Valle-Inclán's aging Don Juan and his memoirs the continued creation of Irigaray's "sexual imaginary." In this instance, the texts represent fantasies that have grown increasingly deadly.

Of course, it's also possible to argue that the pronounced presence of death in Valle-Inclán's *Sonatas* responds not only to the vicissitudes of Don Juan's story but to *fin de siècle* decadence. But Lou Charnon-Deutsch's work on nineteenth-century visual images of women in the popular press goes a long way towards demonstrating how the women portrayed in the *Sonatas* all correspond to various types of women found throughout all forms of representation in the nineteenth century and well into the twentieth (*Fictions of the Feminine*). María Rosario and especially María Nieves of the first *Sonata* respond to the sexualized images of girls so disturbingly common in nineteenth-century visual culture (Image 1). The Niña Chole of the *Sonata de estío* is yet one more example of the exotic woman. Concha fulfills the promise of the fragile or sickly woman in her timely death in the *Sonata de otoño* (Image 2). And what about the *Sonata de invierno*?

The last of the *Sonatas* is perhaps somewhat trickier to read in terms of death because the Marqués de Bradomín's own mortality figures most prominently. But even this story reveals the familiar image of the engendering of chastity in the person of Hermana Maximina. In fact, it is around the enigma of Hermana Maximina that much of this *Sonata* turns and so it is in this character that the issue of death finds a tentative resolution. When the Marqués is recuperating in the convent, the young novice who cares for him is clearly his daughter, the result of his affair with the Duquesa de Uclés. On the one hand, Hermana Maximina—who is "feúcha," a point reiterated by the text—is a novice, indicating that the outcome of Don Juan's seductions are procreative only to a certain extent and productive of something relatively unattractive. On the other, Hermana Maximina is linked to knowledge and literary creation and then mortality; when Sor Simona reveals her surprise at the Marqués's recognition of his daughter, knowledge leads to a deathlike sensation and then to revelation:

La monja, juntando las manos, clamó con horror:
—¡Lo sabía usted!
Y su voz, embargada por el espanto de mi culpa, me estremeció. Parecíame estar muerto y escucharla dentro del sepulcro, como una acusación del mundo. El misterio de los dulces ojos aterciopelados y tristes era el misterio de mis melancolías en aquellos tiempos, cuando fuí galán y poeta. ¡Ojos queridos! Yo los había amado porque encontraba en ellos

los suspiros románticos de mi juventud, las ansias sentimentales que al malograrse me dieron el escepticismo de todas las cosas, la perversión melancólica y donjuanesca que hace las víctimas y llora con ellas. (*Sonata de otoño; Sonata de invierno* 196)

This is the moment of the Marqués's own figured death, the realization of his past as a "galán y poeta." Hermana Maximina thus functions in at least two ways. She reminds us of the novice of Zorrilla's *Don Juan Tenorio*, Doña Inés, the instrument of Don Juan's salvation, and she serves to thwart the eventuality of the Marqués's own death, since a part of him and his past will survive in her. In the end, these are both the same thing, since, in the eyes of Hermana Maximina, the Marqués redeems himself. She is like a *tabula rasa* awaiting the projection of his fantasy.

What the *Sonatas* narrate time and again, therefore, is the overcoming of the belatedness dogging Don Juan as the Marqués situates his own sexual gratification in the mortality of the women to whom he makes love. In terms of Harold Bloom's revisionary poetics of literary history (*The Anxiety of Influence, A Map of Misreading*), Valle-Inclán's reworking of the tropes of Don Juan, mysticism, and decadence recreate the classic image of intellectual procreation found in Plato's *Symposium*—homosocial relations between men— in terms of a decidedly decadent seductive imaginary. Yet the conjunction of Don Juan and death in the *Sonatas* suggests another reading that ties in with Eros and Thanatos, with Laplanche's distinction between Eros as a mature drive and bound relationships, and Thanatos as rampant libido moving towards death. The displacement of death onto the woman in the *Sonatas* allows Valle-Inclán's version of Don Juan to posit, despite the seriality of his relationships with women, his own bounded and binding ties to adult sexuality and thus society, confirming the precedence that the erotic takes over the death instinct. At the same time, death lurks in the women in whom desire runs relatively unchecked. In this way, Don Juan once again articulates the necessary importance of enduring social ties and arrogates those ties for himself. By allowing the women to die for him, Don Juan saves himself. And Valle-Inclán not only grafts the discourse of mystic desire onto the tradition of Don Juan, but sexual pleasure onto death, giving voice to the erotic dimensions of mortality.

Valle-Inclán's *Sonatas* therefore toy with the odd mixture of carnality and spirituality common to mystic discourse but advocate a reversion to the division of the two as found in the story of Don Juan and the seduction of social norms, which is perhaps why the two contradictory aspects of the Marqués

and the *Sonatas*—the emphasis on seduction and the divine—prove so difficult to reconcile. True, the Marqués can be understood to liberate women
from the strictures of social convention, as in the case of Concha:

Culpaba [mi madre] a Concha de todos mis extravíos y la tenía horror.
Recordaba, como una afrenta a sus canas, que nuestros amores habían
comenzado en el Palacio de Bradomín, un verano que Concha pasó allí,
acompañándola. Mi madre era su madrina, y en aquel tiempo la quería
mucho. Después no volvió a verla. Un día, estando yo de caza, Concha
abandonó para siempre el Palacio. Salió sola, con la cabeza cubierta y
llorando, como los herejes que la Inquisición expulsaba de las viejas ciudades españolas. Mi madre la maldecía desde el fondo del corredor. . . .
Concha no cesaba de lamentarse:
—¡Bien castigada estoy! . . . ¡Bien castigada estoy! (*Sonata de otoño;
Sonata de invierno* 96)

But, the punishment that falls on these women is their exclusion from the
folds of society, as we see in the case of Concha. The Marqués brings pleasure
at the expense of the "liberation" and thus the marginalization of the women
he seduces even as this carnality does not bring them closer to what is con-
ventionally identified as the divine. In the end, the love that the Marqués
proffers distances the women he woos from that which is eternal.

In this way, Valle-Inclán's *Sonatas* continue the tradition of the *burlador*.
That is, they are part of what I have referred to as an "ongoing consideration
of Don Juan [that] reveals itself as a form of ideological (mis)representa-
tion, as the means by which society conceals—even as it explains and vindi-
cates—itself and its mechanisms" (268). The spirituality in which Valle-Inclán cloaks his Marqués and the seductions is quite simply that, a cloak that
serves to conceal the specifically carnal, and not vaguely spiritual, aspects of
the Marqués's desires. And if Eros conceals Thanatos, we find that, with the
displacement of death on to his lovers, the Marqués, in the winter of his life,
reflecting on his past from the proximity of death, refuses to die. He returns
again in Valle-Inclán's dramatic pastiche *El Marqués de Bradomín* (1907) and
in the much later *Luces de Bohemia* (1924), where he speculates on death
with "Rubén Darío" and comments that he expects to be eternal because of
his sins. The Marqués's mortality is figured in the mortality of the women he
has seduced; but his immortality rests in the literary texts that bear him and
his name and in the literary tradition of which these texts are a part.

Still, as the literature surrounding Don Juan enters into the realm of parody and irony, the very implication of a force similar to that of Thanatos lurking behind Eros creates the possibility of entropy, or the ultimate reduction of tension, which would entail the end of patriarchal society, of society and culture as we know them. This is why, in the end, the redemptive role played by women in the later Don Juan leads them to their death and its eroticization in the late Don Juan. Were it otherwise, we might have the utopian vision of which Feal speaks, but we would not have Don Juan. And this is why, contrary to what my title might have implied, Valle-Inclán cannot go beyond the pleasure principle. The pleasures of desire, or Eros, may indeed conceal death, or Thanatos, but, in the end, pleasure can never allow death to speak in its own voice.

Images

IMAGE 1: Pedro Saenz, "Inocencia," *La Ilustracion Artistica* 3 July 1899 (Charnon-Deutsch fig. 117).

IMAGE 2: Romañach, *La Ilustración Artística* 6 May 1895 (Charnon-Deutsch fig. 173).

Works Cited

Anderson, Andrew A. "Sex, Flippancy, Autobiography: Existential Palliatives in Valle-Inclán's *Sonatas*." *Hispanic Review* 78.3 (Summer 2010): 387-409.

Bloom, Harold. *The Anxiety of Influence: A Theory of Poetry*. London: Oxford UP, 1973.

———. *A Map of Misreading*. Oxford: Oxford University Press, 1975.

Charnon-Deutsch, Lou. *Fictions of the Feminine in the Nineteenth-Century Spanish Press*. Penn State Studies in Romance Literatures. University Park: The Pennsylvania State University Press, 2000.

Feal, Carlos. *En nombre de don Juan (Estructura de un mito literario)*. Purdue University Monographs in Romance Languages 16. Amsterdam: John Benjamins, 1984.

Freud, Sigmund. *The Standard Edition of the Complete Psychological Works of Sigmund Freud*. Ed. and trans. James Strachey with Anna Freud. 24 vols. London: Hogarth, 1966-74.

Irigaray, Luce. *This Sex Which Is Not One*. Trans. Catherine Porter with Carolyn Burke. Ithaca: Cornell University Press, 1985.

Juan de la Cruz, San. *Obras completas*. Ed. Lucinio Ruano de la Iglesia. 11th ed. Biblioteca de Autores Cristianos 15. Madrid: Editorial Católica, 1982.

Laplanche, Jean. *Life and Death in Psychoanalysis.* Trans. Jeffrey Mehlman. Baltimore and London: The Johns Hopkins University Press, 1976.

Laplanche, Jean, and Jean-Bertrand Pontalis. *Diccionario de psicoanálisis.* Trans. Fernando Cervantes Gimeno. Barcelona: Labor, 1981.

Lev, Leora. "'Tis Pity She's a Corpse: Modernism, Remembering, and Dismemberment in Valle-Inclán's *Sonatas." Revista Canadiese de Estudios Hispánicos* 24.3 (Primavera 2000): 473-90.

———. "Valle-Inclán como *bricoleur*: topografías del deseo en las *Sonatas." Actas del Primer Congreso Internacional sobre Valle-Inclán y su obra.* Ed. Manuel Aznar Soler and Juan Rodríguez. Barcelona: Associació d'Idees, 1995. 269-73.

López, Ignacio-Javier. *Caballero de novela: Ensayo sobre el donjuanismo en la novela española moderna, 1880-1930.* Barcelona: Puvill, 1986.

Mandrell, James. *Don Juan and the Point of Honor: Seduction, Patriarchal Society, and Literary Tradition.* University Park: Pennsylvania State University Press, 1992.

Marrast, Robert. "Religiosidad y satanismo, sadismo y masoquismo en la 'Sonata de otoño.'" *Cuadernos hispanoamericanos* 199-200 (1966): 482-92.

Pérez-Firmat, Gustavo. *Literature and Liminality: Festive Readings in the Hispanic Tradition.* Durham: Duke UP, 1986.

Rousset, Jean. *Le Mythe de Don Juan.* Paris: Colin, 1978.

Serrano, Carlos. *Carnaval en noviembre: parodias teatrales españolas de* Don Juan Tenorio. Alicante: Instituto de Cultura Juan Gil-Albert-Diputación Provincial de Alicante, 1996.

Tirso de Molina. *El burlador de Sevilla y convidado de piedra.* Ed. Joaquín Casalduero. Madrid: Cátedra, 1986.

Unamuno, Miguel de. *Obras completas.* Ed. Manuel García Blanco. 9 vols. Madrid: Escelicer, 1966-1971.

Valle-Inclán, Ramón del. *La marquesa Rosalinda.* Ed. César Oliva. 5th ed. Colección Austral 113. Madrid: Espasa-Calpe, 1990.

———. *Sonata de otoño; Sonata de invierno: memorias del Marqués de Bradomín.* Ed. Leda Schiavo. 36th ed. Austral Narrativa 61. Madrid: Espasa-Calpe, 2007.

———. *Sonata de primavera; Sonata de estío: memorias del Marqués de Bradomín.* Ed. Pere Gimferrer. 37th ed. Austral Narrativa 37. Madrid: Espasa-Calpe, 2009.

Zorrilla, José. *Don Juan Tenorio.* Ed. Luis Fernández Cifuentes. Biblioteca Clásica 95. Barcelona: Crítica, 1993.

José Zorrilla's Don Juan and His Games

RICARDO DE LA FUENTE BALLESTEROS
Universidad de Valladolid

ORRILLA EXEMPLIFIES THE IDEAL nature of the Romantic individual, that is to say, a theatrical nature; so theatrical that, seen from
the distance of our time, it may appear inauthentic to us. For him,
however, it formed part of his deepest self. He was a priest of art, a seer, as
Victor Hugo showed his own generation and the following one in "Los ma-
gos." *Don Juan Tenorio* is a display of this theatrical nature, which is typical of
the period's pattern and even more typical of Zorrilla's world view, but with a
profound significance to which the following pages are dedicated.

As Maffesoli recalls, there have been many who have connected the "concepción trágica de la existencia" [tragic conception of existence] and "el retorno de la pasión" [the return of passion] (Maffesoli, 2005: 85). At the same
time, he brings into comparison Sherer, who saw Don Juan as "el Dionisos
de los tiempos modernos" [the Dionysus of modern times] (Maffesoli, 2005:
90), and the lesson of the tragic, which is "dar su lugar a la alegría demoníaca
del vivir" [to give place to the demonic happiness of living] (Maffesoli, 1996:
90). All of this arises on the premise that in certain moments of cultural history "el juego y los juegos, el placer y los placeres, la emoción y las emociones,
retoman un lugar de importancia en la estructuración social" [the game and
games, pleasure and pleasures, emotion and the emotions, regain a place of
importance in the social structure], so that "la vida como juego es una especie
de aceptación de un mundo tal cual es" [life as a game is a kind of acceptance
of the world as it is]. The symbolic aspect of a popular festivity, which is
the ceremonial representation of this work, is what Zorrilla's *Don Juan Tenorio* seems to embody, which follows and updates Zamora's earlier version.
Maffesoli himself says that the ludic is the clearest evidence of the desire to
live (Maffesoli, 1996: 35); without meaning, however, this act, which is also

127

called "polifónico" [polyphonic] and "polisémico" [polysemic], is also tragic (Maffesoli, 1996: 39)--we will return to this topic later--in the same way that Dionysus bears within himself the desire of life and of death.

There is no doubt that the Dionysian is found at the heart of tragedy, pre-constituting its specific essence: the tragic as myth, as the essence of tragedy, is the Dionysian mode, its game. The tragic is already in *El nacimiento de la tragedia* a form of Dionysian circularity of ebb and flow (Jarauta 108). A few years ago, in my critical edition (Zorrilla 2003), I already suggested a reading of the *Tenorio* as a game, following Maeztu's opinion, and I based that game not only on the embodiment of the character but also on what has been called its theatricality.

But in the light of what has been set out above, I believe the tragic modality is even clearer, together with the theatricality that Zorrilla's work contains; the "diablo a las puertas del cielo" [devil at heaven's gates] shows us its *daemon*, the scandal that always follows Don Juan, who is like "ruidoso Dionisos" [sensational Dionysus] who, wherever he goes, spreads confusion. Don Juan, in turn, is the corporeality destined for death, already from the origin of the myth, and for this reason its acceleration, as a character who knows deep down his destination. Out of this arises the need of creating, as an accumulation of predicaments, the action that leads to madness--Ortega y Gasset says: "Pasan en ella [la obra] muchas cosas--muchas más de las que pasarían en una obra *literaria* normal" [Many things happen in it (the work)--many more than would happen in a normal *literary* work] [5: 247]. Diego Marín and I have also pointed this out (Zorrilla 2003), with the play's 200-minute hours that make sense as much because of the monstrous body in which they are enclosed as because of the carnivalesque transgression of the textual frame (Firmat 1983). This act of condensing works, doubtless, as a theatrical factor. It makes the mimetic time, on the one hand, coincide (almost) with that of the staging, in both the first and second parts of the play; and, on the other hand, it imposes a special dynamism on Don Juan's actions, who, a little before eight in the evening, is already in the Hostería del Laurel--where he will return punctually as the clock marks that hour. At nine he is with Doña Inés in the convent, trying to seduce her; at ten he approaches Doña Ana's house to deceive her and Don Luis; in the early morning--after midnight--he is in his country house, where he awaits Doña Inés, etc. This temporal condensation is repeated in the second part: in a few hours Don Juan carries out his defiance of the dead by inviting Don Gonzalo to dinner; he eats dinner at home; he receives a visit from his beloved's spirit; and finally, he is saved. This temporal condensation, so productive for theatrical-

ity, was criticized by Zorrilla himself, who realized the inverisimilitude with
which it had been acted out: "El primer acto comienza a las ocho; pasa todo:
prenden a Don Juan y a Don Luis; cuenta cómo se ha arreglado para salir de
prisión; preparan Don Juan y Ciutti la traición contra Don Luis, y concluye
el acto segundo diciendo Don Juan: *A las nueve en el convento, / a las diez en
esta calle*. Reloj en la mano, y había uno en la embocadura del teatro en que se
estrenó, son las nueve y tres cuartos; dando de barato que en el entreacto haya
podido pasar lo que pasa. Estas horas de doscientos minutos son exclusivas de
mi Don Juan" [The first act begins at eight; everything happens: they catch
Don Juan and Don Luis; he tells how he has arranged to get out of prison;
Don Juan and Ciutti prepare their betrayal of Don Luis, and the second act
concludes with Don Juan saying: *At nine in the convent, / at ten in this street*.
With a watch in hand, and there was one in the entrance of the theater where
it premiered, it is only a quarter to ten; taking for granted the fact that in
the intermission everything was able to happen. These 200-minute hours are
exclusive to my Don Juan" (O.C., II, 1802).

Let us remember that since we are talking about games, everything begins with a bet, and that Don Juan and Don Luis end by "betting" their lives,
at the same time that Don Juan wagers, on more than one occasion, everything he has on a card. Don Juan must be killed as tradition commands, he
must fulfill his destiny, but in Zorrilla's work there is a transcendental break,
since his death is followed by his salvation. This greatly upset some critics,
which seems significant to me. Manuel de la Revilla said this:

> que un desenfrenado, libertino, seductor, violento, asesino, espadachín,
> traidor, hijo desnaturalizado, amigo desleal y mal caballero (que todo
> esto es *D. Juan Tenorio* de Zorrilla), vaya a desafiar a sus víctimas después
> de muertas, y cuando llega la hora de la expiación, un momento de arre-
> pentimiento arrancado por el miedo y la influencia de una mujer enamo-
> rada basten para que alma tan impura alcance la salvación mientras se
> condenan sus víctimas, a los ojos de la moral, cualquiera que esta sea, es
> absurdo, irritante e impío. (451)

> ¿Qué ha hecho Zorrilla del carácter de Don Juan Tenorio? No le bastaba
> romper abiertamente con la tradición, salvándole en el final, sino que le
> pareció necesario falsearlo por completo. D. Juan es, ante todo, un gran
> carácter, y el personaje de Zorrilla no es carácter siquiera, sino un con-
> junto estraño [*sic*] de inexplicables contradicciones." (452)

[that an insatiable man, a libertine, a seducer, a violent man, a murderer, a swashbuckler, a traitor, an unnatural son, a disloyal friend, and a bad gentleman (all of which applies to Zorrilla's *D. Juan Tenorio*), should provoke his victims after they have died, and when the hour of atonement arrives, a moment's repentance dragged out by fear and the influence of an enamored woman are sufficient for such an impure soul to reach salvation while his victims are damned, in the eyes of any morality, whatever it might be, is absurd, irritating, and ungodly. (451)

What has Zorrilla done with Don Juan Tenorio's personality? It was not enough for him to break openly with tradition, saving him at the end, but it also seemed necessary to falsify him completely. Don Juan is, above all, a great personality, and Zorrilla's character is no personality at all, but rather a strange conglomeration of inexplicable contradictions. (452)]

Negative judgments of this kind have been frequent. Zorrilla's work was attacked from all sides, for example, from a religious aspect in *La Censura* (III-1844):

El autor ha hecho bien de añadir al epíteto *religioso* con que quiso calificar su drama, el de *fantástico*, porque la fantasía del poeta se ha forjado allá a su modo un plan a todas luces irreligioso para quien considere la religión como una institución divina y no como una invención poética. En efecto, sólo dos desenlaces podía tener este drama, conforme con lo que exigen nuestra creencia, la sana razón y hasta las reglas rigurosas del arte; a saber, o que el impío y desalmado don Juan acabase como había vivido recibiendo el merecido castigo de sus crímenes y de su ateísmo, o que arrepintiéndose a tiempo y en vista de los avisos del cielo, expiase con una sincera y dura penitencia su vida licenciosa y criminal.

[The author has done well in adding to the epithet *religious*, with which he sought to qualify his drama, that of fantastic, because the poet's fantasy has shaped therein, in its own way, a plan that is irreligious in any light, for anyone who considers religion a divine institution and not a poetic invention. In effect, this drama could have only two endings, according to what our belief, sound reason, and even the rigorous rules of art demands; that is, either that the ungodly and heartless Don Juan ends as he has lived, receiving the punishment that his crimes and his godlessness deserve, or that by repenting in time and in the face of heaven's warnings, he atone with a sincere and difficult penitence his licentious, criminal life.]

In sum, Zorrilla "ideó otro desenlace que sobre extravagante e inverosímil repugna a nuestra fe" [devised another ending that, on top of being extravagant and inverisimilar, sickens our faith]. In this same line of thought that explores Zorrilla's heterodoxy, Pi y Margall have lingered--always negative with regard to this work of the native poet of Valladolid--as well as Revilla and, closer to us, Mazzeo y Salgot.

In any case, *Clarín* in *Palique* summarizes everything there is in the Tenorio that makes it function as it has throughout the years and that makes us omit the errors that may have slipped into the work, something that appeals to the emotions, to the strangely seductive nature that defines this work by Zorrilla, to the secret concealed by a form some might call defective, and contents, of which we have already seen some of the objections:

Una buena prueba de gusto fuerte, original, se puede dar entusiasmándose todos los años, la noche de las ánimas, entre el vulgo bonachón y nada crítico, al ver a don Juan seducir a doña Inés y burlarse de todas las leyes. Parece mentira que sin recurrir a la ternura piadosa se pueda llegar tan dentro en el alma como llegan la frescura y el esplendor de la primera parte del *Don Juan*. La *seducción* graduada de doña Inés la siente el espectador, ve su verdad porque la experimenta. Triunfo extraño, tratándose del público de los varones, porque por lo común a los hombres nos cuesta trabajo figurarnos lo que las mujeres sienten al enamorarse de los demás. ¿Cómo puede gustar el varón? se dice el varón constante. Pues cuando el arte llega muy arriba vemos el amor de la mujer explicado, porque de cierta manera anafrodítica nos enamoramos también de los héroes. Este es el triunfo del *Tenorio*; que nos seduce y por esta seducción se lo perdonamos todo: pecados morales y pecados estéticos. (120)

[A good sign of strong, original taste may be given by being excited every year on All Saints' Day, among the good-natured common man, who is no critic, upon seeing Don Juan seduce Doña Inés and mock every law. It seems a lie that anything, without resorting to pious tenderness, might enter so deeply in the soul as the freshness and splendor of the first part of *Don Juan*. The spectator feels the gradual *seduction* of Doña Inés, he sees its truth because he experiences it himself. A strange triumph, when speaking of a public full of men, since commonly it takes some work for men to imagine what women feel when they fall in love with others. How can a man be pleasing? men say to themselves constantly. For when art reaches very high, we see women's love explained, because in a certain anaphrodite way, we too fall in love with the heroes. This is the *Tenorio's* triumph; it seduces us and through this seduction, we forgive it everything: moral sins and aesthetic sins. (120)

Standing in the face of opinions that insist on the structural failings of the work[1] are its enduring success and the critics who try to justify the *Tenorio's* defects in a new context, in which the errors appear as harmonious elements, coherent, in a final, uncommon design that is justified by the temporal dislocations and by Carnival (Firmat).

Donald Shaw foresaw that "la significación y gran parte del éxito popular de esta obra se debe al modo con que Zorrilla reconcilia el ideal de amor romántico con los valores tradicionales en que creía y con los que alentaba su público" [the significance and greater part of this work's popular success is due to the way in which Zorrilla reconciles the ideal of romantic love with the traditional values in which the public believed and which they supported] (69). But there is another aspect that should be noted, which is that the work deals with Don Juan up to that moment--although some preceded Zamora in this, and it is obvious that Hoffman begins with this matter--in which he suffers a transformation, a change, one of the conditions of classical tragedy and one that disqualifies many works that have been considered tragedies within the canon, as León Febres Cordero notes in his reflection on the tragic genre. As a result, this transformation gives place for triumph in the face of his destiny, without losing that possibility, since the character dies and accepts his mortal condition in order to live forever in the work.

But, in the end, all this is a paradox, since the monument to life and death that we call *Don Juan Tenorio* is nothing more than a play, the theatricality to which we alluded earlier and that causes Ruiz Ramón to say, "El acierto de Zorrilla está, pues, en haber recalcado con máxima intensidad la teatralidad de Don Juan como forma propia de la vida, en haber elevado la teatralidad a modo de existencia" [Zorrilla's best decision is his having stressed with the greatest intensity the theatricality of Don Juan as a particular form of life, in having elevated theatricality to a mode of existence] (1983: 436). That theatricality is the "parece un juego ilusorio" [it seems an illusory game] to which

---

1   Something that has also been said about Tirso's work; for example, Maurice Molho describes the structure of the work "aberrant" (XIV).

a character refers because everything is seen through the lens of theater. We will soon see that the reader/spectator also, without realizing (or without desiring) it, participates in this game because we make ourselves an echo of the anonymous faces in the crowd that gathers at Buttarelli's tavern to witness the final result of Don Juan and Don Luis's rivalry (Arias: 15-16), something that Roberto Sánchez indicated when he stressed the histrionic aspect of this confrontation between protagonist and antagonist.

In short: what are the secrets of this work that have kept it alive on Spanish stages in spite of the innumerable faults that have been attributed to it? Logically, there cannot be only one explanation. For example, it is evident that the repeated updating of the myth crafted by Zorrilla seems to form a homology with the public's expectations, the role of the woman, also the qualities of the verse in spite of the accusations of facility laid against it, etc. But there are more elements that resolve this enigma, such as its ludic value, and its accommodation to the symbolic universe of popular culture, a work that as a celebration is already a common creation—something with which we began when we referred to Maffesoli's ideas.

The ludic element is the theatrical game that we might call the theatricality (Zorrilla 2003: 62ff.) of the drama and that is already in process from the first scenes of the work. For Roland Barthes, "La *teatralidad* es el teatro sin el texto, es un espesor de signos y sensaciones que se edifica en la escena a partir del argumento escrito, esa especie de percepción ecuménica de los artificios sensuales, gestos, tonos, distancias, sustancias, luces, que sumerge el texto bajo la plenitud de su lenguaje emisor [...] no existe gran teatro sin una teatralidad devoradora" [Theatricality is theater without the text, a density of signs and sensations that is built on stage and based on the written text, that type of ecumenical perception of sensual artifice, gestures, tones, distances, substances, lights, that the text submerges under the fullness of its issuing language [...] no great theater exists without a devouring theatricality] (50). A. Adamov, for his part, defines it as "la proyección en el mundo sensible de los estados e imágenes que constituyen sus resortes ocultos... la manifestación del contenido oculto, latente, que contiene los gérmenes del drama" [the projection in the sensible world of states and images that constitute hidden resources . . . the manifestation of hidden, latent content, that contains the seeds of drama] (13). In both cases, more attention is given to the staged projection of the work, to everything related with the staging, rather than to the dialogic text and the story. But one should note the importance of the emphasis towards the conventional, towards the fictional break that supposes a game and metatheatrical elements. Everything is a game for Don

Juan: life, love... Everything begins with a bet, and Don Juan and Don Luis end by "betting" their lives, at the same time that Don Juan wagers, on more than one occasion, everything he has on a card. Don Juan must be killed as tradition commands, he must fulfill his destiny, but in Zorrilla's work there is a transcendental break, since his death is followed by his salvation.

Guillermo Díaz-Plaja had already indicated this when he said: "Lo interesante es el juego—casi casi diría que a Don Juan le interesa más la *burla* que el placer" [What is interesting is the game—almost, almost I would say that mockery interests Don Juan more than pleasure] (47). This is also applied to Tirso's Burlador, even if that particular mockery becomes weaker with time, as can be seen in Romanticism (Brunel: 135-137). This does not mean that the spirit of the game disappears. Ramiro de Maeztu had already indicated this when he says, "Don Juan es el jugador que juega a las mujeres" [Don Juan is the player who plays with women] (95). Modern editors of the work also highlight this idea: "La burla es, asimismo, juego. Don Juan es jugador y su burla es lúdica—*gana me da de reír*, dice el protagonista de nuestra comedia ante sus hazañas-, como subrayarán Mozart y Da Ponte en su versión del mito" [Mockery is, thus, a game. Don Juan is a player and his mockery is ludic—*it makes me want to laugh*, the protagonist of our comedy says about his deeds—as Mozart and Da Ponte highlight in their version of the myth] (Brioso: 23). But this assertion is a constant in the criticism, as can be seen in Brunel, Turienzo— "Don Juan tiene un concepto deportivo de la vida; concibe la vida como un juego. Lo que él quiere es entregarse plenamente al juego, mientras dure la vida, desentendiéndose de toda posible consecuencia..." [Don Juan has a sporting concept of life; he conceives of life as a game. What he wants is to give himself fully to the game, so long as life lasts, avoiding any possible consequence] (285)—Márquez Villanueva—"Todo es un constante juego de todo o nada" [Everything is a constant game of all or nothing] (32)—Picoche, etc., who saw how in Tirso this *sema* was already clearly planted: "Sirviendo, jugando estás / y si quieres ganarlo luego, / haz siempre, porque en el juego / quien más hace gana más" [Serving, you are playing / and if you want to win / always do something, because in the game / whoever does most wins most] (II, vv. 322-325). Espronceda's and Dumas's versions, clear antecedents of Zorrilla's work, also present him as a player. Don Juan, overflowing with vitality, seems to find rest in the game, in that endless, unproductive act that for Baudelaire was the ultimate reason for life: "La vie n'a qu'un charme vrai: c'est le charme du Jeu" [Life has only one true charm: the charm of the game] (*Fusées*).[2]

---

2   "La vida sólo tiene un encanto auténtico; el encanto del Juego" (*Cohetes*), according to Javier del Prado and José A. Millán Alba's translation (18).

Perhaps the first to see the potential of Zorrilla's drama, in the sense that I am drawing out, was Torrente Ballester, who says that the essence of theater resides in "el ritmo rápido de la acción combinado a los efectos sorpresa y a la cohetería deslumbradora de la palabra [...]. Es un sistema de efectos externos totalmente independientes de la constitución interna del drama" [the rapid rhythm of action combined with the effects of surprise and the dazzling rocketry of the word [...] It is a system of external effects totally independent of the internal constitution of the drama" (81). Linking this concept to *Don Juan Tenorio*, he wonders, "¿Hay alguien que niega teatralidad al *Tenorio* de Zorrilla? Todos los caracteres que acabo de señalar se encuentran en él, sobre todo en su primera parte. Actos y palabras parecen desprenderse del drama, cobrar vida propia, constituir una unidad de efectos autónoma" [Is there anyone who denies the theatricality of Zorrilla's *Tenorio*? All of the traits I have just pointed out are found in it, especially in the first part. Acts and words seem to come free from the drama, taking on their own life, to constitute a unity of autonomous effects] (Baudelaire: 81-82). Roberto Sánchez also indicates in the same direction, the "virtud artística" [artistic virtue] of the text would be based on the "teatralidad romántica" [Romantic theatricality] of the play, applying this criterion almost exclusively to its first part: "*Don Juan Tenorio* consta de dos partes, y la primera es infinitamente superior a la segunda. Así lo veía José Yxart a fines del XIX, y así lo ve la crítica de nuestros días" [*Don Juan Tenorio* has two parts, and the first is infinitely superior to the second. This is how José Yxart saw it at the end of the nineteenth century, and this is how criticism in our day sees it as well] (21-23). In the same way, F. Ruiz Ramón points out: "La virtud fundamental del teatro zorrillesco es la poderosa capacidad de teatralización de su autor. [...] La única verdad, con valor de pervivencia, de su teatro es su propia teatralidad, su esencial teatralidad. Zorrilla, en su obra capital *Don Juan Tenorio* (1844), ha conseguido lo que ningún otro dramaturgo romántico: seguir vivo en los escenarios" [The fundamental virtue of Zorrilla's theater is the author's powerful capacity to create theatricality. [...] The only truth, in terms of survival value, of his theater is its very theatricality, its essential theatricality. Zorrilla, in his masterpiece *Don Juan Tenorio* (1844), has achieved what no other Romantic playwright has: to stay alive on the stage] (329). And further on he adds:

Zorrilla ha sabido encarnar esa pura teatralidad de Don Juan. Su Don Juan Tenorio habla teatralmente, siente teatralmente, piensa, las raras veces que le ocurre, teatralmente, escribe teatralmente su carta en la posada, cuenta teatralmente su historia de libertinaje, enamora teatralmen-

te, maldice teatralmente, siente angustia y pavor teatralmente, son pura
teatralidad sus desplantes a los vivos y a los muertos, a la Muerte y a Dios,
y se salva teatralmente. Don Juan Tenorio es Don Juan Tenorio a fuerza
de ser teatral. El acierto de Zorrilla está, pues, en haber recalcado con
máxima intensidad la teatralidad de Don Juan como forma de vida, en
haber elevado la teatralidad a modo de existencia. (330)

[Zorrilla knew how to embody Don Juan's pure theatricality. His Don
Juan Tenorio speaks theatrically, feels theatrically, thinks, the rare times
that this occurs, theatrically, writes theatrically his letter in the inn, tells
the story of his libertine life theatrically, falls in love theatrically, curses
theatrically, feels anguish and fear theatrically, his affronts to the living
and the dead, to Death and to God, are pure theatricality, and he is saved
theatrically. Don Juan Tenorio is Don Juan Tenorio by the strength of
being theatrical. Zorrilla hits the mark in having underscored with greatest intensity Don Juan's theatricality as a way of life, in having elevated
theatricality to a mode of existence.]

In this way, everything is seen through the prism of the theater, and the
work is conceived in a theatrical tone. We all participate in this game. Thus,
Feal Deibe shows: "La hostería de Buttarelli, donde se produce el enfrenta-
miento entre Don Juan y Don Luis, funciona de esta manera como un teatro
dentro del teatro. Los dos personajes se ven rodeados de un coro, un público
ante el que exponen sus hazañas" [Buttarelli's inn, where the confrontation
between Don Juan and Don Luis occurs, functions in this way as a theater
within the theater. The two characters are surrounded by a chorus, a public
before whom they lay out their deeds] (35). The theatrical game is in place
from the first scene in which we find ourselves in Carnival. This period of the
year is one that justifies the mask, the disguise, and therefore the anagnorisis, that effective mechanism upon which the whole work is built (Castillo),
and which will even be used in the second part—let us remember the play
of scenes with the Sculptor and with Centellas and Avellaneda in the first
act of the Second Part. The whole work is built towards this anagnorisis in a
game of disguising and then recognizing typical of comedies *de capa y espada*,
which is the structural frame of this piece. This has led to interpretations like
that of Horst, for whom the existence of Don Juan is a Carnival that does
not end. And this is what had led to that "carnival" of maskings, personality
games that are identified with that annual festivity. This, let us remember, is
also inherent in Baroque comedy, whose dynamism lies in deceit and illu-

sion. As Scholes says, these proceedings "aumenta[n] en los espectadores el sentimiento de privilegio, el placer de una perspectiva secreta" [increase in the spectators the feeling of privilege, the pleasure of a secret perspective]. And as Ruiz Ramón highlights (1984) while discussing Calderón, the game of anagnorisis marks a contrast between the ignorance of the stage and the knowledge of the audience (84).

Don Juan presents himself with his mask as an excellent actor who dominates every kind of performance (Souiller). For this reason he includes cross-dressings, character binaries, supplantings, symmetries, similarities, everything that underlines the theatrical game and the actor's control of the stage. The work's first act is paradigmatic of all this; when Don Luis Mejía and Don Juan lay out their "deeds," they do it symmetrically, interpolating the lines. Don Juan goes to Italy, in Rome he posts a sign ("Aquí está don Juan Tenorio / para quien quiera algo de él" [Here is Don Juan Tenorio / for whoever wants something from him], vv.459-460, 1ª, I, E12), in Naples he posts a second ("Aquí está don Juan Tenorio, / y no hay hombre para él. / Desde la princesa altiva / a la que pesca en ruin barca, / no hay hembra a quien no suscriba; / y a cualquier empresa abarca, / si en oro o valor estriba. / Búsquenle los reñidores; / cérquenle los jugadores; / quien se precie que le ataje, / a ver si hay quien le aventaje / en juego, lid o en amores" [Here is Don Juan Tenorio, / and there is no man for him. / From the highest princess / to the girl who fishes in a contemptible boat, / there is no woman to whom he does not subscribe; / and he undertakes any business, / if it is based on gold or valor. / Let quarrelsome people seek him; / let the players surround him; / whoever prides himself, let him hold back, / to see if there is any who best him / in game, battle, or in love] vv. 484-495, idem). Don Luis changes, logically, the space, but the discourse's structure is identical, and he concludes it in the same way as Don Juan. Later, the game continues, both calling their respective servants in order to denounce the other man to the authorities, which will lead to both being detained (scenes 14 and 15 of the first act); the final two interventions of the act with Avellaneda ("Pues yo apuesto por Mejía" [I'm betting on Mejía]) and Centellas ("Y yo pongo por Tenorio" [And I'm betting on Tenorio]); and even Buttarelli's asides are given in parallel, first before Don Diego, and later before Don Gonzalo (that intervene, in turn, with lines very similar to those of Don Gonzalo). These parallels continue in the second part, in the décimas vv. 2924-3033 and vv. 3770-3805, or the antinomious dinner: Don Juan's earthly dinner and the hellish dinner offered by the Comendador (Mansour).[3]

---

3   In the same way, Vicente Lloréns says: "El contraste domina toda la composición. En la hostería, a un lado los jóvenes don Juan y don Luis con sus amigos y

On the other hand, the narrative syntax of the *Tenorio* shows the predominance of staged action over narrated action, something typical of *capa y espada* comedies (Márquez Villanueva: 29), and which fits to perfection the work's rhythm, its dynamism, which translates the whirlwind of action that is Don Juan, who cannot watch his step with any degree of caution. He is impulsive, impatient, brusque. Mozart's Don Giovanni says to Zerline: "Orsu, non perdiam tempo; / in questo istante / io ti voglio sposar" [Come now, let's not waste time; / in this instant / I want to marry you], in the same way that Don Juan does not want to lose a "day" in conversation with Brígida, since time drives him on and he has a date with Death. The deadline, as Ermanno Caldera pointed out, is a constant in Romantic drama (1993), and more so in Don Juan (in which everything is "un sucederse de plazos" [a succession of deadlines], because as with his predecessor, they warn him of a future supreme judgment ("... no te olvides/ de que hay un Dios justiciero" [... do not forget / that there is a just God], vv.772-773, 1ª, I, E12) and as he responds: "Largo el plazo me ponéis" [The deadline you've set for me is long] (v. 792, 1ª, I, E12). For this reason, Don Juan must continue plotting and carrying out immediate projects to express his instantaneous quality, his pleasure in the now, his mobility that causes him to go beyond the barriers of time and space until the supreme moment.

In this way the dialogue participates in this velocity, through the shortness of the speeches, particularly in the confrontations between Don Juan and Don Luis. The use of *esticomitia* is also a strong, dynamic force of dramatic time.[4] Let us see, as an example, the dialogue between Buttarelli and Ciutti, in which Don Juan is presented to us:

---

admiradores, sus estadísticas femeninas y sus fanfarronadas; al otro, dos viejos, don Diego y don Gonzalo, respetables padres de familia, obedientes a la ley moral conculcada por los otros. Luego, tras la frívola Ana de Pantoja, aparece la celestial y pura doña Inés" [Contrast controls the whole composition. In the inn, on one side sit the two young men, Don Juan and Don Luis, with their Friends and admirers, their feminine statistics and their boasting. On the other side are two old men, Don Diego and Don Gonzalo, respectable heads of household, obedient to the moral law violated by the other two. Later, coming after the frivolous Ana de Pantoja, appears the pure, celestial Doña Inés] (366).

4   This process also goes back to the theatricality of the comedy of predicaments, but it was also used much by Victor Hugo (Chahine: 279).

BUTTARELLI.- ¿A su servicio estás?   BUTTARELLI.- You are in his service?
    CIUTTI.- Ya ha un año   CIUTTI.- For a year now.
B.-   ¿Y qué tal te sale?   B.-   And how has it gone?
C.- No hay prior que se me iguale;   C.- Nothing before this comes close;
   tengo tiempo cuanto quiero, y más.   have as much time as I want, and more.
   Tiempo libre, bolsa llena,   Free time, a full purse,
   buenas mozas y buen vino.   good girls, and good wine.
B.- ¡Cuerpo de tal, qué destino!   B.- Good God! What a fate!
C.- (Señalando a Don Juan)   C.- (Pointing to Don Juan)
   Y todo ello a costa ajena.   And all of it paid for by someone else.
B.- ¿Rico, eh?   B.- Rich, huh?
C.-   Varea la plata   C.-   He knocks silver off trees.
B.- ¿Franco?   B.- Generous?
C.-   Como un estudiante.   C.-   Like a student.
B.- ¿Y noble?   B.- And noble?
C.-   Como un infante   C.-   Like a prince.
B.- ¿Y bravo?   B.- And fierce?
C.-   Como un pirata.   C.-   Like a pirate.
B.- ¿Español?   B.- ¿A Spaniard?
C.-   Creo que sí.   C.-   I believe so.
B.- ¿Su nombre?   B.- His name?
C.-   Lo ignoro en suma.   C.-   I don't know it in full.
B.- ¡Bribón! ¿Y dónde va?   B.- Rascal! And where is he going?
C.-   Aquí   C.-   Here.
B.- Largo plumea.   B.- He's writing a lot.
C.-   Es gran pluma.   C.-   He's a great writer.
B.- ¿Y a quién mil diablos escribe   B.- And who the hell is he writing to
   tan cuidadoso y prolijo?   so carefully and so much?
C.- A su padre.   C.- To his father.
B.-   ¡Vaya un hijo!   B.-   What a son!
C.- Para el tiempo en que se vive,   C.- For the time in which he lives,
   es un hombre extraordinario;   he is an extraordinary man.
   mas, silencio." (vv. 18-39, 1ª, I, E1)   But, silence." (vv. 18-39, 1ª, I, E1)

In this way, there is a series of speeches written and specifically designed so that the actor shines, or to seduce the public, in the manner of an operatic aria that will be performed so that the spectator, in the end, will plead for an encore. This can be a resource of great effect, as the *Tenorio* will demonstrate. The Tenorio's language has been reviled by countless critics who have let themselves be led astray by the rhyme Tenorio/notorio—already present in Tirso's Burlador—and who have not ceased to point out defects in the work, including the *performative* nature of Zorrilla's lines. They refused to see, or could not see, this language's vitality that, because it is theatrical, is an *imago* of life. Life and tragedy do nothing more than teach us the insubstantial quality of what we are, of the world, that is to say, the impossibility of reducing life to reason. It is the gay science, the force of laughter that seeks order in the body of existence (Jarauta: 111). On the other hand, in this poetic language words operate on the margin of being deciphered (Baudrillard: 19), beyond the value of signifying. Poetic creation goes beyond its limits. It is a game that is processed as an act of seduction. It is what Derrida calls "lenguaje inflacionado" [inflated language], a language that exceeds its limits; theatrical dialogue goes beyond an interchange since it contains a theatrical action and reflects the characters, their essence, by developing that action (Ubersfeld). In those terms, literary language is a subterfuge, whose objective is to transform the world. In this case, Don Juan's language is emotion, not an exchange; it is a game in which we all participate because we all know the rules. The seducer changes the value of words in order to enter into the game of appearances. We also must not forget that the Romantic poetics aspire simply to move, to produce emotion. As we can see in the famous sofa scene, which forms part of our cultural reserve, like all the work, and therefore has been parodied to such an extent:

[...] ¡Cálmate, pues, vida mía!	[...] Calm down, my life.
Reposa aquí; y un momento	Rest here; and for a moment
olvida de tu convento	forget your convent
la triste cárcel sombría.	that sad, shadowy prison.
¡Ah! ¿No es cierto, ángel de amor,	Ah! Is it not certain, angel of love,
que en esta apartada orilla	that on this distant shore
más pura la luna brilla	the moon shines more purely
y se respira mejor?	and one can breathe better?
Esta aura que vaga, llena	This breeze that wanders, full
de los sencillos olores	of the simple smells
de las campesinas flores	of flowers from the field
que brota esa orilla amena;	that this pleasant shore sprouts;
esa agua limpia y serena	this clean and serene water
que atraviesa sin temor	that the fisherman's boat
la barca del pescador	crosses without fear,
que espera cantando el día,	the fisherman who waits, singing, for day,
¿no es cierto, paloma mía,	is it not certain, my dove,
que están respirando amor?	that they are breathing love?
Esa armonía que el viento	This harmony that the wind
recoge entre esos millares	gathers among those thousands

de floridos olivares,
que agita con manso aliento;
ese dulcísimo acento
con que trina el ruiseñor
de sus copas morador,
llamando al cercano día,
¿no es verdad, gacela mía,
que están respirando amor? [...]
(vv. 257-284, 1ª, IV, E3)

of flowering olive groves,
that it stirs with soft breath;
this sweetest accent
with which the nightingale trills,
the dweller at the top of the trees,
calling the nearby day,
is it not true, my gazelle,
that they are breathing love? [...]
(vv. 257-284, 1ª, IV, E3)

Ana Ozores, the protagonist of *La Regenta*, becomes emotional as she contemplates the performance of the Tenorio, in a shrew observation of the Asturian narrator who knew so well how to capture the essence of drama:

Estos versos que ha querido hacer ridículos y vulgares, manchándolos con su baba, la necesidad prosaica, pasándolos mil y mil veces por sus labios viscosos como vientre de sapo, sonaron en los oídos de Ana aquella noche como frases sublimes de un amor inocente y puro que se entrega con la fe en el objeto amado, natural en todo gran amor. Ana, entonces, no pudo evitarlo; lloró, lloró, sintiendo por aquella Inés una compasión infinita. No era una escena erótica la que ella veía allí: era algo religioso; el alma saltaba a las ideas más altas, al sentimiento purísimo de la caridad universal... no sabía a qué; ello era que se sentía desfallecer de tanta emoción"(*Clarín*, 1981: 51-52).

[These lines that he tried to make ridiculous and vulgar, staining them with his spittle, with prosaic necessity, passing them thousands of times through thick lips like a frog's belly, sounded in Ana's ears that night like sublime sentences of an innocent, pure love that delivers itself up with faith in the beloved object, which is natural in every great love. Ana, then, could not avoid it: she wept, wept, feeling for that Inés an infinite compassion. It was not an erotic scene that she saw there: it was something religious; her soul leaped to the highest ideas, to the purest feeling of universal charity...she did not know to what; it was that she felt herself fainting from so much emotion (*Clarín*, 1981: 51-52).]

This emotion is also communicated by the manner of speaking the lines, by the effectiveness of the diction, by the way in which the Tenorio was and should be performed, with an effectiveness that intended to please, to surprise, to amaze the audience. Vocal inflections, transitions, irregular posture, all of this is innate in this drama. For this reason there is disagreement between Romea and Zorrilla about the way of performing his dramas, since the author demands passion, and the truth of poetry is always above the truth of nature (Fuente Ballesteros 2009).

The speech is, on the other hand, what most resembles a musical unit, if a work in verse does not cease being a musical piece, or where music has an important place, although it does not accompany the words. These units, so important for the development of classical theater and theatrical conventions in general and of theater in verse, find an explanation in Baudelaire, in his text titled "Richard Wagner y Tannhäuser en París" and his idea of music:

> Bientôt j'éprouvai la sensation d'une *clarté* plus vive, *d'une intensité de lumière* croissant avec une telle rapidité, que les nuances fournies par le dictionnaire ne suffiraient pas à exprimer *ce surcroît toujours renaissant d'ardeur et de blancheur.* Alors je conçus pleinement l'idée d'une âme se mouvant dans un milieu lumineux, d'une extase *faite de volupté et de connaissance,* et planant au-dessus et bien loin du monde naturel."[5]

[I soon experienced the sensation of a more lively *clarity, of an intensity of light* that grew with such speed that the shades of color provided by the dictionary would not be sufficient to express *that continually-renewing increase of heat and of whiteness.* Then I understood fully the idea of a soul that is moving through a luminous space, of an ecstasy *made of voluptuousness and of knowledge,* and that soars above and very distant from the natural world]

The mysticism associated with music leads the French poet to say, "La Musique creuse le ciel" ("La Música socava el cielo") [Music undermines heaven] (Baudelaire 18). The musical value of Zorrilla's lines may be joined with the performative nature of some of the *Tenorio*'s speeches.[6] That is, be-

---

5   Prado and Millán: "Pronto experimenté la sensación de una claridad más viva, de una *intensidad de* luz que crecía con tal rapidez que los matices proporcionados por el diccionario no bastarían para expresar *ese aumento siempre renaciente de ardor y de* blancura. Entonces concebí plenamente la idea de un alma que se va moviendo por un medio luminoso, de un *éxtasis hecho de voluptuosidad y de conocimiento,* y que planea por encima y muy lejos del mundo natural" (1450).

6   I refer here to the ideas expressed by J. L. Austin on this type of "emissions" and that has given rise to a series of works on this theme applied to the myth of

yond the value of words, the inner truth hidden in the human heart and that which leads us to the mystery according to the French poet are present in Zorrilla's work. What for Unamuno was the music of the tabor and what distanced him from the poet of Valladolid, in reality is a music by which the poet has found the path to be as much a seducer as Don Juan, and to bear us on the wings of mystery to fall in love once more with the value of words.

Another aspect to consider is the issue related to time. While the diegetic content extends for six years—one must add to the five years already mentioned the intervening year that Don Juan and Don Luis recall in Act I—the mimetic time is reduced to two nights separated, it is true, by five years. That is, there is an enormous temporal condensation that generates, again, an emphasis on the conventionality of the performance, of empowering the theatricality, of accelerating the action—something pointed out earlier. But it is more. The maintenance of the unity of time (Fuente Ballesteros, 1995) in many of Zorrilla's pieces is an element derived from the comedies *de capa y espada*—the Golden Age filiation of Zorrilla's structure is evidence. Serralta, Moir, and especially Arellano have dwelled on this aspect (1995: 129-139),[7] who points out correctly how the use of this unity pursues, contrary to the classical precept, an effect of inverisimilitude, which makes obvious the playwright's skill and inventiveness, that is to say the dramaturgical convention, which is what surprises and amazes the public. All this serves in classical authors to strengthen the intrigue and the surprise of the public. Moir insists on the same point in relation to maintaining the unity of time and place: "son muy útiles para crear y aumentar la tensión dramática y para inducir al público teatral a experimentar física, mental y emocionalmente una marcada impresión de urgencia" [They are very useful for creating and increasing the

Don Juan. In synthesis, Fernández Cifuentes wonders if Don Juan's words are simply comedy or, on the contrary, are "constative" language (96). Francisco LaRubia-Prado, in turn, criticizes this earlier work and set out a reading of the double ending of the work (symbolic and allegorical), according to the theory of acts of which Austin speaks, and which influences Don Juan's theatrical vision. This theme of Don Juan's empty language is also dealt with by Sarah Kofman and Jean Yves.

7   Arellano himself (1988: 47) says: "Objetivo final de la comedia de capa y espada me parece ser la construcción de un juego de enredo, muestra del ingenio del dramaturgo, capaz de entretener—suspender—eutrapélicamente al auditorio" [The final objective of comedy *de capa y espada* seems to me to be the construction of a game of entrapment, a display of the playwright's inventiveness, capable of entertaining—suspending—the audience in *eutrapelia*] (47).

dramatic tension and for inducing the theater-going public to experience physically, mentally, and emotionally a marked impression of urgency] (68). In short, the accumulation of predicaments, the discovery of the stage mechanics, the artificial entanglement, the ingenuities, the apotheosis of the word, etc.; what all this brings into the open is the convention and the break of verisimilitude, changing the comedy into an intelligent, recognizable game. Or, to borrow from Ruiz Ramón's criticism of *La dama duende*: "la vigencia teatral de estas comedias no reside [...] ni en la significación de los conflictos, ni en la psicología de los personajes, ni en el interés de su temática, ni en ningún otro elemento del contenido, sino en su pura forma teatral, en lo que en ellas es juego teatral químicamente puro, es decir, teatro puro" [the theatrical currency of these comedies does not reside [...] in the significance of the conflicts, or in the psychology of the characters, or in their thematic interest, or in any other element of their contents, but rather in their pure theatrical form, in what is, in them, a theatrical game that is chemically pure, that is to say, pure theater] (Ruiz Ramón, 1983: 342).

Pérez Firmat (1986) approaches the temporal dislocation of the *Tenorio*, the condensation that we have pointed out, within his carnivalesque thesis, the distance between the time of Carnival and the real chronology. He manages to justify the errors in the work's structure that seem coherent with the design for the ending.

In sum, Don Juan is "libertinaje y escándalo" [licentiousness and scandal], a game, a maximum amorous drive, an image of desire without hindrance. The Tenorio's performance is a collective celebration, repeated, and the spectators are enthusiastic voyeurs of the Burlador's deeds. Just as Christians celebrate the Day of the Dead, which brings the dead to memory and reminds us the respect we owe them, in the same way Don Juan's sacrificial figure and his story refer us to death and to resurrection—every year renewed by the performance—order and chaos, life and death are celebrated. Don Juan the transgressor, the image of chaos, ends up being defeated by order. With order established, we can wait until the next year for the cycle to be repeated. This is also the meaning of Carnival. The first of November has been, for many years, since the premiere of Zorrilla's version in 1844, a celebration, a ceremony, a ritual in which the return of the myth has lived in Spain and Spanish-America. Don Juan, representing life, carries within himself the tragedy of death[8]—Bataille saw it years earlier in his *L'experience intérieur* when he identified Don Giovanni with the festival. In this way, the

---

8   As Maffesoli says in *El instante eterno* "la avidez con que se vive la vida a la vez que la visión de la Fortuna como ente irracional, esto es lo puramente trágico"

Carnival of the work's first part, with all its theatrical games that have been shown, with its sacrificial figures (Mejía, el Comendador), is followed by the Lent of the second part (Alcolea). In his extraordinary intuition, Zorrilla has been able to give shape to the cycle's change. In this way, over the unstoppable rhythm that our Dionysus imposes on the work, manifesting his desire to live without measure, his passionate game without clocks that mark the hour, in the second part the author lays the slow diction of the Statues of Doña Inés and of the Comendador. The speeches grow longer—the *esticomitia* is now an anecdote, as are the *ovillejos*;[9] the discourse is more reflexive, the words seem to acquire a value before the first part's effervescence, because of the sure presence of death, which already from the scene of the first act where we find that the palace has become a pantheon and the figures such as Don Juan's father, Mejía, the Comendador, and Doña Inés changed into statues, waiting for Don Juan to accompany his victims to the next world. The Burlador's chaos, his rebellion, has been controlled; the order disturbed by the flesh (Carnival) has become abstinence and pure spirit (Lent). The first part's speed is now directed towards death, immobility.[10] The volatile Don Juan loses momentum before the Comendador's statue, immobile by nature. The return to his place of origin, in Don Juan's return to Seville at the beginning of the second part, is a return to the past, to the root of the crime; the first part's quickened time slows as the grains of sand in the clock begin to run out and the character enters a frozen timelessness.

Don Juan is a hero of appearances, of disguise; he is an actor, a frivolous one perhaps, and just like his bodily exhibition, his body disappears into the collective body (of the festival). As with Carnival, his exaggerated happiness, his corporeality, his carnality, remains in the fleeting brilliance of the celebrations to then disappear in the temporal cycle that follows, until its resurrection the next year. As Maffesoli recalls, "la brillantez de la apariencia

---

[the greediness with which life is lived at the same time as the vision of Fortune as an irrational entity, this is the purely tragic] (2005: 25).

9   The *ovillejos* that are used in the first part are a very theatrical game that sets before the spectator's eyes a display of inventiveness to which the work gives itself up without condition, but in the second part, with a totally different rhythm and sense than the first, they disappear.

10   The whole second part is marked by the staging effects, and as the reviewers already noted in the premiere, the model that is used in this part is the comedy of magic. I will not linger on this topic, which clearly also influences the performance's rhythm. A summary of this topic is found in my introduction to the work (Zorrilla 2003).

no tiene otras funciones, sino la de recordar [la] finitud, la impermanencia, mostrando que ésta puede engendrar una especie de júbilo" [the brilliance of the appearance has no other functions except that of recalling finitude, impermanence, showing that this can engender a kind of jubilance] (Maffesoli, 2005: 121). The Statue's marble quiet dissolves the inconstancy of the actor/character's body. We have lived a homeopathic process in which life and death meet and will return, again, to exist in the next festivity, in a new performance of the work.

Works Cited

Adamov, A. *Aquí y Ahora*. Buenos Aires: Losada, 1967.

Alas "Clarín," Leopoldo. *Mis plagios. Un discurso de Núñez de Arce (Folletos literarios IV)*. Madrid: Fernando Fé, 1888.

———. *Palique*. Ed. José María Martínez Cachero. Barcelona: Labor, 1973.

———. *La Regenta*. Ed. Gonzalo Sobejano. 2 vols. Madrid: Castalia, 1981.

Alcolea, Ana. "El *Don Juan Tenorio* de Zorrilla: entre el Carnaval y la Cuaresma." *Verba hispanica*. 8 (1999): 101-114.

Arellano. Ignacio. *Historia del teatro español del siglo XVII*. Madrid: Cátedra, 1995.

———. "Convenciones y rasgos genéricos en la comedia de capa y espada." *Cuadernos de Teatro Clásico* 1 (1988): 27-49.

Arias, Judith H. "The Devil at Heaven's Door: Metaphysical Desire in Don Juan Tenorio" *HR* 61 (1993): 15-34.

Austin, J. L. *How to Do Things with Words*. Cambridge: Harvard University Press, 1962.

Barthes, Roland. *Ensayos críticos*. Barcelona: Seix Barral, 1983.

Baudelaire, Charles. *Poesía completa. Escritos autobiográficos. Los paraísos perdidos. Crítica artística, literaria y musical*. Javier del Prado y José A. Millán Alba (Traducción y ed.). Madrid: Espasa, 2000.

Baudrillard, Jean. *De la seducción*. Madrid: Cátedra, 1981.

Brunel, Pierre. "Burla/Burlador." Pierre Brunel (dir.). *Dictionnaire de Don Juan*. París: Robert Laffont, 1999: 135-137.

Caldera, Ermanno. "El tiempo de Don Juan." *Ínsula*. 564 (1993): 14-15.

———. *El teatro español en la época romántica*. Madrid: Castalia, 2001.

Castillo, Homero. "Algunos recursos escénicos de *Don Juan Tenorio*". *Estudios* 3.9-10 (1954): 15-21.

Chahine, Samia. *La dramaturgie de Victor Hugo (1816-1843)*. Paris: Nizet, 1971.

Díaz-Plaja, Guillermo. *Nuevo asedio a Don Juan*. Buenos Aires: Editorial Sudamericana, 1947.

Feal Deibe, Carlos. *En nombre de don Juan (Estructura de un mito literario)*. Amsterdam and Filadelfia: John Benjamins Publishing Company, 1984.

Fernández Cifuentes, Luis, "Don Juan y las palabras." *Revista de Estudios Hispánicos* 25 (1991) 77-101.

Fernández Turienzo, Francisco. "El Burlador: mito y realidad." *Romanische Forschungen* 86.3-4 (1974): 265-300.

Fuente Ballesteros, Ricardo de la. "Aspectos de la teatralidad romántica: las comedias de Zorrilla." Ana Sofía Pérez-Bustamante Mourier, Alberto Romero Ferrer y Marieta Cantos Casenave (eds.). *El Siglo XIX... y la burguesía también se divierte*. El Puerto de Santa María: Fundación Pedro Muñoz Seca y Ayuntamiento de El Puerto de Santa María, 1995: 237-251.

———. "La verdad de la naturaleza frente a la poesía: Zorrilla y sus memorias frente al actor." *Hecho teatral* 9 (2009): 53-78.

Horst, Robert Ter. "Ritual Time Regained in Zorrilla's *Don Juan Tenorio*," *Romanic Review* LXX (1979): 80-93.

Jarauta, Francisco. "Nietzsche: tragedia y filosofía." *Revista de Occidente* 226 (2000): 102-115.

Kofman, Sarah and Jean Yves Masson. *Don Juan, ou, Le refus de la dette*. París: Galilée, 1991.

LaRubia-Prado, Francisco. "Actos de habla y lenguaje figurativo: La doble historia de *Don Juan Tenorio*." *Letras Peninsulares*. Fall (2000): 441-466.

López Núñez, Juan. *"Don Juan Tenorio" en el teatro, la novela y la poesía. Origen, antecedentes, historia y anécdotas de esta famosa obra*. Madrid: Ediciones Castellanas, 1946.

Lloréns, Vicente. "El oportunismo de Zorrilla." *Homenaje a José Manuel Blecua*. Madrid: Gredos, 1983: 359-369.

Maeztu, Ramiro de. *Don Quijote, Don Juan y la Celestina*. Madrid: Calpe, 1926.

Maffesoli, Michel. *El instante eterno. El retorno de lo trágico en las sociedades postmodernas*. Buenos Aires: Paidós, 1ª reimpresión, 2005: 85.

———. *De la orgía. Una aproximación sociológica*. Barcelona: Ariel, 1996.

Mandrell, James. "Malevolent Insemination: *Don Juan Tenorio* in *La Regenta*." *"Malevolent Insemination" and Other Essays on Clarín*. Ed. Noël Valis. Ann Arbor: Michigan Romance Studies, 1990. 1-27.

————. "Nostalgia and the Popularity of Don Juan Tenorio: Reading Zorrilla through Clarín." *Hispanic Review* 59.1 (Winter 1991): 37-55.

Mansour, George P. "Parallelism in *Don Juan Tenorio.*" *Hispania.* 61.2 (1978): 245-253.

Marín, Diego. "La versatilidad del mito de don Juan." *Revista Canadiense de Estudios Hispánicos* 6.3 (Primavera 1982): 389-403.

Márquez Villanueva, Francisco. *Orígenes y elaboración de "El burlador de Sevilla."* Salamanca: Universidad de Salamanca, 1996.

Mazzeo, Guido E. *"Don Juan Tenorio*: Salvation or Damnation?" *Romance Notes* 51 (1963): 151-55.

Moir, D. "Las comedias regulares de Calderón, ¿unos amoríos con el sistema neoclásico?" *Hacia Calderón.* B. Flasche (ed.). Berlín: W. de Gruyter, 1973. II: 61-70.

Molho, Maurice. *Mitologías. Don Juan. Segismundo.* Madrid: Siglo XXI, 1993.

Molina, Tirso. *El burlador de Sevilla y convidado de piedra.* Héctor Brioso Santos, (ed). Madrid: Alianza Editorial, 1999.

Ortega y Gasset, José. *Obras completas.* 11 vols. Madrid: Revista de Occidente, 1963-69.

Pérez de Ayala, Ramón. "Don Juan." *La máscaras. Obras completas.* Ed. José García Mercadal. 4 vols. Madrid: Aguilar, 1963. 3: 170-75.

Pérez Firmat, Gustavo. *Literature and Liminality. Festive Readings in the Hispanic Tradition.* Durham: Duke U P, 1986.

————. "Carnival in *Don Juan Tenorio.*" *Hispanic Review* (51) 1983: 269-281.

Picoche Jean-Louis. "Le joueur dans le théâtre de Zorrilla (vers une définition d'un romantisme espagnol)." *Mélanges offers à Charles Vicent Aubrun.* II. Paris: Editions Hispanique, 1975: 167-183.

Pi y Margall. Francisco. "Observaciones sobre el carácter de *Don Juan Tenorio.*" *Trabajos Sueltos.* Barcelona: Librería Española, 1895: 139-190.

Revilla, Manuel de la. "El tipo legendario del Tenorio y sus manifestaciones en las modernas literaturas." *Obras.* Madrid: Ateneo Científico, Literario y Artístico, 1883: 431-456.

Rodríguez Cuadros, Evangelina. "Antes que todo es la acción: para una lectura de *No hay cosa como callar*, de Calderón." *Cuadernos de Teatro Clásico* 1 (1988): 143-152.

Ruiz Ramón, Francisco. *Historia del teatro español (Desde sus orígenes hasta 1900).* Madrid: Cátedra, 1983.

————. *Calderón y la tragedia,* Madrid, Alhambra, 1984.

Salgot, Antonio de. *Don Juan Tenorio y el donjuanismo*. Barcelona: Juventud, 1953.

Sánchez, Roberto G. "Cara y cruz de la teatralidad romántica: Don Álvaro y Don Juan Tenorio." *Ínsula* 336 (1974): 21-23.

Scholes, Robert. "A Semiotic Approach to Irony in Drama and Fiction." *Semiotics and Interpretation*. New Haven: Yale University Press, 1982.

Serralta, F. *Antonio de Solís et la comedia d'intrigue*. Toulouse: Universidad de Toulouse, 1987.

Suiller, D. "Théâtralité." Pierre Brunel (dir.). *Dictionnaire de Don Juan*. París: Robert Laffont, 1999: 905-911.

Torrente Ballester, Gonzalo. *Teatro español contemporáneo*. Madrid: Guadarrama, 2ª ed., 1968.

Ubersfeld, Anne. *Semiótica teatral*. Madrid: Cátedra, 1989.

Unamuno, Miguel de. "El zorrillismo estético." *Obras Completas*. Madrid: Afrodisio Aguado, 1952. V: 89-96.

Zorrilla, José. *Obras Completas*. Narciso Alonso Cortés (ed.). Valladolid: Santarén, 1943, 2 vols.

———. *Don Juan Tenorio*. Ricardo de la Fuente Ballesteros (ed.). Madrid: Biblioteca Nueva, 2003.

SECTION FOUR

The Classic Playboy
Under the Feminist Gaze

When Women Say No:
Don Juan and Language of Protest

MARGARET E. BOYLE
Bowdoin College

"Pues jura que cumplirás/
la palabra prometida."
- Tisbea, lines 2086-87

"Words without value are worse than silence:
one can be punished for them"
- Rebecca Solnit (27)

L ANGUAGE IS AT THE center of persuasion in *El Burlador de Sevilla y convidado de piedra* and Don Juan's masterful talent with words—his construction and declaration of false promises and broken oaths— is inextricably linked with his devastating ability to deceive. But what relationship do women have with words in Tirso de Molina's seventeenth-century play? The plot of the three acts certainly hinges on women's ability to be "tricked" by Don Juan although the directionality of his linguistic damage is not strictly linear.[1] Harm travels in multiple directions throughout the three acts, often initiated from Don Juan to a female victim, but subsequently

---

1   The quotation marks here indicate uneasiness with the word "trick." Although commonly used to describe Don Juan's actions, it does so without any explicit description of the content of these actions, also without emphasizing seriousness or severity. Yet the word "trick" is useful in a theatrical context, where repeated action or motif is a plot device. Certainly, Don Juan's behaviors are central to the dramatic arc of the play.

moving in dizzying form and course, effectively demonstrating the ways in which Don Juan's crimes wreak havoc on full family structures.

Still, a number of questions about language use within the play remain: how do women themselves make use of words in relationship to Don Juan? How is women's sexual consent manifest through language use as theory and practice both within the world of the play and within the social world in which Tirso was playwright? What relationship do these instances of consent have to do with displays of protest throughout the play? Building on past scholarship concerning women's roles within the dramatic world of the play, this essay will explore the complex ways in which language and sexual consent are tied together within character dialogue: overt and expressive declarations and accusations; scenes of misunderstanding, silencing or obscuring; and finally, how words relate to modes of being and knowing. Hence this exploration makes good use of contemporary feminist theorists, with attention to the ties between gender, language, victimization and resistance.[2]

Although critics have not generally described the start of *El burlador* as a scene of sexual assault, instead characterizing Don Juan's actions more ambiguously—emphasizing concepts such as deception or trickery—in fact the play begins with a scene of sexual assault and the subsequent processes of recognition and resolution.[3] Right from the start, the Duquesa Isabela is strategic in her responses, taking control of the scene as soon as she is able. Her request for a light to see her lover's face foreshadows the confusion of identity that is about to transpire, and establishes the Duquesa's active role with her literal and symbolic access to light as knowledge.[4] Of course horrified to realize what has just transpired, she uses her words to confirm what she and

---

2   On this last term, Carine Mardorossian has helpfully implored scholars "to reconceptualize and reappropriate the word *victimization* and its meaning. We need to resist the facile opposition between passivity and agency that has motivated popular and academic discussions of violence against women" (771, *Toward*). Throughout, this essay will take heed of this reconceptualization, aiming to bring to light the dynamic and sometimes contradictory processes at play in the construction of victimization.

3   Stacey L. Parker Aronson is an exception to this analytical trend. Her 2007 study on Leonor de la Cueva's *La Firmeza en la Ausencia* for example identifies rape as "an all too common motif in the literature of the Golden Age" (141).

4   In this context, consider Valerie Traub's 2015 assertion that in the early modern period "sex is likened to a form of knowledge... shar[ing] with feminist philosophers of epistemology a concern with what is known, how it is known, differential access to knowledge, and the terms by which knowledge is expressed. It departs from their collective project by concerning itself less with establishment of

the audience should have already known: "¿Qué no eres el duque?" (ln. 16), insisting upon her duty and obligation to her spouse and family name. The words that form this short question are powerful for the way they put into conversation agency and blame: the not knowing, the believing that Don Juan was her husband (and it is critical that she *names* him as a way of displaying her own knowledge to multiple levels of authority, including the audience of the play). When Don Juan tries to physically restrain her, insisting: "Détente: dame, duquesa, la mano" (ln. 18) her language and bodily response displays an even more forceful presence: "No me detengas, villano" (ln. 19). She refuses to be held down, calls out and insults Don Juan, and finally works to secure a position from which she can request the presence of authorities to restore order to the scene: "Ay del rey! Soldados, gente!" (ln. 20). Isabela's use of language and choice of actions demonstrate to the audience that she knows better than to be alone with her dishonor. She clearly identifies the established hierarchy as well as her place within it. Thus, *El burlador* begins by foregrounding Don Juan as "trickster" and by dramatizing a victimized woman's protest and her search for a sense of justice.

The encounter between Don Juan and the Duquesa Isabela is just the first in a series of victimizations present on and off the stage throughout the three acts of the play. Duquesa Isabela is deceived alongside another noblewoman Doña Ana, as well as the *villanas* Tisbea and Aminta, providing a representation of women's victimization that transcends traditional class lines.[5] Also present are a series of women whose voices are mediated through stories told about them by other characters in the play. For example we can locate "at least one other anonymous *burlada*—a Spaniard and noble" (1.5.636), as Susana Pendzik has demonstrated "some of these women are anonymous; others, like Beatriz, possess names but are 'invisible'. To this second category belongs the long list of prostitutes: Inés, Constanza, Teodora, Julia, the two sisters and their mother, and several others still who are harder to identify who are referred to as a group (*el barrio de Cantarranas*)" (167). Although women's access to language varies widely in the play, it is clear that language use is a critical tool for women's sexual/social self-definition, protection and recovery. This insistence on recovering the representation of women as dra-

---

truth claims (or their contestation) than in exploring the techniques of knowledge production educed by sex" (9).

5   James Mandrell provides a foundation for this reading when he describes this intersection as "dramatic symmetry created by the four seductions" (60) and points the reader to examine how these acts provide the space for "a progressively complex exploration of the nature of language as it functions in the world" (61).

matic subjects, fictional and real, is inspired by Marcia Welles' rereading of rape narratives in early modern Spain, "entail[ing] returning violence to the language, which, with its brilliant strategies of circumlocution, so often seeks to disguise, rather than express, pain." (38). This reading of *El burlador* carefully attends to the words, moments of silence, and words not yet part of the vernacular used to describe the sexual crimes throughout the play.

To return to the first scene, from the moment Duquesa Isabela recognizes Don Juan for who he is, she makes known her offense first to Don Juan and subsequently to a series of authority figures. It is useful to contextualize her actions within Sebastián de Covarrubias's 1611 definition of *manifestar*: "declarar aquella de que no se tenía noticia" (1235). The contemporary definition is compelling for the way it insists on expression as productive in two interrelated spheres: the creation of knowledge and a way to move action forward. This scene of recognition is extremely vocal, replete with the *gritos* Covarrubias defines by the challenging tie between complaint, threat and evidence: ["quejándose o amenazando o avisando"] (1003). In fact, Isabela's public declaration functions as testimony to crime, one that becomes even more provocative when considered through the lens of Leigh Gilmore's 2017 work on women as witnesses:

Testimony does not begin and end with a single speech act, nor is its lifespan limited to its duration within a particular forum of judgment. Rather, testimony moves—sometimes haltingly, sometimes urgently in search of an adequate witness. An adequate witness is one who will receive testimony without deforming it by doubt and without substituting different terms of value for the ones offered by the witness herself. (5, Gilmore)

This construction of testimony relative to witness is especially captivating in a theatrical context because it presses on the role of spectator both onstage and the audience, implicating both parties as critical participants in the making of truth and knowledge. Moreover, this reading of testimony presents a method of interpretation that resists both singularity (testimony occurs over and over again and it is the witnesses' obligation to observe, steadily and over an extended period of time) and stagnation (testimony is dynamic and process-based).

Through the study of women's language use within *El burlador,* this essay argues for a more fully contextualized reading of this play within the sexual politics of consent and protest as they are tied to rape culture, although it was not yet conceptually framed with this terminology. The word "violar" is completely absent from Covarrubias's 1611 *Tesoro de la lengua castellana o española* and even by 1739 the word is still not included within the *diccionario de autoridades*. Even today, the language we use to define rape is fraught and contentious, although nearly all social and legal understandings of rape are tied to consent. Don Juan uses language to satisfy his own desires, and women use language to negotiate around the harm done to themselves and their families. Attention to women's consent and protest provides a framework through which early modernists can consider sexual consent as well as the control and protection of women's bodies. In our own era, rife with debates concerning "locker room talk," the power of language over action, and most recently the #metoo movement, the provocative and sometimes resistive model raised within *El burlador* becomes an even more fascinating object of study.

Although *violar* is not a word we can clearly locate, we do find the word *consentimiento* both expressed overtly within the action of the play, and as a concept within the known vernacular of the period. Covarrubias defines *consentimiento* with an emphasis on the relationship between choice and action: "el asenso y voluntad que se da para que se haga alguna cosa" (596). In the context of *El burlador*'s opening scene, this raises the question: does Isabela express consent, and if so how?

One way to answer this question is by examining how sexual consent was legally understood during the period when *El burlador* was written. Here, Renato Baranhona's 2003 *Sex Crimes, Honour and the Law in Early Modern Spain* is a fundamental resource, offering both details and context for routine litigation of sex crimes, particularly the form of sexual misconduct known as *estupro*. Baranhona defines this sex crime by the following five elements:

1) courtship, persuasions and offers; 2) seduction and premarital sexual relations—relations, it should be underscored, generally carried out under the promise and assurance of matrimony; 3) a breach of promise to marry by the defendant (sometimes accompanied by his flight—in effect, by abandonment of the female); 4) assertions of shame and dishonor to the plaintiff in the aftermath of the deception and desertion; and 5) claims of damages. (6)

Audiences familiar with *El burlador* will clearly recognize all of these actions as repeated motifs throughout the course of the play, making *estupro* and the language, action, and gender dynamics it encompasses as critical points of study for accessing the world of Tirso's play.[6] It also provides readers with the legalistic framework necessary to explore how the play's plot may have resonated with contemporary audiences.

Throughout the three acts, public claims of damages are made by all four of *El burlador's* most visible female protagonists. Tisbea, for example, describes her betrayal in the following terms: "¡Ah falso huésped, que dejas/ una mujer deshonrada" (lns. 1009-10). Her accusation emphasizes Don Juan's responsibility for both her abandonment and dishonor, and the insult of "fake" paired with "host" is revealing for the way it undermines the moral concept of hospitality, demonstrating to the audience that Don Juan's tricks are not just about false romantic seduction, but a threat and assault to social structures at large. She is also quick to request the intervention of authorities to restore justice to the scene, "Seguidle todos, seguidle./ Mas no importa que se vaya,/ que en presencia del rey/ tengo de pedir venganza" (lns. 1027-30). With this twice-repeated command to pursue Don Juan, Aminta simultaneously appeals to her social and political hierarchy (the king) with her cry for revenge.

Similarly, Ana emphasizes the trickery, lies and betrayal that have led to her conquest. "¡Falso!, no eres el marqués,/ que me has engañado...¡Fiero enemigo, mientes, mientes!" (lns. 1556-7). There could not be any more clarity in the synonymous constellation of words Ana chooses to describe Don Juan: "Liar," "you've tricked me" and "you lie" "you lie." The choice adjective of "fierce" is likewise revealing for the way it emphasizes the exceptionality of Don Juan's character- even the already apparent "enemy" requires this modifier. Like Tisbea, she calls for retributive justice, although she is more public about her call: "¿No hay quien mate este traidor,/homicida de mi honor?" "Matalde" (lns. 1562-63). Aminta too clearly names both her dishonor and her rights: "El señor don Juan Tenorio,/ con quien vengo a desposarme,/ por-

---

6   Covarrubias also includes *Estupro* in his dictionary, offering further insight into the contemporary understanding of the concept. He writes, "El concúbito y ayuntamiento con la mujer doncella, bien como llamamos adulterio el que se comete con la mujer casada... y como semejantes ayuntamientos sean en las camas, pudo tomarse el nombre del estrado compuesto sobre hierbas secas y sobre las strupas o verbenas; porque los estrados, *thoros* o camas, son el campo ordinario deste conflicto. Y así decimos violador del *thoro* ajeno, el que ha cometido adulterio con la mujer casada; ultra de que la novia, cuando iba a casarse, llevaba debajo del velo una corona de verbena llamada *strupo*, y, como el incesto tomó nombre del cesto, que era la cinta con que iba ceñida la novia, pudo también dar el de estupro la corona que llevaba, dicha *strupo*, permutadas las letras, como tenemos dicho" (857).

que me debe el honor,/ y es noble y no ha de negarme./ Manda que nos desposemos" (lns. 2839-44). Her plea is distinguished from the prior examples because she locates her revenge in marriage rather than bodily punishment, marking the institution as the vehicle through which she can recover her lost honor.

At the end of his definition of the verb *consentir,* Covarrubias makes reference to a proverb that may offer a provisional model for the politics of sexual consent as dramatized by *El burlador.* He writes: "Hacientes y conscientes, pena por igual." Punishment acts as equalizing arbiter for both seducer and seduced, although Don Juan's punishment is spectacularly accumulated given the volume of his crimes. As Tisbea famously repeats, and then is joined in chorus by others betrayed by Don Juan: "¡Mal haya la mujer que en hombre fía!" (2209). Women are responsible for their own victimization because of unwarranted trust. The utmost guardedness and circumspection are constant demands placed on respectable women who must protect their name and status. Clearly, those who do not adhere to these demands will suffer.

Tisbea's betrayal is powerful because her lapse is both momentary and out of character. She is keenly aware of her vulnerability and has a strong track record of exercising appropriate caution (not surprisingly, the responsibility here falls on women). For example, an earlier monologue reveals how diligently she has rejected the overtures of other men: she actively defends herself from their advances, she snubs men's charms, and is unmoved by their words. Even their pleas and promises fall on deaf ears: "De cuantos pescadores/ con fuego Tarragona/ de piratas defiende/ en la argentada costa,/ desprecio soy y encanto;/ a sus suspiros, sorda;/ a sus ruegos, terrible;/a sus promesas, roca" (lns. 427-34). Yet in the case of Don Juan, Tisbea falls victim to almost identical tricks, all predicated on language as weapon of seduction.

To best understand the additional layer of consequences tied to this sexual crime, it is valuable to examine the social significance of virginity, here again turning to Covarrubias as a starting point:

Virgen: Por otro nombre, la llamamos doncella; deste estado y de la virginidad y castidad había mucho que decir, pero es lugar común y así me contento con lo dicho y con remitir al lector curioso a un emblema mío cuya figura es una azucena rodeada de un seto rompido y ella destroncada, con la letra «nulla reparabilis arte». (1533)

Several aspects of this definition are noteworthy. First, virginity is defined exclusively for women. Second, Covarrubias nearly avoids defining the term since it is so central to other texts (curiously the same rhetorical strategy appears in his definition of "woman"). Finally, with his Latin caption, the reader is reminded that virginity is reparable or fixable by no art. The stress is on the fact that there's no method that can "fix" the entity being described. The emphasis on the negative is stronger than in the equally valid "irreparabilis ulla arte" (irreparable by any art). The placement of "nulla" in front adds to the emphasis on the negative (similar if we were to say "by *no* art can this be fixed").[7] Certainly this emphasis on permanent injury saturates the protests made by women throughout this play.

Don Juan lies to seduce women, rendering his language not only precursor to the crime, but part and parcel of sexual assault. Here, contemporary readers may find a new point of access and insight into the world of *El burlador* as we celebrate the 400th anniversary of its first performance, given contemporary discussions of the relationship between language and action or more precisely what has been termed "locker room talk" versus sexual assault.

President Donald Trump bragged in vulgar terms about kissing, groping and trying to have sex with women during a 2005 conversation caught on tape, saying for example "when you're a star, they let you do it," a comment which provides clear evidence of the significance of status and power in processes of victimization. During the second presidential debate in 2016, Trump addressed the comments in the following conversation with moderator Anderson Cooper:

AC: "You described kissing women without consent, grabbing their genitals. That is sexual assault. You bragged that you have sexually assaulted women. Do you understand that?"

DT: "No, I didn't say that at all. I don't think you understood what was—this was locker room talk. I'm not proud of it. I apologize to my family. I apologize to the American people. Certainly I'm not proud of it. But this is locker room talk."

The introduction of "locker room talk" received significant attention in the weeks that followed, but seems particularly consequential in the context of *El burlador* for its attempts at erasure and normalization. Trump's defense moves actions clearly understood in plain English to another realm of protected speech where power dynamics are made invisible, namely the

---

7   "Ars" is also a dynamic term. Depending on context it can mean "art," "technical skill," "craft," "ability," "artifice."

enclosure of "the locker room," where language concerning or embodying hyper masculine, aggressive assault is permitted, celebrated, and harms no one. (For what it's worth, several athletes came forward to speak out against the fiction of this space). The pairing of the locker room talk defense with two apologies—one personal and another public—as well the statement about the lack of pride (note he does not suggest humiliation) is also provocative; Trump admits to the potential for damage caused by the activity, but insists this behavior is normal, harmless and therefore excusable: "But this is locker room talk."

In a subsequent interview with the Weekly Standard in 2016, Trump surrogate and then-Senator Jeff Sessions (R-AL) said he wouldn't "characterize" the behavior described in the tapes "as sexual assault:"

SESSIONS: This was very improper language, and he's acknowledged that.

TWS: But beyond the language, would you characterize the behavior described in that [video] as sexual assault if that behavior actually took place?

SESSIONS: I don't characterize that as sexual assault. I think that's a stretch. I don't know what he meant—

TWS: So if you grab a woman by the genitals, that's not sexual assault?

SESSIONS: I don't know. It's not clear that he—how that would occur.

This exchange is fascinating for several reasons: the devaluing of language use as a potentially hostile act, the overall separation between language and behavior, the refusal to locate sexual assault, and the insistence on ambiguity even when such ambiguity devalues, or even erases completely, the place of consent (language and action) or the position of victims.

Public discourse around sexual assault in the US context continues to be dynamic and controversial with the fervor of the #metoo campaign looming large locally and globally, and the seemingly daily toppling of "patriarchs, but not patriarchy" as we were recently reminded by feminist historian and cultural critic Susan Faludi. Considering just two other highly publicized topics from the summer of 2017, it should be apparent the ways in which the current cultural moment has the potential to dramatically inflect the impact and relevance of *El burlador* 400 years later. The first example considers the sexual assault trials of comedian Bill Cosby and the fervent debates they have generated across a variety of audiences, including media outlets, sexual assault support groups, comedy fans, and Cosby's fellow celebrities. These trials have forced a public wrestling with the conversion of the well-known celebrity ideal of Bill Cosby embodied as Cliff Huxtable, to serial rapist, rupturing not only the icon of "America's Dad" but also the dream of the happy family projected onto the cultural imagination via *The Cosby Show*. As of June 17, Cosby's most recent sexual assault case ended in a mistrial, reflecting an ongoing inability to reconcile these contradictions and perhaps move towards resolution.

To complicate matters further, several days after the announcement of the mistrial the *New York Times* reported, to the outrage of sexual assault groups, that the comedian "is planning a series of town hall meetings this summer to educate people, including young athletes and married men, on how to avoid accusations of sexual assault" (Bowley and Hagney). Again, revealing the powerful intersection between celebrity, reputation and negotiation, these town hall meetings would levy the power of language use as a way to negotiate potential accusations, contributing to the myth that reports of sexual assault are often untrue. Just ten days later it was then reported that the town halls would focus on the legacy of the comedian and his beliefs about education, not sexual assault. (Bowley)

The details of these reversals are compelling for the way they put into public conversation the weight of celebrity and its implications even in the realm of the courtroom, highlighting the long and complicated intersections between legal trials and public figures. Perhaps most critically, the trials are momentous for making visible the power dynamics—economic, racial, and gendered—that come into play for all victims of sexual assault, some groups going as far to claim that the lack of resolution in the ongoing trials is an injustice universally: damaging and painful to the women who are directly implicated in the Cosby trials, as well as all victims of sexual assault who have not been legally recognized. The discussion around avoiding and/or negotiating with accusation is especially revealing in the context of *El burlador* for its parallel strategies, pressing on the relevance of language as critical component for negotiating identity and reputation from both accuser and accused.

For a second related topic of considerable public interest, consider title IX. Modifications to the law's implementation made in 2011 by the Obama administration require schools to combat sexual discrimination, recognizing that rape and other forms of gender-based violence demonstrate inequality. In July 2017, Department of Education Secretary Betsy DeVos began review of the policy and its implementation, consulting with victims' advocacy groups, organizations for the rights of the accused as well as men's rights groups, in order to hear from "all sides of the issues." On July 12 Candice E. Jackson, the head of Department of Education's Office of Civil Rights, discussed her rationale for reconsidering investigative processes and implementation, suggesting that current practices

> have not been "fairly balanced between the accusing victim and the accused student," Ms. Jackson argued, and students have been branded rapists "when the facts just don't back that up." In most investigations, she said, there's "not even an accusation that these accused students overrode the will of a young woman. Rather, the accusations—90 percent of them—fall into the category of 'we were both drunk; we broke up, and six months later I found myself under a Title IX investigation because she just decided that our last sleeping together was not quite right.'"

These statements were received with considerable upset, with many advocacy groups pointing to the very low statistics concerning the reporting of false information in sexual assault cases. Jackson subsequently revised her comments to insist that all accusations should be investigated seriously. The interview as well as the larger reconsideration of title IX policy within the aim of "balanced" conversation again point to the powerful role of language *use* (both the words chosen and access to language) as well as the composition of "restorative justice practices" broadly defined, including how the compositions of these conversations have the power to substantially impact the construction of meaning, as well as the scenes of recognition, reconciliation, and reporting happening today or throughout history as documented in cases of *Estupro* or dramatized in a play like *El burlador*.

The dramatic and punitive resolution of *El burlador* clearly locates the power of language as it is capable of intersecting with gender and victimization. When Don Gonzalo reaches out for Don Juan's hand in a gesture foreshadowing punishment rather than marriage, he asks directly: "¿Cumplirásme una palabra/ como caballero?" (lns. 2467-68) intentionally, and likely with some irony, reversing the power dynamic staged throughout the course of the play and reinstating a series of expectations appropriate to rank and class. Don Juan, true to form, replies simply and to the point: "Honor/ tengo y las palabras cumplo, porque caballero soy" (lns. 2469-70). Or is it because of the gender and class privilege he embodies that he is allowed, at least up until this moment, to repeatedly break his promises? This comment provides key evidence for the slippery relationship between a subject and his word, the play over and over again demanding an attentive audience capable of deciphering at the highest level. In this context, Rebecca Solnit's 2017 call to feminist readers is apt:

The task of calling things by their true names, of telling the truth to the best of our abilities, of knowing how we got here, of listening particularly to those who have been silenced in the past, of seeing how the myriad stories fit together and break apart, of using any privilege we may have been handed to undo privilege or expand its scope is each of our tasks. It's how we make the world. (66, Solnit)

At a moment in time that threatens to erase the passionate protests that fill the pages and stages *El burlador*, it is even more critical to locate, and even safeguard these literary, historical and theatrical accounts of women's protest and sexual consent. Four hundred years later, both readings and performances of *El burlador* offer contemporary audiences the critical opportunity to play witness, with all of the responsibilities that the job entails. Moreover, the play posits language as the critical axis between gender and victimization. With its own furious play with words, it asks its audience to do the same: naming and renaming, giving words the meaning they may have lost along the way.

Works Cited

Barahona, Renato. *Sex Crimes, Honour, and the Law in Early Modern Spain: Vizcaya, 1528-1735.* Toronto: University of Toronto Press, 2013.

Bowley, Graham and Sophey Hagney. "Bill Cosby, Fresh From Trial, Plans Talks on Avoiding Assault Accusations." *The New York Times,* June 2017. Accessed 23 June 2017. Web.

Bowley, Graham. "Cosby Team Says His Talks Will Not Be About Sexual Assault." *The New York Times,* June 2017. Accessed 13 July 2017. Web.

Covarrubias Horozco, Sebastián de. *Tesoro de la lengua castellana o española.* Madrid: Iberoamericana, 2006.

Faludi, Susan. "The Patriarchs are Falling. The Patriarchy is Stronger than Ever." *The New York Times,* December 2017. Accessed 28 December 2017. Web.

Gilmore, Leigh. *Tainted Witness: Why We Doubt What Women Say About Their Lives.* New York: Columbia University Press, 2017.

Green, Erica and Sheryl Gay Stohlberg. "Campus Rape Policies Get a New Look as the Accused Get DeVos's Ear." *The New York Times.* July 2017. Accessed 13 July 2017. Web.

Mandrell, James. *Don Juan and the Point of Honor; Seduction, Patriarchal Society and Literary Tradition.* University Park, PA: Pennsylvania State University Press, 1992.

Mardorossian, Carine M. "Toward a New Feminist Theory of Rape." *Signs* 27.3 (2002) 743-775.

Maroto Camino, Mercedes. "'Las naves de la conquista': Woman and the Fatherland in *El burlador de Sevilla.*" *Bulletin of the Comediantes* 55.1 (2003): 69-86.

McCormack, John. "Jeff Sessions: Behavior Described by Trump in 'Grab them by the P———y' Tape isn't Sexual Assault." *The Weekly Standard,* October 2016. Accessed 3 March 2017. Web.

Molina, Tirso de. *El burlador de Sevilla.* Ed. Alfredo Rodríguez López-Vásquez. Madrid: Catedra, 2002.

Parker Aronson, Stacey L. "The Threat of Rape in Leonor de la Cueva's *La Firmeza en la Ausencia.*" *Romance Notes* 47.2 (2007): 141-152.

Pendzik, Susana. "Female Presence in Tirso's *El burlador de Sevilla.*" *Bulletin of the Comediantes* 47.2 (1995): 165-81.

Solnit, Rebecca. *The Mother of All Questions.* Chicago: Haymarket Books, 2017.

Sullivan, Shaun. "Trump Supporter Sen. Jeff Sessions reportedly said behavior Trump described in 2005 video is not sexual assault." *The Washington Post,* October 2016. Accessed 3 March 2017. Web.

Traub, Valerie. *Thinking Sex with the Early Moderns.* Philadelphia: University of Pennsylvania Press, 2016.

Welles, Marcia C. *Persephone's Girdle: Narratives of Rape in Seventeenth-Century Spanish Literature.* Nashville: Vanderbilt University Press, 2000.

Taking Back the Night:
El burlador de Sevilla and
Twenty-First Century Feminisms

ROBERT BAYLISS
University of Kansas

I F WE ACCEPT THE premise that a text comes to be known as a "classic" insofar as it continues to engage audiences no matter how far removed they are from the original circumstances of its composition, that persistent engagement across generations of readers ensures for the "classic" a continuously evolving meaning. The master narratives of the early modern period, for example, acquire new resonances with the arrival of each social movement of lasting cultural impact, and in turn for each generation of readers whose identities and experiences are shaped by such movements. As a case in point, consider the interplay between contemporary feminism and *El burlador de Sevilla*, one of the most canonical and influential codifications of misogyny and sexual abuse of the Western tradition—indeed a text that exposes many of the hallmarks of the patriarchy against which feminism defined itself over the course of the twentieth century and against which it continues to work today. In light of both how scholarship has evolved in its treatment of the text and my own recent experiences engaging with college students in the study of it, I argue that the play remains a vital tool for prompting all of us—teachers and students alike—to take measure of our own cultural moment in the ongoing struggle against the vestiges of the ideological system that first rendered Don Juan a compelling protagonist four centuries ago.

Our contemporary cultural circumstances bear witness to considerable flexibility in usage of the term "feminism," which I analyze here as both a social movement and a framework of critical theory. Discourses outside the

Academy muddy the waters of how the very word "feminism" is understood today, as for example when Kellyanne Conway, advisor to President Trump, speaks of an emerging "conservative feminism" to counter what she terms the "very anti-male" and "pro-abortion" feminist movement of the left. (Merriam-Webster's reply on twitter was appropriately short and sweet: "'Feminism' is defined as 'the belief that men and women should have equal rights and opportunities.'") These different perspectives speak to longstanding cultural tensions between discourses that would frame feminism either as a social evolution meant to normalize gender equality as requisite for modern society, or as an invasive threat to traditional social structures.

Unfortunately, within Academia the waters surrounding contemporary feminism can be similarly opaque. While the field of Women's and Gender Studies remains committed to research on the history and persistence of gender inequality, a number of scholars including Angela McRobbie, Wendy Brown and Charlotte Brunsdon speak of the new century as an era of "post-feminism," not to distance themselves ideologically from the movement but rather to signal that its gains for women in the last several decades require us to rethink its place in contemporary society. As a result of gains made by earlier generations or "waves" of feminism, much of the activism and work done today for feminist causes addresses inequalities in practice (sexual harassment in the workplace, domestic abuse, the pay gap between genders, etc.) that were overcome—in theory—decades ago with the civil-rights accomplishments of the 1960s and 1970s. A counterargument against speaking of our age as "postfeminist" is that it invites the assumption that this earlier work rendered the goal of gender equality already fully realized, and that it therefore invites the dismissal of the movement as no longer relevant. Such casting aside of feminism as anachronistic was a sustaining argument in the so-called feminist backlash of the Reagan era, a conservative campaign against feminism described in Susan Faludi's book *Backlash: The Undeclared War Against Women*. In this context, feminist scholars have been well aware of the plasticity of the term "feminism," that it means very different things to different people.

While beyond my scope here, it is worth noting that this lexical instability coincides in the U.S. with an increasingly polarized political and cultural climate featuring competing narratives of what some might call our "postfeminist condition." It is a climate, in other words, in which contradictory narratives would have us believe either that equality has been achieved or that it remains stubbornly elusive at an institutional level; either that feminism constitutes a threat to traditional cultural values or that it remains our best hope for progress. Most recently, it is a climate in which one presidential candidate's attempt to shatter the ultimate "glass ceiling" won the popular vote by millions, but also in which the opponent of that "nasty woman" formally won the election with a majority of Electoral College votes, despite being caught on tape boasting of sexual assault in terms that would have made Don Juan himself blush. Indeed, notwithstanding the clarity of Merriam-Webster's tweet referenced above, "feminism" remains a hotly contested term.

In the current decade, college campuses across the United States and Canada have become the front lines of this culture war. In the U.S., because federal funding of campuses and campus programs is tied to compliance with Title IX (a law that stands among the greatest legal accomplishments of feminism in the 1970s but which is now cast in doubt by questions about the ways in which it will be enforced going forward), campus administrators are obligated to comply with the law's prohibition of discriminatory practices on the basis of gender that would impact access to education. After decades of legal action involving the ACLU, the law was explicitly linked to the issue of sexual violence when the Department of Education's Office of Civil Rights declared in 2011 that "sexual harassment of students, including sexual violence, interferes with students' right to receive an education free from discrimination and, in the case of sexual violence, is a crime." In short, college and university administrations were informed that by failing to address the occurrence of sexual violence at an institutional level, they risked losing federal funding. The very solvency of the American Academy required it to unequivocally punish students found guilty of sexual assault and to develop initiatives to prevent such crimes.

The intensified institutional focus on the problem of sexual violence, we should note, comes a full forty years after the original passage of Title IX in 1972, and suggests that, despite the law, problems associated with sexual violence have persisted for decades. According to the National Sexual Violence Resource Center, 1 in 5 women is sexually assaulted while in college, and ninety percent of those assaults are not reported (Krebs et al). The 2011 Civil Rights memo can therefore be seen as an attempt to address an institutional myopia that feminists have worked intensely to expose for decades. If the work of feminists in the 1960s and 1970s made the letter of the Title IX law possible, feminist activism of the last three decades often has been dedicated to making its enforcement match the spirit in which it was enacted.

A key force in the movement to address the epidemic of campus sexual assault has been the community of activists known as "Take Back the Night," a loose global network of locally organized efforts to call public attention to the problem of sexual assault. To date the organization has focused its efforts in the U.S. on college campuses by staging protests, marches and rallies. The earliest events associated with it reach back to the 1970s, but in the last two decades these activities have increased from being sporadic to ubiquitous on university campuses across North America. The Take Back the Night Foundation, in addition to calling for (and often organizing) further protests, has developed into a broad community of feminists eager to offer support and strategies to local activists. An upcoming event organized by the foundation, for example, includes "The Sexual Misconduct Policy Institute: Training on Title IX, Investigations, and Response Protocol." The foundation, in short, consists of twenty-first century activists seeking to empower citizens across the U.S., by informing them of the legal recourses made possible by the efforts of previous generations of feminists, in order to make the theory of gender equality a reality in practice.

El burlador de Sevilla and its Reception
Returning to a pre-feminist master narrative of a decidedly misogynistic protagonist's exploits in a markedly patriarchal social system offers the opportunity to see how feminism has impacted the critical reception of *El burlador de Sevilla* over the course of several generations, to see if this feminist social and critical footprint can allow us to read the play differently than have previous generations of scholars, and finally to use the play as a kind of gauge for how we understand feminism today amid the cacophony of the term's usage described above. Questions of how we read the play today and how we understand the legacy and ongoing work of feminism, I would argue, can be mutually illuminating, not by an anachronistic ascription of twenty-first century values or motives to the seventeenth-century text and its author, but because of the ultimately elusive sense of closure that it offered in its early modern public performances.

Given the subject of the play, it should come as no surprise that the history of scholarship dedicated to *El burlador* is impacted by the development of feminist critical theory and its integration into literary and cultural studies. While the play had long been read as a function of its protagonist and the moral lesson attributed to his story, interest in the play's female characters became increasingly common with the arrival of feminism's so-called "second-wave" in the 1960s, for example with José María de Navarro Adriaensens's 1960 article "Los personajes femeninos en el *Burlador* de Tirso de Molina." While many other disciplinary and theoretical developments can

be attributed to the change from approaching the play as the dramatization
of more "universal" (i.e. decontextualized and un-historicized) moral questions regarding the nature of providence, redemption and condemnation, it
is clear that critical treatments of the play take a historical turn at the same
time that second-wave feminism takes root in Hispanism. John Varey's seminal article "Social Criticism in *El burlador de Sevilla*" (1977), for example,
reorients the critical tradition by pointing to the play's multiple targets of critique from Tirso's *milieu*, most notably the court of Naples (which he takes
as a proxy for the Castilian court). Like Ruth Lundelius, Carlos Feal and
Vicente Cabrera, all of whom published articles on the subject within seven
years of Varey's study, he does not spare the play's female characters from
criticism, but only as contributors to a larger vision of social problems for
which male and female characters are equally symptomatic.

   Although this turn to history will eventually have important implications for feminist approaches to the text in the 1990s, the immediate impact
of second-wave feminism's arrival in literary criticism for the tradition of
Burlador scholarship is more closely tied to critical focus (i.e., what guiding questions underlie the scholarship) than it is to methodology. In other
words, scholarship first began to follow the general direction of Navarro's
article in 1960 by focusing on female characters in Tirso's play, before eventually incorporating feminist critical theory in a more rigorous and comprehensive manner. Articles like those named above by Lundelius, Feal and
Cabrera during the 1970s and 1980s reflect an understanding that the representation of women had emerged as a valid and important topic of study,
regardless of the particular theoretical orientation adopted. It is in the 1990s
that we witness a turn in *Burlador* studies that takes more fully into account
the implication of feminist theory and the emerging field of Gender Studies,
even if the explicit goal of many studies is not "feminist," as with the example
of James Mandrell's 1992 book, *Don Juan and the Point of Honor*. By contrast,
Susana Pendzik's article "Female Presence in Tirso's *El burlador de Sevilla*"
(1995) represents a methodological sea change wherein "feminist readings"
of the play are both placed in dialogue with feminist critical theory and contribute to a broader feminist rethinking of early modern Spanish cultural
production.

   Pendzik engages Adrienne Munich's work on the paradoxes inherent
in the entrance of female voices into the phallogocentric realm of literary
discourse to treat the presence (implicit and explicit) in the play, in combination with Julia Kristeva's work on the gendered nature of the Symbolic
Order. In short, if the patriarchy assigns for women a passive and silent role,

their attempts to speak or write render their identities as women (as defined by the patriarchy) problematic. (This line of argumentation dovetails with postcolonial theory as well, we should note, as it echoes Gayatri Spivak's seminal question of "Can the Subaltern Speak?.") Munich's concept of "invisible women" is likewise engaged to show "gaps" in Tirso's representation of Spanish society, and that even "from offstage" women influence such representations.

Pendzik's article reveals just how ripe for feminist analysis the play is, as her consideration of implicit female presence (via references to Ana and other *burladas* who never actually appear on stage) allow us to resituate the story of Don Juan according to its implications for early modern women, and indeed according to its implications for the more contemporary struggles of feminism and the institutional biases and fault lines that preclude gender equality. In this sense, it is not only *El burlador* but also the tradition of scholarship dedicated to it that Pendzik's study takes to task. She refutes, for example, the "victim-blaming" indictments of Don Juan's victims made by critics during the 1970s and 1980s, but also the broader tradition of reading Don Juan as the consummate rebel, for such a reading fails to account for the patriarchy's complicity in his *burlas*: "rather than rebelling against the norms, Don Juan plays with his power to enforce them to the extreme" (179). In the end, this feminist reading of the play replaces traditional readings of Don Juan's final demise: what was invariably read as "divine justice" is for Pendzik far less resolved, and far more open-ended. "The system is not repaired, either by Don Juan's death or by the marriages. The restoration of justice and cosmic balance needs more than one scapegoat and a few happily married couples" (180).

Significant contributions have been made in the intervening years between Pendzik's article and now, and those contributions continue to prompt a reevaluation of *El burlador* and the society in which it was written. A more historicized treatment of gender underscores Elizabeth Rhodes's "Gender and the Monstruous in *El burlador de Sevilla*" (2002), in which the author examines early modern understandings of the male/female gender binary and argues against traditional readings of Don Juan as a paragon of masculinity. A more explicitly feminist reading of the play is offered in Mercedes Maroto Camino's "Las naves de la conquista: Woman and the Fatherland in *El burlador de Sevilla*" (2003). For Maroto Camino, Don Juan's sexual conquests are inextricably linked to military conquest and the "patriarchal gaze" inherent in colonialism. "This male-dominated society clearly rests on the subjugation of a nature gendered as female, and maintains itself united by means of pacts between men sealed on the exchange of women" (79). In this way, *Burlador* criticism thus evolves from an early twentieth-century tradition of male-centered critical treatments of Don Juan, to a midcentury recognition of the importance of also studying the play's female characters, and eventually to a more properly described "feminist" treatment of the play engaged with the full implications of feminist critical theory. Those full implications, we will see, reverse earlier tendencies to see the play as a historically distant cultural artifact and instead suggest that how we read *El burlador* has everything to do with today's feminist struggles for gender equality.

DON JUAN AND FEMINISM, BEYOND *EL BURLADOR*

I suspect that today, a full forty years after it was published, Varey's argument in his seminal "Social Criticism" article would be made with greater attention paid to the gender dynamics represented in these objects of social critique, in other words to how that critique implicates the inherent gender inequality of the patriarchy in all eras and cultures. This connection to the here-and-now certainly seems to be in mind as Pendzik concludes her study: "...the story of Don Juan has repeated itself so many times in Western literature that it is difficult to believe that anything has yet been resolved" (180). She no doubt refers to the countless adaptations and re-casting of Tirso's story over the centuries, both in Spain (Zorrilla, Valle-Inclán, Torrente Ballester, etc.) and beyond (Molière, Byron, Lorenzo da Ponte's libretto for Mozart's opera, and many more). But an even more compelling case can be made that the abuse of patriarchal authority for purposes of sexual conquest and gratification remains a persistent problem in our contemporary culture, that much of the current work of contemporary feminism is directed toward the institutions that allow such abuses to persist, and that these patriarchal institutions (like the court at Naples in *El burlador*) stubbornly resist calls to address the problem unless they are held legally and financially accountable. In light of this work, the lack of closure for which Pendzik argues serves as an invitation to consider how *El burlador*'s dramatization of Don Juan's *burlas* might illuminate our understanding of current efforts to take back the night.

J. Douglas Canfield's 1997 study of three pre-romantic versions of the Don Juan legend offers a useful conceptual framework for such a project of bringing the early modern text to bear on twenty-first century cultural problems. What *El burlador*, Molière's seventeenth-century adaptation for the French stage, and Lorenzo da Ponte's libretto for Mozart's *Don Giovanni* all share is that, in what he terms a "sociopolitical interpretation," Don Juan "remains throughout this late feudal epoch a trope, a figure, a necessary negation that affirms the very code it denies... he paradoxically reaffirms a system of shared power between men—at the expense of women and oppressed classes" (43). Unlike the more modern adaptations of the legend, from which critics generally take Zorrilla's Romantic play as point of departure and in which Don Juan ultimately repents and is converted into a heroic figure, these early modern versions of the legend close with a clear rebuke of the protagonist. Canfield's analysis undermines the simplistic notion that *El burlador de Sevilla* constitutes a cautionary tale with a clear rebuke of the threat to social order that Don Juan poses. Instead, not unlike Pendzik's argument from a more explicitly feminist perspective, Canfield notes the deeply unsettling sense of "order restored" by the Stone Guest's final act of castigation, and its implications for *El burlador*'s audience. Not unlike the social critique outlined in Varey's study, Canfield sees the ultimate legacy of Don Juan's *burlas* as the destruction of a system of male homosocial control dependent on what he calls "word-as-bond." This destructive impact, to apply the insights of James Mandrell and Shoshana Felman, signals a disconnect between performative and constative speech acts, and it is symptomatic of a baroque crisis of social stability that would see its ultimate resolution more than a century later with the French Revolution.

Indeed, from this angle the Stone Guest's *deus ex machina* intervention can be read as necessary to bring down a cycle of abuse that human institutions of law and justice prove impotent to stop. We should note that the peripatetic structure of *El burlador*'s third act, in which dramatic action oscillates between sites of negotiation for human (the king's court) and divine (Gonzalo's tomb) justice, suggests that divine providence only steps in to punish Don Juan after human institutions fail to do so. Like Varey before him, Canfield reads Don Juan's defiance of "word-as-bond as a system of reproductive control" (45) as evidence of that system's precarious balance of power in early modern Europe. But unlike Varey, whose historical analysis limits its scope to the playwright and his historically distant and abstract social milieu, Canfield suggests a more direct implication of the play's audience. "Don Juan is not the only misogynist, I am arguing. The male bonding in the plays themselves and between actors and audience entails us all, even the women who laugh, in the inherent misogyny of this system of reproductive control" (54). Just as Betty Friedan's seminal book *The Feminine Mystique* would implicate the complicity of women in the persistent sexism and misogyny of mid-twentieth century western society, Canfield suggests that *El burlador*'s most devastating social critique is of its own audience in the *gusto* derived from witnessing Don Juan's exploits.

As Lope de Vega's *Arte nuevo de hacer comedias* explains, the true function of early modern Spanish comedy is to please its audiences while holding
a mirror up to society, and the canonical status of *El burlador* suggests that
for centuries male and female spectators have derived pleasure from witnessing representations of Don Juan's daring efforts to subvert (while paradoxically reinforcing, as we have seen above) patriarchal authority. For evidence
of this audience complicity, we need look no further than Catalinón, whose
metatheatrical asides and comical reactions to his master's exploits can be
read as a gloss on the play's main action. Edward Friedman describes this role
as one that "enhances" Don Juan's character, as it leaves spectators continually aware of how the actions they witness run against propriety and decorum. Catalinón names Don Juan, of course (he literally coins the moniker
"el burlador de España"), but more importantly his constant admonitions
regarding the divine retribution that his acts are sure to elicit keep the audience aware of the serious moral consequences of his *burlas*; in this way,
the *criado* ensures that his master's rebellious acts are fully understood and
appreciated. Given this metatheatrical communicative role, it is also instructive to consider Catalinón as a kind of aesthetic guide for the audience as he
cowers, warns, and laments in his glosses, in effect modeling the kinds of reactions that the playwright would have his public experience throughout the
play. Thus, while the play's conclusion might offer an ideologically orthodox
rebuke of his actions, we would do well to remember that those reprehensible
actions have also provided compelling entertainment for audiences across
the globe over the last five centuries.

The paradox of an engaging and compelling representation of Don Juan's
reprehensible "negative exemplarity" becomes more complicated in the cycle
of recastings, adaptations and *refundiciones* that would proliferate in the
nineteenth and twentieth centuries. While it lies beyond the scope of this
essay to explore these complications in detail, we should note that, beginning
with Zorrilla's Romantic *refundición*, Don Juan's narrative trajectory shifts
from that of a castigated *chivo expiatorio* to that of a rebellious hero whose
final submission to divine authority ensures his redemption. And while it
can ostensibly be argued that a more central role for women is afforded by
Zorrilla's rewriting of the final scene, as Inés's purity and virtue make Don
Juan's final conversion possible, a more persuasive case can be made that this
more important role depends on the same gendered hierarchy and reduc-
tionist view of women—virgin or whore, guardian or destroyer of familial
honor—that underlies the early modern original. Even if we accept the reading offered by Guido E. Mazzeo and others that Inés heroically leverages the

destiny of her own innocent soul to make Don Juan's conversion possible, she is still defined as an instrument of his narrative. Zorrilla's *refundición* and all subsequent cultural production influenced by it may "save" Don Juan by replacing Tirso's *deus ex machina* with a *dama ex machina*, but the underlying vision of male sexual conquest and female victimhood is only reinforced, if not strengthened, in the process. The fact that Zorrilla's play would eventually become a fixture in annual celebrations throughout the Spanish-speaking world—for example, as staples of festivities surrounding the *Día de los santos* in Spain and *Día de los difuntos* in Latin America—speaks to how, for more than 150 years and counting, Don Juan's narrative and its implications for women remain vital elements in the Hispanic cultural zeitgeist. The presence of Don Juan beyond the Spanish-speaking world, from Molière's public theater to recent Hollywood adaptations, suggests furthermore that his narrative remains vital and relevant in a global context.

CLASSROOM INTERVENTIONS AND TWENTY-FIRST CENTURY FEMINISM
Of the many versions of the Don Juan narrative impacted by Zorrilla's play, it is instructive to cite one example to demonstrate how that narrative is applied to twentieth-century cultural circumstances, particularly in light of our concerns with the trickster-hero's dialogue with the work of contemporary feminism. Carlos Morton's *Johnny Tenorio* (originally written and performed in 1983, published in 1994) grafts the narrative onto a Chicano cultural context, with a twist: Berta, a female bartender and *curandera*, celebrates the Day of the Dead by reviving Johnny's spirit from an altar/*ofrenda* made of relics from his famously libertine life. Johnny appears and dramatizes key moments from his life in San Antonio and New York, and in the process the audience is invited to consider how the original Don Juan's life would translate into this new context. Johnny is a womanizer, of course, but he is also a pimp and a deadbeat father. In short, *donjuanismo* is presented by Morton as a primal source of many of the societal challenges faced by the Chicano community in the 1980s—to name a few, violence, drug abuse and trafficking, human trafficking, domestic abuse, single parenthood, and prostitution:

> BERTA: Here is Johnny Tenorio, el Don Juan, a thorn in the soul of la Raza since time immemorial. Ha traicionado a mujeres, asesinado a hombres y causado gran dolor. Por eso decimos...que muera!

> CHORUS: ¡Que muera!

BERTA: But he also stood alone, defied all the rules, and fought the
best he knew how. His heart pounds fiercely inside all of us—the
men who desire to be like him, the women who lust after him. He
is our lover, brother, father and son. Por eso decimos—¡que viva!

CHORUS: ¡Que viva!
(51-52)

In this way, Morton's adaptation avoids the kind of closure with which
Zorrillas's version ended and against which Pendzik argues in her reading of
El burlador. Furthermore, it effectively identifies *donjuanismo* as an endemic
feature of Chicano American culture—a destructive and yet still irresistible
part of the community's identity.

As part of a First Year Seminar program recently started at the University of Kansas, I offered a course on contemporary adaptations of canonical literary texts and included *El burlador* in a "Don Juan cycle" that also
included Zorrilla's *Don Juan Tenorio* and Morton's *Johnny Tenorio*. The goal
of this cycle was to examine the impact of social movements like feminism
on the way that the Don Juan legend is repackaged for modern audiences. To
enhance our studies and take advantage of her visit to KU for other reasons,
I invited Lidia Falcón to attend our class for the session in which we would
discuss *El burlador*. Because Falcón was a founding mother of Spain's "second-wave" feminist movement in the 1960s, because her activism landed her
in prison under the Franco regime, and because she remains an active voice in
the *Alianza feminista*'s current political participation in the *Izquierda Unida*
party, I anticipated that her presence would serve the program's goal of providing "experiential learning" for college freshmen while also enhancing my
seminar's engagement with our object of study. What better way to engage
the Spanish Golden Age narrative most clearly connected to the institutional
repression of women's voices and gender equality than to pick the brain of
such an important Spanish feminist?

Falcón's visit occurred in 2012, a year before a series of disturbing incidents on KU's campus involving off-campus parties, binge drinking and
sexual assault. Prior to those events, the university administration had established clear "zero tolerance" policies regarding sexual assault by its students,
but those policies had not yet been tested publicly as they would soon be in
2013. Our 2012 class session dedicated to *El burlador* reflected many of the
ideas discussed here regarding critical reception of the play in recent decades:
Don Juan posed a threat to the social order, his final demise was an act of

divine justice, and so forth. As we wrapped up Falcón's pleasant and informative class visit, I asked her to describe what *moraleja* she hoped that our study of Don Juan narratives would teach us. Because this class of freshmen had participated in a newly revamped set of campus programs and events targeting first-year students, including mandatory online tutorials regarding sexual harassment, I expected Falcón's answer to reflect much of this messaging and campus programming, especially regarding the need to protect women from assault or abuse, the need to report such abuse to the police, and how alcohol use can amplify these dangers.

Falcón's response to my question, however, was directed specifically to the women in the class. Don Juan's victims, she argued, did bear part of the blame for allowing themselves to be so manipulated, and she hoped that my female students would learn from their negative example. The answer implied that such predatory behavior was a given, and that it was imperative for women to anticipate it and take steps to avoid situations that would leave them especially vulnerable. Women needed to understand the dangers that they faced, and they needed to look out for one another when a potential "Don Juan" approached any of them. In short, I found the answer surprising because it seemed to swim against the current of campus programming and messaging regarding the issue of sexual violence, and indeed against the broader cultural currents that have exposed abusive behavior in private corporations and institutions. In the spirit of the "Take Back the Night" movement, after all, women were urged to resist the kind of "victim blaming" that Pendzik sees as endemic of earlier criticism of *El burlador* and to instead demand that institutions of higher learning do more to allow women to participate in campus life without feeling threatened. Was Falcón, the quintessential second-wave Spanish feminist, arguing against third-wave calls to take back the night?

During the two weeks following Falcón's visit and our reading of *El burlador*, we studied both Zorrilla's *refundición* and Morton's *Johnny Tenorio*. And while the class did not enter into a detailed study of the history of feminism and so could not comment on the philosophical differences between these different "waves" of feminism, they did seem to understand instinctively that the disconnect between Falcón's *moraleja* and the "take back the night" messaging across campus spoke above all else to personal experience, and perhaps also to generational and national differences exacerbated by the especially strong opposition to feminism experienced by Falcón during the dictatorship. Twenty-first century students can appreciate that the kinds of sanctioned abuses and institutional myopia first articulated in John Varey's article are especially unfair to the play's powerless women, but they are also taught to see these problems as unacceptable, unjust, and in need of repair. Millennial feminists and their sympathizers, in other words, are less likely to see these problems as unavoidable facts of life, and they see the responsibility to fix them as falling equally on all members of society, public and private.

For Falcón, however, whose efforts in the 1960s to advocate for equal rights for women resulted in serious personal consequences, institutional sexism was a more vivid reality and hardly constituted "news." If such problems were a given for much of Falcón's life, the solidarity of a feminist movement was the only hope for protection against them. Rather than repeat the obvious message that Don Juan abused women with the consent of a rigged patriarchal system, she chose to offer an alternative to passive acceptance of the abuse—namely, for women to understand that their participation in society is not unlike playing a game in which the rules are biased against them. Acting in concert to succeed in spite of that bias, and to reverse it whenever possible, is a lesson far more in tune with her life's work.

It should be said that Falcón's activism has certainly evolved from its *antifranquista* origins. After a career that witnessed the fall of the dictatorship, the reinstitution of democracy, and the rise of her *Partido Feminista de España* from an underground protest movement into a powerful arm of the Spanish Left, it is natural that her views on politics and the potential to bring about social progress would change. After decades of work with the *Partido* to promote feminist causes from the outside of the political system, she has brought her party into the fold of the progressive coalition known as the *Izquierda Unida* and now sees government institutions as the most effective vehicle for tangible change. She currently maintains a blog with the leftist publication *Público*, in which, as recently as March 2017, she enumerated a comprehensive list of provisions to be included in new legislative effort to combat and prevent domestic abuse.

Unfortunately for Don Juan's victims in *El burlador*, legal recourses for women were far more limited. But in the context of heightened awareness of sexual violence and now annual "Take Back the Night" marches in Lawrence, Kansas, it is difficult to avoid seeing the growing crescendo of *burladas* in Act Three as an early modern analogue to this kind of twenty-first century feminist activism. Tisbea, Aminta, Ana and Isabel all converge upon the court to seek redress for the dishonor brought upon them by Don Juan. The king works to address their grievances in typical third-act *Comedia* fashion, by hastily arranging marriages. Of course, what the king is unable to do— control and hold to account Don Juan himself—is the only true remedy for these victims to feel that justice has been served. Varey sees the fact that the king cannot deliver justice in this way as an indictment of the corruption and impotence of his own court, and in our "postfeminist" context today such a reading resonates as a function of gender inequality. The patriarch, after all, is the least likely to reform the patriarchy.

El burlador's Gordian knot of justice is ultimately untied by the stone hand of God Himself, which allows for the articulation of an unequivocal moral: "Quien tal hace, que tal pague" (ll. 2772-2773). The *deus ex machina*'s sure-handed imposition of divine justice resolves the play's central problem of containing and stopping Don Juan, but there is little evidence to indicate that in lieu of divine intervention Don Juan would have not continued to trick with impunity. If we see "Take Back the Night" marches as analogous to the appeals of the play's *burladas*, we may better understand these contemporary efforts as an extension of a struggle that has gone on for centuries between *burladores* and *burladas*, and between patriarchal institutions and the women they are too slow to protect. Taking such a long view also makes Lidia Falcón's advice seem wiser than I had originally understood it to be. When considered in light of her continued efforts to work within a political system that had previously excluded her, her words seem especially apt: protect yourself, be vigilant, and work together to cure the patriarchy of its myopia. Taking back the night is important, but so is reforming the system in the light of day so that such protections are no longer needed.

Works Cited

Bayliss, Robert. "The Best Man in the Play: Female Agency in a Gender-Inclusive *Comedia* Studies." *Bulletin of the Comediantes* 59.2 (2008): 303-23.

Brown, Wendy. "The Impossibility of Women's Studies." *Differences: A Journal of Feminist Cultural Studies* 9 (1997): 79–102.

Brunsdon, Charlotte. "Feminism, Post-Feminism: Martha, Martha, and Nigella." *Cinema Journal* 44.2 (2004): 110-16.

Cabrera, Vicente. "Doña Ana's Seduction in *El burlador de Sevilla*." *Bulletin of the Comediantes* 26.2 (1974): 49-51.

Canfield, J. Douglas. "The Classical Treatment of Don Juan in Tirso, Moliere, and Mozart: What Cultural Work Does It Perform?" *Comparative Drama* 31.1 (1997): 42-64.

Feal, Carlos. "*El burlador* de Tirso y la mujer." *Symposium* 29 (1973): 300-313.

———. *En nombre de don Juan: estructura de un mito literario*. Amsterdam /Philadelphia: Purdue University Monographs in Romance Languages, Vol. 16, 1984.

Friedan, Betty. *The Feminine Mystique*. New York: W.W. Norton & Co., 1963.

Friedman, Edward. "Redressing the Trickster: *El burlador de Sevilla* and Critical Transitions." *Revista Canadiense de Estudios Hispánicos*, 29.1 (2004): 61-77.

Faludi, Susan. *Backlash: The Undeclared War Against American Women*. New York: Crown Publishing Group, 1991.

Krebs, C. P., Lindquist, C., Warner, T., Fisher, B., & Martin, S. *The Campus Sexual Assault (CSA) Study: Final Report, 2007*. Retrieved 18 March 2017 from the National Criminal Justice Reference Service: http://www.ncjrs.gov/pdffiles1/nij/grants/221153.pdf

Kristeva, Julia. "About Chinese Women." *The Kristeva Reader*. Ed. Toril Moi. Trans. Sean Hand. New York: Columbia UP, 1986. 138-59.

Lundelius, Ruth. "Tirso's View of Women in *El burlador de Sevilla*." *Bulletin of the Comediantes* 27.1 (1975): 5-14.

Mandrell, James. *Don Juan and the Point of Honor: Seduction, Patriarchal Society, and Literary Tradition*. University Park, PA: Penn State UP, 1992.

Maroto Camino, Mercedes. "'Las naves de la conquista': Woman and the Fatherland in *El burlador de Sevilla*." *Bulletin of the Comediantes* 55.1 (2003): 69-86.

Mazzeo, Guido E. "Don Juan Tenorio: Salvation or Damnation?" *Romance Notes* 5.2 (1964): 151-55.

McRobbie, Angela. "Post Feminism and Popular Culture." *Feminist Media Studies* 4.3 (2004): 255-64.

Morton, Carlos. *Johnny Tenorio and Other plays*. Houston, TX: Arte Público Press, 1994.

Munich, Adrianne. "Notorious Signs: Feminist Criticism and Literary Tradition." *Making a Difference: Feminist Literary Criticism*. Ed. Gayle Greene and Coppella Kahan. London: Routledge, 1988. 238-59.

Navarro de Adriaensens, José María. "Los personajes femeninos en el *Burlador* de Tirso de Molina." *Romanistisches Jahrbuch* 11 (1960): 376-396.

Pendzik, Susana. "Female Presence in Tirso's *El burlador de Sevilla*." *Bulletin of the Comediantes* 47.2 (1995): 65-181.

Rhodes, Elizabeth. "Gender and the Monstruous in *El burlador de Sevilla*." *Modern Language Notes* 117.2 (2002): 267-85.

Spivak, Gayatri. "Can the Subaltern Speak?," in *Marxism and the Interpretation of Culture*, eds. C. Nelson & L. Grossberg. Chicago: University of Illinois Press, 1988. 271–31.

Tirso de Molina. *El burlador de Sevilla*. Ed. Alfredo Rodríguez López-Vázquez. 7th ed. Madrid: Cátedra , 1995.

Varey, John. "Social Criticism in *El burlador de Sevilla*." *Theatre Research International* 2 (1977): 197–221.

Don Juan's Protean Legacy

The Myth of Don Juan from a Foucauldian Perspective: Relations of Power during the Baroque and the Romantic Periods

Daniel Lorca
Oakland University

R ELATIONS OF POWER AS understood by Foucault offer a meaningful way of understanding some key differences between the literature of the Baroque and the Romantic period. More precisely, a Foucauldian approach allows for the discovery of the power structures that shaped the literary production of both types of literature. To do so, this paper focuses our attention on the notions of justice that were prevalent in both periods, as those notions influenced relations of power.

This analysis is a comparison/contrast between *El Burlador de Sevilla*, by Tirso, and *El Estudiante de Salamanca*, by Espronceda. Those works are selected for three reasons: First, both are fair representatives of the literary periods in which they were written; second, both works are versions of the myth of Don Juan, and finally, third, the treatment of the myth in each work is, everybody agrees, drastically different; therefore, given all three reasons, the differences in the power relations operating within both literary periods, as captured in the relevant notions of justice, should become easier to identify.

It should perhaps be added that this paper is not about what Tirso and Espronceda *intended* with the literary production. A Foucauldian approach, by necessity, leaves the author behind (using instead an author-function, which is basically a convenient way to refer to a text or a collection, and *not* to the actual author).[1] Instead, a Foucauldian analysis takes into account the

---

1 In this paper the use of the names of authors follow the procedure explained by Foucault in his article "What Is an Author?" For example, he writes: "[the name]

discourse itself, without reference to intentions.[2] Considering this clarification, the main question of this paper can be phrased as follows: how did the
changes in power structures through history, as those changes are captured
in notions of justice, influence the transformation of the myth of don Juan
from the Baroque (as captured in *El burlador*) to the Romantic period (as
captured in *El estudiante*)?

RELATIONS OF POWER DURING THE BAROQUE
Critical opinions about *El burlador de Sevilla* may be classified into two
broad categories. For the sake of convenience let us say that the first category is the classical view, and the second is the opposition. The classical view,
judging by the number of critics who hold it, is by far the most popular. It
maintains that the main theme of the play is the implementation of divine
justice. Don Juan receives the punishment he deserves. The opinion of James
D. Wilson is a fair representative of the classical view:

[Don Juan] seems determined only to indulge his lust as often as possible and still achieve salvation within a traditional Christian framework.
Tirso's theme is that the libertine is mistaken; he cannot plot sin with an
eye open to eventual repentance. There is, in the end, little doubt that
Don Juan merits the punishment he receives; as the statue says when he

---

performs a certain role with regard to narrative discourse, assuring a classificatory
function. Such a name permits one to group together a certain number of texts,
define them, differentiate them from and contrast them from others" (145). In other
words, the names are not referring to humans, but to the classification of discourse.
    2 In *The Archeology of Knoweldge* Foucault explains his method and goals
in detail. There he makes clear that his method leaves behind the mental states
(intentions) of authors, and concentrates instead on what the discourse itself shows.
For example, he writes: "Archeology tries to define not the thoughts, representations,
images. themes, preoccupations that are concealed or revealed in discourses; but
those discourses themselves, those discourses obeying certain rules. It does not
treat discourse as a *document*, as a sign of something else [...]; it is concerned with
discourse in its own volume, as a *monument*. It is not an interpretative discipline"
(139)." He also states that his goal is "to describe a group of statements not as the
closed, plethoric totality of a meaning, but as an incomplete, fragmented figure; to
describe a group of statements not with reference to the interiority of intention, a
thought, or a subject, but in accordance with the dispersion of an exteriority [i.e.,
discourse]" (120).

comes to drag the hero off into hell: 'Esta es la justicia de Dios! / quien tal hace, que tal pague'. (247)[3]

On the other hand, the opposition does not have a fair representative, but, rather, it is composed of several objections against the classical view. We may use the opinion held by Trevor J. Dadson to illustrate the kind of objections that have been proposed: "Tirso [...] raised [...] serious questions in the play—about the role and power of woman, about the failings of the monarchs, about justice human or divine—that responded more closely to the realities of his time" (123).

Let us begin by taking a closer look at the classical view. Foucault's book *Discipline and Punish* explains the functioning of justice within Western societies. The book begins with an anecdote that captures justice during the Baroque:

Damiens the regicide was condemned 'to make the *amende honorable* before the main door of the Church of Paris' [a very public place], [...]

---

3   There are, of course, variations, but the following list of critics hold that, at the very least, a version of divine justice is an important element to understand Tirso's play: María-Paz Yáñez states that in the play we have a "God of revenge, a God who [...] is bent on punishment [which may be seen as an] excessive [...] judgment of God" (109); Gerald E. Wade: "To Tirso he [Don Juan] was so vile that his author sent him to hell at the end of the play" (33); Dionisia Tejera Llano: "The two heroes [Dr. Faustus and Don Juan] defy the power of God, and in doing so, bring about their downfall; they are condemned for eternity" (245); Paul M. Lloyd: "la característica más esencial [de Don Juan es] la *perversidad*, el deseo de desafiar todas las costumbres y todas las leyes, humanas y divinas" (448); J. Douglas Canfield: "Despite all the warnings that divine justice is impending, he believes he will have plenty of time for a deathbed repentance when he is old" (46). Other critics who hold similar views about the importance of divine justice are: Karl C. Gregg (358); Youssef Saad (306); Roberta Quance (103); Andreas Flurschütz da Cruz (3); Dorothy Clothelle Clarke (all of her essay, tracing divine Justice to the Middle Ages, especially in 12 and 19); Mathé Allain (divine justice explained in terms of Platonism 196, and also as joke on Don Juan's 183); Rosa Navarro (27); Peggy Von Mayer Ch. (123); Francisco Fernández-Turienzo (52, 55); Gerald E. Wade (675); María Jesús García Garrosa (52); Elizabeth Teresa Howe (divine justice supported with Aquinas on 214, and later on 218); Markus Bandur (89-90); Sandra L. Brown (64); Antonio Gómez-Moriana (35, 44); Robert E. McDowell (53); Ruth Lundelius (12-13); James D. Wilson (247); Jeanne J. Smoot (43); Carol Lazzaro-Weis (37); Ester Abreu Vieira de Oliveira (177) Robert Bayliss (209); and Ruth Plaut Weinreb (428).

[where] the flesh will be torn from his breasts, arms, thighs and calves with red-hot pincers, his right hand, holding the knife with which he committed the said parricide, burnt with Sulphur, and on those where the flesh will be torn away, poured molten lead, boiling oil, burning resin, [...] and then his body drawn and quartered by four horses [...]. (3)

During this punishment "the clerk of the Court" approached Damiens and asked him "if he had anything to say" (4). Damiens responded that "he had not" (4) and then "he cried out, as the damned in hell are supposed to cry out, 'Pardon, my God! Pardon, Lord!'" (4). The punishment continued, and then "several confessors wend up to him and spoke to him at length; he willingly kissed the crucifix that was held out to him; he opened his lips and repeated: 'pardon, Lord'" (4). The four horses were insufficient to quarter Damiens, so two more horses were brought, and after several attempts, his punishment was carried to the end (see 4-5).

The similarities between the punishment of don Juan and Damiens the regicide are striking. Both are horrible deaths, easily seen as forms of torture: Damiens's body is torn, burned and quartered, and don Juan's is burnt by the hand of the statue, and then taken straight to hell. Both ask for forgiveness to God, to no avail: the sentences are carried to the bitter end as prescribed by the ritual. Both are spectacles, and the purpose of both is the same from a Foucauldian perspective: "its aim [of the spectacle] is not so much to re-establish the balance as to bring into play, as its extreme point, the dissymmetry between the subject who has dared to violate the law and the all-powerful sovereign who displays his strength" (48-49). In the case of Damiens's execution, the one displaying his power is the new sovereign, and in the case of Don Juan, it is God all-mighty. Furthermore, Damiens's execution is public (carried out in front of a Church), and don Juan's is public three times: first, it is seen by the audience of the play, it is also seen by Catalinón, and finally, it is made public a third time when Catalinón informs all the main characters of how and why don Juan was taken to hell, a narration, which, by the way, is also seen by the audience. According to Foucault the public nature of executions is important because it "enables us to understand [...] the importance of a ritual that was to deploy its pomp in public. Nothing was to be hidden of this triumph of the law" (49).

The three main elements mentioned above about Baroque justice work together to create a whole that is greater than its parts. First, the function of justice is to establish the dissymmetry of power between the sentenced man and the judge; second, in order to leave little doubt about the existence of that dissymmetry of power, the execution is as public as possible. Finally, third, the execution is spectacular to awe the audience with the dissymmetry of power. The necessity of all three elements working together can be appreciated even more in the case of the torture and execution of Massola, which "took place almost entirely after [his] death [[...] justice did little more than deploy its magnificent theatre, the ritual praise of its force, on a corpse" (51). Thus, establishing the dissymmetry of power by way of having a spectacularly public and highly ritualized execution is so important that it takes place even when the condemned is already dead.

Therefore, at least initially, it is reasonable to hold that the classical view is not without support: from a Foucauldian perspective, we can say that Don Juan's public execution is carried out in spectacular and public fashion because the main purpose of justice during the period (according to Foucault) is to establish the dissymmetry of power between the judge and the condemned.

Furthermore, we need to take into account that Baroque justice is a very personal affair. The one holding the power is the king. Crimes are considered personal offences against the monarch; therefore, ultimately, the one carrying out the sentence is the king. The personal character of justice is made clear by Foucault:

> He [the king] must remain master, he alone could wash away the offences committed on his person; although it is true that he delegated to the courts the task of exercising his power to dispense justice, he had not transferred it; he retained it in its entirety and he could suspend the sentence or increase it at will.
>
> [...] It was a logical inscribed system of punishment, in which the sovereign, directly or indirectly, decided and carried out punishment, in so far as it was he who, through the law, had been injured by the crime. (53)

The same holds in the play but at the spiritual level: Don Juan has committed a sin against God; he has dared to challenge *the power of God*.[4] Throughout the play he has acted as if God's holy laws about matrimony did not matter; therefore, the one offended is God, and given the dissymmetrical and personal nature of Baroque justice, the one that must carry out the sentence is

---

4   As further support, Dionisia Tejera Llano also points out explicitly that Don Juan challenges the power of God.: "The two heroes [Dr. Faustus and Don Juan] defy the power of God, and in doing so, bring about their downfall" (245).

God, and not the king. In the same manner that, according to Foucault, the delegates of the court have the power to dispense justice, but the one who carries out the punishment is the king, in the play the delegated person to dispense justice is the Statue, but the one who carries out the punishment is God. The personal nature of justice within the play is explained by the Statue to Don Juan when his punishment is taking place: "Las maravillas de Dios / son, Don Juan, investigables, / y así quiere que tus culpas / a manos de un muerto pagues; / y así pagas de esta suerte / las doncellas que burlaste. / Esta es la justicia de Dios, / *quien tal hace que tal pague*" (2890-2897).[5]

To sum up, the relations of power during the Baroque as explained by Foucault give strong support to the classical view. In the play, the execution of don Juan exemplifies that Baroque divine justice is personal, spectacular, public and dissymmetrical. It is now time to look at the opposition.

As mentioned previously, the opposition is made of a collection of opinions that find the classical view problematic. It is important to keep in mind that the main claim of the opposition *is not* that divine justice does not have a function within the play (obviously, it does), but rather, the opposition holds, for some reason or another, that *divine justice is problematized, and even contravened, by other elements of the play.*

If we consider Foucault's views about the functioning of discourses, then what follows it that the opposition is *also* right. To understand why both the classical view and the opposition can be right at the same time (from a Foucauldian perspective, of course) we need to consider the role of contradictions within a discourse. Foucault wrote a chapter to explain that role in his book *The Archeology of Knowledge* (149-156). Summing up his view, Foucault holds that contradictions are a necessary aspect of any discourse, an integral part of it: a discourse, any discourse, will generate its own contradictions, and, as such, the contradictions are as much a part of the discourse as the parts that cohere. We can therefore say that the opposition is right because, on the one hand, divine justice in the play is regulated by the power relations of the Baroque, but, at the same time, the power relations that are regulated in that way *necessarily* create contradictions, or problems, which are pointed out by the opposition.

---

5   Given the obvious connection between the notion of God and the relations of power during the Baroque, the fact that Foucault does not consider that connection is very surprising, to say the least. Keeping in mind that Foucault is silent about the power of God during the Baroque, in this paper I extrapolate, arguing that what applies to the king applies, analogously, to God.

The aim of a Foucauldian analysis is not to make the contradictions disappear. Post-Modernism in general is suspicious of coherent grand-narratives; deconstruction, a sub-set of post-modernism, is a manner of reading that brings the contradictions to the forefront. Foucault is not an exception to this strong post-modern trend. In *The Archeology of Knowledge*, in the abovementioned chapter, Foucault makes clear that the task of the archeologist is to *describe* the function of the contradictions (and not to make them disappear): "The task of archeology, therefore, is not to get rid of those contradictions, but rather, to describe them as an essential aspect of the discourse. For archaeological analysis, contradictions are neither appearances to be overcome, nor secret principles to be uncovered. They are objects to be described for themselves, without any attempt being made to discover from what point of view they can be dissipated" (151).

We must therefore avoid getting rid of the contradictions that the opposing view has identified. A more productive endeavor is to describe the function they serve. This paper will consider three contradictions advanced by the critics.

Barbara Simerka's view in her 1997 article is that during the Baroque skepticism was a strong shaping force. It was a popular philosophy with the power to mold the minds of at least some readers. A skeptical reader will naturally be inclined to exercise an attitude of doubt, and consequently, for the skeptical reader, the spectacular, miraculous and supernatural execution of Don Juan, is to be doubted. Thus, the skeptic will put into question the functioning of baroque divine justice. For example, she writes: "For the already skeptical viewer, it could not have been difficult to find affirmation of heterodox convictions in these self-conscious, parodic representations of human contact with the afterlife" (63).

Simerka is right: it is a historical fact that skepticism was very popular during the period; therefore, divine justice as represented in the play is *a problem* for the skeptical mind. This is a contradiction, and it is important to realize that it cannot be resolved during the Baroque, precisely because it is created by the discourse of the Baroque: on the one hand, the discourse of that period shows divine justice as personal, public and spectacular, and on the other, the skeptic of the Baroque necessarily doubts that divine justice has those attributes.[6]

---

6   Barbara A. Simerka offers a similar objection in a second article ("Eros and Atheism: Providential Ideology in the Don Juan Plays by Tirso de Molina and Thomas Shadwell" (2002, p. 220- 233). The main difference is that in the version

Judith H. Arias identifies the following contradiction in the play:

the most disturbing paradox of the resolution [of the play] is the forth-right association between the sacred and violence [...]. The commander's role as a messenger of God openly links the issue of divine justice with revenge, deceit, and murder: the statue tricks Don Juan into taking his hand, ignores his plea for divine absolution and the chance for a final confession, kills the unsuspecting victim, and imputes his murderous act to divine injunction. (369)

Judith H. Arias resolves this paradox denying that divine justice is a true example of divine justice. According to her, divine justice cannot have the attributes of "revenge, deceit and murder" and, consequently, the type of justice present in the play must be of another kind: "We must, accordingly, question the notion that the statue is a messenger of God, as he claims, and suspect instead that he represents the community [to obtain the needed sacrifice to restore social order] [...] the vilified statue, as Tirso presents him, is vengeance" (371).[7]

From a Foucauldian perspective, Arias's argument and evidence lead to different conclusions. If we accept that Baroque divine justice is personal, dissymmetrical, ritualized, spectacular and public, then it follows that it can also be, depending on the crime, murderous and vengeful, as well as deceitful. For example, in the case of Damiens the regicide, we saw that he suffered extreme torture that lead to murder, so that the king could take personal vengeance on the affront to his power, and also that the ritual of his execution is deceitful because Damiens's appeals to God's mercy are consistently ignored. The analogous applies to the implementation of divine justice in the case of Don Juan. God, in the play, commits murder because he does kill a man by way of torture, he does so as an act of vengeance to demonstrate that *all* the power resides with him, and finally, we can say that God has been deceitful

---

quoted in the main body the objection is more focused on the Baroque skeptical attitude, and in the second version skepticism shares the stage with eros and atheism.

7   Several critics have observed that Don Juan is a social rebel. For example, following A. A. Parker, Alfred Rodríguez and Charles M. Burton conclude in their article that "so consistent is the social (as differentiated from the ethico-theological) defiance in *El Burlador de Sevilla*, [...] that it is difficult not to conclude that the playwright consciously considered its projection a major finality of his master piece" (52) However, unlike, Judith H. Arias, Alfred Rodríguez and Charles M. Burton do not make an explicit connection with divine justice.

because, indeed, the pleas of Don Juan are ignored by God, and also because Don Gonzalo does tell Don Juan that he should not fear taking his hand, the hand that will burn Don Juan and take him to hell. Instead of trying to resolve the contradiction, as Arias has done, in this investigation we must accept the contradiction as a natural part of the discourse: on the one hand, God is supposed to be merciful and truthful (i.e., benevolent) but, on the other, the notion of divine justice during the period allows for the literary creation of a vengeful, murderous and even deceitful God. He is therefore contradictory because God must serve two functions that oppose each other: to be just in the manner demanded by the power relations of the Baroque, and to be benevolent, as demanded by Christian doctrine of the same period.

Another objection advanced by the opposition begins by pointing out that the justice of the king is, at best, ineffective, and at worst, harmful. The defects of the king's justice make us see the defects of divine justice by way of analogy. Therefore, the overall conclusion is that divine justice is as bad as the justice of the king. For example, Alberto Prieto-Calixto remarks first that the justice of the king is corrupt: "Conviene señalar que el rey que el dramaturgo nos presenta en el drama, como varios estudiosos han señalado, no es sino un personaje arbitrario, inoperante e injusto, máximo representante de una sociedad corrupta" (784), and then, after arguing that the behavior of the statue is morally questionable , he concludes that "la supuesta justicia divina, máximo órgano sancionador, parece no ser más que un remedo, una copia desvirtuada de la a su vez contradictoria y nada fiable justicia terrenal, de la que el rey de Castilla es exponente" (786).

Alberto Prieto-Calixto does not try to get rid of the contradiction that he has uncovered on the text. On the contrary, he actually embraces it as a necessary expression of Baroque society:

> Como ya he mencionado varias veces a lo largo de este estudio, la ambigüedad presente en las escenas finales del drama, responde, como parte integrante del mismo, a una función específica [...]. Estudios de reconocidos historiadores especialistas en el periodo, como John Elliot, Fernand Braudel o Bartolomé Benassar, coinciden en señalar las contradicciones, complejidades, problemas y crisis sociales que jalonan este periodo. (787)

Given all of the above, the function of the myth of Don Juan during this period is best described by accepting the classical view and the opposition at

the same time.[8] That myth offers a clear example of divine justice. The punishment that Don Juan receives is not only what he deserves, but it is also
carried out in the correct manner, and by the right being (God). However,
precisely because he deserves it and the punishment is carried according to
the ritual, the end of the play also uncovers some of the contradictions created by Baroque divine justice. Those contradictions cannot be resolved during the Baroque because the discourse of that period is what created them in
the first place; they will be solved later in history, with the Enlightenment
and the Romantic period.[9]

THE MYTH OF DON JUAN DURING THE ROMANTIC PERIOD
According to Foucault in *The Archeology of Knowledge,* one of the most important functions of contradictions is to change the discourse through time,
a change that results in the historical process: "contradiction is always anteri-
or to the discourse, and because it can never therefore entirely escape it, that
discourse changes, undergoes transformation, and escapes of itself from its

---

8   Américo Castro advances an objection against the classical view that
is not considered in here. His objection is similar to Alberto Prieto-Calixto's and
Judith Arias's in that all three view the actions of the statue (and hence God) as
morally questionable. Thus, Castro writes: "el pétreo Gonzalo se conduce aquí con
bastante incorrección. [...] La Estatua en cambio se queda muy por bajo de lo que
esperaríamos de un agente de la divinidad" (96). Castro's versión of the objection has
not been considered here because his emphsasis is not the notion of divine justice
per se (or justice, for that matter), but rather a discussion of Baroque aesthetics: "la
forma artística [con el comportamiento de la Estatua] se lanza a un vuelo frenético,
pensando el autor más en maravillas que en otra cosa" (97).
9   There are other Foucauldian analyses of Tirso's play that must be mentioned
here. It should be noted that, in all cases, the focus of the mentioned critics is not
divine justice as it applies to the myth of Don Juan, but rather some other aspect
of the play. Catherine Connor Swietlickj explains from a Foucauldian approach
the meaning of the word "trickster" and its importance in the play (see especially
83, 85 and 100); James F. Burke combines the tradition of carnival with Foucault's
ideas on knowledge by way of resemblance and analogy, as explained in his book
The Order of Things, to explain "Don Juan and the Evolution of the Self "; Judith
H. Arias, in her 1995 article, argues that Don Juan represents pure human evil and
extreme domination, and her approach relies in part on Foucault's philosophy (see
for example 1112); Ann Davies writes an article grounded on Foucault's approach to
power to explain the way in which the women in the play try "to attain their own
desires and survive a hostile environment" (159); finally, Robert Bayliss relies on the
ideas of Foucault about discourses to explain the notion of Decorum in Tirso's play,
as well as Molière (see for example 193 and 195).

own continuity. Contradiction, then, functions throughout discourse, as the principle of its historicity" (158). Therefore, in many ways the Enlightenment can be seen as the end-product of trying to resolve the contradictions of the Baroque, and the Romantic period as the attempt to resolve the contradictions created during the Enlightenment. This process ought to be taken into account to understand the transformation of the myth of Don Juan (from a Foucauldian perspective). The process is explained in detail by Foucault in his book *Discipline and Punish*.

First, many penal codes were introduced around the same period in various European countries and the United States:

> In Europe and the United States, the entire economy of punishment was redistributed. It was a time for great 'scandals' for traditional [Baroque] justice, a time for innumerable projects for reform. It saw a new theory of law and crime, a new moral or political justification of the right to punish; old laws were abolished, old customs died out. 'Modern' codes were planned or drawn up: Russia, 1769; Prussia, 1780; Pennsylvania and Tuscany, 1786; Austria, 1788; France 1791, Year IV, 1808 and 1810. It was a new age for penal justice. (7)

Second, the "reforms" of the new Enlightened penal codes were attempts to resolve the "scandals" of the previous judicial system:

> 'Let penalties be regulated and proportioned to the offences, let the death sentence be passed only on those convicted of murder, and let the tortures that revolt humanity be abolished.' Thus, in 1789, the chancellery summed up the general position of the petitions addressed to the authorities concerning tortures and executions. [...]. Protest against public executions proliferated [...]. Another form of punishment was needed: the physical confrontation between the sovereign and the condemned man must end. (73)

Given that God is supposed to be benevolent and perfectly just by definition, what applies to the sovereign applies even more to God; therefore, God's punishment of Don Juan as envisioned by minds of the baroque becomes unacceptable during this new era (a "scandal" in need of "reform"). To put it in another way, the reforms of the Enlightenment were attempts to solve the contradictions of Baroque justice, which affects notions regarding divine justice as well.

Third, during the Enlightenment there is still a strong interest in maintaining the dissymmetry of power between the judges and the condemned. However, during the Enlightenment that dissymmetry was obtained using different means. Foucault explains the shift as follows:

> In effect, the offence opposes an individual to the entire social body; in order to punish him, society has the right to oppose him in its entirety. It is an unequal struggle; on one side are all the forces, all the power, all the rights. And this is how it should be, since the defence of each individual is involved. Thus a formidable right to punish is established, since the offender becomes the common enemy. Indeed, he is worse than the enemy, for it is from within society that delivers his blows—he is nothing less than a traitor, a 'monster'. (90)

Thus, the personal nature of Baroque justice is substituted by the impersonal justice of the law. All the power now resides in this abstract code of regulations. The dissymmetry of power becomes in many ways the opposite of what it was during the Baroque. More precisely, the function of the public and spectacular executions during the Baroque was to demonstrate that all the power resided with the ruler (or God), but because the new system of justice replaces the power of the ruler with the power of the law, then there is no longer a need of public, spectacular executions. In other words, given that the law represents *all*, but it is, in itself, *no-one*, the punishment becomes impersonal because it is carried by *no*-one in particular (it is carried by *the law*). Thus, Foucault writes: "The right to punish has been shifted from the vengeance of the sovereign to the defense of society [by the law]" (90).

Finally (fourth), Baroque justice was always a personal affair between the judge and the accused, but given that the law becomes this impersonal force that acts in the defense of all (and therefore of no-one in particular), this element of justice is abandoned as well. If, during the Baroque, the body of the condemned had to be publicly punished by way of torture to re-assert the power of the king, under this new system the body of the condemned becomes a burden for society to manage and take care of:

> The punishment-body relations is not the same as it was in the torture during public executions. The body now serves as an instrument or intermediary: if one intervenes upon it to imprison it, or to make it work, it is in order to deprive the individual of a liberty that is regarded as a right and as property. [...] As a result of this new restraint, a whole army

of technicians took over [to take care of the imprisoned body]: warders, doctors, chaplains, psychiatrists, educationalists. (11)

All the elements mentioned above creates a system of punishment and control that, in my opinion, has a terrifying consequence: from the perspective of justice, individual humans become *irrelevant*. What is important under this impersonal system is not *a person*, but the betterment of society at large as dictated by a set of universal, abstract, laws. In this new system, the bodies of people are managed, fed and clothed because the goal of the punishment is no longer to inflict torture on the body, but rather to cause great pain *in the mind*: "the power to punish [...] provoke a shift in the point of application [...]: it is no longer the body, with the ritual play to excessive pains [...]; it is the mind or rather a play of representations and signs circulating discreetly by and evidently in the minds of all. It is no longer the body [that is being punished], but the soul" (101).

From a Foucauldian perspective, therefore, the contradiction that defines the Romantic period is the tension created between the basic, fundamental need of individual humans to be recognized as such, and a system that is all-powerful, completely impersonal, and that operates for the betterment of society at large. In other words, keeping in mind the regulation of the power relations during the period, Romanticism can be defined as a *rebellion* of individual selves against a system that maintains an absolute dissymmetry of power by way of universal, impersonal means: the more impersonal the system of power becomes, the more rebellious the individual selves that are affected by that crushing, impersonal power. Don Félix can therefore be seen as a great romantic hero because he will fight the impersonal power that is in operation throughout the entirety of the poem with all his might, never giving up. What is truly admirable in Don Félix is that he never loses a sense of the self, of who he is, even though he is being managed at all times by an impersonal, all-mighty force. To see this in more detail we may consider the poem from two perspectives: first, the way in which Don Félix understands the power in control of the events, and second, the reactions and attitudes that Don Félix has against that impersonal power.

The poem begins with a duel (see 42-45). Later we learn that Don Félix died in this duel because he sees his own body as it is taken to the cemetery (see 1004- 1007); therefore, most of the events happen when Don Félix is already dead. The body of Don Félix must be managed, that is, it must be placed in its proper resting place. To obtain that result an emissary is sent: the woman dressed in white. She will be his guide, throughout almost the entire poem, until Don Félix reaches his proper resting place (see 1594-1601). From the perspective of the accused, the implementation of justice is completely impersonal. More specifically, even though it is true that the poem identifies God as the being dictating the events, what is relevant in this management of justice is that Don Félix *does not know who or what that power is*. From Félix's perspective, it could be God, but it could also be the Devil. This is an important theme in the poem. For example, he asks the woman in white the following question when he is in the catacomb, and he receives no answer: "siquier de parte de Dios, / siquier de parte del diablo, ¿quién nos trajo aquí a los dos?" (1370-1372); furthermore, he does not even know who his guide is for most of the poem, since he also asks her "Decidme en fin ¿Quién sois vos?" (1373) and once more, there is no answer; finally, when Don Diego appears dead towards the end of the poem, Don Félix asks him the following question, and again there is no answer: "mas antes decidme si Dios o el demonio / me trajo a este sitio, que quisiera ver al uno o al otro" (1543-1544). In short, all Don Félix knows is this: "Que un poder aquí supremo / invisible se ha mezclado" (1380-1381).

At the same time, in this system of justice there is no execution of the condemned. As mentioned above, Don Félix died on a duel, and throughout the poem it appears that the main concern of the impersonal power dictating the events is the proper management of Don Félix's body: he is led so that he can rest, at the end of the poem, with his wife for eternity. In the same way that the body of a prisoner is send to a prison cell to carry out his or her sentence, Don Juan is sent to his tomb because that is where his body belongs.

Furthermore, in this impersonal system of justice the goal is no longer to cause pain to the body of Don Félix, but, rather, to cause great pain *in his mind*. Thus, the pain is psychological rather than physical. This is seen, for example, when Don Juan touches the hand of the woman in white by the end of the poem, only to feel a horrible sensation: "al fiero Montemar tendió una mano, / y era su tacto de cripsante hielo, / y resistirlo audaz intentó en vano: / [...] / histérica y horrible sensación" (1503-1507). It is also seen when we keep in mind that throughout the poem it does not appear that Don Félix is in any kind of physical pain (he does not even know that he died: that is how little physical pain there is).

Finally, from the perspective of the impersonal power Don Félix is seen as a monster, as an enemy of society that needs to be stopped. This is made clear at the beginning of the poem when we read about Don Félix's qualities: "alma fiera e insolente / irreligioso y valiente / altanero y reñidor: siempre el insulto en los ojos, / en los labios la ironía, / nada teme y todo fía / de su espada y su valor" (101-108). In addition, he is a gambler and a womanizer. The management of Don Félix's body, the pain inflicted in his mind, can therefore be seen as a response of society to defend itself against this monster. The fact that the poem ends with Don Félix's body resting in its proper place, according to the standards of society, gives further support.

In short, according to this Foucauldian analysis the first part of the contradictory state of the Romantic Condition appears to be present in the poem: Justice, from the perspective of Don Félix, is represented as the management of his body by an impersonal system that causes great psychological pain. Furthermore, there is no public execution and there is no physical torture.[10]

The response of Don Félix to this all-powerful impersonal force is the other side of the Romantic contradiction. First, it is true that according to the mores of society Don Félix is a monster, and as such society has the duty to defend itself; but is it is equally true that Don Félix is admirable according to the poem. The contrast is clear because his positive qualities are introduced in the same part of the poem where he is described as a monster: Therefore, in addition to a monster, "por su vida y buen talante, / al atrevido estudiante / le señalan entre mil;" (124-127); furthermore, he possesses "caballeresca apostura, / agilidad y bravura" (133-134) so that "hasta en sus crímenes mismos, en su impiedad y altiveza, / pone un sello de grandeza" (136-137).

We have seen above that the force guiding his voyage is impersonal from the perspective of Don Félix, but, at the same time, it is equally true that the reason why Don Félix embarks in his journey is very personal *to him*.

---

10   As further support, the following critics also see a strong connection between the Romantic Condition and judicial systems of the period: Ana Vian explain the poem in terms of the power relations created by the law: "Por lo tanto la libertad (o rebelión) de Don Félix es una libertad metafórica, testimonial, pues es, al mismo tiempo, la marca de su opresion [...]. Los poderes supremos—Dios y el Diablo—están al lado de la LEY" (147); Abraham Martín-Maestro uses notions about the law in order to conclude that "frente a la Ley el valor del yo se ejerce como rebelión" (192); Elizabeth Scarlett first identifies Catholicism as the legislator and legitimizer of power in the poem (see 32) which created a system of law in 1812 (see 31). This in turn is then combined with notions of capitalism (see 42-3) in order to conclude at the end of the essay that "while the habitus generates structures that give compelling and lasting form to the poem, as its rituals and laws shape life in society, it ultimately kills freedom" (43). James D. Wilson expresses the romantic condition as a rebellion against ethical universal laws created during the late Enlightenment, specifically by Kant (see 246).

He follows the woman in white, no matter where, because he chooses to do so, no matter what. This is made very clear when the woman in white actually warns him that following her is dangerous, and Don Félix ignores the warning (see 915-923). Don Félix continues following her because he seeks immediate pleasure: "Basta de sermón / [...], y háblame de amores, que es más dulce hablar / [...] la vida es la vida: cuando ella acaba, / acaba con ella también el placer" (926-933).

We have seen above that the impersonal force managing the events dictates that don Félix and the woman in white should rest together as husband and wife, because that is the proper place for his body for eternity. But at the same time, that event happens because Don Félix agrees to it, and he agrees not because it is the right thing to do (according to the mores of society) but because he thinks that marrying a dead woman is less boring than marrying a live one: "Por mujer la tomo, porque es cosa cierta, / y espero no salga fallido mi plan, / que en caso tan raro y mi esposa muerta, / tanto como viva no me cansará" (1538-1540).

We have also seen that in this system of justice the impersonal force maintains power by causing psychological pain, but at the same time Don Félix resists that pain at every turn. It is not that he does not feel that pain, but rather, that he is able to control it and continues in the journey he has chosen for himself. Thus, for example, he feels horror when he touches the hand of the woman in white, but then he controls that horror and does what he is determined to do: "y a su despecho y maldiciendo al cielo, / de ella apartó su mano Montemar, / y temerario alzándola su velo, / tirando de él la descubrió la faz" (1510-1504).

To understand Don Félix's situation, it may be useful to take into account Foucault's discussion of the panopticon in *Discipline and Punish*. The panopticon is a building conceived by Jeremy Bentham, one of the founders of utilitarianism. The building is designed so that one person can control the movements of everybody else in the building, at all times. "In the peripheric ring [of the building], one is totally seen, without ever seeing [the power in control]; in the central tower, one sees everything, without ever being seen" (202). Thus, all the power resides with the individual who happens to be in the central tower; furthermore, it does not matter who that person is, since it could be anyone: "there is a machinery that assures dissymmetry [of power], disequilibrium, difference. Consequently, it does not matter who exercises power. Any individual, taken almost at random, can operate the machine" (202). The panopticon is an all-powerful *impersonal* arrangement, since the person in the tower is never seen, and also because it could be anyone. The panopticon captures the situation in which Don Félix happens to find himself in, since the being dictating the events is not only all powerful, but also, as Don Félix says, that power is "invisible" as well. However, Don Félix is not your typical inmate in the panopticon: he is a Romantic hero, and consequently, his will to be who he chooses to be will be unbreakable. We can therefore say that the impersonal power managing Don Félix's journey has met its match in Don Félix, because he is equally powerful at a personal level. On the one hand, the unknown power manages the body of Don Félix at every turn, causing him great psychological pain, but on the other hand, Don Félix is also powerful, not only because he always chooses his own path, but also because he continues being who he has chosen to be *despite of the pain* inflicted on him.[11]

CONCLUSION

The evolution of the myth of don Juan as captured by the two texts discussed above may be explained by taking into account the relations of power from a Foucauldian perspective. Given the notions of justice and divine justice during the Baroque, we discover that Don Juan's punishment is not only fitting, but also that it gives rise to a number of contradictions, or problems, which are endemic to the Baroque. In this relation it is very clear that the one with

---

11   Of course, many other critics have explained the Romantic Condition in the context of this poem in different ways. The analysis in the main body should not be taken to imply the absurdity that a Foucauldian approach as it applies to justice is the only way to explain that condition. María-Paz Yáñez explains it in terms of Satanism and society: "El yo romántico, centro del universo, hostil a la sociedad [...] tiene que ser necesariamente soberbio, y sabido es que la soberbia encarna en la tradición cristiana el ángel caído" (124); Carlos Feal explains it as a confrontation with God: "El héroe esproncediano necesita enfrentarse con Dios para exponer su rechazo del mundo en que vive" (28); Eric A. Blackall sees it as a negation of idealism: "a malicious exultation in his own destructive power and cynical defiance of all idealism" (77); Zachary R. Ludington sees don Félix's death as a true expression of romanticism because he dies as a true human being: "Muere como hombre, torturado, loco, poco loable, quizá; pero muere como un individuo y no un maniquí" (482); Richard A. Cardwell sees it as a quest for an absolute: "[Don Félix is] the stature for the modern existentialist hero in search of an absolute in an absurd universe" (39-40); Victoria León Varela's perspective is to take into account *desengaño*: "Cada personaje obedece a un destino común e ineludible, el de perseguir un deseo inalcanzable, una ilusión quimérica que los conduce [...] al desengaño" (1019); more briefly, José C. Paulino sees the voyage undertaken by Don Félix as central (see 66-67); Russell P. Sebold sees Don Félix as the anti-Christ (see 454, 456 and 464).

all the power is God, despite of all the contradictions created by that notion of power. Then, due to the influence of the Enlightened codes of justice, the problems with justice associated with the Baroque disappeared, becoming irrelevant. But this in turn created the central contradiction that defined the Romantic condition: the rebellion of the self against an impersonal, all-powerful, managerial, judicial system. Don Félix captures the romantic condition with incredible precision: on the one hand, there is no question that an impersonal power is dictating the events of the poem in its entirety, but, at the same time, there is no doubt that Don Félix resists with all his might. Thus, it is hard to decide which of the two is more powerful: the force managing Don Félix body and mind, or the rebellious spirit of the hero who refuses to give up.

Works cited

Allain, Mathe. "'El Burlador Burlado': Tirso de Molina's *Don Juan.*" *Language Quarterly* 27 (1966): 174-184.

Arias, H. Judith. "Don Juan, Cupid, the Devil." *Hispania: A Journal Devoted to the Teaching of Spanish and Portuguese* 75.5 (1995): 1107-1115.

———— "Doubles in Hell: 'El burlador de Sevilla y convidado de piedra.'" *Hispanic Review* 58.3 (1990): 361-377.

Bandur, Markus; Janés, Alfonsina (translator). "De *El Burlador de Sevilla* a *Don Giovanni*: Presentación de la mentira y la seducción en el teatro, la ópera y la ópera filmada." *Studi Ispanici* 31 (2006): 89-102.

Bayliss, Robert. "Serving Don Juan: Decorum in Tirso de Molina and Molière." *Comparative Drama* 40.2 (2006): 191-215.

Blackall, A. Eric. "Don Juan and Faust." *Seminar: A Journal of Germanic Studies* 14 (1978): 71-83.

Brown, L. Sandra. "Lucifer and El burlador de Sevilla." *Bulletin of the Comediantes* 26 (1974): 63-64.

Burke, James F. "*Don Juan* and the Evolution of the Self." In *"Never Ending Adventure": Studies in Medieval and Early Modern Spanish Literature in Honor of Peter N. Dunn.* Edited by Edward Friedman and Harlan Sturm H. Edward. Newark: Juan de la Cuesta Hispanic Monographs, 2002. pp. 309-324.

Canfield, J. Douglas. "The Classical Treatment of *Don Juan* in Tirso, Molière, and Mozart: What Cultural Work Does It Perform?" *Comparative Drama* 31.1 (1997): 42-64.

Cardwell, Richard A. "Introduction." José de Espronceda. *The Student of Salamanca/El estudiante de Salamanca*. Trad. C. K. Davies. Warminster (England): Aris & Phillips, 1991. 1-40.

Castro, Américo. "El *Don Juan* de Tirso y el de Molière como personajes barrocos." In *Hommage à Ernest Martinenche: Etudes Hispaniques et Amèricaines*. Paris, 1939. pp. 93-111.

Clarke, Dorothy Clothelle. "Tirso's *Don Juan* and Juan Ruiz's *Don Amor*." *Folio: Essays on Foreign Languages and Literatures* 12 (1980): 12-29.

Connor Swietlicki, Catherine. "*Don Juan*: Cultural Trickster in the *Burlador* Text." In *New Historicism and de Comedia: Poetics, Politics and Praxis*. Edited by José A. Madrigal. Boudler: Society of Spanish and Spanish-American Studies, U of Colorado, 1997. pp. 83-109.

Cruz, Andreas Flurschütz da. "El personaje del *Don Juan* y su desenvolvimiento desde Tirso de Molina 1630 a José Zorrilla 1844." *Espéculo: Revista de Estudios Literarios* 45 (2010): no pag.

Dadson, J. Trevor. "Don Juan and Some Myths of the Spanish Golden Age." *Hispanic Research Journal: Iberian and Latin American Studies* 9.2 (2008): 107-124.

Davies, Ann. "Don Juan and Foucauldian Sexual Discourse: Changing Attitudes to Female Sexuality." *European Studies: A Journal of European Culture, History, and Politics* 17 (2001): 159-170.

Espronceda, José de. *El estudiante de Salamanca*. Ed. Benito Varela Jácome. ed. Madrid: Cátedra, 2001.

Feal, Carlos. "El oscuro sujeto del deseo romántico: De Espronceda a Rosalía." *Revista Hispánica Moderna* 47.1 (1994): 15-29.

Fernández-Turienzo, Francisco. "El Convidado de Piedra: Don Juan pierde el juego." *Hispanic Review* 45.1 (1977): 43-60.

Foucault, Michel. *The Archeology of Knowledge and The Discourse on Language*. Trans. A. M. Sheridan Smith. New York: Pantheon Books, 1972.

———. *The Order of Things: An Archeology of the Human Sciences*. Trans. Alan. Sheridan. New York: Vintage Press, 1973.

———. *Discipline and Punish: The Birth of the Prison*. Trans. Alan Sheridan. New York: Vintage Books, 1979.

———. "What is an Author?" In *Textual Strategies: Perspectives on Post-Structuralist Criticism*. Ed. Josué V. Harari. Ithaca: Cornell U Press, 1979, pp.141-160.

García Garrosa, María Jesús. "No hay plazo que no se cumpla ni deduda que no se pague, y convidado de piedra: La Evolución de un mito de Tirso a

Zorrilla." *Castilla: Boletín del Departamento de Literatura Española* 9-10 (1985): 45-64.

Gómez-Moriana, Antonio. "Discourse Pregmatics and Reciprocity of Perspective: Sobre las Promesas de Don Juan y el desenlace del *Burlador*." *Gestos: Teoría y Práctica del Teatro Hispanico* 4.7 (1989): 33-46.

Gregg, C. Karl. "Del Poyo's Judas and Tirso's Don Juan." *Symposium* 29 (1975): 345-360.

Howe, Elizabeth Teresa. "Hell or Heaven? Providence and *Don Juan*." *Renascence: Essays on Values in Literature* 37.5 (1985) 212-219.

Lazzaro-Weis, Carol. "Parody and Farce in the *Don Juan* Myth in the Eighteenth Century." *Eighteenth-Century Life* 8.3 (1983) 35-48.

León Varela, Victoria. "*El Estudiante de Salamanca* y el *Canto a Teresa*: La Sehnsucht titánica de Espronceda." *Revista de Estudios Extremeños* 59.3 (2003): 1017-106.

Lloyd, M. Paul. "Contribución al estudio de tema de Don Juan and las comedias de Tirso de Molina." In *Homenaje a William L. Fichter: Estudios sobre el teatro antiguo hispánico y otros ensayos*. Edited by David A. Kossoff, David A. Amor and José Vásquez. Madrid: Castalia, 1971. pp. 447-451.

Ludington, R. Zachary. "El sueño siniestro de don Félix de Montemar." *RILCE: Revista de Filología Hispánica* 28.2 (2012): 469-491.

Lundelius, Ruth. "Tirso's View of Women in *El Burlador de Sevilla*." *Bulletin of the Comediantes* 27 (1975): 5-14.

Martín-Maestro, Abraham. "Lectura conjunta de *El Estudiante de Salamanca* de José de Espronceda: análisis narrativo." In *Organizaciones textuales (textos hispánicos): Actas del III Simposio del Séminaire d'Edudes Littéraires del'Universitè de Tolouse-Le Mirail (Tolouse, mayo de 1980)*. U de Toulouse-Le Mirail, U Computense de Madrid, 1981. pp. 159-166.

Mayer Ch. Peggy von. "El Erotismo en *Don Juan*." *Kañina: Revista de Artes y Letras de la Universidad de Costa Rica* 16.1 (1992): 119-124.

McDowell, E. Robert. "Tirso, Byron and the *Don Juan* Tradition." *Arlington Quarterly* 1.1 (1967): 52-68.

Navarro, Rosa. "La mirada de Tisbea: El nacimiento de Don Juan Tenorio." In *Hombres escritos por mujeres*. Edited by Angels Carabí and Marta Segarra. Barcelona: Icaria, 2003. pp. 11-30.

Oliveira, Ester Abreu Vieira de. "El mito y su desmitificación: Temas recurrentes de *Don Juan* Tenorio a Juanito Ventolera." *Anuario Brasileño de Estudios Hispánicos* 11 (2001): 175-188.

Paulino, C. José. "La aventura interior de don Félix de Montemar." *Revista de Literatura* 44.48 (1982): 57-67.

Prieto-Calixto, Alberto. "La función de la ambigüedad en los convites y el castigo de Don Juan en *El burlador de Sevilla y convidado de piedra*." *RLA: Romance Languages Annual* 10.2 (1998): 783-788.

Quance, Roberta. "Don Juan's Last Supper." In *Betwixt-and-Between: Essays in Liminal Geography*. Edited by Philip C. Sutton. Madrid: Gateway, 2002. 101-112.

Rodríguez, Alfred; Burton, M. Charles. "Algo más sobre el satanismo del *Don Juan* de Tirso." *Neophilologus* 76.2 (1992): 234-236.

Saad, Youssef. "The *Don Juan* of Classical Arabia." *Comparative Literature Studies* 13 (1976): 304-314.

Scarlett, Elizabeth. "The Metaphysics of Espronceda's Romanticism in *El Estudiante de Salamanca*." *Bulletin of Hispanic Studies* 93.1 (2016): 29-44.

Sebold, P. Russell. "El infernal arcano de Félix de Montemar." *Hispanic Review* 46.4 (1978): 447-464.

Simerka, Barbara. "Early Modern Skepticism and Unbelief and the Demystification of Providential Ideology in *El Burlador de Sevilla*." *Gestos: Teoría y Práctica del Teatro Hispánico* 12.23 (1997): 39-66.

———."Eros and Atheism: Providential Ideology in the Don Juan Plays by Tirso de Molina and Thomas Shadwell." In *Echoes and Inscriptions: Comparative Approaches to Early Modern Spanish Literatures*. Edited by Barbara Simerka and Christopher Weimer B. Lewisburg: Bucknell UP, 2002. pp. 220- 233.

Smoot, J. Jeanne. " 'Young Goodman Brown'—Puritan *Don Juan*: Faith and Hawthorne." *Postscript* 1 (1983): 42-48.

Tejera Llano, Dionisia. "Dr. Faustus and Don Juan, Two Baroque Heroes." *Sederi: Journal of the Spanish Society for English Renaissance Studies* 4 (1993): 243-250.

Tirso, Molina de. *El burlador de Sevilla*. Ed. Alfredo Rodríguez López-Vázquez. Madrid: Cátedra, 2000.

Vian, Ana. "Lectura conjunta de *El Estudiante de Salamanca* de José de Espronceda: Los contenidos." In *Organizaciones textuales (textos hispánicos): Actas del III Simposio del Séminaire d'Edudes Littéraires del'Université de Tolouse-Le Mirail (Tolouse, mayo de 1980)*. U de Toulouse-Le Mirail, U Computense de Madrid, 1981. pp. 137-147.

Wade, E. Gerald. "Hacia una comprensión del tema de Don Juan y *El burlador*." *Revista de Archivos, Bibliotecas y Museos* 77 (1974): 665-708.

Weinreb, Ruth Plaut. "In Defense of Don Juan: Deceit and Hypocrisy in Tirso de Molina, Molière, Mozart and G.B. Shaw." *Romantic Review* 74.4 (1983) 425-440.

Wilson, James D. "Tirso, Molière, and Byron: The Emergence of Don Juan as Romantic Hero." *South Central Bulletin* 32.4(1972): 246-248.

Yáñez, María-Paz. "El cambio de valorización del satanismo en la cosmovisión romántica: El estudiante de Salamanca de Espronceda." *Revista de lletres* 19 (1996): 116-126.

A Don Juan's Afterlife:
The Ethics and Aesthetics of (Failed) Seduction in Fernando Pessoa's *The Book of Disquiet*

FERNANDO BELEZA
Newcastle University

Some triumph in love, some triumph in politics, and some triumph in art. The first group has the advantage of storytelling, since one can be highly successful in love without there being public knowledge of what happened. Of course, on hearing one of these men recount his sexual marathons, we begin to have our doubts after about the seventh conquest. Those who are the lovers of aristocratic or well-known ladies (and it seems to be the case for nearly all of them) ravage so many countesses that a tally of their seductions would shatter the gravity and composure of even great-grandmothers of young women with titles.
- Fernando Pessoa, *The Book of Disquiet*.

If at first you don't succeed, failure may be your style.
- Quentin Crisp, *The Naked Civil Servant*.

Seduction is that which extracts meaning from discourse and detracts it from its truth. It would this be the opposite of the psychoanalytic distinction between manifest and latent discourse. For latent discourse diverts manifest discourse not *from* its truth but *towards* it and makes it say what did not wish to say. It uncovers determinations and deep-seated lack of determinations. It always suspects depth behind the rupture; always suspects meaning behind the bar. Manifest discourse has the status of a labored appearance, traversed by the emergence of meaning. Interpretation is that which, shattering appearances and the play of manifest discourse, will set meaning free by remaking connections with latent discourse.

In seduction, conversely, it is somehow the manifest discourse, the most "superficial" aspect of discourse, which acts upon the underlying prohibition (conscious or unconscious) in order to nullify it and to substitute for it the charms and traps of appearances.
- Jean Baudrillard, "On Seduction."

I N *O MITO DE Don Juan e o donjuanismo em Portugal* [The Myth of Don
Juan and Donjuanism in Portugal]—a short yet the most comprehensive study of the myth of Don Juan in Portuguese literature and culture
written to date—Urbano Tavares Rodrigues argues that with the exception of António Patrício's brilliant "D. João e a mascara" [Don Juan and the
Mask], published in 1924, the representations of Don Juan in Portuguese
literature occupy a rather marginal place and are often uninspired. Tavares
Rodrigues's explanation for this is eloquent: "D. Juan autêntico repugna à
sensibilidade portuguesa" [Portuguese sensibility loathes the authentic Don
Juan] (31). More precisely, according to Tavares Rodrigues, "uma disposição
natural para a brandura, para a circunspecção, para as relações de piedade
e ironia, conducentes à moderação, uma complexidade perturbadora [...]—
são obstáculos na alma nacional ao surto daquele donjuanismo" [a natural
disposition for gentleness, for circumspection, for relating with pity and
irony, which lead to moderation; a disrupting complexity (...)—all these are
obstacles within the national soul to the eruption of the spirit of donjua-
nism] (31). This does not mean, however, that there is not a Portuguese Don
Juan, for Tavares Rodrigues. In fact, he adds, "existe, todavia, uma forma de
donjuanismo português" [there is, nevertheless, a Portuguese form of don-
juanism] (31). It is precisely this Portuguese Don Juan that Tavares Rodrigues
tries to describe in his essay, often in a rather impressionist manner. According to the author, "a psique lusitana geralmente [...] desfigura, [...] atenua,
[...] adoça ou [...] sublima atlânticamente [...], essa figura originária e essen-
cialmente castelhana, ainda que universalmente assimilada" [the Lusitanian
psyche tends in general to disfigure, [...] attenuate, [...] sweeten or [...] subli-
mate atlantically [...] that character originally from and essentially Castilian,
even though universally assimilated] (44).

Tavares Rodrigues's argument may be considered as being too influenced
by a certain centuries-old desire in Portuguese culture to affirm in terms as
strong as possible its difference in relation to Spain, Spanish literature, art,
and culture. In order to essentialize Portuguese anti-donjuanism, the author
overlooks, for example, more critical representations of Don Juan in Spanish and other European cultures, while focusing mostly on Portuguese anti-
donjuanism, such as that of the poets of the second Romantic generation (e.
i. Guerra Junqueiro: "A morte de D. João" [1874].) It is beyond the scope of
this chapter to discuss Tavares Rodrigues's argument in depth and his choice
not to approach examples of Portuguese critical representation of donjuanismo alongside similar manifestations from abroad. However, I do not wish to
depart completely from his contribution. In fact he draws the contours of a

certain tradition of Portuguese representations of the Don Juan archetype—which he claims to be an exception in national culture—that will assist me in providing the background against which Fernando Pessoa's *The Book of Disquiet* proposes a modernist rethinking of donjuanism and the ethics and aesthetics of seduction. This tradition, according to Tavares Rodrigues, starts with Eça de Queirós's *Cousin Basílio*, to whose gender and sexual politics I will turn now briefly.

The critique of predatory masculinity and the destructive powers of donjuanesque seductive skills and sexuality emerged with relevance in late nineteenth century Portuguese literature, in tandem with broader social, cultural, and scientific concerns regarding the relationship between gender, sexuality, and the nation. As Tavares Rodrigues point out, Eça de Queirós' s *Cousin Basílio*, first published in 1878, is indeed the most paradigmatic case in this context. Basilio is a donjuanesque dandy, whose return to Portugal from Brazil marks the beginning of the end of Luisa and Jorge domestic harmony—a recently married, bourgeois couple. Eça's Don Juan is a quintessential embodiment of the destructive powers of donjuanesque seduction skills and deception as seen through a Realist/Naturalist lens with typical late nineteenth century social and national concerns with the future of the nation. Basilio's seduction of his cousin, Luisa, leads not only to adultery, blackmail, and chaos within the household (with the all-knowing maid making endless demands on a frightened Luisa), but even to Luisa's untimely death.

Joining forces with other disciplinary discourses that were shaping modern sexuality and gender identities, such as sexology (and later on psychoanalysis), Eça's representation of male uncontrolled, extra-marital desire and Basílio's seduction abilities expose in the most eloquent manner the social and national evils of Don Juan's seduction skills and deception, while locating donjuanesque masculinities within the realm of gender performances to be reformed with the contribution of the Realist/Naturalist novel. Along with Basilio, a significantly vast gallery of late nineteenth century male characters in Portuguese literature resemble Don Juan's archetype, with different degrees of proximity, but more often than not shaped by national concerns similar to Eça's. Yet, as we turn to the early twentieth century, particularly to the Modernist generation of Fernando Pessoa, Mario de Sá-Carneiro, and Almada Negreiros (to mention only a few), there seems to be an abrupt loss of interest in representing donjuanesque masculinities in Portuguese cultural production, at least as far as Tavares Rodrigues is concerned, who is almost completely silent about this particular period.

Portuguese Modernism, more precisely what became known as the *Orpheu* generation, represented a radical break with the politics of gender and sexuality that contributed to shape the Realist/Naturalist novel from the previous century. This became particularly clear as early as 1914, when Mário de Sá-Carneiro published *Lucio's Confession*, which provides the first taste of things to come regarding the queer politics of a significant portion of the literary production of Portuguese modernists, particularly of the *Orpheu* generation. This radical change in gender and sexual politics could be pointed out as the main cause for the loss of interest in the figure of the heterosexual trickster in the literary production of this generation. This would be, however, a rather simplistic and superficial conclusion that wouldn't have in consideration rather more complex articulations of donjuanismo, seduction, and desire in Modernism, as well as the importance of donjuanesque masculinities and subjectivities for literary and cultural analysis.

Questioning Tavares Rodrigues's reading of Portuguese anti-donjuanism and his reasons to neglect the *Orpheu* generation, in this chapter I will focus on what I will call the afterlife of Don Juan in Portuguese Modernism. More precisely, I will argue that, in fact, Don Juan's seduction skills, deception abilities, and game of appearances occupy a relevant place in Portuguese Modernism, particularly in the work of Fernando Pessoa. This incarnation of Don Juan is, however, less destructive when compared to late nineteenth century Realism/Naturalism. Pessoa, in particular, as I will be arguing in this chapter, displaces seduction, desire, and the donjuanesque game of appearances from the plot to the text itself. Contrarily to late nineteenth century critiques of the social dangers of Don Juan, this trend in Modernism provides an attack on the donjuanesque archetype that offers what I will be defining as an ethics and aesthetics of (failed) seduction. Moreover, by focusing my attention on Fernando Pessoa's *The Book of Disquiet*, I will propose that this process of relocating desire and seduction from the plot to the text and its materiality emerges as a relevant current in Modernism that has so far been neglected by scholars of early twentieth century literature.

Before I start, some words on the particularities of *The Book of Disquiet* (largely a posthumous work) are in order. To put it very briefly, *The Book of Disquiet* was a title Fernando Pessoa (1888-1935) gave to significantly different literary projects, between 1913 and 1935. The first project, which he initiated in 1913, was signed under his own name. This early project, with its obvious decadent and aestheticist influences, was soon replaced by Vicente Guedes's *The Book of Disquiet*. The emergence of Guedes as the fictional author of the book contributed to transform the project considerably, having then emerged as a personal diary. Pessoa, however, abandons Guedes's *The Book of Disquiet* in the early 1920s and the same title will reemerge only in late 1928. In 1928, *The Book of Disquiet* became an "autobiography without facts" (*Disquiet* 9) [uma autobiografia sem factos], written by Bernardo Soares, Pessoa's last full-fledged heteronym. The writing of the book ended abruptly the year Pessoa died, 1935, without providing it with any final form. I will return to the problematics of *The Book of Disquiet* later on, in the second part of this chapter. This very short introduction to the problematics of *The Book of Disquiet* was, yet, necessary at this point for two main reasons. The first is mostly a question of methodology: I will be focusing only in the writings that were produced in the so-called third phase: that of Bernardo Soares. The second reason is that, as we will see, the fact that *The Book of Disquiet* was left unfinished and not prepared for publication raises several questions that I will address in the last part of this chapter, still in relation to the relocation of desire and seduction to the text.

Soares is a lonely, celibate bookkeeper who works, lives, and writes his autobiography in a single street of Lisbon's downtown district (Rua dos Douradores), which he rarely ever leaves. Soares is to say the least an unlikely candidate for a place in the canon of donjuanesque figures in Portuguese literature, as it emerges from the nineteenth century. His social context is that of the office of the firm where he works. It is an overwhelmingly male dominated one, where he rarely comes across any woman. Any reader will note from the very beginning that Soares is obviously an uncommon autobiographical subject, a man without apparent qualities, whose autobiography without facts turns again and again to the unremarkable in a particularly postmodern manner. But he is not only a man with very little or even nothing to tell, regarding facts at least. Quentin Crisp's famous line from his autobiographical *The Naked Civil Servant*, "if you don't succeed at first, failure may be your style," could be used to describe Soares (189). Crisp's association between failure and style echoes Modernism's love affair with failure, which emerges in Pessoa's *The Book of Disquiet* in an eloquent manner. Moreover, like his tedious, unaccomplished social and professional lives, the book he is writing is in itself a fantastic, modernist failure: an unfinished masterpiece, which was left by Pessoa, when he died in 1935, on a trunk, in two large envelopes. This is in itself particularly important for the argument here in question and will allow me to present an expanded theory of seduction in the last section of this chapter. For now, I will turn my attention to Soares's inability to seduce and the relevance this aspect has in a broader context.

Soares addresses his inability to seduce in one of his fragments. This particular fragment starts suggestively with the topic of failure in broader terms: "Tenho assistido, incognito, ao desfalecimento gradual da minha vida, ao sossobro lento de tudo quanto quiz ser" (*Desassossego* 193) [I've witnessed, incognito, the gradual collapse of my life, the slow foundering of all I wanted to be (*Disquiet* 170)]. Before even trying to seduce, Soares knows he will fail, as he states shortly after:

Tem-me perseguido, como um ente maligno, o destino de não poder desejar sem saber que terei que não ter. Se um momento vejo na rua um vulto nubil de rapariga, e, indifferentemente que seja, tenho um momento de suppor o que seria se elle fosse meu, é sempre certo que, a dez passos do meu sonho, aquella rapariga encontra o homem que vejo que é o marido ou o amante. Um romantico faria disto uma tragédia . . . (193)

[My destiny, which has pursued me like a malevolent creature, is to desire only what I know I will never get. If I see the nubile figure of a girl in the street and imagine for the slightest moment, however nonchalantly, what it would be like if she were mine, it's a dead certainty that ten steps past my dream she'll meet the man who's obviously her husband or lover. A romantic would make a tragedy out of this . . . (171)]

More precisely, Soares does not even try to seduce because he knows he will fail. Only in dreams he is able to imagine himself seducing a girl; reality, however, always puts an end to it. It is precisely this complete inability to seduce and a sense of failure (in every single aspect of life) that suggestively, for the argument here in question, shapes his modernist, fragmented subjectivity in *The Book of Disquiet*—one that is radically different from both the donjuanesque archetype and the typical Romantic, male subject. In fact, as we will see in more detail, it is his acceptance of failure and its inevitability that allows him to reject a Romantic model of masculinity and male subjectivity.

In the two sections that follow this rather long introduction, I will start by focusing on Soares's making of failure his own style—to use Crisp's formulation—and its ethical implications. This process, I argue, is crucial for Pessoa's modernist critique and rejection of the Don Juan archetype in the pages of Soares's autobiography. As we will see in more detail, Soares does not write his masterpiece to transcend his failed, impoverished, and solitary condition. Nor does he undergo any period of learning and maturation—he makes no progress in his social, professional, and sentimental life, as autobiographical subjects commonly do. He works with rather than against failure. When it comes to seduction and sentimental life, he does not envy the Don Juan of early twentieth-century Lisbon, who he actually mocks, as we will also see in more detail shortly. In fact, Soares mocks, disqualifies, and radically displaces the figure of Don Juan—particularly in its Romantic materialization—when writing in his fictional autobiography a quintessentially modernist self. Furthermore, I will argue that Pessoa's mocking and radical exclusion of Don Juan from modernism, in tandem with the Romantic male subject—both presented as outdated forms of masculine subjectivity with no place in Pessoa's modernist literary imagination—aligns *The Book of Disquiet*, as well as Pessoa's Modernism, with recent work by scholars of failure, such as Judith Halberstam and her discussion of the politics of failure in *The Queer Art of Failure*. Proposing this alignment will allow me, in turn, to suggest that the radical rejection of Don Juan and his archetype in *The Book of Disquiet*, an autobiography itself, represents an attempt by Pessoa to think ways of life, or "new ways of being," to quote Halberstam, that differ from what is normally considered to be models of success under capitalism and heteronormativity (Halberstam 55).

Halberstam's project provides both a critique and theoretical alternatives to what she defines as the capitalist, heteronormative model of success that is particularly useful for a first approach to failure in *The Book of Disquiet*. As Halberstam puts it, "success in a heteronormative, capitalist society equates too easily to specific forms of reproductive maturity combined with wealth accumulation" (2). Halberstam responds to this model of success by proposing that "under certain circumstances failing, losing, forgetting, unmaking, undoing, unbecoming, not knowing may in fact offer more creative, more cooperative, more surprising ways of being in the world" (2-3). More precisely, for Halberstam "failure [is] . . . a way of refusing . . . dominant logics of power and discipline and as a form of critique. As a practice, failure recognizes that alternatives are embedded already in the dominant and that power is never total or consistent; indeed failure can exploit the unpredictability of ideology and its indeterminate qualities" (88). The archetype of the Don Juan I am discussing here does not correlate absolutely with Halberstam definition of success under heteronormative capitalism. However, I argue, it does correlate with the spirit of Halberstam project and perspective on heteronormative capitalist society, by emerging as a form of success that depends on conquest and accumulation.

Toward a Class Theory of Failure: Don Juan, Capitalism, and Literary Value in *The Book of Disquiet*
Seduction is not the only thing that Soares is not (apparently) good at, or in what he does not succeed. The topic of failure, in varied myriad of forms, has an overwhelming presence in *The Book of Disquiet*. Before turning in more detail to Soares's inability to seduce, allow me to focus briefly on Soares' theorization on failure as this will allow me to suggest a broader understanding of the relationship between failure, seduction, and ethics in *The Book of Disquiet*. Failure for Soares is first and foremost linked to a notion of inability to adapt to life, particularly to social life. In his discussions of failure, the bookkeeper goes as far as presenting a complete political and class theory of failure, which suggestively attempts at replacing the Marxist tradition of social analysis and its typical class distinction. Soares refuses the revolutionary distinction between bourgeoisie and the working class, between government and those who are governed. As for Soares: "A distinção é entre adaptados e inadaptados: o mais é literatura, e má literatura" [The only distinction is between those who adapt and those who don't: the rest is literature, and bad literature (240)] "Inadaptados" [those who don't] are, as he makes clear, those who are unable to perform according to social norms and to what is expected. He, a bookkeeper writing his own autobiography, obviously positions himself on the side of those who are unable to adapt:

De um lado estão os reis, com o seu prestigio, os imperadores, com a sua glória, os génios, com a sua aura, os santos, com a sua auréola, os chefes do povo, com o seu domínio, as prostitutas, os profetas e os ricos... Do outro estamos nós—os moços de fretes da esquina, o dramaturgo atabalhoado William Shakespeare, o barbeiro das anedotas, o mestre-escola John Milton, o marçano da tenda, o vadio Dante Alighieri, os que a morte esquece ou consagra, e a vida esquece sem consagrar. (274)

[On the one hand there are the kings with their prestige, the emperors with their glory, the geniuses with their aura, the saints with their halos, the political leaders with their power, the prostitutes, the prophets and the rich... On the other hand there's us—the delivery boy on the corner, the reckless playwright William Shakespeare, the barber with his jokes, John Milton the schoolteacher, the shop assistant, Dante Alighieri the tram, those whom death forgets or venerates and whom life forgot without any veneration. (241)]

Those who are unable to adapt to life are, however, those who, as Soares writes in the same fragment, create the consciousness of the world—as Shakespeare and Milton did. Knowing so is precisely what consoles the lonely bookkeeper: "Isto me consola neste escriptorio estreito, cujas janellas mal lavadas dão sobre uma rua sem alegria. Isto me consola, em que tenho por irmãos os creadores da consciência do mundo" [These thoughts console me in this cramped office, whose grimy windows overlook a joyless street. These thoughts console me, and for my brothers I have my fellow creators of the world's consciousness (240-1)]. Two crucial aspects for my argument emerge in this passage. On the one hand, Soares, the writer of his own autobiography, is also imagining his own place in World Literature, finding a community of like-minded, failed subjects with whom he shares that same style—the style of failure, as Quentin Crisp puts it. These failed individuals provide us, however, with a very particular kind of what Foucault defined as subjugated knowledge, which, according to Soares, forms the consciousness of the world. Goethe and Victor Hugo, for example, are excluded from this community; as Soares writes: "Os outros são de outra espécie—o conselheiro de estado Johann Wolfgang von Goethe, o senador Victor Hugo, o chefe Lenine, o chefe Mussolini" [Quite a different class of men is formed by the likes of the state councilor Johann Wolfgang Goethe, the senator Victor Hugo, the Chief of state Lenin, the chief of state Mussolini. . . (241)]. *The Book of Disquiet* proposes, thus, a community of cultural producers who fail to adapt and exist beyond the glittering surface of market valued success, and who, by doing so, create the consciousness of the world.

Don Juan, and the donjuanesque archetype, belongs precisely to this "different class" [outra espécie], whose ability to succeed, conquest, and impose their will Soares rejects in his autobiographical discourse. Donjuanismo is thus part of what we might define, following Soares suggestion, as the heteronormative performance of masculinity, emerging as part of the regime of compulsory heterosexuality, which Soares ends up criticizing through his rejection of donjuanismo. Moreover, the radical rejection of the Don Juan archetype, in *The Book of Disquiet*, as I hope to show in some detail in what follows, is closely linked precisely to this critique of capitalist value and the models of success that it sanctions. In doing so, Soares makes one fierce attack on Don Juan, stating that his model of subjectivity is nothing more than that of the average man under capitalism and compulsory heterosexuality, above whom he, the failed bookkeeper and the very opposite of the donjuanesque seducer, stands.

DON JUAN, SEDUCTION, AND THE ROMANTIC IMAGINATION

Soares is not only a failed seducer, but he also despises those who either seduce or even lie about their seduction skills and sexual affairs: those who are "sedutores e até as mulheres que nunca viram lhes não ousaram resistir" (59) [seducers to whom even non-existing women have surrendered (61)]. On a fragment, Lisbon's Don Juanes fall victim to Soares's wit in a very suggestive manner:

Há os que vencem no amor, há os que vencem na política, há os que vencem na arte. Os primeiros têm a vantagem da narrativa, pois se pode vencer largamente no amor sem haver conhecimento célebre do que sucedeu. É certo que, ao ouvir contar a qualquer desses indivíduos as suas Maratonas sexuais, uma vaga suspeita nos invade, pela altura do sétimo desfloramento. Os que são amantes de senhoras de título, ou muito conhecidas (são, aliás, quase todos), fazem um tal gasto de condessas que uma estatística das suas conquistas não deixaria sérias e comedidas nem as bisavós dos títulos presentes. (277)

[Some triumph in love, some triumph in politics, and some triumph in art. The first group has the advantage of storytelling, since one can be highly successful in love without there being public knowledge of what happened. Of course, on hearing one of these men recount his sexual marathons, we begin to have our doubts after about the seventh conquest. Those who are the lovers of aristocratic or well-known ladies (and it seems to be the case for nearly all of them) ravage so many countesses that a tally of their seductions would shatter the gravity and composure of even great-grandmothers of young women with titles. (243)]

Soares's attack and parody of the figure of Don Juan is also a modernist attack on the Romantic imagination and masculinity—it is, thus, not surprising that Goethe is a target of Soares's disdain for those who succeed in life—for the overachievers. In an important fragment to illustrate this aspect, Soares starts by trivializing and mocking the Romantic subject, as follows:

A personagem individual e imponente, que os romanticos figuravam em si mesmos, varias vezes, em sonho, a tentei viver, e, tantas vezes, quantas a tentei viver, me encontrei a rir alto, da minha ideia de vive-la. O homem fatal, afinal, existe nos sonhos proprios de todos os homens vulgares, e o romantismo não é senão o virar do avesso do dominio quotidiano de nós mesmos. Quasi todos os homens sonham, nos secretos do se ser, um grande imperialismo seu, a sujeição de todos os homens, a entrega de todas as mulheres, a adoração dos povos, e, nos mais nobres, de todas [as] eras... Poucos / são / como eu ... lucidos bastante para rir da possibilidade esthetica de se sonhar assim.

A maior acusação ao romantismo não se fez ainda: é a de que elle representa a verdade interior da natureza humana. Os seus exaggeros, os seus ridiculos, os seus poderes varios de commover e de seduzir, residem em que elle é a figuração exterior do que ha mais dentro na alma... (54)

[In my dreams I've sometimes tried to be the unique and imposing individual that the Romantics envisage in themselves, and I always end up laughing out loud at the very idea. The ultimate man in the dreams of all ordinary men, and Romanticism is merely the turning inside out of the empire we normally carry around inside us. Nearly all men dream, deep down, of their own mighty imperialism: the subjection of all men, the surrender of all women, the adoration of all peoples and—for the noblest dreamers—of all eras. Few men devoted, like me, are lucid enough to laugh at the aesthetic possibility of dreaming themselves in this way.

The gravest accusation against Romanticism has still not been made: that it plays out the inner truth of human nature. Its excesses, its absurdities and its ability to seduce and move hearts all come from the fact that it outwardly represents what's deepest in the soul ... (53-54)]

Don Juan is here the "homem fatal" [ultimate man] that Soares mocks—of which he laughs out loud. But more important than the attack on the "homem fatal" is the trivialization of the Romantic spirit that the "homem fatal," and concomitantly the donjuanesque archetype, embodies. This is perhaps one of the most devastating accusations ever made to the romantic subject and to Don Juan himself: that, despite all his dreams of grandeur, he is nothing but a common man. His powers to seduce come precisely from being just that. According to Soares: he embodies the interior of the human soul. Donjuanism is thus part of male subjectivity and Romanticism is no more than the aesthetic revelation of the male subject in all his desire to seduce and conquer.

Suggestively, in this passage, rejecting Don Juan also implies a non-imperialist, anti-authoritarian position, which is in part also an anti-capitalist position, at least regarding cultural production. As for Soares, he is certainly not the common man, at least as long as he laughs at those who desire to subject all the women and man alike. In sum, in Pessoa's *The Book of Desquiet*, rejecting Don Juan means first and foremost to reject the norms of hetero-normative male subjectivity on which it is based. In turn, Pessoa offers an ethics of failed seduction, one that does not only offer a radical critique of the don Juan but also provides a quintessential modernist attack on notion of literary value and the place of the writer in society. Failure and the impossibility to seduce are, to use Haberstam's words, ways of being in the world that open to "new ways of being in relation to time, truth, being, living, and dying" (Halberstam 55).

This chapter has, so far, exposed Pessoa's rejection of donjuanesque masculinity through Soares's embracing of failure. In what remains of this chapter, I will focus on how the rejection of seduction at the level of the plot allows for its dislocation to the level of the text. Crucial for this process is Soares's rejection of a model of subjectivity and desires based on the Oedipal structure, according to which traditional masculinity as well as its donjuanesque incarnation are structured. Modernism, according to Pessoa's *The Book of Disquiet*, displaces seduction from the plot to the text itself and, concomitantly, rejects interpretation, turning the very materiality of the text the privileged locus for seduction and game of appearances that Don Juan embodies.

ANTI-OEDIPUS AND THE SEDUCTION OF DISQUIET

If, as psychoanalysis has taught us, sex is always the ultimate truth of any autobiographical account, then where the ultimate truth of Soares's autobiography should be, there is nothing. On a fragment of *The Book of Disquiet*, Soares goes as far as denying having any sexual drive. More precisely, for him, "sensualidade real" [real sensuality] has no interest at all—"nem sequer mental ou de sonho" [not even intellectually or in my dreams]. This rejection of "sensualidade real" does not prevent, however, other forms of pleasure and seduction. A different form of pleasure is precisely what Soares affirms when he writes: "gosto de palavrar... As palavras são para mim corpos tocáveis,... sensualidades incorporadas... [T]ransmudou-se-me o desejo para aquilo que em mim cria ritmos verbais, ou os escuta de outros" [I enjoy wording. Words for me are tangible bodies... incarnate sensualities... (D)esire in me metamorphosed into my aptitude for creating verbal rhythms and for noting them in the speech of others. (228)]. Soares's use of the word "transmudado" (which Zenith translated perhaps not very accurately as "metamorphosed") echoes Freud's notion of sublimation. It is certainly not surprising, since Pessoa knew Freud's work. Yet Pessoa's notion of sublimation in this particular passage is different from Freud's. This "transmudado" desire is more accurately described as a model of desire and pleasure that establishes what I propose to define as a process of *jouissance* that goes beyond the pleasures of "sensualidade real":

Tal página de Fialho, tal página de Chateaubriand, fazem formigar toda a minha vida em todas as veias, fazem-me raivar tremulamente quieto de um prazer inatingível que estou tendo. Tal página, até, de Vieira, na sua fria perfeição de engenharia sintática, me faz tremer como um ramo ao vento, num delírio passivo de coisa movida. (259)

[Certain pages from Fialho and from Chateaubriand make my whole being tingle in all of its pores, make me rave in a still shiver with impossible pleasure. Even certain pages of Vieira, in the cold perfection of their syntactical engineering, make me quiver like a branch in the wind, with the passive delirium of something shaken. (228)]

This pleasure in being seduced by pages from Fialho, Chateubriand, and Vieira establishes (and I am now following Freud's suggestion in *Three Essays on the Theory of Sexuality*) a polymorphously perverse body—without a center for pleasure. As Freud argues, in the initial stages of the teleological development of sexuality "the quality of erotogenicity [resides in] all parts of the body and [in] all the internal organs" (*Three Essays* 284). According to this perspective, the teleological development of sexuality leads to the genitalization of pleasure—to its territorialization. The body of Soares-the-reader, or to put it differently, Soares the seduced reader, is, thus, a polymorphously perverse body, through which flows the pleasure of literary reception/seduction—one whose pre-Oedipal model of desire and pleasure rejects the teleological process and structure that according to Freudian psychoanalysis shapes normative male identity and masculine mastery. Moreover, this polymorphous perverse body, I argue, imitates the fluid and open narrative structure of *The Book of Disquiet*; or perhaps we should say that it is the structure of Soares's autobiographical account that mimics the decentered desire of the autobiographical subject of Pessoa's text.

When Pessoa died, in January 1935, *The Book of Disquiet* was very far from a publishable form. Pessoa's untimely death prevented him from organizing its fragments, and thus *The Book of Disquiet* remained unorganized and open to a myriad of different possibilities for the combination of its fragments by its editors. This state of affairs has contributed to the existence of very different editions of the book and fierce theoretical discussions. Richard Zenith, whose edition I am following in this chapter, has opted for a thematical organization, when other editors have followed different options. Despite these attempts at organizing posthumously *The Book of Disquiet*, what remains is a clear consciousness that the book itself, as it was left by Pessoa at the time of his death, is an object without a center and whose organization is always a question of editorial options and, thus, contingencial. In other words, the nature of *The Book of Disquiet* is first and foremost a polymorphously perverse one, always-giving rise to new connections and organizations. Moreover, Soares's inability to seduce is compensated to the text's radical ability to seduce its readers, scholars and editors, who keep looking for its inner truth, without finding any. At the same time, Pessoa's text, like Don Juan himself, keeps telling us that everything only exists in the realm of appearances.

Let me make this last argument regarding the materiality of the book clearer. In his essay "On Seduction," Jean Baudrillard offers a discussion of the relationship between seduction and psychoanalysis that is particularly relevant to read Soares's rejection of the Oedipal development of sexuality and his theory of reading and writing as seduction. Baudrillard proposes that seduction is the "opposite of the psychoanalytic distinction between manifest and latent discourse. For latent discourse diverts manifest discourse not *from* its truth but towards it and makes it say what it did not wish to say... In seduction, conversely, it is somehow the manifest discourse, the most "superficial" aspect of discourse, which acts upon the underlying prohibition (conscious or unconscious) in order to nullify it and to substitute for it the charms and traps of appearances" (152). Baudrillard's theory of seduction provides thus a way to read Soares's rejection of an ultimate truth in the *Book of Disquiet*. More precisely, his rejection of an Oedipal subjectivity is thus an affirmation of the charms of appearance, of the pure play of seduction in the text that constantly negates a final form. In doing so, *The Book of Disquiet* posits itself against the obsession with interpretation and meaning, which Baudrillard finds in the psychoanalytic enterprise. The reader, as well as generations of scholars and editors, are thus victims of Pessoa's seduction, who keeps being tricked by the seductive charm of a text whose ultimate truth is always negated. In fact, there is no ultimate truth, only interpretations and editorial possibilities that will always remain as such.

More than focusing on anti-donjuanism, as Tavares Rodrigues did, this chapter offered a reading that suggests a very particular contribution given by Portuguese Modernism to the many lives and afterlives of Don Juan. While late nineteenth century Portuguese literature focused on donjuanesque masculinities in order to discipline gender and sexual desire and provide a solution for what was considered to be part of national decadence, Pessoa's Modernism radically rejected the traditional figure of the Don Juan and displaced his attributes from the plot to the text itself, in his prose masterpiece. Through his rejection of the Oedipal plot and the displacing of seduction and desire to the realm of the textual, Pessoa provided a response to emerging psychoanalysis and a modernist example of a text who refuses desire and seduction at the level of the plot, displacing it to the realm of the text creating what may be defined as an aesthetics of seduction.

Works Cited

Baudrillard, Jean. "On Seduction." *Selected Writings*. Ed. And Intro. Mark Poster. Stanford: Stanford UP, 2001. 152-168. Print.

Beleza, Fernando. "Sexologia, desejo e transgressão em *A confissão de Lúcio, de Mário de Sá-Carneiro*." *Mário de Sá-Carneiro et les autres*. Ed. Fernando Curopos and Maria Araujo Silva. Paris: Editions Hispaniques, 2017. Print.

Ciccia, Marie-Noëlle, "As máscaras da vida e da morte em D. João e a máscara (1924), de Antônio Patrício." *Conexão Letras* 7.8 (2012): 11-23. Print.

Crisp, Quentin. *The Naked Civil Servant*. London: Penguin, 1997. Print.

Fitzgibbon, Vanessa C. "O donjuanismo português e o projeto nacionalista de Almada Negreiros em *Nome de guerra*." *Navegações* 6.2 (July-Dec. 2013): 179-187. Print.

Freud, Sigmund. "Three Essays on the Theory of Sexuality." *The Freud Reader*. Ed. Peter Gay. New York: Norton, 1999. 239-93. Print.

Halberstam, Judith. *The Queer Art of Failure*. Durham: Duke UP, 2011. Print.

Queirós, Eça de. *Cousin Bazilio*. Trans. Margaret Jull Costa. Cambridge: Dedalus, 2003. Print.

Pessoa, Fernando. *Livro do desassossego*. Ed. and Intro. Richard Zenith. Lisboa: Assírio & Alvim, 2015. Print.

———. *The Book of Disquiet*. Trans. and Intro. Richard Zenith. London: Penguin, 2015. Print.

Rodrigues, Urbano Tavares. *O mito de Don Juan e o Don Juanismo em Portugal*. Lisboa: Ática, 1960. Print.

Sá-Carneiro, Mário de. *Lucio's Confession*. Trans. Margaret Jull Costa. Dedalus: Cambridge, 2013. Print.

Portrait of Giovanni
as an English Anti-hero

VICENTE PÉREZ DE LEÓN
University of Glasgow

"Mr. English: I like music and foreigners, though I don't understand either of
them; yet still on both I freely spend my cash."
- Giovanni in London, Act II, scene 2

A FEW MONTHS AFTER the premier of Mozart's and Da Ponte's opera
Don Giovanni in 1817, a series of comic melodramas based on the
Don Juan's story were successfully performed in some of London's
most popular theatres. The great freedom and creativity displayed in these
sequels are evidence of the historical and ideological reception of the myth
of Don Juan in England during this period. The 'low cost *burlettas*' were performed at Christmas and on other popular dates for, and in many cases by,
representatives of London's boroughs working class, showing many aspects
of a proud Cockney culture (Davis 1-2). Without the need of an official patent for representing non-comic plays, these burlesque short dramas were a
commercial response to the increasing popularity of operas and Royal patent
plays, whose intended audience was London's middle and high class. In many
cases, both patent and non-patent plays were competing against each other
for a common audience (see, for instance, how *Giovanni in London* successfully replaced a series of Shakespeare plays being represented at *The Olympic*).
Although the popularity of these *burlettas* benefitted particularly from the
timely London presentation of Mozart's operatic version, they are the consequence of a long tradition of the presence of Don Juan in England, initiated
just a few decades after the success of *El burlador de Sevilla.*

Early nineteenth-century England saw a renaissance of popular culture that transformed Don Juan into an irreverent, brave and seductive Cockney working-class hero, highly celebrated by audiences. On the one hand, burlesque plays on the Don Juan topic focused on specific aspects of the myth, such as Giovanni's ability to break the glass ceiling of class mobility, by seducing bourgeois damsels and dueling decadent lady suitors. On the other hand, they offered an opportunity to emphasize the association of libertinage, romanticism and sensuality to Southern European subjects and cultures, which seemed to harmonize with the existing Cockney style and comic worldview. In fact, the humoresque essence of these plays, which mocked radically emotional Romantic opera by adapting the traditional plot of the irredeemable Spanish lover to London's popular culture, satisfied English audiences' expectations.

These *burlettas* not only appropriated Mozart's melodies, but they were also the consequence of the presence in popular culture of different versions of Shadwell's seventeenth- century play, *The Libertine*. Several successful ballet and pantomime sequels during the eighteenth and nineteenth centuries included its plot, specifically Don Juan's condemnation to Hell as punishment for his unrepentant libertinage, in their performances in the same London theatres where the Don Giovanni melodrama series were staged. The burlesque character of Giovanni, a handsome, pragmatic and promiscuous lad, is not only the result of decades of cultural influences, but its polemic reception will anticipate and very possibly influence Lord Byron's own scandalous version of Don Juan as well.

In the first part of this essay, "Don Juan, From Tragedy to Burletta," the proposed study of three major influences in the early reception of the original Spanish myth in England will contribute to contextualize London's comic melodramas of the nineteenth-century Giovanni series:

1.1. On the influence of Shadwell's *The Libertine* (1676).
1.2. Don Juan and the tradition of the harlequin pantomimes series.
1.3. The popular musical extravaganza genre initiated with the *Beggar's opera*, incorporating plebeian, Cockney popular cultural aspects in the fabrication of the stereotypical figure of Don Juan.

The second part of this essay, "Don Giovanni, the Undead Anti-Hero," focuses on several aspects of Don Juan's otherness, which, in addition to its presence in the original *comedia* plot, has also contributed to changes in the burlesque adaptations that were popular with audiences. These include the perception of Giovanni as an anti-hero, a protagonist who lacks the traditional features of a hero (related to the Harlequin series), and the undead nature of the re-born Don Juan and the statue, a trope later associated with Vampire sequels. A close reading of the most significant musical cross-over versions of Don Giovanni in early nineteenth-century London will illustrate the prevalence of Don Juan's otherness in English popular culture. Plays such as the *Harlequin Libertine* pantomime, *Giovanni in London,* and *Giovanni the Vampire* show the creative paths, including the comic (d)evolution of the primitive archetype, that this myth followed in the period. Their popularity confirm the strong presence of Don Juan's otherness as an integral element of London's popular melodrama and, more broadly, its influence on culture.

DON JUAN, FROM TRAGEDY TO BURLETTA

This section explores the different ways the Don Juan myth evolved on English stages, alternating from serious to burlesque, from Shadwell's *Libertine* to the Giovanni *burletta* series. The subsequent study of *Harlequin Libertine, Giovanni in London* and *Giovanni the Vampire,* together with their related musical drama and narrative sequels, confirm a peculiar alternation in the serious/tragic vs. comic reception tradition of the Don Juan myth in nineteenth-century England. The fact that the title of one of the Giovanni *burletta* versions mentions the Spanish *olla podrida* is relevant in regard to the eclecticism of the genre of the play, adding a sense of confusion which was not absent in the original *comedia* either.

The comparative principle used to approach the manifestations of the myth of Don Juan in this period will consider the classification of the different versions in terms of their authenticity, using the language-speech metaphor. According to Claude Lévi-Strauss, "meaning in mythology is not about isolated elements, but how these combine [...] each diachronic version in the history is a kind of speech that unfolds within a synchronous system which would be the language," and, "a version would not be more authentic than other, but they would simply be different parameters of name variants" (*Structural Anthropology*, ii, 217). Whether the origin of a myth, or one of its sequels, these should not be different in importance, but their disparities should contribute to the understanding of the often-contradictory creative process followed by each of the versions. The Don Juan archetype, replicated as an unrepentant killer in both mid-seventeenth century Shadwell's version and Mozart-La Ponte's *Don Giovanni,* becomes a funny and gender ambiguous outcast on early nineteenth-century London stages. But in the end, all these versions contribute to a wider transcultural dissemination of the Don

Juan story, showing a snapshot of the demand of strong, emotional characters, who can sing, dance, and be comic or tragic when needed. Although the meaning of the social criticism embedded in the burlesque plays contributed to the recuperation of Don Juan as an immortal myth in England, at the same time, paradoxically or not, they shared related social fears against the foreign, female seducer vampire archetype as well. The identification of these plays with specific anti-social menaces explains their prevalence as myths.

Criticism of young libertine aristocrats was not uncommon at the time when the original *comedia* of Don Juan was published. Their social perception, in many cases, imbued them with a certain passivity to the tyranny they exercised, sharing with their *pícaro* counterparts the social role of having an "anti-system attitude within the system they were part of." These aristocrats, like the *pícaro*, were apparent rebels who, in the end, contributed to confirm the validity of the *status quo*. Similarly to the protagonist in the opera, the Giovanni of the *burlettas* is depicted as anti-social, as the anti-hero who is able to oppose decadent and weak aristocrats; as it happens with the original Spanish nobleman, judging from their deeds, these *donjuanesque* types do not seem to deserve their present privileges.

The exploration of the cultural context in these Giovanni *burletta* series contributes to a better understanding of the ideological perception of the Don Juan topic in England, such as the mechanisms used to emphasize the stereotypical reception of the tradition of the Southern European myth. On the one hand, both in Shadwell's version and in Mozart's opera, the unrepentance act occurs after the statue episode is preceded by the bizarre actions of the narcissistic womanizer Don Giovanni. On the other hand, the Giovanni *burletta* series show that the appropriation of this Mediterranean myth is directly associated to a reaction of rejection that London privileged class had against Cockney popular culture as well. The lack of a patent to represent serious plays contributed to the commercial theatres' fixation on comic, effective and surely profitable plays, where social discontent was not always dissimulated. These burlesque versions reverted some of the main stereotypes of the Don Juan myth as a result. In two of the sequels, for instance, Don Giovanni is represented by an actress (Miss Vestris) who mocks duels against her effeminate rivals. Don Giovanni is very self-conscious about his own fame and shows an ability to attract audiences to his bold actions on stage. An essential part of his mythical personality refers to his self-praising, thus unconsciously incrementing the possibilities of the play's success, as a way of primitive propaganda. These popular culture Giovanni versions celebrate, and at the same time mock, Don Juan, in a mix of nationalistic and local reactions, which make of this character's evolution in different cultures one of the more complex ones in literary history.

1.1. On the influence of Shadwell's *The Libertine* (1676). Since the original *comedia El burlador de Sevilla*, attributed to Tirso de Molina, where two plots were combined into one, the story of Don Juan has endured in European literature. The first plot is about a young *caballero* who falsely promises marriage to young ladies in order to seduce them. Each time Don Juan deceives a woman, he illustrates the contradictions that enable him to manipulate the honor system. The second plot is the story of the *comendador's* statue, which returns to life to punish Don Juan for his sins. The statue invites Don Juan to a bizarre and repulsive dinner, which is the prelude to his condemnation to hell. The different versions of the Don Juan myth exemplify an appropriation process associated to the hegemonic values of the period. Several sequels were performed since the seventeenth-century iteration of the Don Juan myth. They, like the *comedia* attributed to Tirso de Molina, show a deep understanding of the role of comedy in society, as it happens in, for example, Moliere's version (Bayliss 213).

After the success of the original *comedia* in Spain, a group of Italian *commedia dell' arte* actors appropriated the plot of the *burlador* of Seville to perform in Naples the first sequel of Don Juan, Andrea Cicognini's play titled *Convitato di pietra, opera esemplare* (1630-50). From Italy, the fame of Don Juan spread to France, and then to the rest of Europe. The tradition of the original *comedia* of Don Juan in Spain emphasizes the Sacrament of Confession when the *burlador* pleads for forgiveness of his sins in order to avoid condemnation to Hell. There is a similar focus in Antonio Zamora's *No hay deuda que no se pague y el convidado de Piedra* (1714), which inspired the nineteenth-century Spanish version *Don Juan Tenorio* by José de Zorrilla. In the play by Zamora, published almost a century after the *comedia* by Tirso de Molina, the protagonist burns in Hell after a final repentance, which seems to redeem him from all his sins. This character is irreverent and quarrelsome. His dinner with the ghost recreates the most grotesque and gothic details, such as a serving of a dish of snakes and a glass of human blood. One of the original aspects of the plot is the inclusion of an attempted assassination of Don Juan by Beatriz, a disdained lover, in the fashion of the sentimental drama of the eighteenth century. Other versions in diverse cultures have explored alternative aspects of the myth. On the one hand, the sequel of the myth in *Walpurgis Night* studies the contradiction between being a rebel and a tyrant; on the other hand, works such as La Croix's *L'Inconstance punie*, published in Paris by Jean Corrozet in 1630, focus on an aristocrat who deceives the daughters of a poor family (Carrington Lancaster 474). Erofeev also developed this conflict in his version of Don Juan (Burry 76), which Giovanni melodrama series presents in the context of a comic scene.

The historical presence of Don Juan in England is traditionally associated with the reception of two of the legend's most influential versions: the ideologically charged drama of Shadwell's *The Libertine* and Mozart's *Don Giovanni*. Thomas Shadwell's *The Libertine,* written in 1676, initiated the theatrical tradition of Don Juan in England. Its protagonist is a cruel and ruthless character who never repents. The influence of the *commedia dell'arte* might have contributed to Shadwell's modeling of Don John as a bizarre foreigner who, by being proud and braggadocious, is easily related to the Italian archetype of the *capitano*. In fact, French authors and philosophers, such as Lucretius and Hobbes, had a strong influence on Shadwell (Hermanson 3, 7). *The Libertine* was adapted by Gluck into a ballet and several pantomime series, which have been identified as precedents of Byron's Don Juan (Beaty 395-405 and see Worrall *Politics* and *Harlequin*).

The implicit author refers to the actual influences on *The Libertine* in the prologue of the play, according to which a Don Juan play was originally represented in Spain, and "Italian Comedians took it, and from them the French took it, and several French plays were made upon the story." The author of this introduction believes that his version will provide some originality regarding the traditional approach to the hero: "I had rather try new ways to please, than to write on the same road, as in too many do." What is new in *The Libertine*? Don Juan is a counter-exemplary character ruled by his sensual appetites. Adjectives associated to him in this play are "vicious Spaniard" and "a rash fearless Man, guilty of all Vice," among others. In his first speech, Don John not only rejects the guidance of reason, but also the rule of religion. In his own words, he is an irrational atheist: "Nature gave us our Senses, which we please / Nor does our Reason War against our Sense. / By Nature's order Sense should guide our Reason." In another scene of the play, Don Antonio intervenes to confirm why sensuality rules all of his actions: "We live the life of Sense, which Frey thing, / call'd Reason, shall controul. / D. Lope: My reason tells me I must please my Sense. / D. John.: My appetites are all I'm sure I have from Heaven, / since they are Natural, and I always will obey them." Shadwell's Don Juan is always true to his principles. His attitude is that of a villain who follows an antisocial path, alternative to the mainstream way of thinking, until he unrepentantly dies: "I could not feel the least remorse or fear / To the last instant I would dare thy power /

Here I stand firm, and all thy threats condemn;[...]." The final moral of the play relates to the punishment associated with those who defy God: "Statue: Thus perish all, / Those men, who by their words and actions dare, / Against the will and power of Heaven declares. [(Scene shuts.)]."

The Libertine explores the difficult harmony between desire and reason. Don John shows the bizarreness of the stereotype of an Italian *capitano* from the *commedia dell' arte* theater in his behavior. In a similar way to the original Don Juan and Zamora's, he is brave enough to accept drinking blood with ghosts when invited, but, contrary to other archetypes, he never repents before disappearing into the flames of hell. Don John, presented as an uncontrolled vicious man, lacks the original transgressive flavor of the anteceding versions. The original *comedia*'s hero's actions, for instance, even though reprehensible, expose the flaws of mainstream society from which Don Juan profited. For instance, in the first scene of *El burlador de Sevilla,* Don Juan is in Isabela's room after she had allowed her lover in without her father's consent. Don Juan's lovers Tisbea and Aminta have personal ambitions and expectations, most notably the opportunity to belong to the upper class of society, when they decide to get involved with Don Juan against the will of their actual suitors. The audience finds out about the characters' personalities through their reactions to Don Juan's actions, which unveil his victims' darkest secrets. On the one hand, Don Juan's picaresque attitude reveals others' social aspirations by exposing their selfish love in public, which occurs in *El burlador de Sevilla.* On the other hand, Don John shows a different anti-social behavior which deterministically seems to push him into Hell. His role as the villain challenges audiences to see beyond his cruelty. In fact, while Don Juan makes of libertinage a hegemonic behavior to unveil the dark side of a society ruled by a depreciated honour system, Shadwell's Don John's evident sensuality is perceived as a great evil to society. Shadwell's rigid perception of the myth is confirmed by the equivalence between Don Juan and libertinage present in his play, missing the multiple possibilities of success for a seducer in a part of the society in which principles are based on a double morality.

The rule of sensuality associated with Don John, together with his unrepentant death, did not prevent the recuperation of this myth in early nineteenth-century English society. In fact, he was transformed into a comic character, emphasizing the anti-heroic aspect of the myth. Furthermore, he was appropriated by popular culture, which considered him an eternal archetype that remained in the plot of the numerous sequels that populated British stages in the period.

1.2. DON JUAN AND THE TRADITION OF THE HARLEQUIN PANTOMIMES
SERIES

Advertisement: Giovanni and Leporello, from the delight they have
afforded in every Musical Piece in which they have appeared, have become, in Opera, nearly as much looked for as Harlequin and Pierrot in
Pantomime, (*Giovanni in Ireland* 4)

Montcrieff establishes a direct connection between Giovanni and Harlequin
in his advertisement of *Giovanni in Ireland*, realistically emphasizing the actual presence and fame of Giovanni in English culture. The acknowledgment
that the archetype, style and adventures of Harlequin were commonly appreciated by theatre audiences agree with the frequent presence of this character
in pantomimes during the eighteenth and nineteenth centuries in England.
In fact, theater, in all its subgenres, was the main way of entertainment in
English urban and rural contexts, with an average of 10,000 persons daily in
London only (Worrall *harlequin*, 19), particularly for middle class audiences
who were able to appreciate sophisticated plots and the tradition of complex
political and historical events in comic performances (Worrall *harlequin*,
22). Victorian pantomimes required a specific way of perceiving the actions
happening on stage. Attending these spectacles, which had a pre-determined
view of the world, required a specific and clear ideological position by audiences about some of the topics performed on stage, especially those related
to race, politics and social movements, among others (Davis 1-2). Plays represented by the *commedia dell' arte*'s character Harlequin, such as *Harlequin
Doctor Faustus* (1724), *Harlequin's Opera* (1730) or *Harlequin in China*
(1755), were the favorites of audiences (O' Brien 94). This archetype, widely
performed in English theatres since the eighteenth century, was purely car-
navalesque in Bakhtinian terms (O Brien 58). Added to the opportunity that
Mozart's opera presented for the appropriation of the character of Giovanni
in comic plays, the series of Giovanni *burlettas* in early nineteenth century
London illustrate a related phenomenon to their precedent Harlequin series
as well. Mozart's version combines, in a burlesque way, the adventurous with
the rebellious anti-social traits (Cowgill 45). In fact, in the comic tradition,
the preferred role in the play was the servant, not the protagonist (Pirrotta
60; see Marín on being a *burlador*, trickster, in the period 391-94); although
the origins of *Don Giovanni* are associated with the comic sphere, the success
of the plot of *Le nozze di Figaro* influenced *Don Giovanni* as well. Political
and social events criticized in the story of the Giovanni series relate to the

same phenomena in Harlequin pantomimes, which used a folkloric theme, fable or fashionable event to create a dynamic short drama full of social criticism. In the fashion of the *commedia dell' arte*, pantomimes centered on Harlequin; the *burletta* series capitalized on the success of an archetype, Don Juan. Then, different authors creatively expanded his adventures, represented at different geographical locations on London's most popular theater stages; for instance, the Drudy Lane diary discussed the difficulties of showing an Irish king on stage in *Giovanni in Ireland*, lacking an agreed opinion from the audience (Winston 41). Among the main aspects of Harlequin's sense of otherness that relate to Giovanni's are the following:

a) Being a trickster and a foreigner (O' Brien 58).

b) Thomas Dibdin was the author of several Harlequin sequels and the first play of the Giovanni series, *Don Giovanni; or, A Spectre on Horseback!* as well, although it was Moncrieff who mostly contributed to the imaginative Giovanni series.

c) Among the two extant Harlequin pantomimes that incorporate the original plot of Don Juan, one of them is titled *Harlequin libertine*, and the other one, *Harlequin or the Feast of Statue*. The first one was very influential in the context of the Giovanni *burletta* series:

> By 1787, long before the initiation of melodrama as a distinctive generic description for some types of contemporary performance, the Royalty theatre had successfully adapted Thomas Shadwell's The Libertine, a Tragedy (1676) as Don Juan; or, The Libertine Destroy'd a dance pantomime […] orchestrated with new songs by the prolific theatrical composer William Reeve, but mainly comprised of "The Music composed by Mr. Gluck' from his Don Juan (1761) […]. (Worall *Romantic* 32-3)

Harlequin Libertine was the paradigmatic play which inspired the first of the Don Juan *burletta* series. *Giovanni, A Spectre in a Horseback!* was part of the successful tradition of Harlequin pantomimes, too (Worall *Romantic* 33). On Dec. 16, 1817, Lord Chamberlain granted permission for *Harlequin Libertine* to be performed at the Drudy Lane Theater, as it states on the first page of the extant manuscript of the play (Worall *Harlequin* 3). Its main characters included Don Juan, Leporello, Don Pedro, Elvira, Leonora and Octavio. Similarly to *Giovanni in London*, the play starts with Don Juan pretending to leave Hell, after the Ghost of his father is presented in the "Council Chambers of Pluto" (6), where furriers are summoned as "Children of fire" (8); when asked about why he is in Hell, the ghost responds that he claims "by my son whom yet I love." Meanwhile, Don Juan had seduced Proserpine, who does not hide her love for him: "Juan is mine and mine shall be / Not Pluto's power shall set him free / Return swift-winged Mercury." She asks Mercury for help in order to facilitate Don Juan's escape from Hell using the god's wings. Don Juan and Leporello are taken to the palace of Don Pedro, where Leonora is being promised to Don Octavio. Then, Don Juan is surprised by Leonora and Pedro, right before he tries to seduce Elvira. The presence of Harlequin and Columbina with their associated *lazzi* in the following scenes contribute to additional confusion. In another episode, Don Juan and Leporello board a ship, and from there they jump and swim until they arrive to a fisherman's cottage, where they find two fishermen's wives and Elvira. The Ghost enters and locks the door, then Harlequin and Pantomime create more confusion, so that Don Juan can escape. The next scene takes place in a masquerade in Seville, during a wedding, with Don Juan and Leporello present. After Harlequin enters, he steals Leporello's list and waves his hand with the Ghost on his back.

In the next scene, at a magnificent hall, Harlequin, Columbine and Elvira appear on stage and create confusion again, right before Harlequin changes the scene to a beautiful garden. The Ghost scares Leporello and additional confusion follows. Then, Harlequin moves to scene ten, where he is at a nobleman's house. After some chaotic scenes, a gold ship is set on stage, with Harlequin navigating fearlessly in the middle of a gale; scene fourteen ends with Harlequin and Columbine waving their hands. Then, in scene fifteen, there is a grand saloon and a banquet with Don Juan, Leporello and some ladies, including Elvira. Finally, in a scene at the Styx river, Juan and Leporello travel to the palace of pleasure with Venus, under azure skies. Minerva, Diana, Neptune and Aphrodite, Bachus, and Apollo descend from the Olympus mountain, while the Goddess of love looks victorious. In sum, the creativity displayed in the Don Giovanni *burletta* series had the successful Harlequin pantomime sequels as a precedent, sharing, among other characteristics, a common metatheatrical inclination. The Don Giovanni play starts and concludes in Hell, where Don Juan is rescued. This pattern is necessarily present in most of the Don Giovanni sequels. Harlequin and Columbine have a strong role by intervening in the change of scenes with their *lazzi*, contributing to interrupting the action with their comic interludes and stealing the protagonist roles from Don Juan and Leporello.

1.3. THE POPULAR MUSICAL EXTRAVAGANZA GENRE INITIATED WITH THE BEGGAR'S OPERA, INCORPORATING PLEBEIAN, COCKNEY POPULAR CULTURAL ASPECTS IN THE FABRICATION OF DON JUAN'S STEREOTYPICAL FIGURE.

The series of melodramas performed as a reaction to the performance of *Don Giovanni* by Mozart in London at the beginning of the nineteenth century include several titles such as *Giovanni in London, Giovanni in the Country, Giovanni in Paris, Giovanni the Vampire* and *Giovanni in Botany* (...bay, Sydney, Australia). The success of these *burlettas* is due to a mix of originality and spontaneity that can satisfy the expectations of a public that wants new adventures by the offending and politically incorrect hero. The legendary fame of the protagonist is emphasized by his irreverent and cheerful look, distancing himself from the exemplary ending of the libertine who had been punished for his sins in Shadwell's version.

The early nineteenth-century Giovanni *burlettas* were written by popular musical theatre authors such as Dibdin, Planché and H.M. Milner. But W.T. Moncrieff, considered "one of the most talented writers for the minor theatres" (Worall *Artisan,* 216), was the writer with the most number of successful comic versions of Don Giovanni. His work anticipated Lord Byron's own version of Don Juan; Lord Byron's *Beppo in London* also highlights Moncrieff's use of Giovanni's social mobility in a subversive way (Worrall *Artisan,* 218, 220). Byron, avoiding the original comic play prospect, focused on the tragic presence of the hero, blaming social order instead (Wilson 248).

Moncrieff's plays contain numerous cross-references and allusions to popular culture, enhanced by dozens of tunes and songs that foster the multiple possibilities for improvisation in this musical genre. Both the use of several melodies from Mozart's opera, and the presence of the evocative and romantic character of Constantia Quixotte in *Don Giovanni in London,* denote the aim to address a musical and literary canon recognized by the audience. These *burlettas* are part of the genre tradition of ballads, very popular in early eighteenth century. These plays were theatralized in Gay's and Pepusch's *The Beggar's Opera* in 1728, which was originally a satire against Walpole's government (Rubsamen 551). *The Beggar's Opera* had "undertones of resentment against Italian opera" (Rubsamen 557-58), as is also the case with the Giovanni *burletta* series. In fact, this melodramatic genre, associated with local, underprivileged audiences, was reactionary to foreign, sophisticated and hard to understand entertainment. Humour is simple and based on confusing situations enhanced by fast music and the most ingenious songs.

The *burletta* genre in the eighteenth and nineteenth centuries has been described as "non-royal patent theatre melodrama and artisan radical culture in the Drury Lane vicinity," representing cultural manifestations of a strong raising social class (Worrall *Artisan,* 213, 14). Cockney drama in London included the participation of non-professional actors in plays, which became a popular trend associated with a local cultural reaction (Worall *Artisan,* 135-37). The most successful of all *burlettas* in the series was *Giovanni in London* or *The Libertine Reclaimed,* by W. T Moncrieff, which premiered on December 26, 1817 at the Olympic Theatre. The main characters include Don Giovanni and his servant Leporello, several she-devils with their respective husbands, and mythological figures such as Pluto, Caronthe and Mercury. In the first scene, Don Giovanni, who has paid for his sins, is the object of the wrath of several demons such as Firedrake. He had mitigated his suffering in Hell by seducing other fallen she-devils. One of the Sucubbus is still in love with Don Giovanni, who has been approached by the beautiful Queen of Hell, jealous Proserpine, as well. Don Giovanni finally escapes with Sucubbus, but Pluto is angry with Giovanni after the fact, for his seduction of his own partner Proserpine. Giovanni returns to Earth through the Stygian Lake with three she-devils, in a scene that might remind readers of the three 'anti Graces' female vampires at the opening Bram Stoker's *Dracula.*

The familiar tunes of this melodrama probably make it possible for the audience to anticipate the plot of the story. For instance, before leaving Hell, Don Juan boasts about his achievements: "I've kissed and I' ve prattled with fifty She-devils...." Charonte, familiarly called Cary and Merky (Mercury), in Cockney style, transport the returnees. The hero, along with the group of exiles, tricks Charonte by not paying him, then flying with the wings of Mercury back to Earth. In a different scene, Giovanni, his servant Leporello, and the three she-devils, watch as the husbands of the she-devils enjoy their lives as widowers, living for "Old England and Liberty." While Leporello praises his master to the three attentive husbands, Don Giovanni suddenly appears with the wives of these men, who look angrily at them. Giovanni misses Fanny, an Arminta-like peasant he had deceived in front of her husband and on her wedding day in his previous life; then, he asks "But where's the charming bride I ran away with?" Fanny tells her story about how Giovanni deceived her suitor in La Mancha's plains. That night, at a costume ball, Giovanni and his servant meet Constance, a beautiful romantic Quixotesque character woman who possesses 30,000 pounds. Leporello then realizes that, as Giovanni is still married, he could be considered polygamous if he promises himself to another wife. Nevertheless, Giovanni attempts to kidnap Constance, but he fails. A deputy, the father of Constance, with the symbolic name of "English," is then introduced to Don Giovanni. The plot of *The Libertine* enters the story when the deputy plans to reform Don Giovanni, while the trickster tries to seduce his daughter, who is receptive to him because she thinks that "a reformed rake makes a good husband always." Finally, Leporello appears disguised as a commander, but Giovanni rejects him saying: "Goodbye old Stoney." The servant has a strong interest in an old rich Lady, who is no other than his own wife disguised. He tricks Giovanni by telling him that the statue has informed him that he must either be reformed or immediately return to Hell; then, everyone is forgiven in a grand finale.

Giovanni in London is a melodrama featuring Don Juan as a character with a dark past, but who, in the end, has a second chance to redeem himself, and is then praised by all. This attractive *burletta* has multiple songs, arias and references to known places in the city of London. The Don Juan story is set within Cockney culture, contextualizing the present time of the play with references to past adventures of the myth. Although Don Giovanni needs to be morally reformed, he is nothing like the ruthless murderer in Shadwell's play and the cruel repentant sinner in Zamora's story. Like Harlequin, the fact that he is foreign is not a negative, but this trait makes him wittier, and even more successful when seducing female characters, which the English Deputy observes when he praises Don Giovanni: "I like music and foreigners, though I don' t understand either of them." The light-hearted version of *Giovanni in London* presents a mocking and sympathetic hero, whose subversive tone adds to his attractive sensuality and exoticism. The moral lessons of the Don Giovanni series illustrate that love is more valuable than money, heaven and hell exist as mythical travel destinations, and social rules should be more flexible for the common good.

Giovanni in London and its *burletta* sequels, following Levi Strauss's model for the study of myths, provide a different manifestation of speech that displays the evolution of Don Juan over time and within different circumstances (e.g. Cockney culture in nineteenth-century England); in addition, this speech imagines language, which is the elementary and abstract idea of Don Juan's story. The relevance of these low cost *burlettas* should be considered for their valuable contribution to the comparative literature canon, as they illustrate the multiple possibilities that the original Don Juan plot produced. In this case, after being appropriated, distorted and repackaged, the most irreverent and transgressive aspects of the myth remain.

The second part of this essay, *Don Giovanni, the Undead Anti-hero*, expands on two aspects of Don Juan's myth present in both the original *come-*

dia plot and the burlesque plays, which may have contributed to their successful reception on London's stages. First, it is the expansion of the portrait
of Giovanni as an anti-hero, and second, the interpretation of the presence
of the *comendador*'s statue, and the need to resuscitate Don Juan in most of
its sequels. Among the numerous versions of Don Juan, some of them like
Giovanni the Vampire reflect upon the nature of the actual reception of the
myth in England during this period. This confirms the free, but enthropi-
cally-driven appropriative process, which in the circulation of this literary
archetype followed.

2. DON GIOVANNI, THE UNDEAD ANTI-HERO

Giovanni, like Don Juan in the original *comedia* and opera, is portrayed as
masculine, brave and braggadocious in the *burletta* series. This character was
performed, however, by a famous cross-dressed actress, Miss Vestris, on two
occasions. This confusing transgenderness adds to other comic features associated with the hero, such as his celebration of libertinage and sensuality, all
of which can be interpreted as the result of the influence of the first English
version of the myth, Shadwell's *The Libertine*, where don Juan is precisely
condemned for being as sensual as irredeemable.

Defying and misbehaving aristocrats who creatively take advantage of
the honour system have been associated with Golden Age *pícaros* (see Ruán
and Canfield 48). Their unique ability to manipulate emotions and be able
not to face the evidence of their offensive acts depict these characters as
anti-heroes who go 'against the grain' in their own society, and, thus, react-
ing against Spanish wealthy class. Similarly, the Cockney culture reaction to
bourgeoisie/aristocratic society includes both a parallel social organization
lead by a resuscitated Giovanni and his acolytes, together with a weak bourgeoisie universe against which to oppose. The anti-hero Giovanni is able to
denounce the marginalization of his proud Cockney culture by overempha-
sizing it in each aspect of the play: costumes, places, accent and expressions,
among others.

While in the case of the original Don Juan *comedia*, in which the counter-culture hero ends up not being able to defy God, Giovanni, the *burletta*
anti-hero, demonstrates that his Cockney culture is prevalent, at least in love
relationships, as demonstrated by his success in attracting ladies of all classes
and condition, and finally being able to meet his "true" love. Its picaresque
eagerness to ascend in the social ladder is a reactive anti-heroic proposition
which contributes to overemphasize the hegemony of these Cockney heroes
in society (see, for instance, Kelly's reference to picaresque influence in the

Tom and Jerry series). Self- and class-consciousness are common to the aristocratic and libertine Don Juan character, which relates him to the Spanish *pícaro* character as well. In both cases, they are aware of the possibilities of social mobility through their subsequent female seductions, taking advantage of a social system based on an established set of rules, most notably, an honour code, which they choose to use in their favour.

The original archetype of Don Juan benefited from an existing social debate about the attitude of the *pícaro*. Documented Don-Juanesque protagonists were present in the exemplary novels of Zayas and Cervantes, among others. For instance, the author of *Don Quixote* explored these characters in exemplary novels such as *The Jealous Extremaduran* and *The Gypsy Girl*. Cervantes expanded the cosmovision created around these aristocratic libertines in his portrait of the main characters of *The Illustrious Kitchen Maid* and Fernando in the story of Cardenio in *Don Quixote* as well. Social prejudices against this kind of aristocrat-*pícaro* character naturally relates to the origin and reception of the Don Juan-burlador myth, which is frequently associated with debauchery as well.

Giovanni's *burlettas*, which originated from a musical genre based on ballads that include stories of criminals, have an anti-heroic flavor. They are culturally and thematically related to Spanish Golden Age picaresque short dramas about criminals or *jácaras*. In these interludes, bandits or *jaques,* like the famous Escarramán, were presented and treated as celebrities in their plots. In fact, similarly to *jácaras,* the story of Don Juan focuses on the main character's anti-social behavior in a carnivalesque atmosphere as well. Don Juan frequently self-reflects about his actions in the melodramatic burlesque genre, informing the audience about his feats, and in its sequels. Self-reflection was a typical feature of *jácaras* but also Spanish *comedias de enredo* (Borrego 39). Mandrell has emphasized the importance of Don Juan as a known character to audiences in his different versions, and particularly in Zorrilla's (27, 29). In fact, Don Juan, in his sequels, resembles Don Quixote in Part II, when readers share the opportunity to experience the different dimensions of a character who is aware of his own fame.

Self- and cross-references are frequent in most of Don Juan sequels, thus contributing to elevate the metatheatrical flavour of his plays. For instance, at least one of the costumes of *Giovanni in London* had appeared in Mozart's opera (Cowgill 56), and there are several self-references in the celebrative songs of the Giovanni myth in *Giovanni the Vampire* as well: "Finale, tune / Of Don Giovanni, O! / Surely now the freaks are past, / [...] Can still revive him for an hour [...] Vampire Giovanni, O!" (*Giovanni the Vampire* 15).

In *Giovanni in the Country,* several allusions are made to Giovanni being 'stray again': "Mrs. English: Dear Constantia, is it true, / Does Giovanni stray again? / [...] Mrs. Giovanni: Yes, though, 'tis yet the honey-moon, / Giovanni's at his tricks; / But with your help, I hope, friends soon / The fickle Don to fix" (10). In this same play, there is a hyperbolic allusion to the fame associated with Giovanni and Leporello, and another reference to the protagonist's fame in Europe in the advertisement section of *Giovanni in Ireland*:

> In Italy, Germany, England and Spain / In the Holyhead packet again and again
> At Giovy's conquering name would melt, / Och! Cusbla-machree, we'll presently see, / The loving boy, the ladies' joy: / Nimble footed, black eyed, rosy cheek'd
> Sweet voiced, clean limb'd Don Giovanni! (6)

In *Giovanni in Paris,* there is a reference to the fame of Giovanni in his previous London performances:

> The history of the gay profligate Don Giovanni, (or Juan) is universally known, as it is likewise the disagreeable termination of his adventures, by a trip to the regions below. From that warm residence, he was kindly rescued by the ingenious author of Giovanni in London, by whom he was led through a second series of amorous pranks in our great town, concluding with marriage and repentance. But as an excursion to Paris is considered essential to the accomplishment of every modern beau, the DON is, in this piece, conducted to that gay city, wife, and all, where he goes through a succession of amorous adventures, which it is hoped will be found as entertaining as any of his former exploits. (Paris ad, *Giovanni in Paris,* East London theatre Milner, Nov. 1820)

The ending of this play emphasizes the celebrity status of the Spanish myth: "In Spain, below stairs and in London / Very many ladies he has undone; / To virtue now his wife has won one / Who will never stray again" (Milner 16).

In sum, metatheatre, including self- and cross-references, combined with the existing self-celebratory comic tone of the Giovanni *burletta* series, contributes to remind or inform audiences about Giovanni's past, emphasizing the foreign, libertine and irreverent aspects of the myth and usually conclud-

ing with the reformation of the hero through true love. The main protagonist's awareness of himself as an unrepentant libertine is entrenched within
his feeling of class awareness. Self-praising fame, or better said, infamy, of
being adulterous and libertine, enhances the comic version of the myth, like
it did with *jaques* (criminals) and *pícaros* (tricksters) in the Spanish Golden
Age. As each new *burletta* version claimed to tell something different about
the original story, allusions to previous versions are very present and necessary.

In a similar period of creativity, oriented to create anti-hero archetypes, *jácaras*, picaresque drama and narratives were very fertile in inspiring
sequels about the feats of criminals and *pícaros*, such as in the Escarramán
series, which will end up with the most celebrated Spanish Baroque actor-
archetype, Juan Rana, who originated several interlude versions of his imaginary feats. The celebration of anti-social characters in musical short drama
denotes the need to respond to a neglected view of the world of those who
are marginalized by mainstream society. This relates to a similar phenomenon perceived in aristocratic donjuanesque counter-culture characters in
the Spanish Golden Age who, like Don Juan, attacks the core of the honour
system by seducing insecure ladies.

In order to call attention to this fact, aesthetic resources common in both
Spanish Golden Age and nineteenth-century England include self-praising
and the frequent rebirth of antiheroes in new and most imaginative versions
of the same old stories. Most of these aspects are present in the proposed
case study of *Giovanni the Vampire*. This musical short play illustrates how
metatheatre developed as an essential part of the Giovanni series. The first
scene starts at the actual room of the manager of the Adelphi Theatre, who
has a vision:

The Curtain rises, and discovers the Apartment of the Manager of the
Adelphi Theatre.—Theatrical Properties are scattered about; in the
centre of the Stage is a Lumber Chest. P.S. Bustle, Esq. the Manager,
is asleep in his arm chair—The Scene draws, and the GENIUS of
IMAGINATION appears.
SOLO.- Imagination.- Tune, from the Vampire.
Spirit!—Spirit of Burlesque!
Hear and heed my speel of power,
Hasten in thy shape grotesque,
Hither from thy laughing bow'r

Chorus: Appear! Appear! (3)

The audience finds out about the origin of the plot of the story in the following song:

(Music) The spirit of Burlesque descends and advances
Imagination [...]
This morning a new piece an author brought him, [...]
Imagination. The author rose!
Indignant at the solo on the nose,
That met his ear—and vow'd, as up he started,
A Vampire should revenge him—and departed.
Burlesque. A vampire say'st thou?
Imagination. Aye, Burlesque!—that many!
Liv'd Livertne! That monster!—Don Giovanni:
At every house in turn he rears his head;
In vain, alas! You think him damn'd and dead.
When first the Opera Italian burn'd him,
Into a pantomime some author turn'd him (4)

Giovanni's fame in his different sequels is then celebrated:

Song Miss Bustle Tune Coleen
Although the Adelphi no more I should see,
Yet wherever thou art, is Adelphi to me;
Thy bosom, Giovanni, shall still be my home,
In London, in Dublin, at Paris, or Rome!
To the freezing North Pole, and its ice-cover'd main,
Where no cruel father can shoot thee again;
I'll fly with Giovanni, and think the red snow
As warm as the fire in the green room below.- (12)

In the first act of the play, three authors and a manager dialogue in their songs about potential additions for the success of the plot of the new story of Don Giovanni: "Giovanni tir's of London town / Had travelled to the country down / From stage to stage he runs about" (10). Then, Don Giovanni shows up and sings a song from the original pantomime of Don Juan: "My name's well known to all the town / In the Drury Lane bills you'll find [...]" (11). Afterwards, Miss Bustle invites Giovanni into her room, after celebrating his fame "[...] In London, in Dublin, at Paris or Rome, / To the freezing North Pole [...]" (12). Ms. Bustler then tries to catch Don Giovanni's attention back when Leporello summarizes the traditional plot of Don Giovanni: "Here will stalk a commandant who killed in a duel was / There will walk his daughter, to whom my master cruel was..../ Drawn by Europe, Asia, Africa, America / In the Finale, Gentles, we've got rid at last Of Don Giovanni O!"

Giovanni the Vampire, one of the last *burlettas* in the series, shows an effort to summarize the actual legacy accumulated by Don Giovanni through the sequels, reflecting upon the difficulties to be original "once again," just by adding new content to the myth, and then choosing the use of metatheatre and infamous self-praising widely, to create one of the most original and self-conscious versions.

Don Giovanni is usually presented both as a myth and a human being who is born again in each new *burletta* of the series, celebrated as such in the introduction to the plays by himself, other characters and even the actual author of the drama. For instance, the ballet version used the original story, transforming the myth into a tragedy. In fact, Angiolini focused on the serious aspects of the original plot, keeping the fight with the *comendador* in the new version (Russell 23). The traditional evolution of the Don Juan myth is characterized by the conflict associated with the bizarre acts of the main character, which are combined with the story of the undead statue and the devil: "[...] pienso que el demonio / en él tomó forma humana [...]" (Tirso de Molina).

The long tradition of talking statues and other objects of art originating in the Romantic period started with *The Castle of Otranto* by Walpole (Ziolkowski 952, 962-3). This spectacular aspect of the myth is confirmed in Zorrilla's version, and it is associated with the *comedias de magia* as well (Peña, Don Juan Tenorio 218, cit. en Gies 14). Don Juan's versions show the limits of the human condition; in the end, honour and truth usually prevail when unsuccessfully trying to change their universal rules, using human values (Fernández-Turienzo "burlador," 278, 281). Traditionally, the morality associated with the effect of ghostly appearances is key in *The burlador* (Cull 620).

The renaissance and popularity of the undead hero associates him with the vampire, a myth that mainly became part of popular culture in this same period thanks to Polidori's famous short narrative. In Don Juan's original tradition, the main character dies at the end for defying God. While the concept of permanent progress associates it with fantastic literature, the figure of the vampire is related to Don Juan in that there is, in both cases, a questioning of the power hegemony of the family. In fact, Montague Summers relates Don Juan to Zeus (cit. en Livermore 262) and Ter Horst mentions the relevance of the intergenerational challenge in the duel (260).

The vampire associates to the non-progressive primitive world, which needs to be destroyed to protect society as well. He gets to be rejected as a social disease in its Naturalistic, Protestant, industrial-revolutionary versions, as it is clear in Bram Stoker's *Dracula*. On the contrary, Don Juan holds the free-will possibility to be integrated back into society. In the case of Zorrilla's nineteenth-century Catholic version, repentance is allowed, in confirmation of the need to be generous with sinners in line with some of the burlettas, such as *Giovanni in Paris*: (The devil himself declares, / That if you'll promise to be good / He'll take you in—down stairs) (15). Although the evil side is present in *Giovanni in Ireland* and *the Vampire,* it is associated with a comic fashion as well: "Here a bride and bridegroom, who never yet have married been, / Follow'd by a Libertine, who's to the devil carried been!" (*Giovanni the Vampire* 15); "Dear don, I with Lucifer's compliments come, / Your absence below, Sir, has caused him much pain; [...] / The Black Prince himself, invites you to his ball, / Then come to Old Nick, Don, and Shake yourself" (*Giovanni in Ireland* 21).

The resuscitating statue is one of the most uncanny aspects of the story, even though Don Juan seems to be a character impervious to the laws of men (superpowers) and God (divinity); his lack of fear is one of the keys in the Burlador personality, which associates him with libertinage (Vitse 72). In some aspects of the tradition of the myth, such as in his rivalry with the statue, Don Juan's past actions are judged privately, even though he is self-aware about public opinion as well (Fernández-Turienzo "convidado," 49) (Arias 374). In sum, both Don Juan and the vampire are associated with the devil and redeemed libertinage; in the end, being famous, with or without honour, is another path to immortality.

CONCLUSION: DON GIOVANNI'S OTHERNESS IN LONDON: DEVILISH, GENDER AMBIGUOUS AND VERY SELF-CONSCIOUS

There is certainly still more space for expanding on the different characters and aesthetic manifestations related to the "Donjuanesque" myth that have a clear common ground in both Golden Age Spanish theatre and popular Romantic English musical short-dramas or *burlettas,* with a focus on the exploitation of anti-heroes fictional possibilities. The concentration on the reception of the Don Juan myth originally filtered through Mozart's opera, but having as a precedent Shadwell's drama play, *The Beggar's Opera, Tom and Jerry* and the Harlequin series, among others, has contributed to a better understanding of the Giovanni *burlettas* by contextualizing them within their original literary and cultural complexities. The meaning and intention of the different versions in each specific cultural manifestation during the early nineteenth-century English stage has been equally explored. Choosing several main aspects of the character, genre, social class and identity seems to be a great creative resource to play with in order to cause emotions of fear (tragedy, gothic plays) or happiness (comedy, *burlettas*) in audiences. Other aspects present both in the original and subsequent burlesque sequels are Don Juan's libertinage, his association with evil and his self-awareness as a literary character, among others. This essay has illuminated how and why a burlesque approach to Mozart's version of Don Juan, using comic resources celebrated by London audiences, contributed to demystifying different kinds of social fears, such as genre ambiguity and sexual libertinage, which are paradoxically present both in related cultural phenomena of nineteenth-century England and the Spanish Golden Age.

The burlesque plays represented in London at the beginning of the nineteenth century, initiated by *Giovanni, A Spectre in Horseback!* (1817) responded to Mozart's opera by showing a sympathetic and irreverent Don Giovanni, who mocks Hell, Heaven and even himself, referring to his own prevalence as a myth in a humoristic tone. Paradoxically, some of the core characteristics of Shadwell's Don John are present in the Don Giovanni character; especially his bizarreness and devotion to the sensorial world. The Giovanni melodrama series, as burlesque versions of the myth, created a comic universe around a main character who took advantage of his devoted audiences in a kind of entertainment that nonetheless reveals a snapshot of the audiences' spectacular preferences in the period: interactive, bizarre, grotesque, obscene, merry, with a local flavor, transgressive, self-affirmative and, mostly, entertaining.

Works cited

Anonymous. *Harlequin Libertine: Founded on the Interesting Story of Don Juan, a Pantomime.* 1817.

Arellano, Ignacio. "La degradación de las guras del poder en la comedia burlesca." *Bulletin of the Comediantes,* 65, 2, (2013): 1-19.

Arias, Judith H. "*El burlador de Sevilla y convidado de piedra.*" *Hispanic Review,* 58, 3 (1990): 361-377.

Bayliss, Robert. "Serving Don Juan: Decorum in Tirso de Molina and Molière." *Comparative Drama*, 40, 2 (2006): 191-215.

Beaty, Frederick L. "Harlequin Don Juan." *The Journal of English and Germanic Philology*, 67, 3, (1968): 395-405.

Borrego Gutiérrez, Esther. "Convenciones escénicas y tópicos burlados: el éxito de la comedia burlesca." *Bulletin of the Comediantes*, 65, 2, (2013): 21-41.

Burry, Alexander. "The Poet's Fatal Flaw: Venedikt Erofeev's Don Juan Subtext in *Walpurgis Night, or the Steps of the Commander.*" *The Russian Review*, 64, 1 (2005): 62-76.

Canfield, J. Douglas. "The Classical Treatment of Don Juan in Tirso, Molière, and Mozart: What Cultural Work Does It Perform?" *Comparative Drama*, 31, 1, (1997): 42-64.

Carrington Lancaster, H. "Don Juan in a French Play of 1630." *PMLA*, 38, 3 (1923): 471-478.

Colman, George. *Memoirs of the Life, Public and Private Adventures of Madame Vestris with Interesting and Amusing Anecdotes of Celebrated Characters in the Fashionable World, Detailing an Interesting Variety of Singularly Curious and Amusing Scenes, As Performed Before and Behind the Curtain: In Which Will Be Found Most Curious Notices of Many Eminent Roues and Debauchees of the Day; with Various Others of Public Notoriety.* London: Printed for the Booksellers, 1887.

Cowgill, Rachel. "Re-gendering the Libertine; or, the Taming of the Rake: Lucy Vestris as Don Giovanni on the Early Nineteenth-Century London Stage." *Cambridge Opera Journal* 10, 1, 1998: 45-66.

Cull, John T. "Hablan poco y dicen mucho": The Function of Discovery Scenes in the Drama of Tirso de Molina." *The Modern Language Review*, 91, 3 (1996): 619-634.

Davis, Jim. "Victorian Pantomime." *Victorian Pantomime: A Collection of Critical Essays.* Edited by Jim Davis. Hampshire: Palgrave Macmillan. 2013. 1-19.

Dibdin, Thomas. *Don Giovanni, or, a Spectre on Horseback!: A Comic, Heroic, Operatic, Tragic, Pantomimic, Burletta-Spectacular Extravaganza, in Two Acts, as Performed at the Royal Circus and Surrey Theatre.* London: Printed for J. Miller, by B. Millan, 1818.

Fenner, Theodore. *Opera in London: Views of the Press, 1785-1830.* Carbondale: Southern Illinois University Press, 1994.

Fernández-Turienzo, Francisco. "El burlador: mito y realidad." *Romanische Forschungen*, 86. (1974): 265-300.

————. "El Convidado de piedra: Don Juan pierde el juego." *Hispanic Review*, 45, 1 (1977): 43-60.

Gies, David T. "Don Juan Tenorio y la tradición de la comedia de magia." *Hispanic Review*, 58, 1 (1990) 1-17.

Hermanson, Anne. "Forsaken Justice: Thomas Shadwell's "The Libertine" and the Earl of Rochester's "Lucina's Rape or the Tragedy of Vallentinian."" *Restoration: Studies in English Literary Culture, 1660-1700*, 33, 1 (2009): 3-26.

Kelly, Veronica. *Giovanni in Botany. Australasian Drama Studies* 23, (1993): 101-120.

Lévi-Strauss, Claude. *Structural Anthropology*. London: Alan lane Press, 1968.

Livermore, Ann. "The Origins of Don Juan." *Music & Letters*, 44, 3 (1963): 257-265.

López de Abiada, José Manuel and Rodríguez López-Vázquez, Alfredo. "Claramonte hace un teatro de gran impacto popular": Alfredo Rodríguez López-Vázquez zanja la añeja controversia sobre la autoría del "Burlador de Sevilla." *Iberoamericana* 7, 27 (2007): 173- 179.

Mandrell, James. "Don Juan Tenorio as Refundición: The Question of Repetition and Doubling." *Hispania*, 70, 1 (1987): 22-30.

Marín, Diego. "La versatilidad del mito de Don Juan." *Revista Canadiense de Estudios Hispánicos*, 6, 3 (1982): 389-403.

Milner. Henry M. *Songs, Chorusses, Duets, Parodies, &c. in Giovanni in Paris: An Operatic Burletta Extravaganza in Two Acts*. London: Printed for J. Lowndes, 1820.

Moncrieff, William T. M. *Giovanni in Ireland. An Extravaganza Opera in Three Acts*. London: J. Tabby, Theatre Royal, Drudy Lane, 1821.

————. *Songs, Duets, Chorusses, &c., Serious and Comick, as Sung in the ... Comic Extravaganza Entertainment: In Two Acts Yclept Giovanni in London; Or, the Libertine Reclaimed*. London: Printed for J. Miller by B. M'Millan, 1818.

Monleón, José B. "Vampiros y donjuanes (Sobre la figura del seductor en el siglo XIX)." *Revista Hispánica Moderna*, 48, 1 (1995): 19-30.

Nyholm, K., et al. *Taboo*. Season one. London: BBC, 2018.

O'Brien, John. *Harlequin Britain: Pantomime and Entertainment, 1690-1760*. 2015.

Pirrotta, Nino. "The Traditions of Don Juan Plays and Comic Operas." *Proceedings of the Royal Musical Association*, 107 (1980 - 1981): 60-70.

Planché, James Robinson. *Songs, Duets, Glees, Chorusses, &c. in the New Operatic Burlesque Burletta Entitled Giovanni the Vampire, Or, How Shall We Get Rid of Him?* London: John Lowndes, 1821.

Ruán, Felipe E. *Pícaro and Cortesano: Identity and the Forms of Capital in Early Modern Spanish Picaresque Narrative and Courtesy Literature.* Lewisburg: Bucknell UP, 2011.

Rubsamen, Walter. "The Ballad Burlesques and Extravaganzas." *The Musical Quarterly*, 36, 4, (1950): 551-561.

Russell, Charles C. "The Libertine Reformed: 'Don Juan' by Gluck and Angiolini." *Music & Letters*, 65, 1 (1984): 17-27.

Shadwell, Thomas. *The Libertine: A Tragedy.* Acted by His Royal Highness's Servants. London, Printed by T. N. for Henry Herringman, at the Anchor, in the Lower Walk of the New Exchange. 1676.. *http://tei.it.ox. ac.uk/tcp/TextsHTML/free/A59/A59432.html* (Dec.17, 2016).

Ter Horst, Robert. "Epic Descent: The Filiations of Don Juan." *MLN*, 111, 2, (1996): 255-274.

Tirso de Molina, *El burlador de Sevilla.* Ed. de Francisco Florit Durán. Alicante: Biblioteca Virtual Miguel de Cervantes, 2006. (Dec.17, 2016).

Vitse, Marc. "Don Juan o temor y temeridad. Algunas observaciones más sobre "El Burlador de Sevilla."" *Cahiers du monde hispanique et luso-brésilien*, 13 (1969): 63-82.

Wilson, James D. "Tirso, Molière, and Byron: The Emergence of Don Juan as Romantic Hero." *The South Central Bulletin*, 32, 4, (1972): 246-248.

Winston, James, Nelson, Alfred L. and Cross, Gilbert B. *Drury Lane Journal: Selections from James Winston's Diaries, 1819-1827.* London: Society for Theatre Research, 1974.

Worrall, David. "Artisan Melodrama and the Plebeian Public Sphere: The Political Culture of Drury Lane and Its Environs, 1797-1830." *Studies in Romanticism*, 39, 2 (2000): 213-227.

———. *Harlequin Empire: Race, Ethnicity and the Drama of the Popular Enlightenment.* London: Routledge, 2016.

———. *Politics of Romantic Theatricality 1787-1832: The Road to the Stage.* Hampshire: Palgrave Macmillan, 2014.

Ziolkowski, Theodore. "Talking Statues?" *The Modern Language Review*, 110, 4 (2015): 946-968.

From Don Juan to Dracula and Beyond: A Gothic Metamorphosis

FERNANDO GONZÁLEZ DE LEÓN
Springfield College

S AN OUTCAST, A rebel and a wanderer, Don Juan has pride of place within the pantheon of Romantic heroes but his character, "that compound of cruelty and lust" that so fascinated Jane Austen, is not normally seen as a pillar of the Gothic (Austen, 230, Twitchell, 3). To be sure, the most popular and influential creation of that genre, the vampire, has been called in passing "the gothic Don Juan" but without any serious or sustained treatment of the subject by donjuanistas, gothicists or vampirologists (Twitchell, 75). Yet, the topic is of obvious importance and relevance to an understanding of the mutability and reach of the Spanish myth and its impact on contemporary culture, especially considering that the paradox at the core of Don Juan is his capacity to remain himself while in constant transformation. It is perhaps no coincidence that images of Anglo-Celtic Halloween vampires appear so closely before November 2, the traditional Hispanic "day of Don Juan." These two theatrical narcissists associate themselves with the undead; they cannot be put down and endlessly return to thrill, threaten and debauch. This essay intends not just to establish a parallel but to trace the hidden genealogy of this kinship in order to demonstrate that the metamorphosis of the Spanish myth was essential to the Gothic from its inception, leading to a new popular role for the character, that of the vampire.

The earliest literary pathways through which the Spanish play penetrated modern European culture are well known (Weinstein, 35). There were various versions in circulation for as Oscar Mandel affirmed, "one could write a useful history of Western Europe by citing for illustrations nothing but Don Juan text" (Mandel, 21). In my view it is also quite significant that from

247

its premiere the play always linked sexual lust with the undead. It arrived in England through successful adaptations that modified various aspects of the original but did not drastically alter its supernatural, gloomy atmosphere or the essentially predatory nature of its protagonist. The most influential among these is Thomas Shadwell's *The Libertine*, first performed in 1674 and published two years later. The first full English adaptation of the story, it introduces a number of seminal modifications to the Spanish archetype. Shadwell greatly extends the ethical marginality and uniqueness of Don Juan and depicts him not only as a seducer and a cheater but also as a polygamist, an incestuous serial rapist, a thief, an arsonist, a poisoner, a parricide and a serial killer, in other words, a "wonder of cruelty," an out and out criminal, almost a psychopath, in what constitutes a significant ethical hardening of the character and a major expansion of his range, reach and menace (*The Libertine*, 181). Unlike Don Juan, Don John is an all-out atheist who "owns no Deity but his voluptuous appetite, whose satisfaction he will compass by Murders, Rapes, Treasons, or Aught else" as his reluctant servant Jacomo explains (Shadwell, 181). Furthermore, Shadwell endows his protagonist with a pioneering and uncompromising libertine philosophy that is not only materialistic but also aggressively nihilistic and unanswerable by the defenders of faith and morals who can appeal to nothing he respects (Shadwell, 207-210). The notion that what drives him is an uncontrollable sexual urge at the core of his being is not new; the Spanish Don Juan had already proclaimed it, but his English incarnation develops it in much greater detail and uses it quite effectively against those who challenge him (Shadwell, 193, 210). Nevertheless, unlike the rather passive Dom Juan of Moliere, he is a man of intense action not just provocative words and edgy notions. This, the most virulent and radical of all the many theatrical incarnations of the Don past, present and future, is almost Nietzschean in its uncompromising atheism, materialism and determinism and assaults the foundations of the family and of religion in both word and deed, hell-bent not just in privately enjoying himself but also in scandalizing. Shadwell presents him as a dynamic sapper of public morals, a dangerous self-replicator able to persuade or seduce women as well as the young men who follow him and his doctrine of sensuality and impulse. These features and his blatant lewdness would directly and indirectly condition the various versions of the Spanish adventurer in English letters down to Wilde and Shaw and would give rise to a stock character aptly dubbed "the Gothic libertine" (Grey, 76).

   In this proto-Gothic vein, Shadwell places a much darker emphasis than his predecessors on the scene of Don John's shipwreck and dramatizes it with a number of supernatural moments involving apparitions that foreshadow the frisson at the conclusion of the play (Shadwell, 204, 206). The work is the first of which I am aware in the Don Juan tradition to make several direct and graphic allusions to blood-drinking and vampirism and to suggest that the Don turns his victims into vengeful, thirsty spirits: "I will revel in his blood," says Maria, the violated fiancée of the murdered Don Octavio, "Oh I could suck the last drop that warms the Monster's heart" (Shadwell, 200-201, 211). Similar passages appear in the final scene in which the statue offers Don John and his friends "four Glasses full of blood... fit for such bloodthirsty Wretches." And one of the demons who appear to drag them down sings "By Blood and Lust they have deserv'd so well, That they shall feel the hottest flames of Hell" (Shadwell, 246-247). Thomas Shadwell, one of the most prominent playwrights of his day might be forgotten in our own except for the efforts of the pioneering scholar of the Gothic Montague Summers who not surprisingly was the first to produce a modern edition of his work. It has led to more specialized studies by Borgmann, Wheatley and others although one of the most authoritative collective works on its subject, *The Encyclopedia of the Gothic*, contains not a single mention of his name (Borgmann, Wheatley). Nevertheless, he should be credited not just with the first English stage adaptation of the Spanish myth, but also with having foreshadowed and preconditioned the immensely influential Gothic version of Don Juan.

The Shadwellian Don remained popular in England in the eighteenth century in a variety of guises and it was one of its versions that thrilled Jane Austen in 1792 (Mandel, 232, Austen, 228, 230 487, note 7). It eventually transcended the stage and contributed significantly to a new literary genre, the Gothic. In 1764 Horace Walpole issued the first Gothic novel, *The Castle of Otranto*, a work that incorporated major legacies of this play in the creation of the first Gothic villain, Manfred. This key determinant figure for the future of the genre, especially for its protagonists, is compelled by his passions to violate all human and divine laws from hospitality to incest, to persecute scandalized and alluring young women and to imprison their lovers while disregarding the claims and warnings of a social and religious justice that will eventually destroy him. The sign of Don Juan clearly hangs upon him.

As Walpole coyly suggests in the "Preface" to his first edition, his story contains a number of Spanish elements that provide clues to its origins. The actual castle of Otranto, site of the novel, is Spanish (specifically Aragonese) as are the names of characters such as Diego, Ricardo, Manuel, Matilda, Victoria, etc. (Walpole, 3). Elsewhere I have argued that these and other features partially derived, as Walter Scott was the first to indicate, from Spanish romances of chivalry help ground the Gothic in the Black Legend of Spain and would exert a very strong pull on later novels (González de León; Walpole, Appendix 12, 132-133). Also in this seminal work one finds crucial aspects of the Don Juan myth that would take center stage in the formulation of the genre. Though Walpole does not mention the Don anywhere in *The Castle of Otranto*, he was inclined to play a wide variety of textual games such as presenting his narrative as a late medieval translation from the Italian or daring his readers to guess the locale of the story (his own palace at Strawberry Hill), or suggesting that his narrative would have made a fine play (Walpole, 5, 7, 108, note 15). Walpole, an amateur playwright who, while expressly denying it in his Preface, impregnated his novel with theatricality and called his characters "actors," admired the blood-drinking scene in *The Libertine* (Walpole, 6, *Correspondence*, 9, 256). His use of the Don Juan tradition he hid in plain sight.

The core plot of *The Castle of Otranto* is the long-delayed vengeance of the dead lord Alfonso the Good (a name out of Spanish medieval history) on the descendants of his murderer, especially on the willful and lustful usurper Manfred, the aristocratic villain of the story (Walpole, 112, note 1). Ultimate justice occurs through the agency of Don Alfonso's black marble funerary statue, a living sculpture that intervenes in the opening pages by smashing with his stone helmet Manfred's son Conrad as he is about to wed the fair Isabella. Later that day it materializes from a portrait to thwart Manfred's efforts to seduce (or rape) his late son's bride (Walpole, 24-25). Undaunted and in the style of Don Juan's defiant response to the Stone Guest, Manfred challenges this ultra-representation, the specter of the painting of a man, to "Lead on... I will follow thee to the gulph of perdition" (Walpole, 23-25). The dreadful and ghostly statue, preternaturally grown in size, will stalk through the novel in gigantic and immensely disruptive ways and will ultimately deliver divine punishment by ruining the castle thus forcing Manfred to abandon his libidinous designs on Isabella and acknowledge his illegitimacy (Walpole, 98-99). Although Walpole and successive commentators point to Shakespeare as his major theatrical source (specifically to the ghost of Hamlet's father), the trope of the living and vengeful work of art does not appear in the works of the Bard as it so famously and clearly does in the Don Juan tradition. This makes sense within a Catholic versus Protestant context: Shakespeare's ghost is not a hybrid supernatural—yet-physical object in the Catholic sense and does not personally carry out justice, all of which the statue of Don Alfonso and the Stone Guest are and do (Walpole, 10, Punter, 45, Hogle, 497). The trope came to encapsulate the life-in-death fascination of the Gothic and would become a very heavy favorite of writers and poets and, rather appropriately given its nature, an emblem of the new genre. Almost all of the canonic Gothic narratives, Ann Radcliffe's *The Mysteries of Udolpho* (1794), Matthew Lewis' *The Monk* (1794), Charles Maturin's *Melmoth the Wanderer* (1820), Edgar Allan Poe's "The Oval Portrait" (1842), Oscar Wilde's *The Picture of Dorian Gray* (1890) and many others contain it. It will live on into the present in the work of central figures of twentieth century and contemporary English Gothic such as M.R. James's "The Mezzotint" (1904) and Susan Hill's *The Man in the Picture* (2007). Such a long tradition may obscure the fact that it was Walpole who first invited the Stone Guest to crash, quite literally, his inaugural Gothic feast.

Just as famous and widely imitated as *The Castle of Otranto*, the Mozart/DaPonte's opera *Don Giovanni* (1787) elided the truculent and satanic overtones of the Spanish and English versions and offered a more socially acceptable, sybaritic, suave and charming Don, comfortably at home in the "gallant" Age of Reason, like the Dom Juan of Moliere. Many musical and literary Romantics fascinated by the Spanish myth, such as E.T.A. Hoffmann and Alexander Pushkin, while admiring the dark ending of this grand opera especially evident in the powerful music of the last act, sought sharper thrills and a more rebellious and wilder nature for the seducer (Scullion, 325). These elements only the Gothic could offer. Even so, the operatic Don would exert substantial leverage on the genesis and formulation of the Romantic rake and, as I suggest below, would have its say in the birth of the modern vampire. It also sparked a tradition of musical plays on the subject in the English stage in the form of melodramas, operettas, musical comedies, even parodies (Mandel, 398-399).

Despite these important antecedents, the fulcrum of the Gothic metamorphosis of Don Juan is George Gordon, Lord Byron and his tempestuous relationship with his traveling companion, physician and assistant John Polidori in the late 1810's. Their troubled connection led to Polidori's publication of a seminal novella, "The Vampyre" (1819), at roughly the same time as the appearance of the first cantos of Byron's *Don Juan* (*The Vampyre*, xxvii, French Boyd, 3). The tale, the first lengthy fictional treatment of the myth, partly derived from one of Byron's abortive short stories, depicted the vampire as Lord Ruthven, an errant debaucher who targets innocent young women of various national and social backgrounds, a supernatural being whose "character was dreadfully vicious... and his irresistible powers of seduction, rendered his licentious habits more dangerous to society... in fine, he knew so well how to use the serpent's art" (*The Vampyre*, 7, Twitchell, 106-107). His characteristics and even his itinerary through Europe and the Asia Minor identify him with Lord Byron who had already published a famous poem with a vampire, *The Giaour* (1813), and was at work in his picaresque *Don Juan*. It is by now well known that Byron, although conversant with both the Gothic and the Don Juan traditions, including Shadwell's *Libertine* and Walpole's *Otranto*, introduced significant alterations to the character; nevertheless, his peripatetic Don shared major traits with the proto-vampire Augustus Darvell in his 'Fragment of a Novel': high social rank, restlessness, exoticism, and an ever increasing geographical range including a link with the East (French Boyd, 35-39, 61-62, Walpole, 143). The Byron-Polidori "collaboration" helped to associate in the popular mind the figure of the Balkan blood-sucker with that of the Southern European roué and endowed it with a highly charged and morally subversive eroticism, a symbiosis with lengthy consequences for literature and modern culture. Walpole had made both sex and power the motives of his villain but Polidori 's vampire returned Gothic donjuanism to its erotic roots. Furthermore, as critics have pointed out Polidori (and I would say, also Byron) injected a pathological psycho-physical linkage of the vampire with his prey and turned the rural, folkloric and localized blood-sucker into a cosmopolitan predator roaming from East to West, at ease in both high and low society (Senf, 75, Stuart, 39).

Due to the immediate popularity of Polidori's narrative and the tale of Byron from which it sprang, as well as the renewed interest that *Don Giovanni* had sparked in the legend of the great seducer, the French and English stages filled with a variety of vampires and "Don Juans" and the parallels gained strength and definition (Mandel, 398-401). One of the most prominent French Romantics, Charles Nodier, wrote a sequel to Polidori's narrative and co-authored a block-buster play, *Le Vampire* (1820), that incorporated elements of the Don Juan tradition, including a tremendous ending in which the vampire is engulfed in the thunder and flames of Hell. It played to packed audiences in Paris and would inspire spin-offs and sequels for decades (Stuart, 47-52, 55-58). In London, one of the most successful and prolific playwrights of his day, James Robinson Planché, penned two popular and widely imitated works on this theme, first *The Vampire; or the Bride of the Isles* in 1820, which brought on the scene for the first time in English the Byron-Polidori-Nodier version of the sophisticated and sexually enticing predator. But more importantly for the growing Don Juan-vampire connection, he followed this success in 1821 with another: *Giovanni the Vampire!!! or How Shall We Get Rid of Him?* It was not the first Don Juan parody but actually a musical comedy in what Mandel calls "the buffo tradition of Don

Juan" (Mandel, 399). However, it did inaugurate the vampire parody, a Gothic subgenre springing out of the Don Juan tradition and stretching down to the present day in dozens of films of which perhaps the best is Mel Brooks' *Dracula: Dead and Loving It* (1995). It also broke new ground not only in making explicit the textual and meta-textual parallels between these two mythical figures but, as he explained, in justifying the need to destroy them both through parodic ridicule (Planché, I, 39-40).

> The Public...will readily acknowledge the wonderful resemblance which exists between the notorious Don Giovanni , and the supernatural being aforesaid; not only, in their insatiable thirst for blood, and *penchant* for the fair sex, but in the innumerable resuscitations that both have, and still continue to experience. To put this libertine entirely "*hors de combat*"... as the great Cervantes killed Don Quixotte [sic], to preclude the probability of his adventures being extended by other pens————is the design of the present production, and will doubtless meet the hearty concurrence of the Suppressors of Vice..." (Stuart, 99)

Fortunately for nineteenth-century literature, Planché was no Cervantes and Don Juan no Don Quixote. The great seducer's primordial plasticity and mobility, which Planché shrewdly recognized when he lamented that "he changes climate, and costume, and text," also kept him alive (Stuart, 282). His "Vampire Giovanni" is a self-promoting publicity hound, absolutely dependent on the theater, in dire need of spectators to stay alive, seeking to perpetuate himself through yet one more tiresome invasion of the English stage (Planché, 13). It seems obvious that these two mythical predators are narcissistic vampires of attention, debauchers of the media and destined to become parasites of popular culture. Despite some effective comedic touches, such as replacing the Romantic link between the vampire and the moon with pedestrian and common urban gaslight, what Planché accomplished in his fusion, besides starting vampire parodies, is to reinvigorate the great seducer with a fascinating new disguise and since disguises were at the heart of the Gothic, to move him to center stage in this popular genre (Spooner). Byron, among others, would be inspired by this rebirth to write his Don Juan (Mandel, 447, Spooner, 421). Vice-versa, the figure of "the supernatural being" also drew renewed strength from its new association. As has been pointed out, "the vampire always has a tinge of the foreign and exotic to his persona," and this alien quality was largely the result of his theatrical alliance with the figure of Don Juan (Stuart, 126). Planché's "burletta," to be sure, only made clear and explicit what Byron and Polidori had already sketched. In terms of class, once these authors had elevated the vampire to the aristocracy and made him a traveling seducer, the fusion with the Don became plausible, maybe inevitable. Thus, as he was penning his burlesque, a more potent hybrid monster, the vampire Don, was already on his way back from his too premature grave.

In the realm of the novel it was an Irish playwright personally well acquainted with the London stage who exploited the suggestive potential of this new Gothic fiend, although in a serious key. Among the major early classics of Dark Romanticism Charles Maturin's *Melmoth the Wanderer* (1820) is where the new version of Don Juan more distinctly takes shape. Most of the action takes place in seventeenth-century Spain through which the protagonist, significantly named John Melmoth, roams in search of release from a prior deal with Satan and becomes, as Honoré de Balzac characterized him, one Don Juan's fellow literary outcasts (Balzac, 69). In addition to the re-appearance of the trope of the living portrait and the final passage of Melmoth's death and disappearance, the novel directly reflects the Spanish legend in Melmoth's methodic seduction of an innocent girl first in a desert island and later in Madrid (Maturin, 280-394). In his ceaseless hunt for a victim who will assume his demonic burden, John Melmoth shows his "Don Juanism" not only in his Spanish theater of operations but also in targeting the troubled, the innocent and the naïve, donning various disguises and identities, penetrating private or forbidden spaces such as convents and bedrooms, using language and the social and psychological vulnerabilities of his victims as his primary aids to corruption and feverishly moving through Western Europe and the world without a permanent abode, spreading his gospel of anomie. However, he is also a vampire in his affiliation with the black arts, his supernatural capacity to penetrate enclosed spaces and return from the dead, his hypnotic gaze, dead cold hands and nocturnal existence as well as in his personal experience of past historical eras, the destructive and demonic nature of his love and the quest to turn others into versions of himself (Maturin, 18, 26-27, 43, 45, 54, 60, 71, 230, 322-323, 342-343, 394). Mario Praz correctly described *Melmoth* as "a kind of Wandering Jew crossed with a Byronic vampire" but, as Roxana Stuart points out, he forgot Faust and, I would add, also Don Juan (Stuart, 28). *Melmoth the Wanderer* represents a particularly effective Gothic symbiosis of some of the most potent modern European myths, which accounts for its immediate influence and lasting appeal.

The presence of Don Juan in this fascinating mélange was perfectly coherent. Planché's Vampire Giovanni mentions his upcoming journey to

Dublin in possibly a veiled allusion to his impending Irish reincarnation. His theatricality and the world of the theater permeate and condition the entire narrative, as they do indeed so much of the Gothic from Walpole forward. Maturin was a prominent playwright; in London Lord Byron had promoted his play "Bertram" and he presented his "Spanish" tragedy *Manuel* at the Drury Lane Theater, next door to Planché's Lyceum (Maturin, xxiii-xxiv, French Boyd, 36). Moreover, there are in *Melmoth* direct references, quotes, and significant borrowings not only from the incipient vampire sub-genre, including, of course, Polidori, but also from Spanish Golden Age plays such as Luis de Belmonte Bermúdez's *El Diablo Predicador* (1623) as well as from *Don Giovanni*. Finally, as he approaches his end, Melmoth directly compares himself to Don Juan and narrates the horrific death of this character in a passage allegedly right out of the work of "the Spanish writer" (Maturin, 18, 43, 164-165, 221-222, 244, 262, 369, 377, 395, 440, 508, 517). The author claims in a footnote to have read "the original play, of which there is a curious and very obsolete translation" but I have not been able to locate this text and its reference to blood drinking points straight to Shadwell's *Libertine* (Maturin, 517).

Maturin's novel was a major hit and his supernatural version of Don Juan extremely evocative. Major continental writers with a readership across the Channel, such as Balzac, found inspiration in the explicit connection that dark Romanticism had established between Don Juan and the undead focused on the figure of the wandering, border-crossing, liminal seducer. In "The Elixir of Life" (1830) Balzac borrowed elements from Polidori and from *Melmoth*, (for which he even wrote a sequel, "Melmoth Reconciled (1835)") and created an Italian-Spanish Don Juan who after a life of debauchery mutates into a biting cadaver that preys on the pious and the holy. In Britain, Maturin's masterpiece had substantial impact upon the work of his grandnephew, Oscar Wilde and his *The Picture of Dorian Gray* (1890). Wilde begins his narrative with the Polidorian figure of a sophisticated intellectual corrupter, Lord Henry, who like Don John in *The Libertine*, Lord Ruthven in *The Vampyre* or John Melmoth, uses cynical hedonism to pervert the mind of the young and incite them to explore their sensuality free of ethical or social constraints. As in the cases of Maturin and Stoker, most studies of the sources of Wilde's only novel have emphasized Goethe's *Faust* and Shakespeare or gone farther afield to suggest the presence of the novels of Benjamin Disraeli. In addition to the obvious Dorian-Don Juan alliteration, the work contains a variety of Spanish references but none to *Melmoth* or to Shadwell even though Dorian Gray is a heartless upper-class seducer who preys on females of lower social standing and does not hesitate to kill if need be, managing to elude human justice only to be destroyed, like Walpole's Manfred, through the agency of a living work of art, in this case his own portrait. If any Gothic rake was the son of Shadwell's Don John and the grandson of Don Juan it was Dorian. Coherently, the book has been identified as a potential source for *Dracula* (Leatherdale, 80).

In addition to Wilde, other British writers, such as Charles Dickens, closely engaged in the world of the theater and, working along the margins of the Gothic, also experienced the heavy pull of the myth of Don Juan and crafted their own versions in charming but heartless upper class seducers who prey on lower class females and come to tragic ends filled with poetic justice (Hollington). In the case of Dickens, the handsome, charismatic and domineering James Steerforth in *David Copperfield* is perhaps a more sympathetic and complex character than Shadwell's vicious protagonist and yet almost as harmful for he gives little pleasure but perversely inflicts deep and lasting pain on the women around him. His most notorious exploit is the seduction and abandonment of the naïve daughter of a fisherman previously engaged to be married to a devoted young man of her own class. Fittingly, Steerworth is drowned one night in a violent storm at sea. However, despite this and other contributions to the endurance of the myth in nineteenth-century English literature, Maturin's work looms much larger in the penetration of Don Juan into the Gothic. Only he made it the focus of his novel and renewed its appeal by combining it with other major European legends while underscoring his restless migratory nature at the dawn of the first age of mass travel and communication.

Bram Stoker, Irish admirer of Maturin and *Melmoth* and who, like his friend Wilde and his own most famous creation, migrated to London to pursue his vocation, also registered the impact of the Gothic transformation of the Spanish legend (Belford, 132). The major translators of Don Juan into the language of the Gothic, Walpole, Byron, Planché, Maturin, Balzac, Dickens and Wilde, were virtually all intimately involved in the theater and so was Stoker. Since early youth a student, spectator and critic of the Dublin stage, Stoker became the managing agent of one of the most famous English actors of the nineteenth century, Sir Henry Irving (Murray, 55). In some ways a latter day Catalinón, Snagarelle, Jacomo or Leporello, he devoted himself assiduously to administering the affairs of his master and to presiding over London's Lyceum Theatre, the same venue that Planché had earlier turned into a mecca of staged Gothic (Stuart, 73). In his free time he wrote fiction as a kind of a hobby through which he expressed the anxieties and tensions of his bicultural background and dependent professional and personal position. Despite a number of short stories and novels of varying quality he is known today primarily for one monumentally influential masterpiece that condenses and encapsulates the entire genre as well as the Gothic iteration of Don Juan: *Dracula* (1897).

Although studies of its sources invariably point to Shakespeare and to Goethe's *Faust*, *Dracula* represents the culmination of the Romantic preoccupation with the conjoining of love and fear and is probably the most vivid though lesser studied instance of the Gothic reverberations of Don Juan in English literature (Leatherdale, 77-101, Murray, 179-183, Miller, 149-153, Moss, 143-144, Belford, 258). It is surprising that among the many contexts and influences on Dracula that scholars have explored for decades, Don Juan has been often overlooked, although María do Carmo Mendes and Mercedes González de Sande do offer fascinating parallels (do Carmo Mendes, González de Sande). Both the play and the novel are nocturnal works in which night scenes predominate since both protagonists are primarily equivocal, tenebrous creatures identified with the Prince of Darkness by their attractiveness, seductiveness and treachery; both are narratives of persecution and revenge against two monstrous and inhumane aristocratic transgressors carried out by a combination of natural and supernatural means, especially the growing isolation of the culprit and the work of a coalition of the victims across class and national lines with the aid of the sacred instruments and dogmas of Catholicism.

The demonic Count is, of course, the most notorious in a line of Gothic arch-villains stretching back to Walpole's Manfred but he lies much farther outside social norms and is much more sharply delineated and psychologized. He resembles Shadwell's libertine in that he is uniquely obsessed and dependent on a single (highly sexualized) activity, ruthlessly and maniacally willing not only to violate every human and divine law in his quest but also violently to fling aside his victims once he satisfies his lust. Thus he, like Don John, passes his prey down to his acolytes, as in the case of Jonathan Harker whom he leaves immured in his castle to be bled and violated by his lascivious female associates. In the tradition of Don Juan, he begins by violating the rules of hospitality, both as a host and guest, retaining Harker under false pretenses and against his will in his Transylvanian lair in order to exploit him both physically and mentally and extract actionable information about his social world and the females in his circle. In addition, co-opting a tactic of the treacherous Don that harkens back to the original Spanish play, he wears Jonathan Harker's clothes in order to hide his identity and temporarily adopt his victim's (Tirso, 201-202). When he becomes an immigrant in England his first action, almost as soon as he lands, is to prey on the flower of English womanhood and spread his alien race through his blood-sucking miscegenation, a danger foreshadowed in his alliance with the Gypsies of Transylvania. In the style of his Spanish and English predecessors, Dracula comes ashore after a shipwreck and a storm in a fishing village (Whitby) and begins his labor of seduction by turning the playful and sexual Lucy Westenra (a version of the coquettish and vain Tisbea who also has disdained her former pretenders) into a vampire, which is of course analogous to the *burlas* of Don Juan, a man who lacks honor but destroys that of his victims and converts them into irreparable female versions of himself (Tirso, 100). Most of these features Stoker might have located not in the original Spanish play, probably inaccessible to him, but in *The Libertine*. For instance, besides the references to blood-drinking found in the English work, Shadwell's Don John, like Dracula, takes refuge in a church and preys after his shipwreck on a duo of genteel females (not a lone fisherwoman) who are about to be married and whose portraits, he claims, have awakened his passion (Shadwell, 213-214, 217-218, 220, 233). Moreover, there is in *The Libertine* a clear and sacrilegious allusion to the Catholic Eucharist in which Don John portrays himself as Christ, freely giving his body to his devotees, and the use of Christological tropes is virtually a leitmotif in the Stoker novel (Shadwell, 195). Nonetheless, Dracula is more animalistic and less philosophical than Shadwell's libertine and in England, except for his association with Renfield, he hunts and lives alone, not with a group of devoted imitators.

In Kantian ethical terms Dracula is like Don Juan, the most evil of all possible beings since he sees all others not as ends in themselves or as obstacles to a further objective but merely as instruments of his sadistic pleasure. Thus, he enslaves not only those he sexually feeds upon but others as well, the best example of which is Renfield, the inmate of the London insane asylum who becomes his helpmate and celestino but who, like Catalinón and his successors, appreciates and yet resents his moral position, understands the innocence of his victims and the evil of his master and tries to warn them, only to be disciplined and silenced (Tirso, 1440-55). However, Don Juan and Dracula, though seemingly in command of their narratives, are both captives and playthings of their intrinsic cravings and thus are ultimately even less free than the victims they in one way or another imprison. *"Qué me preguntas, sabiendo mi condición?"* says Don Juan (Tirso, 983-984); "he is even more prisoner than the slave of the galley, than the madman in his cell" explains Doctor Van Helsing (*Dracula*, Ch. XVIII, 211).

A prisoner of drives and instincts that he does not lament but celebrates, Dracula is an "*ad fontes*" Gothic villain and his story involves the structural element of constant transformation and return. With him the genre recoils to its deepest and oldest sources and thus, alone among the dozens who stalk, seduce and persecute in its thousands of pages, it is he who most closely resembles the original Don. "*El trueco adoro*" proclaims Don Juan and Dracula is an expert in disguise and he too usurps the identities of those he wishes to cuckold and to penetrate the most intimate of female rooms and spaces (Tirso, 1630). In this regard, the Transylvanian nobleman, though like Don Juan a late medieval European tyrant, is a blood relative of the Andalusian nobleman. In their constant frenetic activities, these two predatory aristocrats reveal themselves as essentially protean characters hiding their basic lack of humanity under a variety of shapes, forms and identities, constantly straddling and crossing the boundaries between human and non-human. Don Juan's first words in the play are to equate himself to the wind ("*El viento soy*" Tirso, 3) and the Transylvanian aristocrat is not only master of the winds, but, like the Spaniard described in the play as "*cauta culebra*" (Tirso, 190), is also a reptile in human form, clearly recognized as such by others, beginning with his very name (Dracula, son of the dragon). Stoker exposes this reptilian nature in an early passage in the novel when Harker sees the Count crawling face down from a balcony in a scene redolent of Don Juan's escape from the Neapolitan palace, when he is described as a demon in human form, "*vuelto en humo y polvo*" (Tirso, 367). Perhaps not coincidentally, Dracula turns himself into a wind and a pillar of dust to infiltrate the male-guarded bedroom of Lucy Westenra (*Dracula*, Chapter XI, 131). "He can come in mist which he create...[sic] He comes on moonlight rays as elemental dust" explains the professorial Doctor Van Helsing (*Dracula*, Ch. XVIII, 211). Like these natural phenomena, Don Juan and Dracula, two primeval predators that emerge from the sea, are almost aquatic in their instability, restlessness and fluidity. They are constantly on the move, always on the prowl, qualities that make the play and the novel episodic adventure stories with frequently shifting scenarios. It was not F.W. Murnau, creator of the earliest preserved filmic version of the story with its repulsive and rat-like protagonist, who best understood Dracula's essential Don Juanism but the playwright Hamilton Deane, an Irish-born friend of Stoker, and director Tod Browning, who turned the Count, on the stage and on the screen, into an urbane, suave and seductive creature, irresistible to women and with a barely hidden predatory side. It is what David Skal calls "the perfect amalgam of Rudolph Valentino and the grave" and nonetheless unsentimentally erotic like Don Juan that is responsible for the contemporary popular image of the vampire (Stuart, 194-200, 218-224, 325; Skal, 297, Menegaldo, 115-116, Holte, 320).

In creating what has been justly called "the most potent literary myth of the twentieth century" did Stoker knowingly use the story of Don Juan as one of the matrices for his masterpiece? (Leatherdale, 10). It would have been very odd indeed, actually almost impossible, if Stoker, a man who dedicated most of his adult life to the theater, and one of whose duties was to read plays in search of potential roles for his boss, had been ignorant of such a prominent work at least in Shadwell's version, especially since Don Juan was a staple of the English theater throughout the nineteenth century, including variations such as *Don Giovanni in London, Don Giovanni in Venice*, etc. That he did not know the work of Planché, his most famous predecessor at the Lyceum and a major cultural figure in London, seems also extremely unlikely. In addition, two other Anglo-Irish members of Stoker's circle in London in the 1890's had written or would write Don Juan stories: Oscar Wilde and Bernard Shaw (*Man and Superman*, 1903) (Murray, 120-124, Richards, 166). (This curious and persistent interest of Anglo-Irish writers from Maturin to Shaw in a protean insider-outsider like Don Juan suggests a variety of interesting interpretations and deserves scholarly attention). Furthermore, there is evidence that he at least was aware of its main outline, as when he mentions Lord Byron's *Don Juan* in his novel, in a context that juxtaposes adultery with the predations of the blood-sucker (*Dracula*, Ch. XV, 173-174). In other words, Dracula appears as a version of the handsome foreigner irresistible to local brides and wives but to realize that one has been cuckolded is as hard to accept as that one's lover has become a vampire. The connection between the two characters was never too far from Stoker's mind.

The final Gothic metamorphosis of Don Juan, one that confirms my suspicions regarding Dracula, occurs in Stoker's next Gothic novel, *The Mystery of the Sea* (1902), set in the appropriately liminal rugged northeastern coast of Scotland during the Spanish-American War. Stoker laces his novel with elements of esoteric lore and the supernatural, Gnosticism to second sight to reincarnation to a lurid procession of ghostly Spanish soldiers marching out of the sea from their sunken galleon like the famous vampire from the Demeter (*Mystery*, 37-39). It is worth noting as a clue to the presence of the infamous Don in this novel that this is a version of the "*Santa Compaña*" of northern Spanish folklore and was already a traditional feature of the myth, widely publicized in the English-speaking world by Washington Irving's "Don Juan: A Spectral Research," first published in 1841 and frequently reprinted throughout the nineteenth century on both sides of the Atlantic

(Irving; Alvarez Peña, 97-111). A more proto-Jungian representation of the threatening return of the repressed past it would be hard to find in all of Gothic fiction (Jung, 18).

In contrast with the constant shifts of location in *Dracula* most events here occur within a small, circumscribed and conflictive landscape, where elements and places, (sea, land, surfaces, caves, passages) eras, nations, races, ideologies and classes clash. However, in a variety of ways *The Mystery of the Sea* is a novel of Don Juan and the locus of his ultimate Gothic metamorphosis, as he has assumed a new guise that simultaneously projects him backward and forward in historical time, like Melmoth or Dracula or Bernard Shaw's John Tanner. Much less read or studied than *Dracula* but containing major clues to the origin and meaning of the earlier work, *The Mystery of the Sea* features the love affair and clandestine marriage of a highly patriotic American girl, a direct descendant of Francis Drake, and Archibald Hunter, an Englishman who greatly resembles a young Stoker, as well as their joint quest for the treasure of sunken galleon of the Spanish Armada hidden by the Spaniards three centuries earlier (Mystery, 4, Smith). These riches include a magnificent naval figurehead of Saint Christopher that the decadent Renaissance artist Benvenuto Cellini had carved, gift of the Pope to the invading Spanish force to be set up in Westminster Abbey after the victory: a symbol of the latent danger of foreign corruption of pure British morals only waiting to be rediscovered in a coastal cave (*Mystery*, 118-119). Their quest is threatened by Don Bernardino de Escoban, (or Don Escoban, a suggestive alliteration of Don Juan), whose castle, as Paul Murray notices, greatly resembles Castle Dracula and whose features minutely recall those of the infamous Count, a wealthy nobleman of Spanish descent whose family has resided in Scotland ever since the Armada with a steady nefarious purpose, to recover the treasure, restore the might of Spain and defeat Protestantism and England (Murray, 224, *Mystery*, 269). In the context of the moment, Don Escoban's mission is to help his country fight the United States in the war over Cuba, which Stoker presents as a female victim of male Spanish imperialism, a rather draculesque representation, since the emaciated images of the Cuban reconcentrados from the contemporary media, mentioned several times in the text, resemble the wasted casualties of a vampire (*Mystery*, 149, 270-271).

His personal obsession and sense of ethnic mission, family duty and personal honor compel the fanatic Escoban to break any taboo as much as his erotic drive does Don Juan. As in the case of Dracula, the supremacy of the trans-Atlantic Anglo-Saxon race is at stake and the symbolic couple must resist the efforts of an unassimilated intruder who, though a nobleman like the Count, is a serpentine alien guest who repeatedly violates the rules of hospitality and is willing to murder (*Mystery*, 328-331). Stoker is obviously projecting anxieties about his own identity into both male antagonists since his Irish ancestors had helped the Spanish Armada and he certainly grasped his personal lack of "pure" English genealogy and "tainted" religious and cultural background (Murray, 8). In this regard the book represents an exorcism of familiar ethnic, political and religious demons at a moment of intensifying Irish nationalism which Stoker rejected and also a *cri de coeur* against his wife's approaching conversion to Catholicism, further proof if any were needed of the enduring seductions of the Latin faith (Murray, 51, 131). How to thwart Don Juan the international seducer and Don Juan the ideological invader, these are the foci of *The Mystery of the Sea*. As in *Dracula* it takes a grand progressive coalition of American bourgeois and English aristocrats, aided by the US Navy and Secret Service using the latest technologies and the finest legal thinking, to save the girl and appropriate the treasure for Anglosaxondom.

Although in the end Don Escoban, like a quintessential Spanish protagonist from a Golden Age honor drama, dies trying to defend Marjory Drake against a gang of international multi-racial rapists and kidnappers who are only baser versions of himself (including "a half-bred Spaniard"), Stoker puts forward one of the most aggressive indictments of Spain, its people, culture, history, legacy, and enduring menace in all of Gothic literature (Stoker, 1902: 379). Born and raised in Scotland where his family has resided for centuries, the Don is curiously unable to express himself in idiomatic English and though "grave and dignified" his facial features and character exhibit traces, of all things, black African ancestry which, Stoker informs us, is common among the Spanish aristocracy. To underline even more sharply Escoban and his nation's separation from "the West" and even from humanity at large, Stoker also comments on his ghostly cat-like "eyes of hate" and on his "canine teeth," which as in the case of Dracula are signs of his "old diabolism" (*Mystery*, 323-324, 327-328). This animalization, racialization and Africanizing of the alien rest upon the affinities between the Spanish seducer and the Transylvanian vampire and, as has been suggested, make this novel a hybrid of the traditional and the imperial Gothic of Wilkie Collins, Arthur Conan Doyle, Joseph Conrad, and Henry Rider Haggard (Warwick).

What Stoker sought and found in the figure of Don Juan was not only the amatory characteristics which he put to good use in *Dracula* and left out of *The Mystery of the Sea*, but his drive to violate the laws of hospitality and friendship, to subvert traditional social norms, to live clandestinely but persistently against the principles of established doctrine, to provoke matrimonial disruption, betrayal and death everywhere and, more importantly, to reverse the course of human development and return mankind to its prehistory, to an earlier more predatory, sexualized and animalistic stage that Stoker associates with Africa and dark corners of Europe such as Spain and Transylvania. But above all, Don Juan's persona allows Stoker to project and, as I said, exorcise menacing personal, collective and historic demons. For the crimes and misdemeanors that Dracula, Don Escoban, and other foreign seducers commit in Stoker's fiction and especially for their unassimilable identities and atavistic socio-cultural designs, they must like Don Juan not just be thwarted in their designs and chased away; to prevent their inevitable return they must also perish in spectacular fashion. *The Mystery of the Sea* is the culmination of the literary metamorphosis of Don Juan (sketched in *El Burlador*, exposed by Shadwell, and fully defined in the Gothic) as Stoker explores the psycho-cultural essence of Don Juan, pulls together the darkest ethnic, sexual and political strains of Hispanophobia, brings them up to date and connects them to a nascent sub-genre in the late Victorian and Edwardian eras: the novel of political seduction, infiltration, alien invasion and espionage. This contemporary offshoot of anti-Catholic Protestant Gothic would have an immense impact on art, literature and popular culture in a new era of ideological confrontation in the West. A procession of wildly successful books and films inspired by this novel such as Erskine Childers's *The Riddle of the Sands* (1903) and Ken Follett's *Eye of the Needle* (1978), which takes place at the same location in Scotland, indicate that not just vampires but also Germans, Russians, Nazis, Soviets and all sorts of unscrupulous, irresistible and invasive secret agents would follow on the footsteps of the Gothic Don and generate another great 20th century myth, the super spy. The ultimate scion of Don Juan is James Bond.

Works Cited

Álvarez Peña, Alberto. *Mitología Asturiana*. Xixon: Picu Urriellu, 2005
Balzac, Honoré de. *Contes Etranges et Fantastiques*. La Flèche: Editions I, 1999.
Belford, Barbara. *Bram Stoker. A Biography of the Author of Dracula*. New York: Alfred A. Knopf, 1996.
Borgmann, A.S. *Thomas Shadwell. His Life and Comedies*. New York: New York University Press, 1928.

Carmo Mendes, María do. "Who's Afraid of Don Juan? Vampirism and Seduction." Isabel Hermida, Editor, *Dracula and the Gothic in Literature, Pop Culture and the Arts*. Leiden: Brill Rodopi, 2016. 271-292.

Childers, Erskine. *The Riddle of the Sands: a Record of Secret Service Recently Achieved*. London: Smith, Elder & Company, 1903.

Follett, Ken. *Eye of the Needle*. New York: Penguin Books, 1978.

French-Boyd, Elizabeth. *Byron's Don Juan. A Critical Study*. New York: The Humanities Press, 1958.

González de Sande, Mercedes. "Drácula y Don Juan: Confrontación de Dos Mitos." In Fidel López Criado, Coord., *Heroes, Mitos y Monstruos en la Literatura Española Contemporánea*. Santiago de Compostela: Ediciones Andavira, 2009. 241-248.

Hogle, Jerrold E. "The Gothic Ghost of the Counterfeit and the Progress of Abjection." *A New Companion to the Gothic*. Edited by David Punter. Chichester: Blackwell Publishing, 2012. 496-509.

Hollington, Michael. "Charles Dickens" 176-181. *The Encyclopedia of the Gothic*. Edited by William Hughes, David Punter, and Andrew Smith. Chichester: Wiley Blackwell, 2016.

Irving, Washington. "Don Juan: A Spectral Research." *The Legend of Sleepy Hollow and Other Macabre Tales*. New York: Fall River Press, 2010. 289-299.

Jung, Carl. *The Archetypes and the Collective Unconscious*. Collected Works of C.J. Jung volume 9, part I. Princeton: Princeton University Press, 1981.

Leatherdale, Clive. *Dracula. The Novel and the Legend. A Study of Bram Stoker's Gothic Masterpiece*. Revised Edition. Brighton: Desert Island Books, 1985.

Mandel, Oscar. *The Theatre of Don Juan. A Collection of Plays and Views, 1630-1963*. Lincoln: University of Nebraska Press, 1963.

Maturin, Charles. *Melmoth the Wanderer*. Edited by Douglas Grant. Oxford: Oxford University Press, 1989.

Menegaldo, Gilles. "L'Ecran Noir de Nos Terreurs." Jean Marigny. *Dracula*. Dirigé par Jean Marigny. Paris: Editions Autrement, 1997. 102-132.

Miller, Elizabeth. "Dracula and Shakespeare. The Count Meets the Bard." *Bram Stoker's Dracula. A Documentary Journey into Vampire Country and the Dracula Phenomenon*. Edited by Elizabeth Miller. New York: Pegasus Books, 2009. 149-153.

Molina, Tirso de (Atribuida a). *El Burlador de Sevilla o El Convidado de Piedra*. Madrid: Ediciones Cátedra, 2014.

Murray, Paul. *From the Shadow of Dracula. A Life of Bram Stoker*. London: Jonathan Cape, 2004.

Punter, David. *The Literature of Terror. A History of Gothic Fictions From 1765 to the Present Day. Volume 1: The Gothic Tradition*. London: Longman, 1996.

Scullion, Val. "Hoffmann, E.T.A. (Ernst Theodor Amadeus)." *The Encyclopedia of the Gothic*. Edited by William Hughes, David Punter, and Andrew Smith. Chichester: Wiley Blackwell, 2016. 324-326.

Stoker, Bram. *The Mystery of the Sea*. New York: Doubleday, Page & Co., 1902.

———. *Dracula*. Edited by Mina Auerbach and David J. Skal. New York: Norton & Company, 1997.

Shadwell, Thomas. *The Complete Works of Thomas Shadwell*. Edited by Montague Summers. London: The Fortune Press, 1927.

———. *The Libertine. A Tragedy in Five Acts. (1676). The Theatre of Don Juan. A Collection of Plays and Views, 1630-1963*. Edited with a Commentary by Oscar Mandel. Lincoln: University of Nebraska Press, 1963. 171-250.

Skal, David J. "'His Hour upon the Stage': Theatrical Adaptations of Dracula." *Bram Stoker's Dracula. A Documentary Journey into Vampire Country and the Dracula Phenomenon*. Edited by Elizabeth Miller. New York: Pegasus Books, 2009.

Spooner, Catherine. "Masks, Veils, and Disguises." *The Encyclopedia of the Gothic*. Edited by William Hughes, David Punter, and Andrew Smith. Chichester: Wiley Blackwell, 2016. 421-424.

Summers, Montague. *The Gothic Quest. A History of the Gothic Novel*. London: The Fortune Press, 1968.

Stuart, Roxana. *Stage Blood. Vampires of the 19th Century Stage*. Bowling Green: Bowling Green State University Popular Press, 1994.

Walpole, Horace. *The Castle of Otranto*. London: Penguin Books, 2001.

Warwick, Alexandra. "Imperial Gothic." *The Encyclopedia of the Gothic*. Edited by William Hughes, David Punter, and Andrew Smith. Chichester: Wiley Blackwell, 2016. 338-342.

Weinstein, Leo. *The Metamorphoses of Don Juan*. Stanford: Stanford University Press, 1959.

Wheatley, Christopher. *Without God or Reason: the Plays of Thomas Shadwell and Secular Ethics in the Restoration*. Lewisburg: Bucknell University Press, 1993.

Don Juan's Reach, Painted and Filmed

Don Juan Interpreted by Great Painters

Carmen García de la Rasilla
University of New Hampshire-Durham

"A man without a name" and without a portrait

WHILE DON QUIXOTE BENEFITS from a unique story that he himself defended against sequels (Cervantes 2.72.926-27) as well as from an indelible image created in a few but well-drawn cervantine sketches (García de la Rasilla), Don Juan has neither a unique visual portrait nor a definitive and unalterable story. This lack of clear delineation has contributed to a situation in which each author and painter has constructed his own version of the character, generating a multiplicity of Don Juans. In Tirso de Molina's *El burlador de Sevilla y convidado de piedra* (1625), Don Juan is described as a "hombre sin nombre" [man without a name] and therefore on the margin of the social order. At the same time, his image, compared to that of the devil, appears as slippery as the serpent's (vv 187-90) and as ethereal as smoke and dust (vv 364-67). This description helps to explain painters' difficulty in capturing his physical appearance and the fact that our great conqueror, in spite of his universal popularity, has not become an icon recognizable at first sight, unlike Don Quixote. It is not, therefore, strange that artists, instead of trying to recreate an impossible image, have been interested in exploring the moral and tragic dimensions of his personality or in representing concrete episodes from the drama (duels, amorous encounters, confrontations with the dead, etc.) in which an actor in the theater might breathe life into Don Juan. The great Spanish painter Ignacio de Zuloaga expressed the difficulties of composing a portrait of Don Juan "lo suficientemente representativo y a la vez lo suficientemente concreto para ser pintado" [sufficiently representative and at the same time sufficiently concrete to be painted], which brought his friend, and a great expert on the

269

topic, Gregorio Marañón to point out that with regard to the visual arts one cannot speak of a Don Juan but instead of many Don Juans (Marañón 83). We will discuss some of these in the first part of this essay, and then we will consider the surrealist transformation of Zorilla's Tenorio carried out by Salvador Dalí.

GOYA, FRAGONARD, AND DON JUAN IN FRONT OF THE STATUE OF THE COMENDADOR

The popular desire to find a historical figure who could have been the flesh-and-blood Don Juan who inspired Tirso de Molina led to the identification of the famous libertine of Seville Don Miguel de Mañara (1627-79), painted by Valdés Leal in 1681 in the regalia of a knight of the Order of Calatrava, with the *Burlador* from the play. Nevertheless, only with great difficulty could that historical Don Juan have served as a model for Tirso because, quite simply, the text predates his birth. This information has dissolved the hopes of those who wanted to see in Mañara's portrait the living image of Don Juan. One must wait, therefore, until the end of the Enlightenment for Don Juan's history to appear in European painting, in the hand of Francisco de Goya, who possibly was attracted by the challenge of delving into the reason of the unreason of that character's bizarre, cruel, and pathological personality, and by the desire to explore his dark, sacrilegious spirit. For this purpose, Goya chose to paint the scene from Act III of Antonio de Zamora's comedy *No hay plazo que no se cumpla ni deuda que no se pague y convidado de piedra* (1714), which was staged with great success in Madrid's theaters between 1784 and 1804. After having killed the Comendador, Don Juan invites him to dine at his house, and throughout the rest of the work the dead man's statue corresponds with another invitation. The painting, which reproduces in precise detail the episode of the funeral banquet that Don Juan attends, has disappeared to some unknown location since it was last auctioned in 1896. Only a black and white photograph remains. In it one can see the arch of the Chapel of the Ulloa where Don Juan appears before the spectral statue of the Comendador with a disrespectful, defiant attitude. The painting, titled *El convidado de piedra*, belongs to the series *Asuntos de brujas* (1797-98), a collection of six paintings that Goya carried out to decorate the country house of the dukes of Osuna in the Alameda. In it he deals with the theme of direct communication with the dead, a practice rejected by the church but common in witchcraft. This explains the inclusion of the painting in the series, in which Goya reflects, in addition to the dark world of witchcraft and superstition, the irrational and terrible aspects of the human spirit.

In his approach to Zamora's drama, the great Aragonese painter captures with masterful lines the cold, indifferent soul of Don Juan, in large part responsible for his death and final condemnation in spite of the warning from heaven sent through Don Gonzalo. Indeed, we can observe how, standing before the terrifying apparition of the statue, Don Juan remains absolutely unmoved, seated with his legs extended and his arms akimbo, indifferent in the face of death and the threat of eternal perdition. Goya reproduces in the painting the passage from Zamora in which Don Juan affirms "que nada puede haber que a mí me espante" [that there can be nothing that frightens me] (Zamora 38), inviting us to reflect on the consequences of the coldness and hardness of Don Juan's soul and to decide, based on the painting's ironic title, which of the characters painted in the scene is the real guest of stone.

Following the classical line of drama, but with a more romantic frame of mind, and inspired in versions created by Molière and Mozart-Da Ponte, Alejandro Evaristo Fragonard, son of the famous French painter Jean-Honoré, also captured, at the beginning of the nineteenth century, Don Juan's encounter with the Comendador's statue in two different scenes of great spectacle and theatricality. The terrifying image of Don Gonzalo, charged with executing divine justice, dominates both canvases, but, while a frightened Don Juan flees in one of these, in the other he confronts, sword in hand, the statue that wants to carry him off to hell. Although Fragonard's oil paintings lack the introspective character of Goya's treatment of the encounter with the stone guest, they draw us closer to the character, who reacts in a comprehensibly human way, fleeing with horror in one case and defending himself, in the other, from the statue's dark intent. Nevertheless, and in spite of the differences that have been marked out, both artists coincide in drawing out the inevitability of the punishment that pertains to classic versions of the play. Beyond the exemplary teaching, with these living statues they also reflect on the artist's capacity to breathe life into inert material and on the power of a work of art to restore a divine order that human justice cannot establish or impose, perhaps because such lies outside its reach.

DELACROIX, BROWN, AND LORD BYRON'S *DON JUAN*.

Lord Byron's epic poem *Don Juan* (1819-24), which captivated with its pathos first the Romantics and then, with its decadence, the Victorians and Pre-Raphaelites, was the most-glossed text of English and French painters of the nineteenth century. Among the Romantic artists most seduced by Byron, Eugène Delacroix stands out. Inspired by Canto II of the poem, he painted *El naufragio de don Juan* (1840), in which he captured one of the conceptually most sublime visions in the history of painting. The canvas shows the moment in which Don Juan and the rest of the survivors of the disaster, aboard a barge and desperate in the face of imminent death from starvation, are deciding by lot the unfortunate one who will serve as food for the others. It shows a catastrophic limit-case in which every vestige of civilization has disappeared, giving way to the crude, savage instinct of survival, symbolic of the value-system that drives Don Juan. Delacroix, in this way, picks up on the fascination with intense and extreme experiences that drew Byron to maritime disaster, so close to the sense of the sublime that produces terror in the middle of the vastness of the sea, as Edmund Burke described it (Burke 102). In the composition, Don Juan stands out even more as the central axis that sets in motion the drama, possessor of an irrational vital force that attracts, like a vortex, all those who surround him, generating chaos and despair.

In the poem, Don Juan, the only survivor, disembarks at the end of his odyssey in the Cyclades of the Aegean, where the beautiful Haidée and her servant Zoe find him and shelter him in a cave on the beach. Don Juan and Haidée fall in love, but her father, the pirate Lambro, comes between them and achieves their separation. The pain caused by the absence of her beloved leads to Haidée's death, but her memory will remain forever in Don Juan's heart. Perhaps this amorous parenthesis in the outlandish history of Byron's character, as well as Haidée's heroism and self-sacrifice, has interested various painters in the romantic episode. Alexandre Marie Colin, Thomas Barker, and Ford Madox Brown chose as the subject of their works this idyllic love story. The version of the latter, *El encuentro de don Juan por Haidée* (1870-73), stands out for its symbolism, in which the unconscious and naked figure of Don Juan stretched out on the beach, with an ambiguous, feminine beauty, evokes the Byronian theme of the hero's martyrdom. Catastrophe and renewal combine in the scene where the shipwrecked young man, rescued by Haidée, arises as a symbol of the Romantic theme of the survival of genius. The composition, very similar to that of a *pietà*, evokes the idea of the woman as saving angel that we will see later in Zorrilla's drama. Nevertheless, in spite of Haidée's compassionate gesture, Don Juan remains cold, distant, and indifferent, as is fitting for Byron's uncorrupted, pure hero. In his comparative analysis of the paintings of Brown and Delacroix, Tim Killick points out the individualist existentialism of the former, in contrast to the latter's emphasis on the hero's situation in moments of social crisis, with both responding to very different attitudes towards the Romantic idea of the power of individual imagination (Killick 96-99). The artists coincide, however, in detecting the lack of solidarity in Don Juan's character, forerunner *avant-la-lettre* of fierce, Nietzschean individualism.

A curious anecdote, and perfectly in keeping with Don Juan's provocative disposition, that deserves to be mentioned is the scandal produced by a spectacular and decadent work that the Italian painter Giacomo Grosso (1860-1934) produced in Venice's first international art exposition. In the canvas, titled *Supremo encuentro* and also known as *Las mujeres en la tumba de Don Giovanni* (1895), five nude young women in lewd poses appeared on a coffin with the body of Don Juan displayed within a church. Clerical indignation came swiftly, and even the patriarch of Venice, Giuseppe Sarto, the future Pope Pius X, intervened. In spite of their protests, the painting not only managed to stay in the exposition but even won a prize by popular vote. The scandal raised public curiosity, and finally the painting was acquired by a society to take it to the United States, where its fame had already spread. Unfortunately, in the crossing it was destroyed in a fire, the "exemplary" punishment for Don Juan's scandals, even for those committed in the sphere of art.

THE SURREALIST TENORIO OF SALVADOR DALÍ

At the beginning of the twentieth century, many painters continued to be interested in the theme of Don Juan. Max Slevogt painted an impressive, impressionist canvas of Don Juan with the Stone Guest in 1906, and Charles Ricketts returns to the encounter with the Comendador in various oil paintings (1905, 1911) inspired by the text of Bernard Shaw, *Don Juan in Hell*, which belonged to his *Man and Superman*. However, neither Slevogt nor Ricketts offers a new perspective of the famous seducer, who will have to wait to be renewed by the surrealist reading of Salvador Dalí. In Spain, a series of lesser known painters who lived between the nineteenth and twentieth centuries, like Rogelio de Esgusquiza, Salvador Sánchez Barbudo, José San Bartolomé Llaneces, and Elías Salvaverría, incorporated scenes from Zorrilla's *Don Juan Tenorio* into their work (Charro García 171). In spite of the inaccessibility of the images in their paintings, their existence speaks for itself of the taste that Spanish artists had for the theme, a taste shared by the painter from Empordà.

Dalí's interpretation of Tenorio is inscribed within a literary-critical tradition that accents the woman's role as enabler, conqueror, or even producer of the myth, when she is not seen as its destroyer. To this tradition belong, for example, Lord Byron's poem, in which Don Juan appears as a victim of women, as well as Bernard Shaw's *Man and Superman*, in which women attempt to possess the protagonist to preserve and improve the species, transforming him into an impotent victim of feminine force. Unamuno himself in *El hermano Juan* reduces Don Juan to a "noluntad" [unwillingness], subject to women and condemned to suffer all the pains he had inflicted on his victims in the past, while the traits normally associated with Don Juan pass to the women. For his part, Edmond Rostard, in his posthumous and unfinished drama *La última noche de Don Juan* (1921), takes this psychological annihilation of the character to its extreme, carried out by the ghosts of his victims, who avenge themselves by making him see that in reality they were the ones who had conquered him.

We know that Dalí recited from memory the lines of the *Tenorio* (Gibson 588) and that his passion for drama was shared by his group of friends from the Residencia de Estudiantes de Madrid (Federico García Lorca, Luis Buñuel, Pepín Bello, etc.). With regard to the sets, designs, and sketches that were carried out for the version of *Don Juan Tenorio* directed by Luis Escobar for the Teatro María Guerrero de Madrid in 1949, Dalí commented: "Estaba escrito que yo tenía que hacer un *Tenorio*. Es una obra típicamente daliniana. Era absolutamente inevitable. Estaba en mi destino" [It was written that I had to do a *Tenorio*. It is a work that is typical of Dalí. It was absolutely inevitable. It was in my destiny] (*Informaciones*, 27 October, 1949). The attraction that the painter felt for the *Tenorio* must have been motivated not only by psycho-autobiographical reasons but also because of a series of Romantic characteristics very much to surrealist tastes, heirs to the end of Romanticism: the exaltation of the Satanic, rebellious individual, contrary to social and religious norms; the triumph of love; and the prominence of the angel-woman. To this one should add that Romantic playwrights conceived their dramas in pictorial and sculptural forms. It is known that Bécquer and the Duke of Rivas were also painters, and in the case of Zorrilla, it is known that he was not, which makes his friendship with painters like Esquivel or Jenaro Villamil significant (Lafuente Ferrari 175). Zorrilla fills his text with pictorio-esthetic notes meant to facilitate the labor of a future painter-scenographer like Dalí. It is important not to forget also the strong visual content of the work, whose lines describe, and generate in an ekphrastic way, the first images of the beloved in the lover, provoking the obsessive feeling of love that moves the action. On the other hand, Zorrilla's drama could not be more surrealist, with its mixture of the real and the unreal, sleeping and waking, life and death, animate and inanimate, where contradictory spaces and times exist, above all in the last scene, in which it remains unclear if Don Juan is alive or dead.

The sets designed by Dalí for his *Don Juan Tenorio* were described in the press as "monstruosos, fabulosos, locos, divinos, insultantes, sugerentes e incongruentes" [monstrous, fabulous, insane, divine, offensive, suggestive, and incongruent] (Gibson 571). Unfortunately, to this day critics have only focused on the images typical of Dalí in these scenes, and none of them has dared draw closer to the terrifying truth that they enclose beneath an absurd, even comical appearance. It is essential to understand first that these magic, dream spaces created by the artist correspond to the concept of the surrealist vision, as formulated by André Breton, that is, as a glance at the interior world. In this way, all its resources are directed towards penetrating and revealing the irrational psycho-tragic spectacle that hides behind the drama of Don Juan, which had been staged from its opening in 1844 only for the exterior gaze. Its objective would be to materialize the images of irrational impulses enclosed in the text, but, towards the middle of the last century, neither the critics nor the spectators seemed to have understood its purpose.

The Catalan artist created doubtless a totally new, unprecedented version of the work, and without modifying so much as a single line. The text was staged unedited, but the reading offered by Dalí through his delirious images permitted the emergence of a Don Juan buried in the text until then, moved by resources of the subconscious. As in his paintings, in which the double or even multiple image makes us constantly suggest to ourselves what we see or what we wish to see, with his double version of the myth on stage, the public felt impelled to decide if they really wanted to see again the staging of the classic *Tenorio*, and in that case becoming exasperated with Dalí's disconcerting sets, or if they would accept the invitation to look inwardly to discover the hidden face of Don Juan.

In the night at Seville of Dalí's *Tenorio*, we note for example gigantic, grotesque, disproportionate fauna and flora, which makes the characters appear like small and insignificant animals or insects. The shadows of giant leaves and the actors' outfits accentuate, if possible, the characters' animalization and underline the strangeness of the atmosphere. Dalí launches Zorrilla's drama in the earliest mists of time, submerging it in an antediluvian world characterized by the coexistence of primitive man with oversized plants and animals and by the absence of civilization. The artist situates his Don Juan in a frame of primitive instincts, savage and without control, and he subjects his characters—reduced, let us not forget, to the size of tiny insects—to a test of the psychic resources that drive them, almost as if this were a matter of an entomologist of the psyche. Curiously, Ortega y Gasset had already spoken in his essay on the *Tenorio* ("La estrangulación de Don Juan") "de la simplicidad y el primitivismo de cuanto allí se dice y cuanto allí se hace" [of the simplicity and primitivism of what is said and done therein]. Dalí intended, in effect, to show that primitivism, that is, drama in all its crudeness, and to carry the story back to the origin of Don Juan's self, diving into the depths of his subconscious world. He followed, in this sense, the connections discovered by psychoanalysis between psychological development and the content of tragedy. Let us remember that for Freud, tragic themes "serían formulaciones de ciertas fantasías subconscientes comunes a todos los hombres" [would be formulations of certain subconscious fantasies common to all men] (11-12).

Having arrived at this point, we must consider the mythopoetic connection between Zorrilla's *Don Juan* and Dalí's own story, who after depicting himself as an irredeemable narcissist, and therefore as someone incapable of loving anyone but himself, tells us in his autobiography, *Vida secreta*, how a woman, in this case his wife, Gala, saved him from the abyss. Although we might not exactly describe Dalí as Don Juan, from a psychoanalytic point of view there exist evident parallels between the story of his life and that of the famous Romantic character, whose common denominator would be flagrant narcissism. In keeping with Freud, the narcissistic condition would be directly connected with the Oedipal complex, which would bring with it an identification of the self with the maternal ideal, and consequently with an atrophy of later psychosexual and emotional development of the individual, keeping him from loving any object different from himself.

In his autobiography, *Vida secreta*, the artist tells how his chronic narcissism, which drove him to annihilate every rival of that *imago* of the maternal ideal with which he identified, condemned him to amatory impotence. Gala, however, was able to break this curse by offering the sacrifice of her own life, making herself an echo of Dalí's desire and therefore of the warning maternal voice, managing to identify herself with the ideal, castrating image of the mother. Only after that moment was the young Dalí capable of loving without fear of renouncing his narcissism.

Curiously, Zorrilla's drama offers a very similar example, for Don Juan begins to love exactly in the moment of hearing the description of Doña Inés's love in Brígida's words, almost as an echo of his own desire. In turn, and following the tradition of *La Celestina*, Brígida has awoken in Doña Inés an idea or obsessive feeling of such a kind that it will cause not only a type of love-madness but also its consequent, salvific action. In the theatrical version of Dalí-Escobar, the over-acting of the actress Mari Carmen Díaz de Mendoza, as can be seen in the version filmed by Alejandro Perla in 1952, clues us in to the hysteria and mental imbalance of the character, visible even after her death: disheveled, her eyes wild, her movements convulsive, her voice and intonation unnatural and exaggerated. In fact, the actress's interventions are so notorious that, even as a ghost, she almost seems to weave, like one of the Fates, the development of the drama from beyond the grave, underlining her role as the feminine creator of the Don Juan's story.

Precisely in his Seminar XVIII (from February 17, 1971), Jacques Lacan, friend of Dalí, reveals that Don Juan was nothing but a woman's dream, or as Diana Rabinovich would say, a servant or slave of the feminine fantasy that imagines a man who is impossible to trap, and therefore, impossible to castrate, in clear reference to the unassailable figure of the father. Perhaps his true seduction as a myth resides in this profound truth, as well as the fascination it has exercised on writers and artists of all times like Dalí. Possibly Tirso de Molina, who knew the feminine mind well because of his office as a confessor to women, would agree with Lacan's thesis, and therefore with Dalí's version of the drama, and likewise Zorrilla, who made his Doña Inés directly responsible for his *Tenorio*. Certainly for Dalí the paranoid imagination of Doña Inés was capable of saving from sure and eternal condemnation Tirso's young and unredeemed libertine. In one of his engravings dedicated to the theme, *The Nude*, the artist pays homage to that eternal feminine, a mixture of the sacred and the profane or erotic, represented by Doña Inés, before whose redemptive, creative, as well as sensual, power, Don Juan himself kneels.

Works cited

Burke, Edmund. *Philosophical Enquiry into the Sublime and Beautiful and Other Pre-Revolutionary Writings*. Ed. David Womersley. London: Penguin, 1998.

Byron, George Gordon. *Don Juan*. Harmondsworth: Penguin Books, 1977.

Cervantes, Miguel de. *Don Quijote de la Mancha*. Ed. John Jay Allen. 2 vols. Madrid: Ediciones Cátedra, 1989.

Charro García, María del Rosario. *Dalí a escena: Obra dedicada a la escenografía, diseño de vestuario y acciones performativas*. Tesis Doctoral. Universidad de Burgos, 2015.

Dalí, Salvador. *Vida secreta de Salvador Dalí*. Figueras (Gerona): Dasa Edicions, 1981.

Freud, Sigmund. Citado en J.A.C. Brown, *Freud and the Post-Freudians*. London: Cassell, 1961. 11-12.

García de la Rasilla, Carmen. "Images from the Reading: Generative and Functional Aspects of the Visual in *Don Quijote*." *A Novel without Boundaries: Sensing Don Quixote 400 Years Later.* Ed. Carmen García de la Rasilla and Jorge Abril Sánchez. Newark, Delaware: Juan de la Cuesta, 2016, 91-107.

Gibson, Ian. *The Shameful Life of Salvador Dalí.* Nueva York: W.W. Norton and Company, 1998.

Killick, Tim. "The Protean Poet: Byron's *Don Juan* in the Visual Arts." *Romantic Textualities: Literature and Print Culture, 1780-1840,* 21 (Winter 2013): 88-107.

Lacan, Jacques. *Libro 18, De un discurso que no fuera del semblante, 1971.* Buenos Aires: Paidós, 2009.

Lafuente Ferrari, Enrique. *Breve historia de la pintura española.* Madrid: Akal, 1987.

Marañón, Gregorio. *Amiel. Don Juan.* Madrid: Espasa Calpe, 2008.

Molina, Tirso de. *El burlador de Sevilla y convidado de piedra.* Ed. Alfredo Rodríguez López- Vázquez. Madrid: Cátedra, 2010.

Ortega y Gasset, José. "La estrangulación de Don Juan." *El Sol,* 17 de noviembre de 1935.

Rabinovich, Diana. "Don Juan As Slave." *NFF,* 5, 1 & 2 (Spring/Fall 1991): 85-95.

Rostand, Edmond. *La dernière nuit de Don Juan: Poème dramatique en deux parties et un prologue.* Paris: Ulan Press, 2012.

Shaw, Bernard. *Man and Superman: A Comedy and A Philosophy.* Harmondsworth: Penguin Books, 1973.

Unamuno, Miguel. *El Otro. El hermano Juan.* Madrid: Espasa Calpe, 1992.

Zamora, Antonio. *No hay plazo que no se cumpla ni deuda que no se pague y convidado de piedra.* Barcelona: J. F. Piferrer, 1831.

Cosmopolitan Don Juan, Mauricio Garcés and the Myth of the Modern Mexican Dandy

Daniel Chávez
The University of New Hampshire

THE HISTORY OF MEXICAN masculinities reflects the different inflections present in western cultures. However, the combination of colonial heritage, cultural *mestizaje*, revolutionary violence and the pressures of capitalist modernity gave rise to contested if not conflicting forms of masculinity in the twentieth century (Domínguez 2007; Macías and Rubenstein 2012). In this context, by a combination of certain cultural tropes embodied as a strategy of cosmopolitanism and sexual ambiguity, Mauricio Garcés established an artistic persona that moved from *donjuanismo* to homosexuality, from chauvinistic bourgeois Mexicaness to affected cosmopolitan dandyism that ensured him an iconic presence in Mexican film and television for more than three decades. In this chapter, by exploring the ethnicity, gender, and class components of Garcés's representations of masculinity I analyze the contemporary and conflicting appropriation of the classic myths and philosophical anxieties of Don Juan's figure in one of the most beloved Mexican comic actors of the twentieth century.

Mauricio Feres Yázbek (1926-1989), aka Mauricio Garcés, born to a Lebanese family from the port city of Tampico, had a distinguished and eventful career in a country where actors of "foreign" cultures from the Middle East were often perceived as "not sufficiently" national. Mauricio Garcés jumped to the screen in an unusual time for Mexican cinema, but his career included more than sixty films, the hosting of iconic TV programs and numerous appearances in theatre and cabaret spectacles (Baca et. al. 2013; Calderón 2011). By the early 1950s when he started acting in film, the industry was entering in the last phase of what is now known as the Golden Age of Mexican cinema.

From 1933 to 1955, the Mexican movie industry had the perfect combination to transform the popular art of film into the most salient spectacle for its national audience and due to a combination of factors the films of this era marked a trend and were warmly received by moviegoers in the rest of Latin America and among the Latino population of the United States (Mora 1982; Noble 2005; cf. Monsiváis 1995). With a good number of well-trained actors and the capital and technology to produce films, a generation of budding filmmakers and screenwriters found a way to craft interesting and aesthetically pleasing images with the quality to compete with any cinematography around the world (Ramírez Berg 2015). Films presented the new ideas and social dreams of a triumphant revolution and the world witnessed the rising of a group of stars and directors that became a reference and an identifiable brand of a rising country in the Americas. Moreover, between 1938 and 1945, due to changing geostrategic perspectives and for reasons of ideological expediency, North American capital supported the development of the Mexican film industry in order to reach the screens of Latin America with a friendly and attractive message that could counteract the penetration of the images and ideas of Fascism and Communism, the actual enemies on the other side of the Atlantic (Fein 1999). However, by the end of World War II, Hollywood went back to its aggressive internationalism and the disinvestment in the Mexican screen productions was exacerbated with skewed monopolistic market conditions that put in crisis the national production at the time that the new and improved competition for screen time from American majors was mounting. By the late 1960s when Mauricio Garcés became an icon of Mexican comedies, American super productions had dwarfed the modest budgets of Mexican and Latin American films (De la Vega Alfaro 1999).

It was at this time that Mauricio Garcés successfully built an image of a cosmopolitan dandy of the Third World, an autumnal seducer that could combine the swagger of James Bond's 007, the magnetism of an Alain Delon and the endearing clumsiness of a Peter Sellers to provoke the laughter of millions and capture the imagination of national audiences in more than sixty films. Furthermore, the permanence of his figure on television, in comedy and variety programs, and the rerun of his films until the early 1980s, made him one of the most memorable actors in the first century of the history of Mexican cinema.

In hindsight, it is not an exaggeration to say that Garcés's borrowing of elements from the myth of Don Juan, with a humorous twist, served him well as a lasting symbolic insertion into the imagination and preference of several generations of moviegoers. As Alfredo Rodríguez has asserted in relation to the enduring figure of the *burlador* not only in the Hispanic but also in the Western tradition:

The [Don Juan] myth, as one can see, is consistent and primeval: reappears according to the era and geography; comes allied to other myths or gets to be reconstructed to explore the territory of collective dreams. (Rodríguez 2004: 50)[1]

As I will show in the next few pages, the recombination of the elements of *donjuanismo* in Mauricio Garcés version does not come exclusively from literary sources but rather it is a recombination of recent versions of masculinity popularized by the silver screen with new responses to gender formation that reflected the anxieties of the changing times. In Mexico as in other countries, the 1960s brought about the movement for the emancipation of women, the questioning of the instant celebrity and respectability of politicians and captains of industry and their militant nationalism, and the enthusiastic embrace in youth culture for new music in different languages, a thirst for cosmopolitan art and an intense curiosity about what everyday life was like in societies of the First World (Monsiváis 2000).

It was at the behest of his uncle Tafic Yázbek, a producer, that the young Mauricio Feres frequented the studios in Mexico City and became an extra. Very soon, the young *tampiquense* abandoned his Chemical Engineering studies and devoted his time to a new passion, acting in film and theatre. Garcés started in minor roles when he was twenty-five (Calderón 2011). His first speaking role was in a film considered among the most memorable comedies from the last period of the Golden Age. In *La muerte enamorada / Death in Love* (1951) a down on his luck salesman (Fernando Fernández) enters into an unusual deal with the grim reaper, a very attractive personification of Lady Death played by Miroslava Stern, one of the most distinguished female actors in Mexican cinema (García Riera 1998). The salesman learns that he is at the end of his days, but he is given two more weeks while the Dark Lady, recently reincarnated in the body of a beautiful woman, gets reacquainted with the world. While strolling the streets the salesman and Lady Death witness the accidental fall of a construction foreman. The victim is quickly declared dead by a young medic. The first responder in charge is none other than Mauricio Garcés in his first speaking part. The astonishing Lady Death declares that the unfortunate man that fell from the fifth floor is not

---

1   My translation

dead, and with this she ridicules the false authority of the young medic. In my view, this role became a prophetic announcement for things to come for the young actor from Tampico. In his first appearance Garcés acted in a dark comedy in which death, love and desire were the main motors of the story and he had to submit to the unfathomable designs of a woman.

It is well known that Garcés's first appearances did not give him the immediate boost to land starring roles. Perhaps due to the fact that comedies were not the most favored genre by producers and audiences at the time, and it was in roles designed to provoke laughter that our actor delivered his best performances. Throughout the 50s and early 60s, Garcés continued working in secondary roles in productions of a variety of genres ranging from westerns, horror, gangster movies and melodramas. In some of these Garcés played memorable characters but did not become trend setting parts for his career (García Riera 1998: 222, 226; Baca et. al. 2013). Nonetheless, in these productions, Garcés's aptitude for comedy became apparent and his performances were noticed and applied in parodies of consolidated genres. In Mexico as in the U.S., westerns lived a second life in the late 1950s and early 1960s. Garcés appeared in some of these second life westerns including *Por querer a una mujer* (1951), *Los hermanos diablo* (1959) and *Una bala es mi testigo* (1960).

In 1960, Garcés played the second fiddle in *El jinete negro,* a western dressed as a comedy of errors in a hypothetic rural town in Mexico directed by Rogelio A. González. In this film, Garcés plays the role of a traveling salesman peddling toys, rummage, and clothing from town to town. However, while Mauricio Elías,[2] the character played by Garcés, is taking a bath in a river bend, the regional avenger, el Jinete Negro, steals his truck and his urbanite outfit and leaves his own "avenging uniform," a set of black cowboy clothing, including a pair of revolvers and a white horse, for the salesman to wear. Mauricio, who after the shock of having been robbed, becomes quite content with the sudden change of clothes, humorously starts toying with the two pistols the hero left for him. Unbeknownst to the salesman now turned into an instant-cowboy, the real hero is fleeing from a hot pursuit since another impersonator has just robbed a store and killed the owner. The local authority assembled a posse that is furiously looking for the "real" Jinete

---

2   The fact that the character keeps the original name of the actor and only adds an Arabic last name (Elías) speaks of the pride Mauricio felt for his Lebanese heritage. Later in his career Garcés invited to collaborate his friend and fellow Mexican—Lebanese actor Antonio Badú. Another thespian with a long career as a singer like Pedro Infante and Jorge Negrete.

Negro, the robin hood turned hoodlum. The script, written by *trasterrados* Fernando Galiana and Janet Alcoriza,[3] presents a series of impersonations and impostures that mocks the narrative of the social bandit with *donjuanesco* traits already exploited in numerous versions of Zorro, Robin Hood, Chucho el Roto and El Charro Negro[4] that had saturated for decades the screens of Mexican theatres and the pages of the massive editions of comics. Furthermore, in the film, the Jinete Negro also has the reputation of a ladies' man. In the case of the role played by Garcés, *donjuanismo* is more a pretension than a defining trait. In a humorous scene, after Mauricio's character has become amnesiac due to a fortuitous gun-shot wound that providentially only scraped his skull, he sees himself surrounded by young girls eager to have him regain consciousness. The scene is reminiscent of important visual moments in the characterization of the quintessential Mexican hypermasculine figure: Pedro Infante. In the *ranchero*-buddy film *Los tres García* (1947), Infante dreams of a situation in which all his past conquests and lovers are begging him to choose one of them. Sergio de la Mora describes the significance of this scene:

A famous dream sequence in *Los tres García* depicts Infante dressed as a *charro* looking away in disdain from a group of women in mourning. He calls them *las abandonadas* (the abandoned women, meaning his ex-girlfriends). They kneel before him, their eyes cast upon him, imploring his attention and affection. . .This film is a tongue-in-cheek celebratory fantasy about the alluring and irresistible charms of the Mexican macho man popularized by the Mexican film industry. (De la Mora 2009: 81)

---

3   Fernando Galiana (Barcelona 1925- Miami 1995) was a Spanish refugee who wrote and successfully produced dozens of films in Mexico. Janet Alcoriza (Viena 1918- Mexico 1998) married Spanish director and producer Luis Alcoriza. Both collaborated with Buñuel while he was making films in Mexico. Janet was a dancer, actress, and successful scriptwriter in her own right (Ciuk 2000: 38).

4   Chucho el Roto is a popular figure from the nineteenth century in Mexico. Jesús "Chucho" Arriaga, 1858-1894, was a sort of a robin hood of the Porfirian era who became a legend and a symbol of the resistance against the abuse and injustice of the dictatorship (Vanderwood 1992: 90). El Charro Negro was the main character of an immensely popular comic book series created by Adolfo Mariño Ruiz. Later on, the comic book was the basis for a successful string of films (Aurrecoechea and Bartra 1994: 158-167). Both the literary and the visual discourse legends borrowed freely from the myth of Don Juan and the discourse of the social bandit.

De la Mora is delineating the masculine attributes that surrounded the most successful male lead of the Mexican Golden Age. Pedro Infante and his buddy-rival Jorge Negrete became the most important masculine figures that Mexican audiences ever knew in the first fifty years of film history. On one hand, Negrete, a baritone with a virile and arrogant presence, exploited his military training and good looks to present himself as the elegant and serious heartthrob in a vernacular version of Clark Gable and Cary Grant combined. On the other hand, Pedro Infante, a lower middle-class carpenter and mechanic, was discovered on the radio as a mellow crooner of ballads and ranchera music and was eventually launched for a film career as the epitome of the popular *muchacho alegre* who is a good friend to his friends, sacrifices everything for his family and as the laugh a minute ladies-man before taking them to bed (De la Mora 2009; Rubenstein 2001). Against these consummated models of traditional virility, Alcoriza and Galiana seem to use the iconic moment in Infante's *Los tres García* in order to dismantle the hyper-masculinity of the silver screen *charro* (Mexican cowboy). The scene played by Garcés gives one more twist to the exaggeration and proposes the disassembling of masculine dominance. In *El jinete negro*, the amnesiac Mauricio is not only surrounded by women but actually being pinched and tenderly slapped in the face while he is still recovering from the minor injury suffered at the hands of a local gunslinger. While he is coming back to his senses the following dialogue takes place:

Girl 1. He has them [eyes] brown
Girl 2. Giant lashes (*pestañudo*)
Girl 3. Lookie here, huge eyebrows
All three. And what a huge sweet snout
Girl 2. But he is not well yet
Girl 1. I don't know why they call him the Black Horseman (*jinete negro*)
Girl 1. They should call him the brown skinned horseman (*jinete moreno*)
Girl 3. [Caressing Mauricio's face] Rather the olive skinned one
    (*apiñonado*)
Girl 4. Do not stifle him!
Mauricio. Just a moment young ladies. Do not think that...
                                     (González *El jinete negro*)

Mauricio, still semiconscious, starts repeating a nonsensical rhyme he was singing in the scene previous to his shooting. He turns his head, looks quizzically at the four women around the couch who are practically fondling him. When he attempts to talk, Rosenda (Girl 4) smothers Mauricio's voice with a forceful kiss that leaves him dumbfound and gasping for air. The damsel is adamantly kissing the accidental impersonator so he could not say outloud that he "is not the Jinete Negro." Rosenda is in reality the Jinete Negro's love interest and wants to protect her lover from the confusion regarding the robbery. She is also willing to keep Mauricio as the fall guy for the robbery and assassination, for the time being, because she is sure he will be found innocent when the investigation of facts concludes. Mauricio, as the second substitute of the Jinete Negro, is not only a sham but also an unwilling hero who fears bullets because "they hurt too much" as he says in a dialogue. He seems to agree to temporarily stay in the role of the horse-mounted avenger at the behest of Rosenda while there is a trial against the first impersonator and true assassin. Beyond the convoluted plot and confusion created by the sudden appearance of three Jinete Negros, the role played by Garcés reveals the wide net of parodizations of the late western as presented in this film. The scene with the women, who dominate and fondle him, the funny description of his brown skin designating him as non-white, closer to a mestizo but also marking him as a possible Middle-eastern salesman by the name of Mauricio Elías, belie any attempt to a facile identification with the stereotypical male superstar of Mexican cinema. A symbolic figure that had a timely death with the demise of its most distinguished impersonators Jorge Negrete, who died in 1953 of liver failure, and Pedro Infante, deceased in 1957 in an aviation accident (Pilcher 2012; Rubenstein 2001).

By 1960, it was clear that any attempt to imitate Infante or Negrete and build a masculinity following Golden Age screen machismo, would have felt anachronistic and boring. In this sense, Mauricio Garcés devised a new perspective on the seduction and stratagems of the trickster from Seville to build a fresh and dynamic version of the male lead. His first stellar role came in 1966 with *Don Juan 67* directed by the Galician filmmaker Carlos Velo. By then, Garcés was forty years old and the image of the autumnal ladies-man was cast as one of the most enduring roles for the actor. The title is very revealing. The number 67 was not only a designator for the year of the film's release, but also suggests that this was a variation, perhaps the 67th version of the play. Most assuredly the number in the series indicated that the classic immortalized by Andrés de Claramonte in the early 1600s, and reprised by José Zorrilla in 1844, was susceptible to actualization, that the film was an attempt at modernizing the Don Juan myth for the Mexico of the 1960s. Moreover, the actual reference to the literary figure became a trademark for the Tampiquense star, since two more movies were released with title variations *Fray Don Juan* (1970) and *Cómo atrapar a Don Juan* or *El dinero tiene miedo* (1972). I selected the final sequence of the first impersonation to illustrate the parodic actualization of the myth of Don Juan and also to analyze the complexity of the deconstructive gestures inscribed in the roles played by Mauricio Garcés.

It is important to recall that it was in Mexico where the first adaptation for the silver screen of Zorrilla's version of Don Juan was ever produced (Gies 2008). In a silent film, a medium still in its infancy, the Mexican director and prominent documentarist Salvador Toscano Barragán released the first cinematographic version of the Spanish myth in 1898. Less than a decade later the legendary director Enrique Rosas produced another version of Don Juan Tenorio in 1909 (García Riera 1998; Gies 2008). For the sound era, the next adaptation was René Cardona's production of 1937. After this, Mexican films did not present a newer version of the Sevillian gentleman until the modernized parodies played by Mauricio Garcés from 1967 and after. However, it is important to recall that other film versions from Spain, the United States and France did circulate in Mexico, and as, it is well known, one of the most enduring traditions in some Mexican cities with a theatre scene, including Mexico City, Guanajuato, Querétaro and Guadalajara among others, was the representation of Zorrilla's or Claramonte's version of the myth of Don Juan during the annual commemoration of the Day of the Dead on November 2nd. These popular theatre and media representations kept the audacity and morally daring actions implicated in the myth of Don Juan fresh in the memory of the public.

Rodríguez has pointed out how the myth of Don Juan is built around the main symbolic sequence of seduction, broken promise-escape, and final punishment of the seducer (Rodríguez 2004: 54). This structuring sequence will be reproduced in Garcés' films, but the actualization of its elements will follow closely many of the sociological and political conditions of modern Mexico. In *Don Juan 67*, at the end of the screenplay devised by Velo and Fernando Galiana, the constant womanizing of Mauricio Galán, a playboy on the verge of bankruptcy, has resulted in the unexpected appearance of a baby at the doorstep of his house. Dimas, the loyal servant, played by David Reynoso, an actor better known for his roles as a tough detective in Mexican film noir, wants his master to accept the kid as the physical and moral consequence of his escapades. Galán refuses to believe the child is his and cannot accept the fact that, from now on, he has to take responsibility for the newborn and completely alter his life style. The Don Juan of Las Lomas—an upper class neighborhood in Mexico City- fearing the "bad publicity" of people knowing he has a son without a mother to take care of him, devises the plan to flee to his country house in Avándaro to avoid scandal. Avándaro, an exclusive sierra destination close to Mexico City, was the weekend resort of choice for the jetsetters of the 1960s. However, Dimas has decided that his master has to man-up once and for all and he should marry the mother of the child. For that, behind his masters' back, he makes calls on every phone number in Mauricio's private directory and tells the women that his master is ready to marry the legitimate mother of the newly found kid. An army of possible brides heeds the call and flocks in sports cars, 4x4s, taxis and limousines to the countryside manor of the playboy. Given the high number of prospects, Mauricio tries various tacks and questions to weed out the real mother. The evasive tactics of the seducer, however, enrage the swarm of women who end up physically attacking the would-be groom, leaving him in bad shape after he has found out that none of them is the real mother. That the instigator of the symbolic sequence of punishment is none other than the faithful servant of Don Juan is already a new twist. Furthermore, the fact that the women mob the seducer and exact a minor revenge on the betrayer by attacking him physically is a sign that the real and imaginary roles of women and the role of the subaltern servant have suffered a significant change in the late twentieth century.

As in a good comedy of errors, the spectator learns that nothing is what it seems at the beginning. The little boy is, in fact, the son of Dimas and one of his lovers (the servant imitating badly the behavior of the master). This aspect is also a minor twist in the role of the servant of the classic *Burlador de Sevilla's* character Catalinón, in Agramonte's work (see Rodríguez 2004). In the film, however, the failure of Dimas as seducer restores the role of the *gracioso* to the faithful servant, and Mauricio laughs hysterically. Mocking the sermons he had heard from his butler, and knowing that the joke is now on him, Mauricio feels relieved from having dodged the responsibility of becoming a father. However, his tribulations are not over. His last two tormentors, his young and attractive lawyer and a young plumber, for whom he feels an intense desire, enter the scene to confront the playboy with the last two symbolic systems he refuses to acknowledge power over him: homosexuality and the law.

One of his main powers and key to the successful practice of seduction, Don Juan is an artist of disguise and a master supplanter. Doña Ana believes she is giving herself to Don Luis, but he is being supplanted by Don Juan, his enemy, in Zorrilla's *Tenorio* (Zorrilla 2014). This aspect could not be left out in a modernization of the myth, but true to the transformative intervention of Alcoriza and Galiana, it is not Don Juan but rather one of his love interests who is supplanting another. Pepe the plumber is in fact an underage girl who has sworn herself to seduce the seducer. From her part, the lawyer has sworn she will be the one who finally marries the eternal runaway groom. These characters become two discursive options that can reverse the potencies and traditional symbolic powers of Don Juan: heterosexual carnal love, and the complete evasion of patriarchal law. Mauricio fears his homosexual desire for Pepe, and knows that, in the secluded location of Avándaro, he will not be able to escape from the enticements of the young boy. Luckily, for him, Pepe reveals himself as a woman in a clumsy striptease. After this revelation, the playboy seems to be back in control of the situation, he is in familiar territory in the symbolic sequence: deception, seduction, satisfaction of desire. Nonetheless, this "restoration" of heterosexuality is symbolically incomplete since the suspicion of homosexuality has already been outed and thrown into the open. In this regard, Garcés's representation takes one step forward in the dismantling of the traditional masculinities of the Mexican screen, by directly representing the possibility of attraction between Don Juan and a young boy.

Recent film criticism from the perspective of queer studies has pointed out that homosocial and homosexual tensions were already built in the discourse of the screen macho of the Golden Age due to the intense and close relations in buddy movies and male subjections of servants to their masters (see De la Mora 2009; Pilcher 2012). But films from that era would never allow a direct association of the male lead with homosexual desire, such possibilities were subjacent or indirectly suggested. In this sense, Garcés's parodies destabilize the rigid limits pre-established by models of masculinity fostered by the previous generation of film performers. The destabilization goes beyond this representation of an "accidental" or "temporary" appearance of homosexual desire and extends to the mechanisms of seduction as I will show next.

Coming back to *Don Juan 67*, as it is usually the case with the movie, there is a constant subplot that functions as a mechanism of "desire interruptus." The female lawyer arrives accompanied by a photographer knowing that her former boss is about to have sex with an underage girl. With photographic evidence of her masters' alleged transgression, in this case statutory rape, the terms of the extortion proposed by the lawyer are simple, confront justice or sign a matrimonial contract with her. To complicate matters further, Pepe wants her honor preserved too—even though nothing has happened yet, or the spectators have not seen it happen- she also wants to marry her supposed

victimizer in a fast shot-gun wedding. The two women quarrel for the possession of their lover while Mauricio shouts he is not marrying anyone, that he
would rather die than get married. In this hour of desperation Dimas comes
to the rescue offering a Tarzan vine which his boss takes hurriedly in order to
escape, but the vine is attached to a tree that is being cut by a lumberjack, a
leitmotif image that has recurrently appeared as a dialectical montage scene
throughout the last three sequences of the film. The obvious phallic references, and the concomitant allusions to castration and loss of male power,
come to converge in the images of the lumberjack progressively downing the
tree. Again, another sign that in the 1960s no single social type is stable and
that the subaltern figures may yet claim agency and sabotage the sweet con-
stancy of hegemony.

In the final sequence of *Don Juan 67*, we see Mauricio land from his vine
jump inside a small boat cushioned and padded as a casket. A beautiful woman dressed in black holds the helm on one hand and a scythe in the other. This
incarnation of Lady Death is of course reminiscent of that of Miroslava Stern
in *La muerte enamorada*, the actual film debut of Garcés back in 1951. In this
case, the *convidado de piedra* is not only female but also the last "conquest" of
Don Juan. Mauricio kisses the Grim Reaper and the "end" title appears. After
the constant jumps of sexual escapades and patriarchal misadventures, the
film goes back to the moral-religious realm of the Don Juan myth.

This was not the first time that Garcés played a role in which the basic te-
nets of the Don Juan myth were somehow invoked. In previous comedies like
Estoy casado, ha, ha / I Am Married Ha, Ha (1959) he combined the role of a
cosmopolitan seducer, helped faithfully by his servant or a minor entourage.
Even in these earlier examples, it was evident that despite his medium height
and regular complexion, Garcés could present himself with poise, with great
assurance and that his fast-talking enticements and innuendo seemed to be
irresistible for women. In recent commentaries about the actor, some critics
refer to Mauricio Garcés as the first "metrosexual" personality of Mexican
cinema, a trait he ably added to the construction of the "traditional" male
lead (Calderón 2011; Baca et. al. 2013). Furthermore, there is very little that
is just traditional or a simple repetition either from Mexican cinema or from
the Renaissance archetype of Don Juan. Invariably, one way or another, the
attitudes, schemes and sexual advances of the seducers played by Garcés include an element of self-parody or secondary dismantling of its affirmative
gestures. This is to say, the hypersexuality of the characters played by Garcés
seems to reaffirm a supposed heteronormative conduct, an aggressive masculinity with an all-out devotion for heterosexual pleasure executed through a

supposed "destruction" or "annihilation of the will" of the women to resist him. However, in the next scene the gestures or discourse of the character would indicate that what the spectator is witnessing is not necessarily the exaltation of *donjuanismo*, but rather a simulation, a discrete process of dismantling the phallocentric residuals of contemporary gender roles. Seduction should now be negotiated, talked over, or outright postponed because one of the participants is not ready and he, she or somebody else, manages to sabotage the advances. For instance, Garcés often used the expression "la voy a hacer pedazos" (I will tear her to pieces) to indicate that Don Juan is ready to cast the full power of his spell in order to consummate the conquest and have sex with the "target" (Baca et. al. 2013). But more often than not, some external situation interrupts the completion of the sequence of seduction. These interruptions could take the form of an external physical impediment, an accidental subplot, or emerge from another character, usually a protective father or jealous suitor—the symbolic re-incarnation of Don Gonzalo and Don Luis in Zorrilla's version of the myth- before whom Don Juan always retreats or finds a way to dodge the confrontation (cf. Zorrilla 2014).

In fact, this long postponement of carnal intimacy becomes the central plot in one of Garcés' favorite films: *24 horas de placer / 24 Hours of Pleasure* (René Cardona 1969) in which the unfaithful couple formed by Silvia Pinal, a dissatisfied wife, and the writer and also unfaithful husband played by Garcés, attempts to make love but their encounter is constantly interrupted by an interminable series of minor and hilarious incidents and annoying obstacles (Aviña 2004: 148). In this as in other comedies, very often the retreat or recoil of the weapons of seduction are of a symbolic quality and quite often seem to be the product of auto-sabotage. Moreover, while the spectator observes the simulations, the charades invoked as masks of innocence to lure the woman, the mellow voice of the seducer, the actual gestures reveal a naïve or hilarious side of performance that makes evident the weak constitution, the tender and almost innocent power of the wannabe heartthrob hidden underneath the skin of the supposed metrosexual wolf. At times, Mauricio seems to become a purring kitten or a frustrated little boy wanting the caresses of his mommy and, in a way, the amatory encounter seems rather a compensatory gift or the emotional alms payed by the woman to a destitute man. These conditions and indirect tactics are hardly in tune with the sexual prowess expected of a full-fledge *burlador*.

Despite the fact that the most memorable roles ever played by Garcés were delivered for light romantic comedies that today would be considered exercises in sexual repression in terms of skin exposure to the camera, Garcés's recourse to politics, class and social commentary, the fast wit and complex references to aspects of cosmopolitan consumption, classic mythology, travel, his humorous use of English, French and German, and the references to Mexican, European and Asian art and philosophy, have made some of his dialogues gems of contextualized humor, filtered expressions of the tensions, economic struggles and political violence of the Mexico of the 1960s.

In *El criado malcriado* (Del Villar 1969) Garcés plays the role of an impoverished globetrotter-turned-bank robber who, due to a botched heist, has to hide in the house of a perfectly dysfunctional family. The aristocratic head of the family brings to her mansion distant relatives who seem to be a humorous microcosm of the social ailments of Mexican society. The supposed uncle of the woman is an elderly general of the last revolution threatening to line up and shoot all those who do not agree with him. An American woman painter, a supposed distant cousin, lives off from the family without contributing to the house, this despite the fact that the household is on the brink of bankruptcy. There is also a nephew and wannabe juvenile delinquent who spends the day on his bike yelling and stealing food. These odd characters are accepted as family by the old heiress who declares herself a widow even though her husband is living in the house. Only the father and the beautiful daughter seem to have a sense of reality. In my view, as I mentioned, the house guests are metaphoric representations of the crisis lived inside the house, a stand in for Mexico as a country. The uncle is the aging authoritarian state that threats and sometimes actually shoots at those who dissent and disobey. The American cousin represents the onerous freeloading of American industry and foreign capital, living off from the meager resources from the household. The young delinquent seems to be a reference to the search of freedom and antisystem tendencies of Mexican youth. The fact that the woman of the house considers herself a widow is indicative of the country having lost the presence of a real father, not as a source of authoritarian ruling but as stabilizing and constructive force. In contradiction to the allusion of an outmoded motherhood, it is the disempowered father and his daughter Ana who are still in charge of the house and trying to prevent the chaos brought about by the "guests."

While fleeing from the botched bank robbery, Mauricio is knocked down by the nephew and is recovering in the house from the youngster's attack. The next day, when he tries to leave the mansion, the old heiress offers him a ride in a Ford A and they have the following dialogue:

Esperanza. Why are you escaping from the house?
Pablo Namnum (Mauricio Garcés). I do not know how to stand still
    anywhere. I have been a croupier in Vegas, a smuggler in Macao,
    guerrilla in the Middle East, diver in Acapulco
Esperanza. What else?
Pablo. A monk in Tibet, Ku Klux Klan in New Orleans, Hippie in San
    Francisco, and once I had to dress as a Geisha in Japan. Oh...if I told
    you, dear lady!!
Esperanza. And now?
Pablo. In a hot mess and trying to get out of it
Esperanza. Have you ever been a cook?
Pablo. On board the Titanic
Esperanza. Do you know how to drive?
Pablo. Cars, ships and planes

Despite the preposterous final responses, since the Titanic sank back in
1912 and it would have been impossible for a man this age to have been in
that historic disaster, the old lady seems to believe him and ends up offering Pablo a job as a butler and cook for the madhouse she calls home. In
contrast with the apparent flirting of this dialogue with absurdist aesthetics, the phrases and the character played by Garcés in this film are a logical
indication of the cosmopolitan ambitions of many of his representations. In
a previous dialogue Pablo declares he is of Lebanese origin and his last name
was "Namnum." This was the actual family name of his real-life friend and
also movie star Antonio Badú, a Lebanese-Mexican performer as himself. As
I mentioned before, the reaffirmation of his ethnic origin in actual dialogue
became a frequent occurrence for the actor in his later films. Furthermore,
it matters little that the list of jobs Pablo cited was only part of an imaginary curriculum because, once confronted with the current issues of the era,
all the supposed professions and trades enlisted seem to make up a map of
hotspots for convulsive societal change and political confrontation.

    By 1969 Las Vegas had become the playground for the corrupt bour-
geoisie in Mexico. Acapulco diving at "la quebrada" was an exploitative form
of spectacle practiced by impoverished local divers in the most fashionable
beach destination of those years. Starting in the late sixties and throughout
the 1970s a massive exodus of Chinese mainlanders fled the Communist regime and were smuggled by boat to Macau and Hong Kong. In 1969 the
Palestinian PLO violently took over some of the refugee camps controlled
by the Lebanese army. The case of Brandenburg vs. Ohio was overturned by

the U.S. Supreme Court in favor of a member of the Ku Klux Klan protecting inflammatory speech unless it can be proven that utterances can cause violence. The Summer of Love occurred in 1967 in California, and in 1969 the Altamont Free Concert or "Woodstock West" took place in San Francisco, both important events for the countercultural movement of that era. The most obvious reference missing from that list, perhaps due to self-censorship, was a profession somehow connected to the massacre of students at the Tlatelolco square in Mexico City the year before. Although a current of strong social criticism was about to enter Mexican cinema from 1970 on, it seems peculiar that in a comedy with certain elements of the absurd, Garcés's dialogue was pointing out some of the most urgent conflicts that were making the headlines in national and global news media (cf. Chávez 2010). From any number of fantastic or heroic trades that could have made believable the profile of the global wanderer for his character, Garcés chose to make reference to the cultural and social storms looming in the background in that year. This sense of being in a contemporary and convulsive world transformed Garcés's characters in male figures that if in a way were repeating most of the sexist discourse prevalent at the time, also seemed widely aware of the limitations of the tyrannical male chauvinism played by stars of previous generations. In one of the most hilarious scenes Pablo *el criado malcriado* receives a beating from Ana who is an expert in martial arts.

Clearly the *donjuanismo* of Garcés's films had also abandoned the militant and rambunctious localism of the *ranchera comedy* for a critical cosmopolitanism, more in tune with the classic internationalism of the original *burlador*, and based on social, historical, and political awareness bespeaking of a progressive spirit and a genuine curiosity for the outside world. I will say more, in his own mundane and lighthearted way, Garcés was effecting similar changes in film acting to those implemented by the young figures of Mexican literature in the narrative art. In the *anno admirabilis* of 1967, Carlos Fuentes published *Cambio de piel*, an experimental novel interspersing dialogue of young cosmopolitan hipsters visiting Cholula with the advance of the Spanish troops over Mexico Tenochtitlan in 1519. Vicente Leñero with *El garabato* (1967) and José Emilio Pacheco with *Morirás lejos* (1967) actualized many of the experiments attempted by the *Nouveau roman* in France while crafting characters who write from the United States, flee from Nazi Germany or revisit the events of the Roman-Jewish wars of Flavius Josephus (cf. Sefchovich 1987: 206). An air of ambitious cosmopolitan exploration was the common trait in the screen art of Garcés, and in the literary craft of these young Mexican writers.

Perhaps, the most important contribution of Mauricio Garcés's sexual comedies was the inauguration of a tactical demolition, still partial and imperfect, but pioneering nonetheless against the long lasting homophobic prejudice prevalent across the popular and middle classes in Mexico. Garcés was the first recognized and beloved male lead to play a role as a gay man in a featured film. In *Modisto de señoras* (1969), D'Maurice is a successful fashion designer who specializes in modern and exquisite garments for married women. Garcés's character pretends to be an effeminate and temperamental gay man, not only to deceive a society who mistrusts a masculine male designer, but also in order to live his life as an undercover Don Juan. He would not only charge exorbitant prices for dressing jetsetters, but he would also get into bed with the wives of corrupt politicians, financiers and captains of industry. True, many of the manners, exaggerations and ideas used by Garcés in his representation of a gay fashion designer seem stereotypical to us today. For this reason, certain critics have seen this gesture of "temporal homosexuality" that dissolves at the end of the film as one more ploy in the long catalogue of oppressing gay representations (see Baca et. al. 2013). In my assessment of the film, however, I pay attention to what I consider effective tactics to question the repressive rigidities of masculine representation in general, and in Mexican film in particular. In a scene in which D'Maurice is taking measures for one of his clients, a cabaret dancer interpreted by the voluptuous Argentinian actress Zulma Faiad,[5] they have the following exchange:

Zulma: I confess that I don't know what to expect from a man like you
D'Maurice: Even in that we are twin souls. I don't know either what to expect from a man like me
Zulma: Sometimes you seem like a Don Juan, other times...
D'Maurice: And other times. . .
Zulma: A. . .*modisto*
D'Maurice: Well ...we *modistos* also have our little heart
Zulma: Ayyy. . . you are a very strange man
D'Maurice: That is because a body like yours is capable of converting the craziest of the craziest among the *modistos*. (Cardona 1969)

---

5   Zulma Faiad (Buenos Aires 1944) is an Argentinian *vedette* and actress of Lebanese origin. She participated in three films starring Mauricio Garcés: *La cama* (1968); *Modisto de señoras* (1969) and *Espérame en Sibera vida mía* (1971). The latter was an adaptation of the novel of the same title by Spanish writer Enrique Jardiel Poncela.

The kiss sealing this scene also seals the seduction. After a cut, the next sequence shows the couple in a high angle long shot in Dutch tilt. They are in opposite sides of the frame, the camera turns around to straighten the angle and we can see them in bed, scantly dressed, talking and eating from a couple of seafood dishes. The allusion is clear, the camera move confirms the refocusing of the relation, this is a post-coital scene that was preceded by a dialogue in which the sexual identity and preferences of two consenting adults was being negotiated. In this and other scenes, not only the female characters have to figure out if their attraction for the effeminate man is corresponded but also the audience has to overcome all the rigid signs that mark D'Maurice as a gay man. Female characters and spectators are challenged by the images to realize that sexual preference, desire and gender, are never one definitive and exclusive category, but rather a complex and fluid reconfirmation of signs and come from a mutual acceptance of the two parties. It is probable that most spectators chose to see Garcés's interpretation of a gay man as a male dominated simulacrum, simply as a ruse in the war of sexes, a masculine masquerade to lower the defenses of the woman and strike at the right moment. This is to say, the sustained deployment of exaggerated gestures of femininity in an artist like Garcés that has until then played the role of a serial womanizer is one more trick in the bag of tricks of the master supplanter that the myth of Don Juan purports. But in my view, there are a couple of important contradictions to this simplified perspective. On one hand, in order to suggest that the macho is simply supplanting the gay man, there was no need to present the pre and post seduction dialogues in which the female characters are questioning their own assumptions, trying to examine their feelings and finding themselves disarmed by their desire for he who is perceived as "different" and supposedly "undesirable" in heteronormative terms. On the other hand, the assurances for heterosexual males that there is "nothing to fear" from the relation of a gay man and a woman are humorously questioned. The verbal musings about women's conflicting feelings and desires uttered by the female characters played by Irma Lozano and Zulma Faiad in *Modisto de señoras* and other Garcés's films are essential for the most explicit scenes of seduction ever allowed in mainstream cinema in Mexico, and were no doubt sowing disquiet and spreading doubts regarding the traditional heteronormative expectations and assurances afforded by Mexican film. Garcés's sex comedies suggested that the comfortably reassuring scopophilic tendencies that film had cultivated for heterosexual male pleasure during seven decades were no longer guaranteed. I contend that even if some of the traits of the representation of a gay person are perhaps a caricature, in *Modisto de señoras*

(1969) by adding D'Maurice to the repertoire of his characters—originally built around the sophisticated and world traveled playboy in previous films-representing a highly ironic, intelligent and strong willed gay man, Mauricio Garcés was contributing to a quiet demolition of the last remnants of the fossilized machismo inherited from the material and imaginary legacy of the Mexican Revolution (1910-1940).

By finding a way to represent a gamut of masculine roles whose sexuality was not fully predetermined: a sophisticated metrosexual Don Juan, a man of delicate taste in clothing, a sybarite gourmet, with a sexuality in question for its fluidity and uncertain preferences, Garcés was putting to rest the affected hypermasculinity of yesteryear stars like Pedro Infante, Jorge Negrete and Pedro Armendariz. These actors would represent on the screen, and sometimes led real lives, as consummated womanizers in roles of strict heteronormative conditions, and until the arrival of Garcés's comedic persona, this seemed the only formula for success for male leads in Mexican cinema. Although personal life hardly ever reflects what is on the screen, at the time of his death, Pedro Infante had four women and contributed to the sustenance of fourteen children (Rubenstein 2001). Negrete married three times and lived through a long string of romances widely covered by the media. In contrast, Mauricio Garcés chose to keep his love life out of the public eye. He never married but all his female co-stars remembered him with love and admiration. Although rumors of his supposed homosexuality or bisexuality were constant, there was never an exposé, a scandal or a denunciation to confirm or deny that aspect of his private life. This might seem not uncommon in a country and in an era when openly declaring homosexuality was tantamount to signing away a career in any field. However, in interviews Garcés always insisted that he loved to stay home and cook for friends, that he was much more reserved in person than in his screen persona. This zealous protection of his privacy, of course, did not prevent him from openly declare he enjoyed tobacco and alcohol, dancing, gambling or betting on the ponies. The latter two were his most costly passions in which he squandered most of his earnings. No doubt in and out of the screen, Garcés had a complex and fascinating personality and, in many ways, that personality contradicted the prescribed formulas of masculinity of his time. In the words of Silvia Pinal, one of his most famous co-stars:

> I was his impossible love, Mauricio always said he loved me, that he was in love with me. My husband at that time (Enrique Guzmán) did not like him to say that...But he and I became best friends and I can only say

that he was and will be the best comedy leading man and I don't believe there will ever be an actor who can take his place. (cited in Calderón 2011)

With the sexual ambiguity of many of his roles, Garcés was opening the door to a methodic doubt regarding the heteronormative beliefs in perfect sexual dichotomies. With incisive humor he was giving expression to some of the most important demands of the sexual revolution of the 1960s: freedom from rigid gender roles, freedom of expression and respect for different ways of becoming a sexual being in the world. Who would have thought that in Mexico the actualization of the Don Juan myth would become a point of departure in the discussion and visualization of gender and sexual rights in the twentieth century.

Works Cited

Aurrecoechea, José Manuel and Armando Bartra. *Puros cuentos III, historia de la historieta en México 1934-1950*. México: Grijalbo / Consejo Nacional para la Cultura y las Artes, 1994.

Aviña, Rafael. *Una mirada insólita, temas y géneros del cine mexicano*. México: Océano, 2004.

Baca Tavira, Norma, Luna Martínez, América and Graciela Vélez Bautista. "Las enseñanzas de *Don Juan 67*. Mauricio Garcés, cine y masculinidad." *La colmena. Revista de la Universidad Autónoma del Estado de México*. 67 (2013): 13-20.

Calderón, Lucero. "Mauricio Garcés, galán de risa." *Excelsior*. December 12, 2011.

Chávez, Daniel. "The Eagle and the Serpent in the Screen, the State as Spectacle in Mexican Cinema." *Latin American Research Review*. 45.3 (2010): 115-141.

Ciuk, Perla. *Diccionario de directores*. México: CONACULTA / Cineteca Nacional, 2000.

Domínguez Ruvalcaba, Héctor. *Modernity and the Nation in Mexican Representations of Masculinity, from Sensuality to Bloodshed*. New York: Palgrave McMillan, 2007.

Fein, Seth. "From Collaboration to Containment: Hollywood and the International Political Economy of Mexican Cinema after the Second World War." in *Mexico's Cinema a Century of Film and Filmmakers*. Edited by

Joanne Hershfield and David R. Maciel. Wilmington, DE: Scholarly Resources. 1999. 165-191.

García Riera, Emilio. *Breve historia del cine mexicano. Primer siglo 1897-1997.* México: Ediciones Mapa / Instituto Mexicano de Cinematografía/ Universidad de Guadalajara, 1998.

Gies, David. "Don Juan Tenorio, estrella de cine: Zorrilla, Marcero, Barrera." In *La literatura española del siglo XIX y las artes.* Edited by Botrel, J.F. , Marisa Sotelo et. al. Barcelona: Universidad de Barcelona, 2008. 163-174.

Macías-González, Víctor and Anne Rubenstein. "Introduction." In *Masculinity and Sexuality in Modern Mexico.* Edited by Víctor M. Macías-González and Anne Rubenstein. Albuquerque: University of New Mexico Press, 2012.

Monsiváis, Carlos. "Mythologies" in *Mexican Cinema.* Edited by Paranaguá, Paulo Antonio. British Film Institute / Instituto Mexicano de Cinematografía, 1995. 117-127.

―――, *Mexican Postcards.* London: Verso, 2000.

Mora, Carl. *Mexican Cinema, Reflections of a Society.* Berkeley: University of California Press, 1982.

Mora, Sergio de la. "Pedro Infante Unveiled." In *Cinemachismo: Masculinities and Sexuality in Mexican Film.* Austin: University of Texas Press, 2009. 68-104.

Noble, Andrea. *Mexican National Cinema.* New York: Routledge, 2005.

Pilcher, Jeffrey M. "The Gay Caballero." In *Masculinity and Sexuality in Modern Mexico.* Edited by Víctor M. Macías-González and Anne Rubenstein. Albuquerque: University of New Mexico Press, 2012.

Ramírez Berg, Charles. *Cinema of Solitude, a Critical Study of Mexican Film 1967-1983.* Austin: University of Texas Press, 1984.

―――, *The Classic Mexican Cinema, the Poetics of the Exceptional Golden Age Films.* Austin: University of Texas Press, 2015.

Rodríguez López-Vázquez, Alfredo. "Introducción." In Molina, Tirso de. *El burlador de Sevilla.* Madrid: Ediciones Cátedra, 2004. 11-99.

Rubenstein, Anne. "Bodies, Cities, Cinema: Pedro Infante's Death as Political Spectacle." In Joseph, Gilbert, Anne Rubenstein et. al. *Fragments of a Golden Age, the Politics of Culture in Mexico Since 1940,* 2001. 199-233.

Sefchovich, Sara. *México: país de ideas, país de novelas.* México: Grijalbo, 1987.

Vanderwood, Paul. *Disorder and Progress. Bandits, Police, and Mexican Development.* Wilmington: Scholarly Resources, 1992.

Vega Alfaro, Eduardo de la. "The Decline of the Golden Age and the Making of the Crisis." In *Mexico's Cinema a Century of Film and Filmmakers*. Edited by Joanne Hershfield and David R. Maciel. Wilmington, DE: Scholarly Resources, 1999. 165-191.

Zorrilla, José. *Don Juan Tenorio*. Edition by Gies, David. Madrid: Clásicos Castalia, 2014.

Filmography

Cardona Jr. René. dir. *Modisto de señoras*. 1969.

Cardona Jr. René. dir. *24 horas de placer*. 1969.

Cortázar, Ernesto. dir. *La muerte enamorada*. 1951.

González, Rogelio. A. dir. *El jinete negro*. 1961.

Velo, Carlos. dir. *Don Juan 67*. 1967.

Villar, Francisco del. *El criado malcriado*. 1969.

Contributors

JORGE ABRIL SÁNCHEZ is an independent scholar whose interests range widely, from the study of legends in the Middle Ages, heresy, folklore, and treatises of demonology in Renaissance Europe to the description of idolatry, paganism and demonolatry upon the exploration and conquest of America and Asia by Spaniards. Abril Sánchez focuses his research on the literature and culture of Medieval and Early Modern Spain, often from a comparative perspective that covers the works of authors on both sides of the Atlantic and their influence on other neighboring nations: Rojas, Cervantes, Lope de Vega, Calderón de la Barca, Tirso de Molina, Sor Juana, Miguel de Luarca, Shakespeare, Dryden, Settle, Behn, Molière, Corneille, etc. Abril Sánchez is especially interested in the occult, magic, the Hermetic tradition, alchemy, astrology, mythology, and the interconnections between the Church and the State during the religious persecutions of the 16th and 17th centuries in Europe and the American territory.

ROBERT E. BAYLISS (PhD, Hispanic Literature and Comparative Literature, Indiana University) is an Associate Professor of Spanish at the University of Kansas. He has published articles in several journals including *Hispanic Review, Comparative Drama, Hispania* and *Comparative Literature Studies.* His book, *The Discourse of Courtly Love in Seventeenth-Century Spanish Theater,* was published in 2008 by Bucknell University Press. His forthcoming book, *The Idea of Spain: Local, National and Global Afterlives of the Spanish Golden Age* addresses the ways in which the "classics" of Spain's Golden Age are adapted, appropriated and consumed in contemporary Spain.

FERNANDO BELEZA is a Lecturer in Portuguese Studies at Newcastle University (U.K.). He holds a B.A. from the University of Coimbra, an M.A. from the University of Porto, and a Ph.D in Luso-Afro-Brazilian Studies and Theory from the University of Massachusetts Dartmouth. He is the co-editor of the volume of essays *Mário de Sá-Carneiro, a Cosmopolitan Modernist*. He has articles and book chapters published on Portuguese modernism, race, gender, and sexuality in Luso-Afro-Brazilian literatures and cultures, and modernist cosmopolitanism. He is also an associate researcher in the Center for Comparative Literature at the University of Porto and a member of the research project *Estranhar Pessoa*, based at the New University of Lisbon. Currently, he is finishing a book project entitled *Modernist Desires: Cosmopolitanism, Sexuality, and the Making of Portuguese Modernism.*

MARGARET E. BOYLE is Associate Professor of Romance Languages and Literatures at Bowdoin College. She is the author of *Unruly Women: Performance, Penitence and Punishment in Early Modern Spain* (University of Toronto Press, 2014) and co-editor of the forthcoming volume *Health and Healing in the Early Modern Iberian World: A Gendered Perspective* (with Sarah E. Owens). She is also an elected member of the committee for 16th- and 17th-Century Spanish and Iberian Drama for the Modern Languages Association, and a delegate member for the MLA's Status of Women in the Profession.

DANIEL CHÁVEZ is Assistant Professor of Latin American and Latino studies at the Department of Languages, Literatures and Cultures at the University of New Hampshire. He obtained a degree in biochemical engineering from the ITESM (Monterrey and Queretaro, Mexico), an M.A. in Spanish and an M.A. Latin American studies from Ohio University, and his Ph.D. in Romance languages from the University of Michigan. He also holds a certification in film studies from the latter. Professor Chávez has taught at the universities of Oregon, Virginia and Kentucky as well as Vassar and Middlebury College. The author of numerous articles on film, Latin American literature and new media studies, he is currently working on book projects regarding cinema and new media representations of Mexican and Mexican American history and culture. Vanderbilt University Press published his book on cultural and political history *Nicaragua and the Politics of Utopia* (2015). His teaching and research interests include Latin American and U.S. Latina/o film and visual culture, 20th & 21st Century Latin American literature and cultural studies, Latina/o crime novel, and Mexican and Central American novel and poetry. His book of poems, *Visiones en luna agreste y nitrato de plata,* received the Efraín Huerta National Poetry Award in Mexico in 2010.

FREDERICK A. DE ARMAS is a literary scholar, critic and novelist whose scholarly work focuses on the literature of the Spanish Golden Age (Cervantes, Calderón, Claramonte, Lope de Vega), often from a comparative perspective. His interests include the politics of astrology; magic and the Hermetic tradition; ekphrasis; the relations between the verbal and the visual particularly between Spanish literature and Italian art; and the interconnections between myth and empire during the rule of the Habsburgs. His books and edited collections include: *The Invisible Mistress: Aspects of Feminism and Fantasy in the Golden Age*; *The Return of Astraea: An Astral-Imperial Myth in Calderón*; *The Prince in the Tower: Perceptions of "La vida es sueño"*; *Heavenly Bodies: The Realms of "La Estrella de Sevilla"*; *A Star-Crossed Golden Age: Myth and the Spanish Comedia*; *Cervantes, Raphael and the Classics* (1998); *Quixotic Frescoes: Cervantes and Italian Renaissance Art* (2006); *Don Quixote among the Saracens: A Clash of Civilizations and Literary Genres* (2011), *La astrología en el teatro clásico europeo: de Lope de Vega a Shakespeare* (2018), among many other works.

EDWARD H. FRIEDMAN is Gertrude Conaway Vanderbilt Professor of Spanish, Professor of Comparative Literature and European Studies, and Director of the Robert Penn Warren Center for the Humanities. He has been editor of the *Bulletin of the Comediantes* since 1999 and is a past president of the Cervantes Society of America. His research has centered on early modern Spanish literature, with special emphasis on Cervantes, picaresque narrative, and the Comedia. Friedman has explored how sixteenth- and seventeenth-century Spanish texts play against tradition and, at the same time, establish directions for future creation, by anticipating forms of contemporary fiction and drama, as well as the preoccupations of contemporary theory. As they establish new modes of fiction, Cervantes and the authors of picaresque narratives find access to social and ideological centers from the margins. While these writers point the way toward narrative realism, they also mirror—paradoxically and precociously—modernist and postmodernist responses to realism. Golden Age drama and poetry create their own, and equally engaging, dialectics of politics and rhetoric, centers and margins. Friedman's most recent monograph examines questions of realism from the anonymous *Lazarillo de Tormes* (1554) to Miguel de Unamuno's *Niebla* (1914), and he is working on a project that focuses on the British critic and historian Gerald Brenan. Friedman has published adaptations for the stage of Lope de Vega's *La dama boba* and Unamuno's *Niebla*, and a translation of Leandro Fernández de Moratín's *El sí de las niñas*. *Wit's End*, adapted from Lope's play, was performed as part of Vanderbilt University Theatre's 2006-2007 season. He received the Jeffrey Nordhaus Award for Excellence in Undergraduate Teaching in 2006 and the College of Arts and Science Graduate Mentoring Award in 2007, and a Fulbright grant to Spain in 2010.

CHARLES GANELIN is Full Professor of Spanish at Miami University of Ohio. He specializes on Early Modern Spanish literature and *Don Quixote* by Miguel de Cervantes. He is the author of *Rewriting Theatre: The Comedia and the Nineteenth-Century Refundición* and the editor of Andrés de Claramonte's *La infelice Dorotea.*

CARMEN GARCÍA DE LA RASILLA is Professor of Spanish language and culture at the University of New Hampshire. She has a Ph.D. in history from the University of Valladolid, Spain and a Ph.D. in literature from The Johns Hopkins University and researches and publishes in both fields. Author of *Salvador Dalí's Literary Self-Portrait: Approaches to a Surrealist Autobiography* (Bucknell University Press 2009), and of *Salvador Dalí: Traditions, Myths and Cultural Modes* (University of Granada Press, 2018); her other publications include a study of twentieth century Spanish urban history, one edited monograph on the Spanish historical novel (Verdelís 2016), one co-edited volume on Cervantes' *Don Quixote* (Juan de la Cuesta 2016), and articles and book chapters on these subjects, as well as on comparative literature, women and painting and on Spanish Surrealism.

FERNANDO GONZÁLEZ DE LEÓN (Ph.D. in History, The Johns Hopkins University, 1992) is Associate Professor of History at Springfield College in Massachusetts and specializes in Spanish and European history and antebellum American culture. He has published widely in the social, military and intellectual history of early modern and modern Spain, particularly on issues of cultural projection, adaptation and transference as in, for instance, *The Road to Rocroi*, (Brill, 2009) a major study of the cultural, social and professional structures of the *tercios* of Flanders in the sixteenth and seventeenth centuries. He is also a book translator and has authored a variety of critical essays on diverse figures and topics such as Diego de Saavedra Fajardo, Edgar Allan Poe, Luis Buñuel, Charles Maturin and Henry Wadsworth Longfellow as well as on the impact of Spanish themes on the Gothic genre. He is currently at work on two book-length manuscripts, one on the political and ethical philosophy of Diego de Saavedra Fajardo and another on the presence of Spanish Golden Age literature in Poe.

ANTONIO GUIJARRO-DONADIÓS is an Assistant Professor of Spanish in the Department of World Languages at Worcester State University. His research focuses on Early Modern Spanish literature, especially in 17th Century Spanish One-Act Plays. He has presented his work at various national and international conferences, and he has also published numerous articles on the topic in edited collections and in journals such as *Hipógrifo, Cálamo-Faspe,* and *Teatro.* Professor Guijarro-Donadiós is currently working on a book tentatively titled: *Comical Spaces: Material Culture and Social Practices in 17th Century Spanish One-Act Plays.* His analysis illuminates the anxieties associated with the behavioral changes provoked by the new habits that emerged in a new society of consumers.

DANIEL LORCA is an Associate Professor of Spanish Renaissance Literature at Oakland University. He holds a Ph.D. in philosophy from Loyola University at Chicago (2007) and a Ph.D. in Cervantine Studies from the University of Chicago (2010). He is the author of *Neo-Stoicism and Skepticism in Part I of* Don Quijote: *Removing the Authority of a Genre* (Lexington Press, 2016). He has published various articles in Philosophy Journals, such as *Philosophy, Phenomenology* and *Philosophia,* as well as Literary Journals, such as *Cervantes, Anales Galdosianos* and *Hispanófila.*

JAMES MANDRELL is the author of *Don Juan and the Point of Honor: Seducion, Patriarchal Society, and Literary Tradition* (Penn State Press, 1992). He teaches Hispanic Studies at Brandeis University, where he also participates in the programs in American Studies, Film Studies, and Latin American and Latino Studies. He has published on Spanish literature and culture, as well as Latin American and comparative literature, and US popular culture.

VICENTE PÉREZ DE LEÓN is Professor of Hispanic Studies and Head of the School of Modern Languages and Cultures at the University of Glasgow. Previously, he was Associate Professor at Oberlin College from 2000 to 2010, and at the University of Melbourne from 2010 to 2017. He has published three books and more than seventy articles on Cervantes's short theater, Cervantes's novel and triumphal entries, among others. His latest book, *Hysteresis Creativa,* 2015, explores the links between courtly and popular culture in times of Cervantes. His present research focuses on essays about anti-superstitious literature, travel narratives in the Pacific, the reception of Cervantes in France, animal studies and the relationship between medicine and literature in the Spanish Golden Age.

ALFREDO RODRÍGUEZ LÒPEZ-VÁZQUEZ is Full Professor of Spanish at the Universidade da Coruña in Spain. He is a specialist in the works of Andrés de Claramonte and the leading scholar in tracking plays by this author often attributed to other playwrights. He has edited *El burlador de Sevilla* twice for Cátedra, and also Calderón's *El príncipe constante*, Tirso's *El condenado por desconfiado* and recently Luciano de Samósata's *El sueño o la vida de Luciano.*

CPSIA information can be obtained
at www.ICGtesting.com
Printed in the USA
BVHW040524030820
585257BV00008B/17